PELICAN BOOKS
A275

THE LETTERS OF
GERTRUDE BELL

THE LETTERS OF
GERTRUDE BELL

*

SELECTED BY
LADY RICHMOND
FROM
LADY BELL'S
STANDARD EDITION

*

PENGUIN BOOKS
MELBOURNE · LONDON · BALTIMORE

This selection first published 1953

TO

Gertrude's Father

*

Made and Printed in Great Britain
for Penguin Books Ltd, Harmondsworth, Middlesex
by Hazell Watson and Viney Ltd, Aylesbury and London

CONTENTS

Contents

PREFATORY NOTE

In the letters contained in this book there will be found many Eastern names, both of people and places, difficult to handle for those, like myself, not conversant with Arabic. The Arabic alphabet has characters for which we have no satisfactory equivalents and the Arab language has sounds which we find it difficult to reproduce. We have therefore in dealing with them to content ourselves with transliterations, some of which, in words more or less frequently used in English, have become translations, such as 'Koran', 'kavass', etc. But even these words (there are many others, but I take these two as an example) which have almost become a part of the English language are now spelt differently by experts, and at first sight it is difficult to recognize them in 'Quran' and 'qawas' – which latter form is I believe in accordance with the standardized spelling now being officially introduced in Bagdad. Gertrude herself in her letters used often to spell the same word in different ways, sometimes because she was trying experiments in transliteration, sometimes deliberately adopting a new way, sometimes because the same word is differently pronounced in Arabic or in Turkish. These variations in spelling have added a good deal to the difficulty of editing her letters, especially as reference to expert opinion has occasionally shown that experts themselves do not always agree as to which form of transliteration is the best.

I have therefore adopted the plan of spelling the names as they are found when they occur in the letters for the first time, and keeping to it. Thus Gertrude used to write at first 'Kaimmakan', in her later letters 'Qaimmaqam'. I have spelt it uniformly with a K for the convenience of the reader, and so with other words in which the Q has now superseded the K.

The word 'Bagdad', which used to be regarded as the English name of the town, a translation and not a transliteration, was spelt as I have given it in Gertrude's first letters long ago. It is now everywhere, even when regarded as a translation, spelt 'Baghdad' and it ought to have been so spelt in this book. The same applies to the name 'Teheran' which is now always spelt 'Tehran' but of which I have preserved the former spelling.

I have omitted the vowel signs altogether.

The formulae beginning and ending the letters have been mostly omitted, to save space and to avoid repetition. The heading H. B. at the top of a letter means that it is addressed to Gertrude's father, and the heading F. B. means that it is addressed to me.

I am most grateful to the people who have given me counsel and help in compiling this book: Sir Valentine Chirol, Mrs W. L. Courtney, H. E. Sir Henry Dobbs, Dr D. G. Hogarth, Elizabeth Robins, and Major-General Sir Percy Cox, who has had the kindness to read and correct many of the proofs.

I am also much indebted to the following for placing at my disposal maps or photographs, letters or portions of letters from Gertrude in their possession, or accounts of her written by themselves: Captain J. P. Farrar, Vice-Admiral Sir Reginald Hall, Mrs Marguerite Harrison, Hon. Mrs Anthony Henley, The Dowager Countess of Jersey, Mary Countess of Lovelace, Hon. Mildred Lowther, Mr Horace Marshall, Hon. Mrs Harold Nicolson, Sir William Ramsay, Mr E. A. Reeves, Miss Flora Russell, Lady Sheffield, Mr Lionel Smith, Mr Sydney Spencer, Lady Spring Rice, Colonel E. L. Strutt. Also for clerical help given me by Mrs D. M. Chapman and my secretary Miss Phyllis S. Owen.

FLORENCE BELL

MOUNT GRACE PRIORY,
August 1927

Note to this Edition

Lady Bell's narrative, which links the letters, has been printed here in small type; her interpolations in the letters themselves are enclosed in square brackets.

Introduction to the Letters of Gertrude Bell

GERTRUDE BELL, happily for her family and friends, was one of the people whose lives can be reconstructed from their correspondence.

Through all her wanderings, whether far or near, she kept in the closest touch with her home, always anxious to share her experiences and impressions with her family, to chronicle for their benefit all that happened to her, important or unimportant: whether a stirring tale of adventure or an account of a dinner party. Those letters, varied, witty, enthralling, were a constant joy through the years to all those who read them. It was fortunate for the recipients that the act of writing, the actual driving of the pen, seemed to be no more of an effort to Gertrude than to remember and record all that the pen set down. She was able at the close of a day of exciting travel to toss a complete account of it on to paper for her family, often covering several closely written quarto pages. And for many years she kept a diary as well. Then the time came when she ceased to write a diary. From 1919 onwards the confidential detailed letters of many pages, often written day by day, took its place. These were usually addressed to her father and dispatched to her family by every mail and by every extra opportunity. Besides these home letters, she found time a for a large and varied correspondence with friends outside her home circle, both male and female, among the former being some of the most distinguished men of her time. But the letters to her family have provided such abundant material for the reconstruction of her story that it has not been found necessary to ask for any others. Short extracts from a few outside letters to some of her intimate friends, however, have been included. The earlier of these letters, written when she was at home and therefore sending no letters to her family, show what her home life and outlook were at the time of her girlhood, when she was living an ordinary life – in so far as her life could ever be called ordinary. They foreshadow the pictures given in her subsequent family letters of her gradual development on all sides through the years, garnering as she went the almost incredible variety of experiences which culminated and ended in Bagdad. Letters written when she was twenty show that after her triumphant return from Oxford with one of the most brilliant Firsts of her year, she threw herself with the greatest zest into all the amusements of her age, sharing in everything, enjoying everything, dancing, skating, fencing, going to London parties; making ardent girl friendships, drawing in to her circle intimates of all kinds. She also loved her country life, in which her occupations included an absorbing amount of gardening, fox hunting – she was a bold rider to hounds – interesting herself in the people at her father's ironworks, and in her country village, making friends in every direction. And when she was wandering far afield (her wanderings began very early – she went to Rumania when she was twenty-two and to Persia when she was twenty-three) she was always ready to take up her urban or country life at home on her return with the same zest as before, carrying with her, wherever she was, her ardent zest for knowledge, turning the flashlight of her eagerness on to one field of the mind after another and making it her own, reading, assimilating, discussing until the years found her ranged on equal terms beside some of the foremost scholars of her time.

To most people outside her own circle Gertrude was chiefly known by her achievements in the East, and it is probably the story of these that they will look for in this book. But the letters here published, from the time she was twenty until the end of her life, show such an amazing range of many-sided ability that they may seem to those who read them to present a picture worth recording at every stage.

Scholar, poet, historian, archaeologist, art critic, mountaineer, explorer, gardener, naturalist, distinguished servant of the State, Gertrude was all of these, and was recognized by experts as an expert in them all.

On the other hand, in some of the letters addressed to her family are references to subjects or events that may seem trivial or unimportant. But Gertrude's keen interest in every detail concerning her home was so delightful, and presents her in such a new light to many who knew her only in public, that these passages have been included.

Her love for her family, for her parents, for her brothers and sisters, her joy in her home life, has always seemed to those who shared that life to be so beautiful that it is worth dwelling on by the side of more exceptional experiences, and by the side of the world-famous achievements of one whose later life especially might well have separated her in mind and sympathy as well as in person from her belongings. But her letters show how unbreakable to the last was the bond between her and her home, and above all between her and her father. The abiding influence in Gertrude's life from the time she was a little child was her relation to her father. Her devotion to him, her whole-hearted admiration, the close and satisfying companionship between them, their deep mutual affection – these were to both the very foundation of existence until the day she died.

CHAPTER I

1874 – 1892

Childhood – Oxford – London

THIS is the earliest letter extant from Gertrude, dictated when she was six years old. It is addressed to me, at a time when she was not yet my little daughter but my 'affectionate little friend'.

Mopsa, about whom she writes, was a large grey Persian cat, who played a very prominent part in the household.

REDBARNS, COATHAM, REDCAR, *Sept. 25th, 1874.*

MY DEAR FLORENCE,

Mopsa has been very naughty this morning. She has been scampering all over the dining-room Cilla says. I had a great chase all over the hall and dining room to catch her and bring her to Papa. She bit and made one little red mark on my hand. During breakfast she hissed at Kitty Scott. Auntie Ada had her on her knee and Kitty was at one side. As Auntie Ada let Mopsa go down she hissed at Kitty and hunted her round to my side of the table. Please Papa says will you ask Auntie Florence if she will order us some honey like her own. I gave Mopsa your message and she sends her love. I forgot to say Kitty was very frightened. I send you my love and to Grandmamma and Auntie Florence.

Your affectionate little friend

GERTRUDE BELL.

At the time that the above letter was written, the two children were living with their father at Redcar on the Yorkshire coast. His unmarried sister, Ada Bell, was then living with them.

Gertrude was eight when her father and I were married. She was a child of spirit and initiative, as may be imagined. Full of daring, she used to lead her little brother, whose tender years were ill equipped for so much enterprise, into the most perilous adventures, such as commanding him, to his terror, to follow her example in jumping from the top of a garden wall nine feet high to the ground. She used to alight on her feet, he very seldom did. Or she would lead a climbing expedition on to the top of the greenhouse, where Maurice was certain to go through the panes while Gertrude clambered down outside them in safety to the bottom.

They both of them rode from a very early age, and their ponies, of which they had a succession, were a constant joy.

From her early years Gertrude was devoted to flowers and to the garden. I have found a diary of hers when she was eleven. It was an imposing-looking quarto volume bound in leather, apparently given her for a Christmas present in 1878 but only kept for a few pages, alas. I have left her own spelling.

Jan 11. 1879 Sunday – we played in liberry morning. Feb. 11. Read Green till 9. Lessons went off rather lazily. We went into the gardin. I looked at flowers. Stilted Feb. 14. 1879. St Valentines Day. I got 12 valentines. The lessons went very badly. the lessons themselves were good. each got twopence … we caught a pigion we put it into a basket.

15 Feb. The pigion was brought into our room it drank some milk Maurice spilt a lot on my bed. so we went into the cuboard. Breakfast. I read all the morning. Dinner. I read all the afternoon. Tea. I played with Hugo. Mother read to us. Taught Maurice geography and read. Went to bed tied, had a little talk not fun and went to sleep.

Feb. 16. . . . . We now have out some yellow crocus and primroses snodrops and primroses. Primroses and snodrops in my garden. Crocus in Papas.

The only remaining entry in the diary is an account of her birthday, the day she was eleven, Monday, 14th of July. The record, the celebrations, and all the presents seem amusingly childish for a little girl who was reading Green's History before breakfast, and devouring every book she could find.

When I woke up I went to see the time. It was a quarter to seven. I woke Maurice. then I hid my face and he got out his presents. he gave me scales a fireplace with pans kitchen furniture. then I found under my pillow a book from nurse then we got up. When we were ready we went into Mother's room and there I found a hopping toad from Auntie Bessie dinner set from Mother, watering can from Papa. Then we went downstairs to breakfast Mother and Maurice and I cooked a dinner because it was wet. we had soup fish mince crockets puding, cheese and butter and desert.

Gertrude never entirely mastered the art of spelling, and all her life long there were certain words in her letters that were always spelt wrong. She always wrote 'siezed', 'excercise', 'exhorbitant'. Sometimes 'priviledge'.

The cooking lessons referred to in the diary and sometimes in the early letters did not have much practical result. She never excelled in this art.

The two or three years following the time described in the diaries were spent happily at Redcar with Maurice – years of playing about, and studying under a German governess, and having pet animals, of which there were always one or two on hand. There were periodical onslaughts of grief when one of these died, grief modified by the imposing funeral procession always organized for them and their burial in a special cemetery in the garden.

Gertrude's and Maurice's earliest and favourite companion from babyhood onwards was Horace Marshall, their first cousin and son of their mother's sister Mrs Thomas Marshall. Then after their father's second marriage the two Lascelles boys came into the circle as intimates and cousins, the sons of my sister Mary spoken of in the letters as Auntie Mary, wife of Sir Frank Lascelles.

Florence Lascelles, my sister's only daughter, is constantly mentioned in the letters. She was a good deal younger than her two brothers and Gertrude, but as she grew up she was always one of Gertrude's chosen friends and companions. She married Cecil Spring Rice in 1904.

When Gertrude was fifteen and Maurice had gone to school she went, first as a day scholar and afterwards as a boarder, to Queen's College in Harley Street, where a friend of her mother's, Camilla Croudace, had just been made Lady Resident. Gertrude lived at first at 95 Sloane Street with my mother Lady Olliffe, who took her and Maurice to her heart as if they had been grandchildren of her own.

The History Lecturer at Queen's College at that time was Mr de Soyres, a distinguished and inspiring teacher. Gertrude's intelligence and aptitude for history impressed him keenly, and he strongly urged us to let her go to Oxford and go in for the History School. The time had not yet come when it was a usual part of a girl's education to go to a University, and it was with some qualms that we consented. But the result justified our decision. Gertrude went to Lady Margaret Hall in 1886 just before she was eighteen, she left it in June 1888 just before she was twenty, and wound up, after those two years, by taking a brilliant First Class in Modern History.

One of her contemporaries at Lady Margaret was Janet Hogarth, now Mrs W. L. Courtney, who, in a delightful article contributed to the *North American Review*, entitled 'Gertrude Bell, a personal study', and also in her interesting book *Recollected in Tranquillity*, has described Gertrude as she was when she first arrived at Lady Margaret Hall – I quote both from the article and the book. ... 'Gertrude Lowthian Bell, the most brilliant student we ever had at Lady Margaret Hall, or indeed I think at any of the women's colleges. Her journeys in Arabia and her achievements in Iraq have passed into history. I need only recall the bright promise of her college days, when the vivid, rather untidy, auburn-haired girl of seventeen first came amongst us and took our hearts by storm with her brilliant talk and her youthful confidence in herself and her belongings. She had a most engaging way of saying "Well you know, my father says so and so" as a final opinion on every question under discussion – [and indeed to the end of her life Gertrude, with the same absolute confidence, would have been capable of still quoting the same authority as final].

'She threw herself with untiring energy into every phase of college life, she swam, she rowed, she played tennis, and hockey, she acted, she danced, she spoke in debates; she kept up with modern literature, and told us tales of modern authors, most of whom were her childhood's friends. Yet all the time she put in seven hours of solid work, and at the end of two years she won as brilliant a First Class in the School of Modern History as has ever been won at Oxford.'

And many years later Mrs Courtney, who had herself taken a First Class (in Moral Philosophy) the same year as Gertrude, writes as follows in the *Brown Book*, which is the organ of Lady Margaret Hall:

'I never lost touch with her for well-nigh forty years "after we parted in the First Class", as she said the day I went round to Sloane Street to wish her joy when the History List appeared.'

The untidiness in Gertrude's appearance referred to by Mrs Courtney gradually gave place to an increasing taste for dress, and she is remembered by more than one person who saw her during the finals of the History School as appearing in different clothes every day. The parents of the candidates were admitted to the 'viva voce' part of the examination, and I have a vivid picture in my memory of Gertrude, showing no trace of nervousness, sitting very upright at a table, beneath which her slender feet in neat brown shoes were crossed. She was, I have since been told, one of the first young women at Oxford to wear brown shoes, of which she set the fashion among her contemporaries.

Mr Arthur Hassall of Christ Church, Oxford, who knew her well, records the following incident of Gertrude's 'viva voce'. I quote from his letter: 'S. R. Gardiner, the famous historian of the times of James I and Charles I, began to "viva voce" Miss Bell. She replied to his first question, "I am afraid I must differ from your estimate of Charles I". This so horrified Professor Gardiner that he at once asked the examiner who sat next to him (I think it was Mr H. O. Wakeman) to continue the "viva voce".'

The result of the whole examination however did her so much credit that she may perhaps be forgiven this lapse into unparalleled audacity.

Mrs Arthur Hassall also writes: 'Gertrude went to the four balls given at Commemoration that week, of which the last was the night before her "viva voce", and danced all the evening looking brilliantly happy.' She also writes: 'She was the only girl I have ever known who took her work for the schools and her examination in a gay way.'

After the happy culmination of her two years at Oxford she rejoined her family in London and then at Redcar.

My sister – Sir Frank Lascelles being at that time Minister at Bucharest – begged me to send Gertrude to stay with them for the winter, after the return from Oxford, opining that frequenting foreign diplomatic Society might be a help for Gertrude 'to get rid of her Oxfordy manner'. My sister was very fond of Gertrude, whom she called her niece and treated like a daughter: they were the greatest friends. The effect however on Gertrude's 'Oxfordy manner' of the society of foreign diplomats was not all that Lady Lascelles had hoped, for it is recorded that on one occasion when a distinguished foreign statesman was discussing some of the international problems of Central Europe, Gertrude said to him, to the stupefaction of her listeners and the dismay of her hostess: 'Il me semble, Monsieur, que vous n'avez pas saisi l'esprit du peuple allemand.'

There is no doubt that according to the ordinary canons of demeanour it was a mistake for Gertrude to proffer, as we have been shown on more occasions than one, her opinions, let alone her criticisms, to her superiors in age and experience.

But it was all part of her entire honesty and independence of judgement: and the time was to come when many a distinguished foreign statesman not only listened to the opinions she proffered but accepted them and acted on them.

Gertrude hardly ever dated her letters except by the day of the week, sometimes not even that, so that where the envelope has not been preserved I have had to guess the year by the context.

Her letters from Bucharest, which had not come to light when this book was first written, can be read in the *Earlier Letters of Gertrude Bell*. Some extracts from two or three are given here:

BUCHAREST, *Dec. 27th, 1888.*

Today is the great day – the first ball day. I am looking forward to seeing all these people very much. Yesterday afternoon Auntie Mary and I called on some of them – first on a Mme Arion – a Roumanian – whom we found in a very nice drawing room opening on to a conservatory. She was a curious lady. She was clothed in a kind of toga of scarlet, embroidered all round the edge, and round her neck a boa, knotted at the waist. As soon as we appeared she called out to her daughter 'Minna! une jeune fille!', whereupon the daughter came out of the next room to entertain me. I imagine she is never allowed to appear unless there is a jeune fille! All the girls wear their waists so ridiculously small, their figures are quite hideous. We then called on a Mrs Mawe, the wife of an English doctor, who is a worthy and tiresome old lady sitting in a patchwork drawing room. She talks in an ascending scale and always about her sons.

BUCHAREST, *Sunday, Dec. 30th, 1888.*

We went to our ball at the Soutzos on Thursday. Auntie Mary and I arrived about 11 and found the rooms full of people. I was introduced to a great many of them, men and women, and danced many turns of the waltz which was going on with different men. This is what happens; your dancer comes up and asks you for a turn. You dance three or four times round the room with him and he then drops you by your chaperone with an elegant bow and someone else comes up and carries you off. I think it is a very amusing

plan. You dance nothing through with one person, except
the square dances, of course, and in the intervals you either
sit with your chaperone or you walk round the rooms with
your last partner. I can't attempt to tell you whom I danced
with for it was impossible to remember them all at once. . . .
The officers all appear in uniform of course and with spurs
on and top boots, but they dance so very well that they don't
tear one in the least. I was introduced and talked to a great
many ladies and their daughters. One of the nicest of the
women was a Mlle Davila who is a maid of honour to the
Queen, is very pretty and dances beautifully. The maids of
honour chaperone themselves and this girl who is about 23
or 24, I should think, is made a great deal of and enjoys herself particularly. She took me with her into the little dressing
room where I found a good many women sitting about on
sofas and chairs and talking to the men who were hanging
round the door. Rather to my surprise Davila proceeded to
powder herself in front of the glass and then, still more to
my surprise, she powdered all the men who were standing in
the doorway! Don't be shocked! She is really nice though
she is a minx! We stayed till about a quarter past three, well
into the cotillon of which I danced the first figures with Billy
and was amused, then we all came away and sat here in the
drawing room eating sandwiches and talking till about 4
then we went to bed. . . .

BUCHAREST, *March 26th, 1889.*

Monday is our day but fortunately not many people came.
The Bibescos, mother and daughter came rather late and
the Hidalgo and we had rather an amusing talk. Auntie
Mary had almost to send them away in the end for we dined
at the Palace at 7 and at ten minutes past six they showed no
signs of going. We hopped into our clothes with great celerity
and arrived at the Palace on the stroke of 7, quite in time.
I was so amused. First of all I was amused by the whole
ceremony and the magnificence of it, and further I was of
course at the one less low of everyone and so had the youngest minister, M. Marghiloman, to take me in, and a very

conversable French secretary, M. Gachet, on the other side
of me. There was a formal cercle before dinner, the King
and Queen coming round to talk to each of us in turn. I was
the only girl there except of course the maids of honour. All
the corps diplomatique was there and all the ministers with
their wives, which made about 70 people. We were received
upstairs and marched down to the dining-room as soon as
the cercle was over. The table was elaborately decorated with
a looking-glass lake, islands of ferns with Greek temples on
all the eminences and imitation water-lilies growing all
round – very ugly indeed. The only nice thing was that
there were heaps of real flowers which one was expected to
take away with one. Everyone had a glass-ful opposite him;
my men gave me all theirs and Urbu and some other people
brought me more after dinner, and upstairs more flowers
were handed to us on china dishes so that we came away
laden. After dinner there was no formal cercle, we all stood
about and talked, the King and Queen chatted with people.
I had a long crack with the Queen whom I suddenly became
conscious of immediately in front of me. However, I don't
really think it was my fault and she need not have talked to
me unless she liked. She told me how she spent her winters –
it sounds dreary enough, poor lady; she hates the cold and
never goes out at all from one end of the winter to the other,
but spends her time indoors and for exercise walks up and
down the long galleries and ball rooms at the Palace. The
whole thing lasted till about half past 10 which was quite
long enough for we were standing all the time.

From Bucharest she returned to London, from London she went
to Redcar, enjoying herself everywhere. At Redcar she shouldered
the housekeeping and also various activities among the women at
the ironworks, Clarence, often mentioned, being Bell Bros ironworks
on the north bank of the Tees.

Her letters of this time give a picture of her relation to the
younger children – her step-brother and her two step-sisters, Hugo,
Elsa, and Molly. Hugo was ten years younger than Gertrude, Elsa
eleven years younger, Molly thirteen years. Her letters often recount what she was doing with her two little sisters who adored her.

Hugo by this time had gone to school. Some letters are here given that she wrote between 1889 and 1892 during the time spent in England in one of our two homes either in London in the house shared with my mother, or at Redcar, where we lived until 1904. These letters are mostly about every-day happenings, always lifted into something new and exciting by Gertrude's youthful zest. Some of these early letters are to her parents, others, of which fragmentary extracts are given, are to Flora Russell, who remained her intimate friend all her life. Flora was the elder daughter of Lord and Lady Arthur Russell, who lived in Audley Square. The Audley Square circle, the house, the hosts, the people who used to assemble there, formed for Gertrude, as for many others, a cherished and congenial surrounding.

To F. B.   RED BARNS, *1889*.

I think the reason the books were so high was because of the dinner party – it was before I began to keep house wasn't it, so I am not responsible, though I feel as if I were.

I paid everything but the butcher with what you sent, and had over £1 balance which I have kept for next time.

I went to Clarence to-day and arranged about the nursing lecture to-morrow, – there were a lot of things to prepare for it. Then I paid some visits and came home with Papa at 4.35. Molly and I have since been picking cowslips in the fields. It is so heavenly here with all the things coming out and the grass growing long. I am glad I'm here.

To F. B.   LONDON, *1889*.

... I must tell you an absurd story. Minnie Hope was sitting with an Oxford man. Presently he grasped her hand and said 'do you see that young lady in a blue jacket?' 'Yes' said Minnie lying low. 'Well' said he in an awe-struck voice, 'she took a first in History!!'

To F. B.   LONDON, *July 5th, 1889*.

Billy [Lascelles] and I sat in the garden and had a long talk so long that he only left himself a quarter of an hour to catch his train. I expect he missed it. He wanted to take me with him to Paddington and send me back in a hansom, don't be afraid, I didn't go – what would have happened if I had, it was ten o'clock!

We drove in hansoms to the exhibition and Captain —— brought me home, I hope that doesn't shock you; I discussed religious beliefs all the way there and very metaphysical conceptions of truth all the way back – that sounds rather steep doesn't it. I love talking to people when they really will talk sensibly and about things which one wants to discuss.

It's so hot this morning, I went into the gardens to be cool, but presently came the babies who announced that they were barons and that they intended to rob me. I was rather surprised at their taking this view of the functions of the aristocracy, till I found that they had just been learning the reign of Stephen. Molly informed me in the pride of newly acquired knowledge that there were at least 11,000 castles in his time! So we all played at jumping over a string, not a very cooling occupation, till fortunately Miss Thomson came and called them in. Did we tell you how Molly puzzled and shocked her dreadfully the other day by asking her suddenly what was the French for 'this horse has the staggers'!

To F. B.   RED BARNS, *October 30, 1889.*

It was so fine this afternoon, a rough sea almost up to the esplanade. I walked a long time and then came in and did history for to-morrow.

i.e. to prepare the children's lesson for the next day. She was then teaching them history.

To F. B.   LONDON, *1889.*

About the little girls frocks, Hunt would like to have one for Molly made of cambric matching the pattern of Elsa, 16d. a yard 40 in. wide; the other two one for each little girl of nainsook which is a shade finer and will she says wash better, 13d. and 38 in. wide. There are two insertions, one at 6¼ not so very pretty, one at 10½ very pretty indeed.

Mr Grimston says that he cannot supply us with mutton at

9d a pound, it is so dear now. I have asked the other butchers and find they are all selling it at 10d or 10½ a pound so I think it would be best to pay him 10d for legs and loins – what say you?...

To F. B.   RED BARNS, *April 2nd, 1890.*

I have just returned from Clarence where I found only a few mothers but some very agreeable ladies amongst them. I walked back with a very friendly lady – I wonder who she was. She lives in the New Cottages and only comes up to the other end of Clarence for the Mothers' Meeting and for confinements!

To F. B.   RED BARNS, *April 17th, 1890.*

... I should like to go to the first drawing room if you could because I shall want some evening gowns and shall have none till I can use my court gown.

To F. B.   LONDON, *Feb. 8th, 1891.*

All the sales are over I'm afraid. I went to Woollands this afternoon for the sashes, they had nothing approaching the colour, but I will find it somewhere. I am much interested about your gown, though as you rightly supposed I'm a little sorry it's black! ...

To F. B.   LONDON, *Feb. 14, 1891.*

Horace came here about three on Saturday and we walked to Kensington Square, where I took him to call on Mrs [J. R.] Green. It was pleasant and amusing. ... Mrs Green told me that Mr York Powell had said to her – this is not a becoming story, and suited for the ears of one's immediate family only – that I was the only girl he had ever examined who knew how to use books or had read things outside the prescribed course and that he thought I had got into the heart of my subject. What a little daring it takes to deceive his misguided sex!

She was at this time staying in London with Lady Lascelles.

To F. B.   LONDON, *Feb. 20, 1891.*

We dined at Devonshire House. There were there Lady Edward, William Egerton, Alfred Lyttelton and Victor Cavendish [afterwards Duke of Devonshire] who came in from the House announcing that he must be back in 30 minutes but finally stayed till ten. Victor C. is tremendously interested in his politics, talks of nothing else; it is very nice to see, as genuine enthusiasm always is.

To F. B.   LONDON, *Feb. 26th, 1891.*

It was pleasant at Mansfield Street, Mr William Peel, Horace, Diana, Harold, Grisel, Mildred Hugh Smith.

Horace Marshall, Diana Russell, Harold Russell, Lady Grisel Ogilvie and Mildred Hugh Smith, afterwards Countess Buxton, G.B.E.

Uncle Lyulph presently went to sleep; Harold, Mildred and I had a long and amusing talk together which lasted all the evening. She is such a nice girl.

On Thursday I walked in the afternoon with Flora and went back with her to tea. . . .

'Uncle Lyulph', then Hon. Lyulph Stanley, afterwards Lord Stanley of Alderley, and later Lord Sheffield.

During 1891 there are very few letters to her family. I have inserted a few extracts from her letters to Flora Russell, recording some of her doings.

To Flora Russell.   RED BARNS, *July 22, 1891.*

The Lascelles are moved to Teheran which is rather thrilling. They are coming back to England now and my uncle goes to Persia in October, my aunt later, I don't know when. I should like her to take me out with her, Persia is the place I have always longed to see, but I don't know if she will.

I expect my aunt will be rather annoyed for she will hate being so far away, but it is a great promotion. As for me if only I go there this winter everything will have turned out for the best.

I wear a blue-green velvet in my hair which is becoming.

To the same.   RED BARNS, *August 13, 1891.*

We spent a madly amusing five days at Canterbury, of which nothing remains to tell except that we danced every night, saw a good deal of cricket and talked a little. . . .

Do you remember discussing what other girls do with their days? Well! I have found out what one particular class does – they spend the entire time in rushing from house to house for cricket weeks, which means cricket all day and dancing all night; your party consists of an eleven and enough girls to pair off with – you discuss byes and wides and Kemp at the wicket and Hearne's batting and any other topic of a similar nature that may occur to you. It seems to me to be rather a restless sort of summer. . . .

To the same.   RED BARNS, *Dec. 23, 1891.*

I have been reading Latin with great energy. It's a language of which I know very little but whose difficulties must be mastered somehow for I constantly find myself brought up against a blank wall by my ignorance of it. It is very interesting to learn but I could wish it were a little easier. . . .

To the same.   RED BARNS, *1891.*

I read a certain amount of history with the children's lessons, for exercise, and the works of Balzac for amusement. Dante for edification. It's an agreeable and a varied programme. . . .

CHAPTER 2

1892 – 1896

Persia – Italy – London

GERTRUDE went to Teheran, to her great joy, in the spring of 1892.

Her letters from Persia of which there were a good many were also only found some years after this book was first published, and may be read in the *Earlier Letters of Gertrude Bell*. The first is given here:

TEHERAN, *Monday 9th May, 1892.*

We arrived on Saturday afternoon in the Garden of Eden with a very comfortable house built in the middle of it and your letter waiting for me inside. You can't think how lovely it all is – outside trees and trees and trees making a thick shade from our house to the garden walls, beneath them a froth of pink monthly roses, climbing masses of briers, yellow and white and scarlet, beds of dark red cabbage roses and hedges of great golden blooms. It's like the Beast's garden, a perfect nightmare of roses. In the middle are three deep tanks with weeping willows hanging over them from which run a network of tiny water channels which the ten Zoroastrians who are the gardeners open and shut most cunningly, sluicing the flowerbeds with water. Inside a big rambling house, long, long passages with liveried people in every corner who rise and bow their heads as we pass, big big rooms opening one out of the other, two dining rooms, two drawing rooms, Uncle Frank's study and bedroom, two rooms for Auntie Mary, a billiard room and countless little sitting rooms and cupboards; two long stone passages opening at each end with chanceries kitchens etc. in them. Florence and I are upstairs; I have a beautiful big room, cool and dark; three narrow windows opening on to the garden, the tops of the trees rustling against them and nodding in, and such a sweet smell of roses. In the evening the nightingales sing and never stop; it's delicious. Behind the

28

house all the garden is ours and no-one comes into it; a long terrace runs before the house with steps leading down; in front of the house is another stretch of garden at the end of which all the secretaries live.

Now the other people who live in our paradise are these: Dr and Mrs Odling, she very scotch, very nice, quite young; he a self-made man with an interesting face and a pleasant straight-forward manner, a little shy. Mr Cadogan, tall and red and very thin, agreeable, intelligent, a great tennis player, a great billiard player, an enthusiast about Bezique, devoted to riding though he can't ride in the least I'm told, smart, clean, well-dressed, looking upon us as his special property to be looked after and amused. I like him. Mr and Mrs Crowe [afterwards Sir Eyre and Lady Crowe]; I don't know what his functions are. Mr Sidney Churchill, the man who brought us from Resht; he's well worth making friends with; he speaks Persian like a Persian, has lived in every part of this country, disguised and undisguised; knows the people and their habits and prejudices as no European does; rides anything and anywhere and is one of the most capable people withal that I have ever come across. He had arranged our journey after such sort that we travelled for seven days and there was never a hitch anywhere; wherever we arrived there were lunch, dinner, rooms, and horses to take us on – no easy matter when there are many people on the road; whatever we wanted was there before we asked for it; on one occasion he produced a looking-glass out of a howling wilderness that I might do my hair which had come down; where he got it from I have never yet been able to discover; our luggage was miles away and there was no sign of human habitation anywhere near; Florence happened to say we liked caviare – there was caviare every night for dinner; if it rained he had half a dozen waterproofs on his saddle; if the sun was hot and we had not put on shady hats he had a Terai in his pocket; we wanted to write – in a second pens, ink and paper were before us; we wanted a good gallop – horses of Mr Churchill's own appeared by magic in the very post-house at which we were. He is one of the Oriental

Secretaries; the other is the Nawab, a polite person who is, I believe, a Persian, dull, grey-haired, obliging; he speaks English very well. 1st Secretary there is none and General Gordon is away. The three unmarried men lunch and dine with us whenever they have no other engagements; it's very amusing and merry!

I'm not going to tell you about our journey because in a day or two we shall post the diary home and you will read it all there. We rode 5 days and drove 2; the weather was not hot at all; two days it rained but not very much; we arrived not the least tired and almost sorry it was all over. For the first four nights we slept in quite bare post-houses; there were always heaps of rooms opening one out of the other, but there was absolutely nothing of any sort in them – four bare walls, a mud floor and a fireplace. We carried camp beds with us, carpets, curtains and a small table, campstools, candles, food; chairs and tables were usually unearthed for us at every place, but not very many of them. As we neared Teheran the post-houses grew more pretentious; the last two nights our rooms were suitably furnished with a carpet, a moth and a toothbrush; but these were really less comfortable, for they were stuffy and dirty, we preferred our bare walled rooms with swallows' nests in the rafters. The journey as we did it presented no difficulties at all; but there, we did it en prince, with two golams, three cooks, 20 servants and a whole caravan of mules; it was one long picnic – a very expensive one, I should think. When you come to the end of it I must say you feel that you have travelled a great deal!

We arrived at 6 on Saturday. Uncle Frank rode out about 4 miles to meet us; two miles further on we found all the legation and the landau waiting for us; they rode and we drove with Uncle Frank. We dined alone that night and went to bed early. No luggage had arrived at all! I had not even any sponges. The small luggage came yesterday and the caravan will be here tomorrow. Yesterday, Sunday, we spent the morning walking in the garden, inspecting the stables, talking to Mr Cadogan and Mr Churchill. After lunch all the Golams' horses were brought out for us to see,

12 of them. Then the English people called; Madame Rosen and her husband came late and when they had gone Uncle Frank and I walked down to the tennis ground where we found the Wells, Mr Cadogan and some foreigners. The three men dined with us; they played billiards which we watched, after which Mr Cadogan and I played Bezique.

Auntie Mary is delighted with everything; Uncle Frank is very well and very glad to have his family with him. It *is* so amusing!

This first letter from Persia shows her delight at arriving, and it sets the scene and introduces the players who were to form Gertrude's world for the next six months.

We have further records of Gertrude's first impressions of the East in a book she wrote the year after her return, published by Bentley in 1894, entitled *Safar Nameh*, i.e. 'Persian Pictures', in which the life of the town and of the bazaars, the desolate places so strangely near them, the dwellers in the tents, the divine Persian gardens and many other aspects of her surroundings, are described with the glowing eagerness of a first experience. The little book attracted attention and was favourably reviewed.

Her own attitude to these first little sketches is shown in a letter to Flora Russell after her return to England:

RED BARNS, *1893.*

This is for the private eye; Bentley wishes to publish my Persian things, but wants more of them, so after much hesitation I have decided to let him and I am writing him another six chapters. It's rather a bore and what's more I would vastly prefer them to remain unpublished. I wrote them you see to amuse myself and I have got all the fun out of them I ever expect to have, for modesty apart they are extraordinarily feeble. Moreover I do so loathe people who rush into print and fill the world with their cheap and nasty work – and now I am going to be one of them. At first I refused, then my mother thought me mistaken and my father was disappointed and as they are generally right I have given way.

But in my heart I hold very firmly to my first opinion. Don't speak of this. I wish them not to be read.

31

Gertrude had, as we have seen in many of the letters, a special and very valuable gift, that of forming extremely rapid impressions, whether of places or of human beings. She would dive beneath the surface, estimating, judging, characterizing in a few words that were not often mistaken. She would ride through a countryside and report on its conditions, human, agricultural, economic, and her report would be adopted. When she came into contact with human beings, whether chiefs of the desert or men and women of her own Western world, she would label them, after her first meeting with them, in a sentence. ·

I am not pretending that her judgements were always infallible. But on the whole they were correct often enough to enable her to thread her way successfully through the labyrinth of her experiences.

It was characteristic of Gertrude, and it was an inestimable advantage to her, that she insisted on learning Persian before going to Teheran. She arrived there 'knowing' as it is commonly called, the language, i.e. able to understand what she heard and what she read. But she had not yet reached the stage in which the learner of a language finds with rapture that a new knowledge has been acquired, the illuminating stage when not the literal meaning only of words is being understood, but their values and differences can be critically appreciated. It was not long before Gertrude was reading Persian poetry by this light and with the added understanding brought to her by her knowledge of Western literature.·

She published a translation of the Divan of Hafiz in 1897. The book includes a life of Hafiz, which is practically a history of his times as well as a critical study of his work. These, and the notes on his poems at the end of the book, show how wide was her field of comparison. She draws a parallel between Hafiz and his contemporary Dante: she notes the similarity of a passage with Goethe: she compares Hafiz with Villon, on every side gathering fructifying examples which link together the inspiration of the West and of the East.

The book on its publication was extremely well received.

I quote here from one of the translations.

TO HAFIZ OF SHIRAZ

(Two first stanzas)

Thus said the Poet: 'When Death comes to you,
All ye whose life-sand through the hour-glass slips,

He lays two fingers on your ears, and two
Upon your eyes he lays, one on your lips,
Whispering: Silence.' Although deaf thine ear,
Thine eye, my Hafiz, suffer Time's eclipse,
The songs thou sangest still all men may hear.

Songs of dead laughter, songs of love once hot,
Songs of a cup once flushed rose-red with wine,
Songs of a rose whose beauty is forgot,
A nightingale that piped hushed lays divine:
And still a graver music runs beneath
The tender love notes of those songs of thine,
Oh, Seeker of the keys of Life and Death!

Gertrude, who was an ardent lover of poetry all her life long,
and who kept abreast of the work of the moderns as well as of their
predecessors, seemed, strangely enough, after the book of Hafiz
had appeared, to consider her own gift of verse as a secondary pursuit, and to our surprise abandoned it altogether. But that gift has
always seemed to me to underlie all she has written. The spirit of
poetry coloured all her prose descriptions, all the pictures that she
herself saw and succeeded in making others see.

It was a strangely interesting ingredient in a character capable
on occasion of very definite hardness, and of a deliberate disregard
of sentiment: and also in a mental equipment which included great
practical ability and a statesmanlike grasp of public affairs.

But in truth the real basis of Gertrude's nature was her capacity
for deep emotion. Great joys came into her life, and also great
sorrows. How could it be otherwise, with a temperament so avid
of experience? Her ardent and magnetic personality drew the lives
of others into hers as she passed along.

She returned to England from Teheran in December of 1892.
The years from 1893 to 1897 were spent partly in England and
partly travelling in Europe with her father or with women friends
(Mrs J. R. Green, Mrs Norman Grosvenor), and in January 1897
we find her starting for the British Embassy in Berlin. Sir Frank
Lascelles had been posted there as Ambassador in the previous
year.

1897

Berlin

To her sister.   BERLIN, *Jan. 22nd, 1897.*

DEAREST ELSA,

I made my bow to the 'Kaizer Paar' on Wednesday. It was a very fine show. We drove to the Schloss in the glass coach and were saluted by the guard when we arrived. We felt very swell! Then we waited for a long time with all the other dips. in a room next to the throne room and at about 8 the doors were thrown open. We all hastily arranged one another's trains and marched in procession while the band played the march out of Lohengrin. The Emperor and Empress were standing on a dais at the end of the room and we walked through a sort of passage made by rows and rows of pages dressed in pink. The 'Allerhöchst' looked extremely well in a red uniform – I couldn't look at the Empress much as I was so busy avoiding Aunt Mary's train. She introduced me and then stood aside while I made two curtseys. Then I wondered what the dickens I should do next, but Aunt Mary made me a little sign to go out behind her, so I 'enjambéd' her train and fled!

To F. B.   BERLIN, *Jan. 24th, 1897.*

... The Princess Frederic Leopold's ladies asked when I was going to be introduced to her ... we arranged that I should be presented during the first polka of the first Court ball....

To F. B.   BERLIN, *Tuesday, 1897.*

... F. and I went to see *Henry IV* last night, the Emperor having invited all the Embassy to come to the royal box. Uncle F. and Aunt M. were dining with the Frederic Leopolds, so they were obliged to decline the box for themselves but the Emperor said that he hoped we should go as we should be chaperoned by Countess Keller, one of the ladies-in-waiting. Accordingly we went off by ourselves and sat very comfortably with Countess Keller in the second row of chairs – no one might sit in the front row even when the royalties were not in the box. All the Embassy and a lot of the Court people were with us, the Emperor and Empress were in a little box at the side. The play was very well done. The Falstaff excellent and the whole thing beautifully staged. There was no pause till the end of the second act when there was a long entr'acte. Countess Keller bustled away and presently came hurrying back and whispered something to Knesebeck and Egloffstein, two of the Court people, and they came and told F. and me that we were sent for. So off we went rather trembling, under the escort of Countess K. and Egloffstein who conducted us into a little tiny room behind the Emperor's box where we found the 'Kaiser Paar' sitting and having tea. We made deep curtseys and kissed the Empress's hand, and then we all sat down, F. next to the Emperor and I next to the Empress and they gave us tea and cakes. It was rather formidable though they were extremely kind. The Emperor talked nearly all the time; he tells us that no plays of Shakespeare were ever acted in London and we must have heard tell that it was only the Germans who had really studied or really understood Shakespeare. One couldn't contradict an Emperor, so we said we had always been told so. Egloffstein's chair broke in the middle of the party and he came flat on to the ground which created a pleasing diversion – I was so glad it wasn't mine! Countess K. was a dear and started a new subject whenever the conversation languished. After about 20 minutes the Empress got up, we curtseyed to her, shook hands with the Emperor. Florence thanked him very prettily for sending for us and we bowed ourselves out. Wasn't it amusing! Florence said she felt shy but she looked perfectly self-possessed and had the prettiest little air in the world as she sat talking to the Emperor. I felt rather frightened, but I did not mind much as I knew I need do nothing but follow Florence's lead. The Empress sits very upright and is rather alarming. He flashes round from one person to the other and talks as fast as possible and is not alarming at all. ... We go again to-night to the second part ... but we shall not be sent for as Uncle Frank and Aunt Mary will be there.

To F. B.   BERLIN, *Feb. 5th, 1897.*

... The Court Ball on Wednesday was a fine show. We were asked for eight o'clock and at a quarter past we formed up for waiting. The ambassadresses sat on a line of chairs to the left of the throne in the Weiser Saal, and we stood meekly behind them. After about half an hour someone tapped on the floor with a wand and in came a long procession of pages followed by the 'Kaiser Paar' and all the 'Fürstliche Personen'. The whole room bobbed down in deep curtseys as they came in. ... In to supper ... back to the ball room. The room was almost empty and the few people that were there were dancing the 'trois temps' – one is only allowed to dance the 'deux temps' when the Empress is there. It was a very delicious half-hour for the floor is peerless and all these officers dance so well. Then followed the gavotte which Florence danced very prettily.

To H. B.   BERLIN, *Feb. 8th, 1897.*

I wish you many many happy returns of your birthday and may your children become less and less tiresome with every succeeding year! ...

The house is all upside down for the ball. Wherever one goes one finds lines and lines of waiters arranging tables. We can seat 340 people at supper. There are to be tables in all the ball rooms, the Chancery ante-room and even the big bedroom. We all intend to bring our partners up to the big bedroom which makes a delightful supper-room. Florence and I went into the kitchen this morning and inspected the food. I never saw so many eatables together. ...

To F. B.   BERLIN, *Feb. 12th, 1897.*

The Court Ball on Wednesday was much nicer than the first one. ... The Emperor wore a gorgeous Austrian uniform in honour of an Austrian Archduke who was there – the brother of the man who is heir to the throne. He will be Emperor himself someday as the heir is sickly and unmarried. The Emperor William is disappointing when one sees him close; he looks puffy and ill and I never saw anyone so jumpy. He is never still a second while he is talking....

Uncle Frank is in a great jig about Crete. He thinks there is going to be red war and an intervention of the Powers and all sorts of fine things. I wonder.

CHAPTER 4

1897 – 1899

Round the World, Dauphiné, etc.

GERTRUDE came back to England at the beginning of March. My sister Mary Lascelles died on April 3rd, after three days' illness. Her death made a terrible gap in Gertrude's life.

To F. B.   REDCAR, *April 7th, 1897.*

I have been to Clarence to-day – it was no use sitting and moping so I thought I had better make myself useful if I could. . . .

In August of that year we all went to the Dauphiné, staying at La Grave under the shadow of the Meije, objective of all Dauphiné climbers. This holiday makes an epoch, as it was the beginning of Gertrude's climbing experiences, although this year she did nothing very adventurous.

She went over the Brèche with two guides, slept at the refuge, came down over the Col des Cavales and proudly strode back into the village next morning between her guides, well pleased with herself.

She was at home with us all the rest of the year.

*

On the 29th December 1897 Gertrude and her brother Maurice left home for Southampton, to embark on a voyage round the world.

Gertrude begins the year 1899 at Redcar, she and Hugo are left together for a few days at Red Barns.

To F. B.   REDCAR, *January 6th, 1899.*

. . . Hugo and I have made an excellent 'ménage' – we get on admirably and I have come to know him much better, chiefly because he has told me all his views as to his future. They are rather a blow to me, I admit. He is one of the most lovable and livable with people I have ever come across.

To her sister Elsa.   LONDON, *Jan. 1899.*

... I thought the braid a little too braidy. A modification of it would be lovely. I should have no braid on the coat just the seams strapped. 'Tis very smart so. I went to Prince's this morning and skated. . . . with Flora and a lot of people. ... Next time I'm in London I shall have a few lessons there. It's silly not to be able to skate well when everybody does.

My new clothes are very dreamy. You will scream with delight when you see me in them!

To F. B.   LONDON, *Thursday, Mar. 17th, 1899.*

... I write from a sofa. This morning at Prince's I fell violently on my knees and when I shortly after took my skate off, I found I couldn't walk. ... Maclagan, however, says I must lie up for a few days. Isn't it boring? I'm writing to all the amusing people to come and see me, having dressed the part well in a Japanese tea gown. . . .

It is so provoking because I was getting to skate really well. . . .

In the spring of the year 1899 Gertrude went abroad again to Northern Italy, by herself, then to Greece, with her father and her uncle Thomas Marshall, a classical scholar and translator of Aristotle, deeply interested at going to Greece for the first time. A most successful tour altogether. In Athens they find Dr Hogarth and go to the Museum, 'where Mr Hogarth showed us his recent finds – pots of 4000 B.C. from Melos. Doesn't that make one's brain reel?' Another distinguished archaeologist, Professor Dörpfeld, is there also. They listen with breathless interest to his lecture on the Acropolis: 'he took us from stone to stone and built up a wonderful chain of evidence with extraordinary ingenuity until we saw the Athens of 600 B.C. I never saw anything better done.'

She also writes from Athens: 'Papa has bought him a grey felt hat, in which he looks a dream of beauty, and some yellow leather gaiters to ride in the Peloponnesus. He will look smart, bless him. . . .'

Then to Constantinople, and back again to England in May.

In August she started with Hugo for Bayreuth, joining on the way Sir Frank Lascelles and his daughter Florence, and Mr Chirol (afterwards Sir Valentine Chirol). They go to Nuremberg and Rothenburg on the way, enjoying themselves ecstatically everywhere. She writes 'this is really too charming. You never met a more delightful travelling party'.

Descriptions of the music follow, and Gertrude also records some personal social experiences.

To F. B.   BAYREUTH.

Frau Cosima has asked us all to a party on Friday evening. Great Larks! ... The restaurant was crowded when the door opened and in came the whole Wagner family in procession, Frau Cosima first on Siegfried's arm. There was a great clapping as she passed down the room to her table.

To F. B.   BAYREUTH, *Wed. Aug. 16th, 1899.*

This morning about half past 8 came a message from the Grand Duke [of Hesse] asking us whether we could be at the theatre at 9 as he would show us the stage. We bustled up and arrived only a few minutes late. It was most entertaining; we were taken into every corner, above and below. We descended through trap doors and mounted into Valhalla. We saw all the properties, and all the mechanism of the Rhine maidens; we explored the dressing rooms, sat in the orchestra and rang the Parsifal bells! The Grand Duke was extremely cheerful and agreeable – he's quite young – and of course everyone was hats off and anxious to show us all we wanted to see. It's a very extraordinary place, the stage; the third scene of Siegfried was set. We shall feel quite at home when we see it to-night. Hugo is delighted with it all. He was much impressed by the Walküre though he says it will take a great deal to make him a Wagnerian.

After Bayreuth the party breaks up, all of them except Gertrude returning to England.

I'm awfully sorry to have parted with Hugo. He really is one of the most delightful people in the world. The Harrachs, you will be glad to hear, thought him very beautiful ... when I told you that they were people of discernment!

After this Gertrude went back through Switzerland to the Dauphiné and fulfilled her year-old purpose of ascending the Meije.

To H. B.   LA GRAVE, *Monday, 28th August, 1899.*

I sent you a telegram this morning ['Meije traversée'] for I thought you would gather from my last that I meant to have a shot at the Meije and would be glad to hear that I had descended in the approved, and in no other manner. Well, I'll tell you – it's awful! I think if I had known exactly what was before me I should not have faced it, but fortunately did not, and I look back on it with unmixed satisfaction – and forward to other things with no further apprehension. . . .

We left here on Friday at 2.30, Mathon, Marius and I, and walked up to the Refuge de l'Alpe in two hours. Two German men turned up at the Refuge. . . . Madame Castillan gave us a very good supper and I went at once to bed. I got off at 4.30 and got to the top of the clot at 8.10. In the afternoon there arrived a young Englishman called Turner with Rodier as guide and a porter. I went out to watch the beautiful red light fading from the snows and rocks. The Meije looked dreadfully forbidding in the dusk. When I came in I found that Mathon had put my rug in a corner of the shelf which was the bed of us all and what with the straw and my cloak for a pillow I made myself very comfortable. We were packed as tight as herrings, Mr Turner next to me, then the two Germans and Rodier. Mathon and the porters lay on the ground beneath us. Our night lasted from 8 till 12, but I didn't sleep at all. Marius lighted a match and looked at his watch. It was ten o'clock. 'Ah, c'est encore trop matin,' said Rodier. It seemed an odd view of 10 p.m. We all got up soon after 12 and I went down to the river and washed a little. It was a perfect night, clear stars and the moon not yet over the hills. . . . We left half an hour later, 1 a.m., just as the moon shone into the valley. Mathon carried a lantern till we got on to the snow when it was light enough with only the moon. . . .

At 1.30 we reached the glacier and all put on our ropes. ... It wasn't really cold, though there was an icy little breath of wind down from the Brèche. This was the first time I had put on the rope ... we went over the glacier for another hour ... we got into the Promontoir, a long crest of rock and rested there ten minutes ... we left there at 2.40. ... We had about three hours up very nice rock, a long chimney first and then most pleasant climbing. Then we rested again for a few minutes. ... I had been in high feather for it was so easy, but ere long my hopes were dashed! We had about two hours and a half of awfully difficult rock, very solid fortunately, but perfectly fearful. There were two places which Mathon and Marius literally pulled me up like a parcel. I didn't a bit mind where it was steep up, but round corners where the rope couldn't help me! ... And it was absolutely sheer down. The first half-hour I gave myself up for lost. It didn't seem possible that I could get up all that wall without ever making a slip. You see, I had practically never been on a rock before. However, I didn't let on and presently it began to seem quite natural to be hanging by my eyelids over an abyss. ... Just before reaching the top we passed over the Pas du Chat, the difficulty of which is much exaggerated. ... It was not till I was over it that Mathon told me that it was the dreaded place. We were now at the foot of the Pyramide Duhamel and we went on till we came in sight of the Glacier Carré, where we sat down on a cornice, 7.45. ... The Germans got up a quarter of an hour later having climbed up the rock a different way. ... At 8.45 we got to the top between the Pic du Glacier Carré and the Grand Pic de la Meije and saw over the other side for the first time. We left at 9 and reached the summit at 10.10, the rock being quite easy except one place called the Cheval Rouge. It is a red flat stone, almost perpendicular, some 15 feet high, up which you swarm as best you may with your feet against the Meije, and you sit astride, facing the Meije, on a very pointed crest. I sat there while Marius and Mathon went on and then followed them up an overhanging rock of 20 feet or more. The rope came in most handy! We stayed on the summit

until 11. It was gorgeous, quite cloudless. . . . I went to sleep
for half-an-hour. It's a very long way up but it's a longer
way down – unless you take the way Mathon's axe took.
The cord by which it was tied to his wrist broke on the
Cheval Rouge and it disappeared into space. There's a bad-
dish place going down the Grand Pic. The guides fastened a
double rope to an iron bolt and let Mr Turner and me down
on to a tiny ledge on which we sat and surveyed the Aiguille
d'Arve with La Grave in the foreground. Then was a very
nasty bit without the double rope – how anyone gets down
those places I can't imagine. However, they do. Then we
crossed the Brèche and found ourselves at the foot of the first
dent. Here comes the worst place on the whole Meije. I sat
on the Brèche and looked down on to the Châtelleret on one
side and La Grave on the other. . . . Then Mathon vanished,
carrying a very long rope, and I waited. . . . Presently I felt
a little tug on the rope. 'Allez, Mademoiselle,' said Marius
from behind and off I went. There were two little lumps to
hold on to on an overhanging rock and there La Grave beneath and there was me in mid-air and Mathon round the
corner holding the rope tight, but the rope was sideways of
course – that's my general impression of those ten minutes.
Added to which I thought at the time how very well I was
climbing and how odd it was that I should not be afraid.
The worst was over then, and the most tedious part was all
to come. It took us three hours to get from the Grand Pic to
the Pic Central – up and down over endless dents. We followed the crest all the way, quite precipitous rock below us
on the Châtelleret side and a steep slope on the other. There
was no difficulty, but there was also no moment when you
had not to pay the strictest attention. . . . I felt rather done
when we got to the Pic Central. . . . There was an hour of ice
and rock till at last we found ourselves on the Glacier du
Tabuchet and with thankfulness I put on my skirt again. It
was then 3 and we got in at 6.30. The glacier was at first
good then much crevassed. We skirted for nearly an hour
the arête leading up to the Pic de l'Homme and it was 5.30
before we unroped. . . . When I got in I found everyone in

the Hotel on the doorstep waiting for me and M. Juge let off crackers, to my great surprise. . . .

I went to bed and knew no more till 6 this morning, when I had five cups of tea and read all your letters and then went to sleep again until ten. I'm really not tired but my shoulders and neck and arms feel rather sore and stiff and my knees are awfully bruised.

After the Meije there is one more letter, too long to insert here, from La Grave, in which she relates her successful ascent of the Écrins. She comes back to England in the middle of September, well pleased, as shown by her letters, with her progress in climbing.

CHAPTER 5

1899 – 1900

Jerusalem: First Desert Journeys

IN November 1899 she starts for Jerusalem, with many hopes and plans, including learning more Arabic.

Dr Fritz Rosen was then German Consul at Jerusalem. He had married Nina Roche, whom we had known since she was a child, the daughter of Mr Roche of the Garden House, Cadogan Place. Charlotte Roche was Nina's sister. They made everything easy for Gertrude.

To H. B.   HOTEL JERUSALEM, *13th December, 1899.*

Here I am most comfortably installed. I am two minutes' walk from the German Consulate. My apartment consists of a very nice bedroom and a big sitting room, both opening on to a small vestibule which in its turn leads out on to the verandah which runs all along the first story of the hotel courtyard with a little garden in it. I pay 7 francs a day including breakfast, which is not excessive. My housemaid is an obliging gentleman in a fez who brings me my hot bath in the morning and is ready at all times to fly round in my service. I spent the morning unpacking and turning out the bed and things out of my sitting room; it is now most cosy – two armchairs, a big writing table, a square table for my books, an enormous Kiepert map of Palestine lent me by Uncle Tom and photographs of my family on the walls. I propose buying a horse! for which I shall pay about £18 and sell him at the end for no less, I hope.

To-day Dr R. and I went for a long walk, I left a card and a letter of introduction on Mrs Dickson at the English consulate. One's first impression of Jerusalem is extremely interesting, but certainly not pleasing. The walls are splendid (Saracenic on Jewish foundations), but all the holy places are terribly marred by being built over with hideous churches of all the different sects.

Gertrude's interest in the Holy places was that of the archaeologist only and not that of the believer.

To F. B.　　　　　　　　　　　　　　　　*December 13th, 1899.*

My days are extremely full and most agreeable. I either have a lesson or work alone every morning for 4 hours – the lesson only lasts 1½ hours. I have 3 morning and 3 afternoon lessons a week. I am just beginning to understand a little of what I hear and to say simple things to the servants, but I find it awfully difficult. The pronunciation is past words, no western throat being constructed to form these extraordinary gutturals. Still it's really interesting. We lunch at 12.30 and go out about 2, generally riding till 5. Then I come home to my work till 7 when I dress and go in to dinner. I aim at being back by 10 to get another hour's work but this doesn't always happen, especially now when Nina is very busy preparing a Xmas tree and we spend our evenings tying up presents and gilding walnuts, Dr R. reading to us, the while, all his travel letters from Persia – extremely interesting.

My horse is much admired. My teacher, also, is a success. He has the most charming fund of beautiful oriental stories and I make him tell them to me by the hour as I want to get used to the sound of words. He is a Christian and his family claims to have been Crusaders.

He has given me a lecture of his, written out in English, on the customs of the Arabs. It begins: 'The Arabs are the oldest race on earth; they date from the Flood!!' Comes my housemaid, 'The hot water is ready for the Presence,' says he. 'Enter and light the candle,' say I. 'On my head,' he has replied – it sound ambiguous in English! That means it's dressing time.

To F. B.　　　　　　　　JERUSALEM, *Thursday, Dec. 28, 1899.*

It has rained quite persistently for 5 days. You may imagine how I say 'Heil dir, Sonne!' this morning when I woke and saw the sun. Yesterday the Rosens had a Xmas tree for all the German children. It was most successful and the children were dears. I am beginning to feel very desperate about Arabic and I am now going to try a new plan. A Syrian girl is to come and spend an hour with me 3 or 4 times a week and talk to me. I shall take her out walks sometimes, if she is satisfactory, and converse with her. It is an awful language.

To F. B.   JERUSALEM, *Jan. 1st, 1900.*

Will you order Heath to send me out a *wide gray felt sun hat* (not double, but it must be a *regular Terai shape* and broad brimmed) to ride in, and to put a black velvet ribbon round it with straight bows. My Syrian girl is charming and talks very prettily but with a strong local accent. It adds enormously to one's difficulties that one has to learn a 'patois' and a purer Arabic at the same time. I took her out for a long walk on Friday afternoon and went photographing about Jerusalem. She was much entertained, though she was no good as a guide, for she had never been in the Jewish quarter though she has lived all her life here! That's typical of them. I knew my way, however, as every Englishwoman would – it's as simple as possible.

She came with us on the following day on a most delightful expedition. We started at 9 in the morning – it was Sunday and therefore a legitimate holiday – and rode down the Valley of Hinnom and all along the brook Kedron (which is dry at this season) through a deep valley full of immensely old olive trees and rock tombs scarcely older.

To H. B.   JERUSALEM, *Jan. 11th, 1900.*

... I am just beginning to feel my feet after a fearful struggle. The first fortnight was perfectly desperate – I thought I should never be able to put two words together. Added to the fact that the language is very difficult there are at least three sounds almost impossible to the European throat. The worst I think is a very much aspirated H. I can only say it by holding down my tongue with one finger, but then you can't carry on a conversation with your finger down your throat, can you? My little girl Ferideh Yamseh is a great success. She talks the dialect, but that is all the better as I want to understand the people of hereabouts.

My Sheikh has just told me that Ladysmith is relieved. I do hope it is true and that this is the beginning of good news. I am sending you a little packet of seeds. They are more interesting for association's sake than for the beauty of the plant – it is the famous and fabulous mandrake. By the way the root of the mandrake grow to a length of 2 yards, so I should think somebody shrieks when it is dug up – if not the mandrake, then the digger.

I took Ferideh for a drive and a walk yesterday and talked Arabic extremely badly and felt desponding about it. However there is nothing to be done but to struggle on with it. I should like to mention that there are five words for a wall and 36 ways of forming the plural. And the rest is like unto it.

To H. B.   JERUSALEM, *Jan. 11th–14th, 1900.*

Sunday 14. This goes to-morrow. It ought to reach you in a week as it goes by a good post via Egypt. The posts are arranged thus: Sunday and Monday outgoing posts and the rest of the week nothing. Dr R. Nina and I rode this afternoon, heavenly weather. We went an exploring expedition through a lovely valley under a place called Malba. The path of course awful. In one place we had to get off, pull down a wall and lead our horses over it. There are no decent paths at all, only the hard high road. I so often wish for you – always when I'm making a nice expedition. Next spring let us come here together. Anyhow let us have a nice travel together soon.

To F. B.   JERUSALEM, *Feb. 18th, 1900.*

There is a regular commerce apart from all others here to supply the Russian pilgrims with relics, souvenirs and the necessities of Russian peasant life. I bless the typewriter. It is such a joy to open an envelope of yours and find long sheets from the typewriter. It is rather terrible to think that Maurice is off; I hoped he wouldn't leave till the end of the month. Anyhow you will telegraph to me on his arrival, won't you, and all items of news you receive from him which can be conveyed by telegram. He writes in great spirits and it may be that it will be good for him, the out-of-door life there. My last letter I have sent home to be forwarded to him. Do you know the way when something disagreeable happens, that one looks back and tries to imagine what it would have been like if it hadn't happened? That's how I feel about his going.

Maurice had gone out to the Boer War in command of the Volunteer Service Company, Yorkshire Regiment. He and Gertrude were bound together with the closest affection and her constant anxiety and solicitude about him is shown in her letters.

Do you know these wet afternoons I have been reading the story of Aladdin to myself for pleasure, without a dictionary! It is not very difficult, I must confess, still it's ordinary good Arabic, not for beginners, and I find it too charming for words. Moreover I see that I really have learnt a good deal since I came for I couldn't read just for fun to save my life. It is satisfactory, isn't it? I look forward to a time when I shall just read Arabic – like that! and then for my histories! I really think that these months here will permanently add to the pleasure and interest of the rest of my days! Honest Injun. Still there is a lot and a lot more to be done first – so to work!

To F. B.   JERUSALEM.

Friday 2. To-day came the joyful news of the relief of Ladysmith. My horse is extremely well. We are going for a long ride to-morrow. The R's and I have been planning expeditions. We mean to go for 10 days into Moab about the 18th. It will be lovely. We shall take tents, Dr R. Nina and I.

To H. B.   AYAN MUSA, *Tuesday, March 20, 1900.*
                                From my tent.

I left Jerusalem yesterday soon after 9, having seen my cook at 7 and arranged that he should go off as soon as he

could get the mules ready. (His name is Hanna – sounds
familiar doesn't it! but that H is such as you have never
heard.) I rode down to Jerusalem alone – the road was full
of tourists, caravans of donkeys carrying tents for cook and
Bedouin escorts. I made friends as I went along and rode
with first one Bedouin and then another, all of them exag-
gerating the dangers I was about to run with the hope of
being taken with me into Moab. Half way down I met my
guide from Salt, east of Jordan, coming up to meet me. His
name is Tarif, he is a servant of the clergyman in Salt and a
Christian therefore, and a perfect dear. We rode along together, sometime, but he was on a tired horse, so I left him
to come on slowly and hurried down into Jericho where I
arrived with a Bedouin at 1 – famished.

This morning I got up at 5 and at 6 was all ready, having
sent on my mules and Hanna to the Jordan bridge. I knocked
up the Mudir and he said he would send a guide to Madeba
to make the necessary arrangements for me. The river valley
is wider on the other side and was full of tamarisks in full
white flower and willows in the newest of leaf, there were
almost no slime pits and when we reached the level of the
Ghor (that is the Jordan plain) behold, the wilderness had
blossomed like the rose. It was the most unforgettable sight
– sheets and sheets of varied and exquisite colour – purple,
white, yellow, and the brightest blue (this was a bristly sort
of plant which I don't know) and fields of scarlet ranunculus.
Nine-tenths of them I didn't know, but there was the yellow
daisy, the sweet-scented mauve wild stock, a great spendid
sort of dark purple onion, the white garlic and purple
mallow, and higher up a tiny blue iris and red anemones
and a dawning pink thing like a linum. We were now joined
by a cheerful couple, from Bethlehem, a portly fair man in
white with a yellow keffiyeh (that's the thing they wear
round their heads bound by ropes of camel hair and falling
over the shoulders) and a fair beard, riding a very small
donkey, and a thinner and darker man walking. The first
one looked like a portly burgher. He asked me if I were a
Christian and said he was, praise be to God! I replied piously

that it was from God. So we all journeyed on together
through the wilderness of flowers and every now and then
the silent but amiable Ismael got off to pick me a new
variety of plant, while the others enlivened the way by
stalking wood pigeons, but the pigeons were far too wily and
they let off their breech loaders in vain and stood waist deep
in flowers watching the birds flying cheerfully away – with
a 'May their house be destroyed!' from my Christian friend.
A little higher up we came to great patches of corn sown by
the Adwan Bedouins – 'Arabs' we call them east of Jordan,
they being the Arabs par excellence, just as we call their
black tents 'houses', there being no others. Then goodbye to
the flowers! Now we saw a group of black tents far away on
a little hill covered with white tombs – Tell Kufrein it is
called – and here the barley was in ear and, in the midst of the
great stretches of it, little watch towers of branches had been
built and a man stood on each to drive away birds and
people. One was playing a pipe as we passed – it was much
more Arcadian than Arcadia. We had now reached the
bottom of the foot-hills, and leaving the Ghor behind us, we
began to mount. We crossed a stream flowing down the
Wady Hisban (which is Heshbon of the fish-pools in the
Song of Songs) at a place called Akweh. It was so wet here
that we rode on to a place where there were a few thorn
trees peopled by immense crowds of resting birds – they seize
on any little bush for there are so few and the Arabs come
and burn the bush and catch and cook the birds all in one!
On the top of the first shoulder we came to spreading cornfields. The plan is this – the 'Arabs' sow one place this year
and go and live somewhere else lest their animals should eat
the growing corn. Next year this lies fallow and the fallow of
the year before is sown. Over the second shoulder we got on
to a stretch of rolling hills and we descended the valley to
Ayun Musa, a collection of beautiful springs with an Arab
camp pitched above them. I found the loveliest iris I have
yet seen – big and sweet-scented and so dark purple that the
hanging down petals are almost black. It decorates my tent
now. Half an hour later my camp was pitched a little lower

down on a lovely grassy plateau. We were soon surrounded by Arabs who sold us a hen and some excellent sour milk, 'laban' it is called. While we bargained the women and children wandered round and ate grass, just like goats. The women are unveiled. They wear a blue cotton gown 6 yards long which is gathered up and bound round their heads and their waists and falls to their feet. Their faces, from the mouth downwards, are tattooed with indigo and their hair hangs down in two long plaits on either side. Our horses and mules were hobbled and groomed. Hanna brought me an excellent cup of tea and at 6 a good dinner consisting of soup made of rice and olive oil (very good!) an Irish stew and raisins from Salt, an offering from Tarif. My camp lies just under Pisgah. Isn't it a joke being able to talk Arabic! We saw a great flock of storks to-day (the Father of Luck, Tarif calls them) and an eagle. I am now amongst the Bilka Arabs but these particular people are the Ghanimat, which Hanna explains as Father of Flocks.

Wed. 21. Well, I can now show you the reverse side of camping. I woke this morning at dawn to find a strong wind blowing up clouds from the east. At 7 it began to rain but I nevertheless started off for the top of Siagheh, which is Pisgah, sending the others straight to Madeba. I could see from it two of the places from which Balaam is supposed to have attempted the cursing of Israel and behind me lay the third, Nebo – Naba in Arabic. The Moses legend is a very touching one. I stood on the top of Pisgah and looked out over the wonderful Jordan valley and the blue sea and the barren hills, veiled and beautified by cloud and thought it was one of the most pathetic stories that have ever been told. I then rode to Nebo, the clouds sweeping down behind me and swallowing up the whole Ghor. As I left Nebo it began to stream. Arrived at Madeba about 11.30, wet through. I sent up to Government House, so to speak, to find out what my Mudir's letter had done for me in the matter of to-morrow's escort. The answer came that this Mudir was away but the Effendi was coming to see me. He appeared, a tall middle-aged Turk; I invited him into my tent with all politeness and offered him cigarettes (you see a bad habit may have its merits!) while Hanna brought him a cup of coffee. But – the soldier was not to be had! There weren't enough. I determined to wait till the coffee and cigarettes had begun to work and turned the conversation to other matters – with as many polite phrases as I could remember. Fortunately I fell upon photography and found that his great desire was to be photographed with his soldiers. I jumped at this and offered to do him and send him copies and so forth and the upshot of it was that *for me* he would send a soldier to-morrow at dawn. I think it's rather a triumph to have conducted so successful a piece of diplomacy in Arabic, don't you? The wind has dropped and sky is clear, but it's cold and dampish. I had the brilliant idea of sending into the town for a brazier which was brought me full of charcoal and put into my tent. I have been drying my habit over it. From my camp I look over great rolling plains of cornfields stretching eastwards.

Thursday 22. This has been a most wonderful day. Hanna woke me at 5.30. By 6.30 I had breakfasted and was ready to start. I sent up to know if my soldier was coming. He arrived in a few minutes, a big handsome cheerful Circassian mounted on a strong white horse, and a little before seven we started off. In a dip we came suddenly upon a great encampment of Christians from Madeba and stopped to photograph them and their sheep. They were milking them, the sheep being tied head to head in a serried line of perhaps forty at a time. We went on and on, the ground rising and falling and always the same beautiful grass – no road, we went straight across country. Another big encampment of Christians. The people were most friendly and one man insisted on mounting his little mare and coming with us, just for love. So we all cantered off together, through many flocks and past companies of dignified storks walking about and eating the locusts, till we came to the road, the pilgrim road to Mecca. Road of course it is not, it is about one-eighth of a mile wide and consists of hundreds of parallel tracks trodden out by the immense caravan which passes over it twice a year. We next came to some camps and flocks of the Beni Sakhr, the most redoubted of all the Arab tribes and the last who submitted to the Sultan's rule – 'Very much not pleasant,' said Tarif – and now we were almost at the foot of the low hills and before us stood the ruins of Mashetta. It is a Persian palace, begun and never finished by Chosroes I, who overran the country in 611 of our era and planned to have a splendid hunting box in there. Grassy plains which abound in game. The beauty of it all was quite past words. It's a thing one will never forget as long as one lives. At last, most reluctantly, we turned back on our four hours' ride home. We hadn't gone more than a few yards before three of the Beni Sakhr came riding towards us, armed to the teeth, black browed and most menacing. When they saw our soldier they threw us the salaam with some disgust, and after a short exchange of politenesses, proceeded on their way – we felt that the interview might have turned differently if we had been unescorted. We got in at 5, quite delighted with our day. Don't think I have ever spent such a wonderful day.

Friday 23. We were on the Roman road all the day – paved on the flat, hewn out of the rock in the gorges. Oh, my camp is too lovely to-night! I am in a great field of yellow daisies by the edge of a rushing stream full of fish and edged with oleanders which are just coming out. (I have a bunch of them in my tent.) On either side rise the great walls of the valley and protect me from every breath of wind. I have just been having a swim in the river under the oleander bushes and Tarif has shot me a partridge for dinner.... There is a very pretty white broom flowering. Mashallah! Oh, the nice sound of water and frogs and a little screaming owl!

Sunday 25. I'm going on to Petra! What with giving out that I'm a German (for they are desperately afraid of the English), I have got permission and a soldier from the Governor and this is always difficult and often impossible, and I can't but think that the finger of Providence points southwards! I would telegraph to ask your permission, but there's no telegraph nearer than Jericho! I think a missionary and his wife, Mr and Mrs Harding, are coming with me; they are nice people and I shall like to have them. He has gone to see about mules, etc., now, and we are off at dawn. I have spent a pleasant day here. ... I photographed and came back to my tent determined to penetrate into the south-west fort which is now used as barracks for the Turkish soldiers. Dr Johnson had told me I could not possibly get permission, so I asked for none, but took Hanna and walked calmly in, in an affable way, greeted all the soldiers politely and was shown all over! As I was walking about I came to the edge of a deep pit and whom should I see at the bottom of it but my poor Madeba friends! It was the prison, there were underground chambers on either side of the pit, but they were all sitting outside to enjoy the sun that straggles down at midday. We greeted each other affectionately. I then went down a long outer stair to a lower floor, so to speak, of the forts, and here again was shown great vaulted rooms cut out of the rock. These are all inhabited by soldiers and mules. I felt I had done a good morning's sight-seeing and came back to my tent where I was presently fetched by a little Turkish girl, the daughter of an Effendi, who told me her mother was sitting down in the shadow of the wall a little below my camp and invited me to come and drink coffee. We went down hand in hand and I found a lot of Turkish women sitting on the ground under a fig tree, so I sat down too and was given coffee and as they all but one talked Arabic, we had a cheerful conversation. We had a glorious view down the valley and across the Dead Sea – it is supposed to be the tomb of Noah and honoured as such. It's a glorious hot night. We bought a lamb to-day for a medijeh – our 4/-, which seems cheap. He was a perfect love and his fate cut me to the heart. I felt if I looked at him any longer I should be like Byron and the goose, so I parted from him hastily – and there were delicious lamb cutlets for supper.

Thursday 29. Wady Musa – at length we have arrived and it is worth all the long long way. We descended to the village of Wady Musa where we hoped to get provisions, but devil a hen there was, so we despatched a man post haste to the nearest Bedouin camp for a lamb, and as yet – 7 p.m. – none has appeared! However, we have got laban and barley and butter so we can support life with our own rice and bread. What the people in Wady Musa live on I can't imagine. They hadn't so much as milk. These things settled, we rode on and soon got into the entrance of the defile which leads to Petra. The Bab es Sik is a passage about half a mile long and in places not more than 8 ft. wide; the rocks rise on either side straight up 100 ft. or so, they are sandstone of the most exquisite red and sometimes almost arch overhead. The stream runs between filling all the path, though it used to flow through conduits and the road was paved; oleanders grew along the stream and here and there a sheaf of ivy hung down over the red rock. We went on in ecstasies until suddenly between the narrow opening of the rocks, we saw the most beautiful sight I have ever seen. Imagine a temple cut out of the solid rock, the charming façade supported on great Corinthian columns standing clear, soaring upwards to the very top of the cliff in the most exquisite proportions and carved with groups of figures almost as fresh as when the chisel left them – all this in the rose red rock, with the sun just touching it and making it look almost transparent. As we went on the gorge widened, on either side the cliffs were cut out into rock tombs of every shape and adorned in every manner, some standing, columned, in the rock, some clear with a pointed roof, some elaborate, some simple, some capped with pointed pyramids, many adorned with a curious form of stair high up over the doorway. ... The gorge opened and brought us out into a kind of square between the cliffs with a rude cut theatre in it and tombs on every side. We went on and got into a great open place the cliffs widening out far on every side and leaving this kind of amphitheatre strewn over with mounds of ruins. And here we camped under a row of the most elaborate tombs, three stories of pillars and cornices and the whole topped by a great funeral urn. They are extremely rococo, just like the kind of thing you see in a Venetian church above a seventeenth century Doge leaning on his elbow, but time has worn them and weather has stained the rock with exquisite colours – and, in short, I never liked Bernini so well! ... It is like a fairy tale city, all pink and wonderful. The great paved roads stretch up to a ruined arch and vanish; a solid wall springs up some 6 ft. 'A rose red city half as old as Time' – I wish the lamb had come! ...

Saturday 31. We left Petra at 7 this morning with great regret.

Monday 2. One of my muleteers, Muhammad, is a Druze. If all his sect are like him, they must be a charming race. He is a great big handsome creature, gentle and quiet and extremely abstemious. He eats nothing but rice and bread and figs. It makes me all the more keen to go to the Hauran which is the chief centre of them, and I want very much to take these two muleteers with me: they are very capable and obliging, and Muhammad would be interesting to have in a Druze country. One mayn't know or see anything of their religious observances, but he has been telling me a great deal about their life and customs. He says nearly all the people in the Lebanon are Druzes. He himself comes from Beyrout, where he lives next door to Ali. They both talk with the pretty, soft, sing-song accent of the Lebanon. I have a good variety of accents with me for Tarif has the Bedouin and Hanna the real cockney of Jerusalem. They appeal to me sometimes to know which is right. I never was so sunburnt in my life; I'm a rich red brown, not at all becoming! in spite of the Quangle Wangle hat you sent me.

Friday 6. Jericho again. Our plans are these: The Rosens and I start off on Monday fortnight, the 23rd, and go up together to the Hauran. It will take us about a fortnight. They come home and I go straight up to Damascus, a couple of days or so, and so perhaps across to Palmyra, and the rest as before, reaching Jerusalem again about the end of May.

To her sister. JERUSALEM, *April 9th, 1900.*

DEAREST ELSA,

It is so amusing to have a letter with photographs in it. I quite understand your impressions of Florence and Venice. To this day I feel more inside Florence myself, but I went to Venice knowing the East and knowing a good deal of Italy and for those reasons I think I found it easier to become a part of it. Also, I was there a month, nearly, you must remember. But it is very strange – 'unheimlich', some silly German said and it's not as silly as it sounds at first. It's a heavenly feeling when suddenly the thing jumps at you and you know you understand. I daresay you don't, but it doesn't matter, the feeling is there. I don't think you get it out of books a bit, though books help to strengthen it, but you certainly get it out of seeing more and more, even of quite different things. The more you see, the more everything falls into a kind of rough and ready perspective, and when you come to a new thing, you haven't so much difficulty in placing it and fitting it into the rest. I'm awfully glad you love the beginnings of things – so do I, most thoroughly, and unless one does, I don't believe one can get as much pleasure out of the ends. The early Florentines are too wonderful – there's such a feeling for beauty even in the woodenest of them, and they are so earnest, bless them, that they carry one with them – well, very nearly up into Paradise and down into Hell!

CHAPTER 6

1900

Desert Excursions from Jerusalem

To H. B.   JERUSALEM, *April 13th, 1900.*

TO-MORROW the Rosens and I are going off after lunch to
Neby Musa, where we are to camp for 2 nights. I think it
will be immensely amusing. Oh, Father dearest, don't I have
a fine time! I'm only overcome by the sense of how much
better it is than I deserve! ...

To H. B.   JERUSALEM, *Sunday, 22nd April, 1900.*

Saturday was the great day here, the day of the annual
miracle of the Holy Fire. Charlotte and I went off to the
Russian Consulate, for we were to go to the Russian balcony
to see the ceremony in the Church of the Holy Sepulchre.
The church was packed, every soul having bunches of
candles in his hand to receive the Holy Fire. There was a
moment of breathless interest – you know the murmur of a
great crowd which is waiting for something to happen? it
was intoxicating, I never felt so excited in my life. Suddenly
the sound of the crowd rose into a deafening roar and I saw
a man running from the corner of the sepulchre with a
blazing torch held high over his head. The crowd parted
before him, the flying figure and the flaming light disappeared into the dark recesses of the church – he had been
the first to receive the heaven-sent fire. Then followed a
most extraordinary scene. On either side of the sepulchre
the people fought like wild beasts to get to the fires, for there
were two issuing from the two windows of the sepulchre, one
for the Greeks and one for the Armenians. In an instant the
fire leapt to the very roof; it was as though one flame had
breathed over the whole mass of men and women. Every
soul was bearing a light, torch or candle or bunch of tapers;
behind us in the Greek church, which is almost dark, there
was nothing but a blaze of light from floor to dome, and the

59

people were washing their faces in the fire. How they are not burnt to death is a real miracle. . . . Then came a man from the sepulchre with a whip, bursting through the crowd, and behind him the Patriarch in his mitre holding two great torches over his head and two priests holding up his arms, and they ran, like men carrying some great tidings, through the narrow passage which had been cleared for them and which closed up behind them like water, and passed below us and up the Greek church to light the candles on the High Altar. I have a vision of looking up into the huge dome and seeing high high up, an open window with men standing in it, and their torches flaming between the bright sun and the dense smoke. Well, I can scarcely tell you about it sensibly, for as I write about it, I am overcome by the horrible thrill

DERAA, *Monday, April 30th, 1900.*

This morning we none of us had a very long way before us, so I didn't get up till 6.30, which was most pleasant. When I looked out of my tent door, there was Mount Hermon gleaming in all its snows, right in front of me. It was so beautiful that I had the greatest difficulty in not turning my face northwards and rushing straight for it, but the Druze mountains were standing mistily on the eastern horizon and I must try for them first. We breakfasted, as usual, in front of the Rosens' tent, with Hermon occupying the fourth place at our table, and at 8.30 we very sadly parted and I went east and they west. I have two muleteers, Muhammad and Yakoub, and Hanna. The maps mark this country as belonging to the Anazeh, a great tribe which stretches to the Euphrates, but they appear to have withdrawn their black tents further eastward, probably because of the encroaching Turkish government. There was a strong, cool west wind, but the sun was blazing hot, so hot that one had to put on a coat to keep it out. I wear a big white keffieh bound over my hat and wound round me so that only my eyes show, and they are partly hidden by a blue veil; but the chief comfort of this journey is my masculine saddle, both to me and to my horse. Never, never again will I travel on anything else; I haven't known real ease in riding till now. Till I speak the people always think I'm a man and address me as Effendim! You mustn't think I haven't got a most elegant and decent divided skirt, however, but as all men wear skirts of sorts too, that doesn't serve to distinguish me. About two we entered Deraa, built of black volcanic stone it is, all bare and dusty, with a black ruined tower. My tents were pitched on a hill by some ruined Roman baths, in sight of Hermon and the Jebel Druze. You wouldn't believe how soon the most unpromising spot changes into a comfy, home-like place as soon as one's tents are up and one's horses tethered.

BOSRAH, *Wednesday, May 2nd.*

I am deep in intrigues! I will tell you all from the beginning. We set off with a soldier for guide across the corn-covered plains; here and there a black village stood out from the green and the ground was covered with black porous stone. The volcanic peaks of the Jebel Druze lay ahead of us eastwards all day. At 11 I got to the first really interesting village, Jizeh, and here I saw the building of this country. You must understand that the peculiarities of it depend on the fact that there was (and is) no wood at all, and when the Romans made a great colony here in the first century, about, they built entirely with stone – the rafters are long bits of stone stretched across from arch to arch over the rooms, the doors are solid blocks of stone with charming patterns carved on them; the windows even are stone perforated with holes and carved between the holes. All this in black basalt; it is curious to see. There was one perfect house in Jizeh, small and four-square, with a cornice running round near the top on the outside, but it had no window at all. There was another, the beautiful walls of which were standing, and the stone roof, but the original door and windows were gone. It was turned into a mosque. Bosrah stood up, black and imposing, before us for miles before we arrived, a mass of columns and triumphal arches with the castle dominating the whole. I went up the square tower of the minaret and looked out over the town – columns and black square towers over every ruined church and mosque, and the big castle and the countless masses of fallen stone. I had been joined by a cheerful, handsome person, the Mamur (the Sultan's land agent) who climbed with me in and out of the churches and the fallen walls and the ruined houses. Such a spectacle of past magnificence and present squalor it would be difficult to conceive. There were inscriptions everywhere, Latin, Greek, Cufic and Arabic, built into the walls of the Fellahin houses, topsy turvy, together with the perforated slabs that were once windows, and bits of columns and capitals of pillars. After two hours of this I began to feel light-headed with fatigue and hunger. At last he took me to the top of the castle to see the view of the town and introduced me to the head of the soldiers, who produced chairs and coffee on his roof-top, and subsequently glasses of arrack and water in his room below. The Mamur is a Beyrouti and talks Arabic, but the other is a pure Turk, and our common tongue is French – most inadequate on his side. At length I induced them to let me go, and retired to my tents below the castle. I found the Mudir (Governor of the town) waiting for me, a handsome, dignified Arab, much looked down on by the whipper-snapper Turkish officials. We exchanged polite greetings and I retired to my dinner and my bed. This morning the Mamur appeared at eight to take me to a ruined village to the north. I went first to see the Mudir, whom I found sitting in his arched and shaded courtyard. He gave me coffee and nego-tiations began. 'Where was I going?' 'To Damascus.' 'God has made it! there is a fine road to the west with such and such places in it, very beautiful ruins.' 'Please God I shall see them! but I wish first to look upon Salkhad.' (This is in the heart of the Druze country, where they don't want me to go.) 'Salkhad! there is nothing there at all, and the road is very dangerous. It cannot happen.' 'It must happen.' 'There has come a telegram from Damascus to bid me to say the Mutussarif fears for the safety of your Presence.' (This isn't true.) 'English women are never afraid.' (This also isn't true!) 'I wish to look upon the ruins.' And so on and so off, till finally I told him I was going nowhere to-day and he said he would come and see me later. We parted, he saying, 'You have honoured me!' and I 'God forbid!' and I rode off with the Mamur to a village called Khurbet, crossing many beautiful Roman bridges on the way. There was nothing of interest there, and we turned east to Jemurrin, where there are some very beautiful ruined houses. They used no mortar, but the walls are built in a most wonderful way, the stones being often notched out and fitted into one another. We got back about 11. I lunched, after which my two Turkish friends came to call, but fortunately did not stay long. While they were with me, a Druze Sheikh was hanging round my tent, but I could not speak to him under the eyes of the officials. A Bedouin has also been here to ask if I want to go east, but I prefer to put myself under the protection of the Druzes. It's awfully amusing, and my servants fully enter into the fun of the thing. If only I could put myself into communication with the Druzes, all would be well. If not, I shall try starting very early to-morrow, and making a dash for them; once into their country I'll move quickly and it will be difficult for the Turks to catch me, for they are horribly afraid of the Druzes. I may fail – God is He who knows! I gather that the two Turks would put nothing in my way to stop me out of jealousy of the Mudir, who is the local authority. But one can't ever tell how much they say is true, and I keep my own counsel as far as possible. As yet I haven't let on that the places I want really to go to are not Salkhad at all, but some ruined towns further north, but I expect they know.

JEBEL DRUZE, *Thursday, May 3rd.*

I've slipped through their fingers, and as yet I can scarcely believe in my good fortune. The story begins last night; you must hear it all. I dined early and as I was sitting reading in my tent, I heard the voice of the Mudir. I blew out my light and when Hanna came to tell me of his coming, I sent him a message that I was very tired and had gone to bed. I heard this conversation: *Hanna.* 'The lady has been awake since the rising of the sun: all day she has walked and ridden, now she sleeps.' *Mudir*. 'Does she march to-morrow?' *Hanna*. 'I couldn't possibly say, Effendim.' *Mudir*. 'Tell her she must let me know before she goes anywhere.' *Hanna*. 'At your pleasure, Effendim.' And he left, but not without having assured me that he meant to stop me. I hastily re-arranged my plans. He knew I was going to Salkhad and when he found that I had flown, he would send after me along that road as far as he dared; I decided, therefore, to strike for a place further north, Areh, where I saw in Murray that a powerful Druze sheikh lived. Moreover the road lay past Jemurrin, which I knew, and whither I could find my way. Providence watched over me, as you will see, in this resolution. I told my servants. Muhammad tried to dissuade me, saying that if I told the Mudir I was going to Suweidah, north of Areh, he would raise no difficulties as there were Turkish soldiers there; but I knew better and besides, what was the good of being passed from the hands of one Turkish official to another? I afterwards found out that Muhammad, poor dear! was terrified out of his life and was trying all he knew to prevent my going. I went to bed, but what with excitement and dogs, I didn't sleep much. At two Hanna called me and I got up into the shivering night. By three I was ready, and the packing up began under the stars. It was bitter cold – one felt it after the heat of the days and in our thin summer clothes. I walked backwards and forwards and prayed Heaven that no soldier would look over the castle wall, see our lantern, and come to enquire what was happening. Fortunately the Mudir lived inside the town. The stars began to pale and that darkest moment of the night, when the east whitens, set in. At 4 we were off. It was a ticklish business finding our way in the dark round the walls to the east. I didn't know this bit of the road, having only seen the beginning and the end of it. The houses seemed to finger out towards us, and suddenly we would find ourselves heading inwards and were obliged to retrace our steps. It took us near an hour, but at last we were past the N.E. corner and I hit on the Jemurrin road. We had met only two men driving out their cows. By this time the little band of cloud in the east had turned pink; half an hour later it was gold and we saw the black ruins of Jemurrin in front of us. The sun rose just as we had passed them. Now we had to find our way by my excellent map; it was not difficult for we had the Roman road for our guide, but oh! it seemed long to the first Druze village. Muhammad was trembling lest he should see either a Druze or a soldier. I feared the latter only, but much. I was borne up by the extraordinary beauty of Hermon, with the dawn touching its snows. The road rose gradually; we could see nothing ahead but the top of the west slope of corn, and a black village where I hoped we should find Druzes, but which turned out to be only a ruin – Deir Zubier was its disappointing name. There was a man among the corn, however, with the white turban and black keffiyeh of the Druze and I greeted him thus (it is the right form) 'Peace be upon you! oh, son of my uncle!' He put us into the path, which we had missed. At length we came to the top of the last slope and saw in front of us a rolling fertile, watered country, scattered over with little volcanic hills, and behind it, higher hills and the pointed peak of the Kulieb rising over all – the Little Heart, the highest of the Jebel Druze. In front of us, not half a mile away was the tiny village of Miyemir. I hurried on. At the foot of the hill on which it lay was a pool and fig trees near by. The women were filling their earthenware jars at the water, Druze women in long blue and red robes and white muslin veils drawn over their heads and round their faces, and by the water stood the most beautiful boy of 19 or 20. I dismounted to water my horse; the boy (his name is Saif ed Din, the Sword of the Faith) came up to me, took my hands and kissed me on both cheeks, rather to my surprise. Several other men and boys came up and shook hands with me; they were all more or less beautiful, and so are the women, when you can see their faces. Their eyes look enormous, blacked with kohl, men and women alike; they are dark, straight browed, straight shouldered, with an alert and gentle air of intelligence which is extraordinarily attractive. I asked Saif ed Din if he would show us the way to Areh, but he said he was busy and it was only half an hour off, so we rode on. But we hadn't gone a quarter of a mile before he repented and came running after us to offer his services, touching his heart and his forehead in token of obedience. So we went on through meadows, cornfields and vineyards in this pleasant country of little hills, and the muleteers began to sing and the kindly white turbaned people working in the vineyards stopped to salute as we passed, and I laughed for joy all the way at the thought of the Mudir and the Turks. And so about 8.30 we reached Areh. Some persons of apparent importance were standing by their house doors at the bottom of the hill, so I rode up and gave them the salaam. They took me by both hands and begged me to alight and drink coffee with them. This was just what I wanted, for I needed information. We walked hand in hand, Druze fashion, with our little fingers clasped, not our hands, to the nearest houses. As I entered they said 'Are you German?' and when I told them I was English they nearly fell on my neck – you need no other introduction here. With many Mashallahs! they piled all their cushions on to a raised seat for me, brought a stool for my feet and water for me to wash my hands, and then sat round in a circle on the clean matted floor making coffee for me. The nicest of them all, Hamma Hamid, sat by me and laid his hand on my shoulder when he talked to me. I told them all my tale and how I escaped from the government and came to them, interrupted by many interjections of welcome and assurance that there was no government here (Turks, that means), and that I was safe with them and might go where I pleased. The sense of comfort and safety and confidence and of being with straight speaking people, was more delightful than I can tell you. They asked about the war and knew the names of all the towns and generals and were very sympathetic about Maurice – were cultivated, civilized human beings. The coffee finished (very good it was) I asked if I could see the Sheikh. 'Sheikh!' said they, 'Yahya Beg is the head of all the Druzes in the land, of course you must visit him.' So we went off to the top of the little hill on which stands the Beg's verandahed house, Hammad and I finger in finger, and as we went he told me that the Beg had been five years in prison in Damascus and had just been let out, three weeks ago, and warned me that I must treat him with great respect. I said my Arabic and not my feelings would be at fault, and indeed I would defy any one not to treat Yahya Beg with respect. He is the most perfect type of the Grand Seigneur, a great big man (40 to 50, I suppose) very handsome and with the most exquisite manners. We walked straight into his reception room, where he was sitting on a carpet with six or eight others eating out of a big plate. He beckoned me into the circle, and I ate too, using the thin slabs of bread for spoon and fork. The food was laban, and an excellent mixture of beans and meat. I should have liked to have eaten much more of it, but the Beg had finished and I was afraid it wouldn't be polite. The plate was removed and he piled up his cushions for me on the floor and I waited till he sat down, very politely, for he's a king, you understand, and a very good king too, though his kingdom doesn't happen to be a large one. Then I had to tell my tale over again and the Beg shut his big eyes and bowed his handsome head from time to time, murmuring 'Daghy, daghy' – it is true – as I spoke. I told him all I wanted to see and that I didn't want to see Suweidah because of the Turks in it – there's a telegraph too, greatest danger of all – and he was most sympathetic and arranged all my travels for me and told me to take Saif ed Din with me and to count on his protection wherever I went. So we drank coffee and then someone suggested I should photograph the Beg (to my great delight) and I posed him in his verandah and very splendid he looked. So we parted, and I walked down to a delicious water meadow where I found my horses and mules grazing and set off with Saif ed Din and another gentleman called Ali, whose functions I don't rightly know, but who seems an agreeable travelling companion. Saif ed Din, walking along briskly while I rode, his embroidered skirts neatly buttoned up over a white petticoat. On the way we met a troop of shining ones, all in their best, carrying guns and lances. They were going to congratulate the Beg on his safe return. They stopped to greet me and bid me every kind of welcome – it's a pleasant change after being with people whose one idea is to tell you not to go anywhere! We went gradually upwards towards the second ridge of hills, Saif ed Din showing me the plain where the great battle was fought, four years ago; they say 500 Druzes fell and 1400 Turks. At first we went through corn and meadows, then up a stony ground with grass between the stones. The country is thinly peopled, but there are Bedouins scattered about, who come in with their flocks for the pasturage and pay rent in money and camels. The Druzes use them as servants. The ruined sites are countless. On the southernmost corner of the ridge, finely situated, is the village of Habran, where I now am. My camp is pitched by a big pond, in a meadow, with evergreen oaks growing about in it and the black village behind. Kulieb stands over me to the north – dear Little Heart! I did not dare to think last night that I should ever be so near it. We got into camp at 12.30. I washed and lunched and slept, and at four went off with Saif ed Din to explore. The village is full of the old stone houses, more or less ruined and built up again. The best house I saw, with its arches inside and stone rafters and corbels supporting them, is now used as the Druze church – Khelweh, they call it. The village is beautifully clean, full of fruit trees, and hay drying on the flat roofs. The women were coming down to the various ponds on all sides with their jars for water on their heads. The Sheikh of the village took me to his house, spread some carpets and cushions outside and made me coffee – a lengthy process, as you begin from the beginning, roast and pound it. I didn't mind, however, as I lay on my cushions talking to all the pleasant friendly people and watching the light fade on Kulieb. Since dinner I have been swimming in the pond – it's almost a lake and quite deep. The women are very shy; they don't unveil even to me, but they let me photograph them. They appear to spend most of their leisure time mending their mud roofs, but the men treat them with great respect and affection even when they are muddy up to their elbows. Isn't this all too wonderful? I'm so delighted with it! But I began my day at 2, so good night. The Sheikh of the village invited me to dinner, but I refused on the plea of fatigue. To-day when I was having my first coffee party in Areh, Hammad asked me to tell them something out of the Bible. I translated for them 'Love thy neighbour as thyself', which seemed a good all round maxim, and they were much pleased with it.

Saturday, 5th.

A Christian lady sent me a delicious dish for breakfast – some flat thin bread with cream rolled up in it, slightly salted.

... There is a Mazar outside the town. I went in and found a charming room with a row of columns supporting the dome roof and lots of little children sitting on the floor, to whom the schoolmaster was teaching reading. The Mazar itself was an inner domed chamber with a tomb in it. I was off at 7.30 with Nusr ed Din. The barley was most beautiful, but alas! lots of locusts eating it. He begged me to come a little out of the route to Sehweh and honour his mother by drinking coffee with her. I sat under a mulberry tree with Nusr ed Din's family, nice handsome people, and ate fried eggs and bread and drank coffee and milk, the whole village crowding round. When one expostulates they say: 'We wish to gaze upon you, because you have honoured us.'

An hour's ride up a hill side, prettily wooded with stunted oak and hawthorn, in full flower, brought us to El Kafr, where I found my tent pitched. Directly I arrived, the Sheikh's son and some other persons of importance came to see me. They were a group of the most beautiful people you would wish to see. Their average height was about 6 ft. 1 in. and their average looks were as though you mixed up Hugo and you, Father.

At 4 I sallied out with Ali, whose native town it is. I don't need him really – it's an absurd luxury to have two guides, but when I tell him to go he replies that he is my brother and must accompany me everywhere – not without recompense, of course! I returned the call of the Sheikh's son and while I was drinking coffee the old Sheikh arrived. He had been to see Yahya Beg, and half expected me because the Beg had asked after me in the following terms: 'Have you seen a queen travelling, a consuless?' They offered me a sheep, but I refused it. I hope I did right; one never knows and I'm terribly afraid of committing solecisms. I feel it would be too silly, under these exceptional conditions, not to see all I can in a country which so few people have seen. It's extraordinarily enjoyable too. They took me to see the Khelweh, which was bigger and better than any I have yet seen. It was divided into two parts by a thin black curtain, one being the Harem for the women. The straw objects are for putting the holy books on.... There came a gentleman with a poem in Arabic which he had composed in my honour. I said I didn't know the custom in his country, but in mine, if anyone wrote a poem about me, I should certainly give him a shilling. He said 'Yes, it would happen'. I gave him a quarter of a medjideh, and he presented me with a copy of the poem, so we were both pleased.... I have told them all that I am going to bring you, Father, here next year, and they are much delighted and bid you 'relationship and ease'.

Monday, 7th.

When you are travelling in hot countries, the primary rule is always to bring your winter clothes. I have had reason to-day to be glad that I had learnt it. I meant to camp another night in the hills, go up Kulieb and be on the spot for the Druze gathering to-morrow, but when I woke I found the west wind colder than ever and the hills wrapped in cloud. I therefore decided to come straight across the ridge and sleep at Kanawat, much to my servants' delight, for a town is a better camping place in rainy weather than a mountain side.

Wednesday, 9th.

Before leaving this morning I went to the house of my friend, Ali el Kady, to drink a cup of tea – these were the terms of his invitation. He was very vague about the tea

making, consulting me as to whether he ought to boil the
water and the milk together. I said that wasn't the way we
did it usually. He gave me an extraordinary variety of foods,
a pudding, some very good fried cakes dipped in honey and
almonds and raisins, both of them swimming in a sweet
syrup – the almonds were excellent. It is fortunate that my
digestion is ostrich-like, for I seem to eat very odd things at
the oddest hours. I parted here with Nusr ed Din. I am
sorry to leave the little hills. Though they are so small, they
have quite the air of a mountain district, and also the climate. The hot, fine weather has come back to-day. We went
on, skirting the hills, north by east. Mount Hermon was a
shining glory across the plain to the west, and beyond him,
northwards, stretched the long line of the Anti-Lebanus,
also snow-topped. The Jebel Druze end in tiny volcanoes,
the beginning of the purely volcanic Lejah. It all looks black
and uncanny – 'unheimlich'.

Friday, 11th.

Damascus, but a long, long day to get to it. We were off at
6, and after an hour's riding we got to Burak and passed the
first Turkish garrison without remark. Then came an endless five hours; we never seemed to gain on the scenery. We
went on to the River Awaj, where we watered man and
beast under the poplars and willows, a charming spot. Here
I rode on alone up the Black Mountains, a low range of hills
separating the Awaj valley from the Abana, and at the top
I saw far away in a green plain and ringed round with
gardens, Damascus. This is the way to arrive at a great eastern city. I journeyed along with the trains of camels carrying
the merchandise of Damascus to and fro, and the Arabs on
their pretty mares, and the donkey boys bringing in grass
and all the varied population of an oriental road. But the
way was very long. It was 4 before I got into the town. I
dawdled up through the bazaars and stopped to eat ices
made of milk and snow and lemonade from a china bowl
half full of snow and half of lemon juice and water – nothing
was ever so good. At 5 I reached my hotel, saw that my

horse was properly looked after and went off to the German Consulate to get the box of clothes I had sent from Jerusalem. There I also, to my joy, found letters from you all. A very civil Oriental secretary has been giving me advice about Palmyra, whither I shall go, if your telegram is satisfactory, on Wednesday, returning here in about a fortnight. Dearest Father! you are a perfect angel to let me do all this! I don't see that the Palmyra journey ought to be much more expensive than all the others. It seems I shan't have to take more than three soldiers at the outside. I've got so many things to say to you, Mother, that I should have to make my letter as long again if I began saying them. It is at times a very odd sensation to be out in the world quite by myself, but mostly I take it as a matter of course now that I'm beginning to be used to it. I don't think I ever feel lonely, though the one person I often wish for is Papa. I think he really would enjoy it. I keep wanting to compare notes with him. You, I want to talk to, but not in a tent with earwigs and black beetles around and muddy water to drink! I don't think you would be your true self under such conditions.... Of course Arabic makes just all the difference. It would be small fun without.

To her family.   DAMASCUS, *May 14th, 1900.*

Beloved Family. – To-day came your telegram which it was a great relief to receive.

I'm off to-morrow with an escort of 3 soldiers and all promises well, I expect to be back in a fortnight.

KUTEIFEH, *May 15th.*

I got off this morning at 9. After the usual difficulties attending the first day's start, an hour's vigorous activity found us all in the saddle. You never can get off the first day, so what's the good of bothering? I have three soldiers. Ali, Musa and Muhammad. Following Lüttiche's excellent advice, I have arranged to give them half a medjideh a day each, and they keep themselves, which is a great simplification for us. They seem pleased, and as I believe they levy food and barley on the inhabitants as they go along, it pays them amply.... At the top of the pass there was a well of rain water, very good, said Ali, and I made Hanna fetch me a cupful. It was, however, full of little red animals swimming cheerfully about, and one must draw the line somewhere, so I did not partake.... There's a cuckoo here; let me quickly write and tell the Spectator.

Wednesday, 16th.

We were off at 5, Ali and I going ahead to see about camels for the desert. At 11.30 we reached Nasariyeh – may God destroy its houses! there was no corn in them. The camels had not come up and anyhow there was nothing to be done but to send back to the village, and accordingly Hanna and Jacoub rode off together. I lunched under a white umbrella, for there was no shade. Nasariyeh is a new place, the property of the Sultan. It lies in the middle of the wide, flat valley between bare hills that we have been following all day, and beyond it there is no water for twelve hours. There was an enormous caravan of camels grazing near their piled up saddles and a little tent in which were seated some merchants from Bagdad, the owners of the caravan. They had been two months on the way, said one of them, who came down to our canal to get water; he walked as slowly as a camel and was about as communicative, answering me in a sort of dazed way as if the desert had got into his brain, and turning slowly, heavily away with his water-skin. Hanna and I, after taking counsel together, had bought eight skins and four leather bottles in Damascus, which was lucky, for we found none here. When they came to fill them, however, they found that one had a big hole in it and came despairingly to tell me. For once I was equal to the occasion. Do you remember, Father, the Greek boy we met as we went over the hills from Sparta, whose skin of oil broke? I had seen him mend it cunningly with a stone and a bit of string and I mended mine with much skill in the same way. It has held, too. The sun was so hot, it burnt one through one's boots. I have gone into linen and khaki. The latter consists of a man's ready-made coat, so big that there is room in it for every wind that blows, and most comfy; great deep pockets. The shopkeeper was very anxious that I should buy the trousers too, but I haven't come to that yet. We got off at 2.30, having sent the three camels on, and rode till 5, when we just pitched down anywhere, in the desert it's all the same. The road was enlivened by Ali and Muhammad, the soldier, who are both extremely intelligent, and who related to me many interesting tales. My soldiers are delighted that I can talk Arabic; they say it's so dull when they can't talk to the 'gentry'. They talk Kurdish together, being of Kurdish parentage, but born in Damascus. Their Arabic is very good. Mine is really getting quite presentable. I think I talk Arabic as well as I talk German (which isn't saying much perhaps!), but I don't understand so well. It's so confoundingly – in the Bible sense! – rich in words. This is my first night in the desert – the first of I wonder how many dozens, scores – Heaven knows! There was a great stretch of shining salt to our right as we passed Nasariyeh, and while we rode I saw immense plaques of water on the horizon – always on the horizon, the further we rode the further they went. We passed a ruined khan half an hour from here – I believe they occur at regular intervals all the way to Palmyra. I meant to be a couple of hours farther on, but the delays prevented it, and start under the moon to-morrow. The smooth, hard ground makes a beautiful floor to my tent. Shall I tell you my chief impression – the silence. It is like the silence of mountain tops, but more intense, for there you know the sound of wind and far away water and falling ice and stones; there is a sort of echo of sound there, you know it, Father. But here nothing.

Sunday, 20th.

Palmyra, for I've got here at last, though after such a ride! We left Karyatein on Friday evening at 5.30. At dusk we found ourselves in the desert region. The night closed in very dark, the west being thick with cloud. My rolling stone which gathers moss all the way had picked up another companion, one Ahmed, white robed and perched up on the top of a

camel. The Agha had provided him as a guide. I was not on
the ordinary road, I must tell you, having decided to make a
'détour' to the south in order to avoid going and coming by
the same route. No tourist ever goes this way. It leads to a
spring called Ain el Wu'ul, the Spring of the Deer, in the S.
hills, which is half way between Karyatein and Palmyra.
This we had to make as soon as possible after sunrise for the
sake of the beasts for whom we had no water. It was very
strange pacing on in the silent dark behind my white robed
guide, the three soldiers, black shadows, beside me and the
mules tinkling behind. For the first few hours there was a
sort of path which one could see white and clear through the
scrubby desert plants; when it left off Ahmed turned off resolutely into the broken ground under the hills, guiding himself by the stars in the clear east and by a black hill which
stood out in front of us, and from which, he said, the spring
was seven hours away. The ground was very rocky; the
horses' hoofs rung out on the rough slabs of stone. We went
on and on and I talked first with one of my men and then
with another, and at intervals I half fell asleep and woke up
to see Ahmed's swaying figure like a kind of beckoning Fate
leading us into a grim waterless world. Across the range of
hills there is a country that no one ever travels over – right
away to Nejd there is not a spring – not a well; 44 waterless
days, said Ahmed. He imparted me scraps of information at
intervals; he knew the name of every hill and every bare furrow – I was surprised to find they had names, but it seems
they have. This was the sort of conversation. 'Where is the
Lady?' 'Here, oh, Ahmed.' 'Oh, Lady, this is the Valley of
the Wild Boar.' There didn't seem anything to say about it
except that it was a horrid sandy little place, so I replied
that God had made it. Ahmed accepted this doubtful statement with a 'God the Exalted is merciful!' on which Ali, the
five times hadji, would break in with 'Praise be to God who
is Great! may he prolong the life of the Sultan!' Soon after
3, Ahmed said 'Oh, Lady! the light rises.' I looked and the
east was beginning to pale. I felt as if I had been sitting in
my saddle for a lifetime and my horse felt so too. He was so

hungry that he began to snatch at the camel's food as he passed – now the names of these plants I know, but only in Arabic, so I think it best not to tell. I was also hungry, and I had a light refection of chocolate and an orange, and then I got off and walked for near an hour, Ahmed walking too to keep me company. The light came quickly across the stony ground in the furrows. We mounted and rode on till 5, when the sun was behind some clouds. We were now coasting along the foot of the hills and Ahmed began to look about and wonder where the spring was. He had only been there once in his life before. The hills consisted of a long range of little stony peaks with a valley running up between them every quarter of a mile or so; in one of these valleys, high up, was the spring; the question was which. Ahmed wasn't sure, so he left me with the camel and set off running into the hills to explore. The others came up, and I made Hanna give me a bit of bread and a cup of milk which had turned into butter and whey (but awfully good) and I fell asleep almost while I was eating it. I had been riding for 12 hours. Half an hour later I heard my men say that Ahmed was beckoning to us. We had gone a good bit too far. We rode back half an hour, entered one of the valleys and climbed up it nearly to the top, and there on a tiny platform between rocks, we found the spring. It was only a very small cup, 6 or 8 feet across, more perhaps, and about 10 feet deep of water, the cup being barely half full. The water was clear and cold but covered with masses of weed and full of swimming things of all kinds. The soldiers and the beasts didn't seem to mind, however, and I shut my eyes and drank too. It was past 7 when we got to it. I had something to eat, climbed up to a shady cave, and slept till 1, quite indifferent to the fact that my bed was thistles and my bed-fellows stinging flies. If we had missed this one spring hidden in the hills, we should have been hard put to it. The good Hanna gave me an excellent lunch of fried croquettes and a partridge that he had killed, and tea. I had told him to cook nothing, but his conscience was too much for him, and he had made a charcoal fire between some stones and prepared these masterpieces, bless him! At 3 we were off again, and down into the plain, and then straight east at the foot of the hills. It had never been really hot all day, fortunately; the sun set without a cloud and it began to be very cold. We rode till 7 and then stopped for the animals to eat, and for us to eat too. I put on gaiters, a second pair of knickerbockers and a covert coat under my thick winter coat, rolled myself up in a blanket and a cape and went to sleep, all the men following my example, rolled up in their long cloaks. The cold and the bright moon woke me at midnight and I roused all my people (with some difficulty!) and at one we were off. Again, you see, we had to reach our water as soon as possible after the sun, so that the animals might not suffer too much from thirst. We went on and on; the dawn came and the sun rose – the evening and the morning of the second day, but I seemed to have been riding since the beginning of time. At sunrise, far away in the distance, on top of one of a group of low hills, I saw the castle of Palmyra. We were still five hours away. They were long hours. Except Petra, Palmyra is the loveliest thing I have seen in this country, but five hours away. They were long hours. The wide plain gradually narrowed and we approached the W. belt of hills, rocky, broken and waterless. It's a fine approach, the hills forming a kind of gigantic avenue with a low range at the end behind which Palmyra stands, and the flat desert, very sandy here, running up to them. My horse was very tired and I was half dazed with sleep. As we drew near Palmyra, the hills were covered with the strangest buildings, great stone towers, four stories high, some more ruined and some less, standing together in groups or bordering the road. They are the famous Palmyrene tower tombs. At length we stood on the end of the col and looked over Palmyra. I wonder if the wide world presents a more singular landscape. It is a mass of columns, ranged into long avenues, grouped into temples, lying broken on the sand or pointing one long solitary finger to Heaven. Beyond them is the immense Temple of Baal; the modern town is built inside it and its rows or columns rise out of a mass of mud roofs. And beyond all is the desert, sand and white stretches of salt and sand again, with the dust clouds whirling over it and the Euphrates five days way. It looks like the white skeleton of a town, standing knee deep in the blown sand. We rode down to one of the two springs to which its owes its existence, a plentiful supply of the clearest water, but so much impregnated with sulphur that the whole world round it smells of sulphur. The horses drank eagerly, however, and we went on down a line of columns to the second spring which is much purer, though it, too, tastes strongly of sulphur. If you let it stand for 12 hours the taste almost goes away, but it remains flat and disagreeable, and I add some lemon juice to it before I drink it. It's very clean, which is a blessing.

Monday, 21st.

I got up feeling extremely brisk, and spent the whole morning exploring Palmyra. Except Petra, Palmyra is the loveliest thing I have seen in this country, but Petra is hard to beat.

Wednesday, 23rd.

We were off at 5, just as the sun rose. As I rode over the hill, Palmyra looked like a beautiful ghost in the pale stormy light. I am returning by the ordinary tourist route, the old high road across the desert. Last night there arrived from the East a big caravan of camels belonging to the Agail Arabs, who are going to sell them in Damascus. The chief man of them is one Sheikh Muhammad. I had met him yesterday in Palmyra, and he told me that please God, who is great, he meant to travel with me. He comes from Nejd, and talks the beautiful Nejd Arabic; there are one or two Bagdadis with him, and the rest of the party are the wildest, unkemptest, Agail camel drivers. The interesting part of it is that the Agail are some of the Rashid's people, and I'm going to lay plans with Sheikh Muhammad as to getting into Nejd next year. I found them breakfasting on dates, camels' milk and the bitter black coffee of the Arabs – a peerless drink. I also made a supplementary breakfast with them and then we all started off together. The reason Sheikh Muhammad wants to travel with me is that he is anxious to have the extra protection of my three soldiers – he has two of his own – fearing a raid of Arabs on his camels on the way to Karyatein. I think it's great sport; I'm not sorry to be able to do a good turn to an Agail, and he and his Bagdadis are very interesting to talk to, with their dragoman on the box and their mules following behind the crowds of tents.

Thursday, 24th.

I wish I could manage to travel on the approved lines, but the fates are against me. I had laid all my plans for coming back from Palmyra like a lady, but no! it was not to be. We got off rather late this morning – 5.30 it was before I left Ain el Baida, and then the mules were not ready. I started without them – a fatal step, as you will see. The Agail were off half an hour before, the good Sheikh Muhammad having put two water skins for me on his camel. Ahmed, my guide, put another two on his camel and I told the muleteers to bring the other four, so that we should have enough water for our beasts and could sleep comfortably in the desert. There is no water between Ain el Baida and Karyatein. At Kasr el Khair we found that the two water skins on Sheikh Muhammad's camel had leaked and were quite empty, and Hanna told me that Yacoub, the muleteer, had refused, after I left, to carry his two skins and had poured the water out on the ground. So here we were with two skins and a couple of leather bottles for ten animals and seven people. There was nothing to be done but to make a dash for Karyatein. The Agail were rather distressed at this, being still terrified for their camels, but what was I to do? They had no water, camels needing none, and after I had watered my beasts at Kasr el Khair, I had none – I couldn't keep my camp 24 hours waterless. We were only seven hours from Karyatein, and we had done barely seven that morning, in fact our horses were so brisk that Ali, Muhammad the soldier, Ahmed the guide and I got into Karyatein in five hours – but we rode for it! I came in the last hour or two on Ahmed's camel – it's the greatest relief after you have been riding a horse for

8 or 9 hours to feel the long comfy swing and the wide soft saddle of a camel. I was glad to get into my tent again and to bed about 11, feeling as if I had had enough of travelling for one day.

Friday.

I found my camp pitched in Mahin near the water, and hundreds of camels drinking near it. A big company of the Hasineh Arabs had just arrived, moving from their winter quarters and their black tents were pitched not far from me. Their Sheikh, Muhammad, came to call on me, a boy of 20 or younger, handsome, rather thick lipped, solemn, his hair hanging in thick plaits from under his keffiyeh. He carried an enormous sword, the sheath inlaid with silver. After he had gone, his sister and some other women appeared in all the trailing dirt of their dark blue cotton robes. Sheikh Muhammad is a great swell. He owns 500 tents and a house in Damascus, and Heaven knows how many horses and camels. After tea, I returned his call and sat on carpets and cushions in the big Sheikh's tent, the Hasineh making a circle round me while I drank coffee. The Sheikh's mother also appeared and was treated with great honour, Muhammad getting up and giving her his place on the carpet and his camel saddle to lean on. After a bit, one of the black browed, white robed Arabs took a rubaba, a single stringed instrument played with a bow, and sang to it long melancholy songs, monotonous, each line of the verse being set to the same time and ending with a drop of the voice which was almost a groan. The murmur of the rubaba ran through it all – weird and sad and beautiful in its way. All the silent people sat round looking at me, unkempt, half-naked, their keffiyehs drawn up over their faces, nothing alive in them but their eyes, and across the smouldering fire of camels' dung, the singer bent his head over the rubaba or looked up at me as he sent the wailing line of his song out into the dark. Sometimes one would come into the open tent (the front is never closed) and standing on the edge of the circle, he greeted the Sheikh with a 'Ya Muhammad!' his hand lifted to his forehead and

the company with 'Peace be upon you', to which we all
answered 'And upon you peace!' Then the circle spread out
a little wider to make room for the new comer. At last I got
up and said good-bye. I hadn't gone more than a few steps
when my soldiers told me I had committed a fearful solecism.
They had killed a sheep for me and were preparing a dinner,
of which I ought to have partaken, and further, said Ali,
'Muhammad is a great Sheikh and you ought to give him a
present.' I went back to my tent rather perturbed, what
could I give? Finally, after thinking things over, I sent one
of my soldiers with Ali's pistol wrapped up in a pocket-
handkerchief (you can give nothing to an Arab but arms
and horses) and a message that I hadn't known he had
meant to do me such honour and would he accept this present (net value £2). He returned answer that he was grateful,
that he was doing nothing but his duty and would I honour
them? So back I went with Athos, Porthos and What's-his-
name, and we all sat down again on the cushions and carpets
and waited. We waited till 9.30! I wasn't bored (though I
was hungry!). One by one, the Arabs dropped in till the circle
stretched all round the big tent; at intervals the talk went
round – the politics of the desert: who had sold horses, who
owned camels, who had been killed in a raid, how much the
blood money would be or where the next battle. It was very
difficult to understand, but I followed it more or less. Besides
the bitter black coffee, we were handed cups of what they
called 'white coffee' – hot water, much sweetened and flav-
oured with almonds. At length came a black slave with a
long spouted water jar in his hand, to me first and then to all
the company. We held out our hands and he poured a little
water over them. And at last dinner – four or five men bearing in an enormous dish heaped up with rice and the meat of
a whole sheep. This was put down on the ground before me,
and I and some ten others sat round it and ate with our
fingers, a black slave standing behind us with a glass which
he filled with water as each guest required it. The food was
pretty nasty, saltless and very tough – but it was 9.30! They
eat extraordinarily little, and I was still hungry when the

first circle got up to make place for the second. More hand-washing, with soap this time, and I bowed myself out and retired to biscuits and bed. It was rather an expensive dinner, but the experience was worth the pistol.

Tuesday, 29th.

I had a very beautiful ride into Damascus. The air was sweet with the smell of figs and vines and chestnuts, the pomegranates were in the most flaming blossom, the valley was full of mills and mill races bordered by long regiments of poplars – lovely, it must be at all times, but when one comes to it out of the desert it seems a paradise. I got to Damascus soon after two and rode through the bazaars, eating apricots, with which all Damascus is full. Now he who has not eaten the apricots of Damascus has not eaten apricots. To my joy I found Charlotte here when I arrived and letters. Telegrams from you and the war news excellent.... 95 [Sloane St] will be splendid! Tell my sisters I love their letters and fly to them as soon as I get my post.... I do fervently hope to be in London about the 21st. I should like a week there because I am somewhat ragged, as you may well imagine. I wish I were as well stocked with clothes as Elsa, tell her! As for my travelling clothes – 'nein!!' Oh, my dear family! I do long to be with you again. I want to have the most fearful long talk about nothing with my sisters and about things with my father and about everything taken together with my mother. By the way, did I mention that Damascus is a singularly beautiful place?

Gertrude's letters until her return to England are very vaguely dated, but it is clear that she remained with the Rosens, making more or less distant excursions with them at intervals.

To H. B.   ARAK EL EMIR, *Wednesday, 30th May, 1900.*

From my Camp.

(Arabia, suggests Dr R., in case you shouldn't know where the above important place is.) Well, we left yesterday after lunch, after a tremendous getting off, such a packing and saying Goodbye! I never had my hand kissed so often!

She describes Baalbek and the Lebanon range. She and her companions ride to the place where the great cedars flourish.

Wednesday, 6th.

There is such an exquisite village in front of me that I can scarcely take my eyes off it to write to you. Its name is Hasrun, and it stands perched up on cliffs over the deep valley Kadisha, the stream being 1,000 feet or more below it, and the mountains rise above it, and the whole is a red gold at this moment, for the sun is busy sinking into the sea out Tripoli way. We spent a delicious lazy morning at the cedars, breakfasted and lunched under the big trees and photographed and drew and listened to the birds. The ground is covered with tiny cedars, but they never grow up under the shadow of their parents (how different from the Belgian Hare!) but wither off when they have reached the height of about 2 inches – which is small for a tree. There were, however, outside the big trees a few saplings which had sprung up of themselves and were growing extraordinarily slowly; they were five years old, said the guardian of the wood, but they were not more than 18 inches high. I have brought a lot of cones away with me. Shall we try and make them grow at Rounton? It would be rather fun to have a real Cedar of Lebanon – only I believe they don't grow more than about 20 feet high in 100 years, so we at least shall not be able to bask much under their shadow. We tore ourselves away at 1, the guardian of the woods making us low salaams as we rode off – a beautiful creature he was – tall and straight and dressed in a red and gold cotton coat and a white felt scull cap on his curly head. There were pale periwinkles growing on the edge of the wood and a sweet-scented pink daphne inside – well, well, we were sorry to go....

Gertrude brought the cones home, and distributed them to her family and friends – and so there is a real Cedar of Lebanon growing on the lawn at Rounton now. It is about 16 ft. high. Another stands on Sir George Trevelyan's lawn at Wallington.

Saturday, 10th.

And so to-day. We set off about 7 – it was already fear-fully hot, we walked 3 hours leading our horses, over the devilish road. Then we got on to the carriage road to Bey-rout and followed it all along the coast arriving at 3 about. We shall go to Jaffa to-morrow, as there is a boat and I am anxious to get home. But you know, dearest Father, I shall be back here before long! One doesn't keep away from the East when one has got into it this far.

CHAPTER 7

1901–1902

Switzerland – Syria – England

SHE had been on the golf links.

To F. B.   REDCAR, *March 5th, 1901.*

... It was a regular March day with a bitter wind. The pools of water on the links were as blue as the cracks in a glacier and the wind shivered them into steely lines. They reminded me of a simile in an Arab war song – 'the folds of their coats of mail were like the surface of a pool which is struck by the pressing wind....'

Gertrude does not seem to have left England again until the late summer of 1901, when she returns to Switzerland for some more climbing.

To H. B.   ROSENLAUI, *Sunday, 8th September, 1901.*

I am now going to give you a history of my adventures. Friday: we set out before dawn, the mists lying low everywhere, on the sporting chance of finding fine weather above them. We walked up the hour and a half of steep wood which is the preface to every climb here, and got to our familiar scene of action, a rocky valley called the Ochsenthal. Our problem was to find a pass over a precipitous wall of rock at the S. end of it. Now this rock wall had been pronounced impossible by the two experts of these parts and by their guides. We cast round and finally decided on a place where the rock wall was extremely smooth, but worn by a number of tiny water channels, sometimes as much as 3 inches deep by 4 across. These gave one a sort of handhold and foothold. Just as we started up it began to snow a little. The first 100 feet were very difficult and took us three quarters of an hour. The rock was excessively smooth and in one place there was a wall some 6 feet high where Ulrich had to stand on Heinrich's shoulder. Above this 100 feet it went comparatively easily and in an hour we found ourselves in a delightful cave, so deep that it sheltered us from the rain and sleet which was now falling thick. Here we breakfasted, gloomily enough. After breakfast things looked a little better and we decided to go on though it was still raining. The next bit was easy, rocks and grass and little ridges, but presently we found ourselves on the wrong side of a smooth arête which gave us no hold at all. We came down a bit, found a possible traverse and got over with some difficulty. A rotten couloir and a still more rotten chimney and we were on the top of the pass, 1 h. 20 m. from the cave. We *were* pleased with ourselves! It was a fine place; about 2000 feet of arête, less perhaps, between the great peak of the Engelhorn on the right and a lower peak on the left, which is the final peak of that arête of 4 peaks we did the other day. We called this 5th peak of our arête the Klein Engelhorn.... The whole place up there is marked with chamois paths, no one, I expect, having ever been there before to disturb them. There is, however, an old old cairn on the low slopes of the Engelhorn, made by some party who, having come over the Engelhorn, tried to traverse down the N. side and turned back at this place. We know that neither the N. nor the S. side of the Gemse Sattel, as we have called it, has ever been done. Indeed the S. side *may* be impossible, but I don't think it is. They say it is, but we know that the experts may be mistaken. It was snowing so hard that we decided we could do no more that day and returned by the way we had come.... We got down the smooth rocks with the help of the extra rope. It was most unpleasant, for the water was streaming down the couloirs in torrents and we had to share the same couloirs with it. It ran down one's neck and up one's sleeves and into one's boots – disgusting! However, we got down and ran home through the woods. In the afternoon it cleared and at dawn on Saturday we were off again. We went again to the top of the Gemse Sattel; it was a beautiful day and we knew our way and did the rocks in an hour and ten minutes less than we had taken the day before. Here we breakfasted and at 10 we started off to make a small peak on the right of the saddle which we had christened beforehand the Klein Engelhorn. We clambered up an easy little buttress peak which we called the Gemse Spitz and the Klein Engelhorn came into full view. It looked most unencouraging; the lower third was composed of quite smooth perpendicular rocks, the next piece of a very steep rock wall with an ill-defined couloir or two, the top of great upright slabs with deep gaps between them. It turned out to be quite as difficult as it looked. We got down the Gemse Spitz on to a small saddle, did a very difficult traverse forwards and upwards above the smooth precipitous rocks, scrabbled up a very shallow crack and halted at the bottom of a smooth bit of overhanging rock. The great difficulty of it all was that it was so exposed, you couldn't ever get yourself comfortably wedged into a chimney, there was nothing but the face of the rock and up you had to go. For this reason I think it more difficult than the Simili Stock. Well, here we were on an awfully steep place under the overhanging place. Ulrich tried it on Heinrich's shoulder and could not reach any hold. I then clambered up on to Heinrich, Ulrich stood on me and fingered up the rock as high as he could. It wasn't high enough. I lifted myself still a little higher – always with Ulrich on me, mind! – and he began to raise himself by his hands. As his foot left my shoulder I put up a hand and straightened out my arm and made a ledge for him. He called out, 'I don't feel at all safe – if you move we are all killed'. I said, 'All right, I can stand here for a week', and up he went by my shoulder and my hand. It was just high enough. Once up he got into a fine safe place and it was now my turn. I was on Heinrich's shoulder still with one foot and with one on the rock. Ulrich could not help me because he hadn't got my rope – I had been the last on the rope, you see, and I was going up second, so that all I had was the rope between the two guides to hold on to. It was pretty hard work, but I got up. Now we had to get Heinrich up. He had a rope round his waist and my rope to hold, but not shoulder, but he could not manage it. The fact was, I think, that he lost his nerve, anyhow, he declared that he could not get up, not with 50 ropes, and there was nothing to do but to leave him. He unroped himself from the big rope and we let down the thin rope to him, with which he tied himself, while we fastened our end firmly on to a rock. There we left him like a second Prometheus – fortunately there were no vultures about! So Ulrich and I went on alone and got as far as the top of the first great slab which was a sort of gendarme.[1]

I must add as a footnote to this letter that when Gertrude came home to us and related the thrilling ascent, still more exciting naturally in the telling, she told us that after it was over Ulrich had said to her, 'If, when I was standing on your shoulders and asked you if you felt safe, you had said you did not, I should have fallen and we should all have gone over.' And Gertrude replied to him, '*I thought I was falling when I spoke.*'

Here Ulrich shouted down to me, 'It won't go!' My heart sank – after all this trouble to be turned back so near the top! Ulrich came down with a very determined face and announced that we must try lower down. We were now on the opposite side of the mountain from that on which we had left Heinrich. We went down a few feet and made a difficult traverse downwards above a precipice till we came to a chimney. I leant into the crack, Ulrich climbed on to my shoulder and got to the top. It was done! a few steps more brought us to the very top of all and we built a cairn and felt very proud. There was a difficult moment coming down the first chimney. We had left our thin rope with Heinrich, so we had to sling the thick rope round a rock for Ulrich to come down on. But it was still wet from the day before and when we got to the bottom the rope stuck. He went up and altered its position and came down and it stuck again. Again he went up, and this time he detached it and threw it down to me and came down without a rope at all. I gave him a shoulder and a knee at the last drop. So we got back and rescued Heinrich and after a great deal of complicated rope work we reached the Gemse Sattel again after 4 hours of as hard rock climbing as it would be possible to find. Lunch was most

[1] Mr Heinrich Fuhrer, the well-known admirable and courageous guide (now of the Sports House, Gstaad, Switzerland), is not the guide of the same name mentioned above. These two were cousins: and it was the latter, since dead, who shared in the ascent.   F. B.

agreeable. Our next business was to get up the Engelhorn by
the arête up which I told you we saw the chamois climb the
other day. This proved quite easy – it has not been done before, however – and at 3.30 we were on the top of the Engelhorn. Now we had to come down the other side – this is the
way the Engelhorn is generally ascended. It's a long climb,
not difficult, but needing care, especially at the end of a hard
day when you have no finger tips left.... It was 7 o'clock
before we reached the foot of the rocks. It was too late and
too dark to think of getting down into the valley so we decided that we would sleep at the Engen Alp at a shepherd's
hut. We wandered over Alps and Alps – not the ghost of a
hut was to be found. It was an exquisite starry night, and I
had almost resigned myself to the prospect of spending the
whole night on the mountain side, when suddenly our lantern
showed us that we had struck a path. At 9.30 we hove up
against a chalet nestled in to the mountain side and looking
exactly like a big rock. We went in and found a tiny light
burning; in a minute 3 tall shepherds, with pipes in their
mouths, joined us and slowly questioned us as to where we
had come from and whither we were going. We said we were
going no further and would like to eat and sleep. One of the
shepherds lighted a blazing wood fire and cooked a quantity
of milk in a 3-legged cauldron and we fell to on bowls of the
most delicious bread and milk I ever tasted. The chalet was
divided into two parts by a wooden partition. The first part
was occupied by some enormous pigs, there was also a ladder
in it leading up to a bit of wooden floor just under the roof,
where the fresh hay was kept. Here I slept. The other room
had a long berth all down one side of it and a shelf along another filled with rows of great milk tins. The floors were just
the hard earth and there was a wooden bench on which we
ate and a low seat by it. I retired to my hayloft, wrapped myself in a new blanket and covered myself over with hay and
slept soundly for 8 hours when my neighbours, the pigs,
woke me by grunting loudly to be let out. The shepherd gave
us an excellent breakfast of milk and coffee – we had our
own bread and jam. It was so enchanting waking up in that

funny little place high up on the mountain side with noisy torrents all round it. The goats came flocking home before we left; they had spent a night out on the mountains, having been caught somewhere in the dark and they bleated loud complaints as they crowded round the hut, licking the shepherd's hand. It was about 7.30 before Ulrich and I set off down the exquisite Urbach Thal; Heinrich had gone on before. We walked down for a couple of hours discussing ways up the Engelhorn and the Communal System! then we turned into the valley of the Aar and dropped down on to Innertkirchen in the green plain below. This is Ulrich's native place. We went to his home and found his old father, a nice old man of 70, who welcomed us with effusion. It was an enchanting house, an old wooden chalet dated 1749, with low rooms and long rows of windows, with muslin curtains, and geranium pots in them. All spotlessly clean. They gave me a large – well, lunch, it was 11.30, of eggs and tea and bread and cheese and bilberry jam, after which Ulrich and I walked up through the woods here and arrived at 2 in the afternoon. I don't think I have ever had two more delightful alpine days. To-morrow I go over to Grindelwald; the weather looks quite settled. Wednesday up to the hut, from whence on Wednesday night we try the Finsteraarhorn arête. If we do it we sleep at another hut on Thursday night, and at the Grimsel on Friday and Saturday. Sunday night we bivouac under the Lauteraarhorn and Monday try the arête to the Schreckhorn. Probably I should leave for England on Tuesday....

I am very sorry to leave this nice place. What do you think is our fortnight's bag? Two old peaks.

Seven new peaks – one of them first-class and four others very good. One new saddle, also first-class.

The traverse of the Engelhorn, also new and first-class. That's not bad going, is it!...

To F. B. *November 27, 1901.*

Of course I will take the Mothers' Meeting on Wednesday. I will find out about sending out the invitations. Will you tell me what you want read – any of the Health Book? – and if so, where is it? I can look out some story....

To F. B.   RED BARNS, *Thursday, December 28, 1901.*

All has gone off quite well. We had over 200 people. Your telegram arrived and I read it out to them in the middle of my speech! The magic lantern slides are lovely, it was most exciting seeing them. . . .

Tell Father I've written to Maurice by every mail *all* about him! He mustn't get to think there's nothing else to write about! Hugo says Prout's an old fogey – that's what he says! *I* say Hugo is a great darling!

1902

Gertrude, her father and Hugo indefatigably start for another sea voyage after the new year, leaving Liverpool January 14 and going by sea to Malta, then to Sicily and up through Italy. Hugo and his father returned and Gertrude made her way into Asia Minor.

She finds a temporary abode at Mount Carmel.

I am now become one of the prophets – at least I make merry in their room so to speak – and it's a very nice room I may add, and I am sitting writing at my own writing table with everything genteel about me.

To H. B.   MOUNT CARMEL, *30th March, 1902.*

... But mind, if ever you think I'm unbearable, just say it straight out and mention what you can't abide and I'll do my best to mend it. To return to the East. I'm having a comic time, but most amusing. I had a delightful afternoon by myself on Friday and rode out from 1 to 6 on the worst horse in the world. I am much entertained to find that I am a Person in this country – one of the first questions everyone seems to ask everyone else is, 'Have you ever met Miss Gertrude Bell?' Renown is not very difficult to acquire here.

Monday, 31. To-day I came down into Haifa early and established myself in my new hotel. I had an Arabic lesson and interviewed a Persian who is to come and teach me every evening after dinner. My hotel is most comfortable, kept by Syrians and I hear and speak nothing but Arabic which is really ideal. I have a large sitting-room – you should see how nice it looks with all my books and things and great pots of mimosa and jasmine and wild flowers.

To H. B.   HAIFA, *April 7th, 1902.*

This afternoon I paid a long call on the mother and sisters of my Persian – their house is my house, you understand, and I am to go and talk Persian whenever I like. This is my day: I get up at 7, at 8 Abu Nimrud comes and teaches me Arabic till 10. I go on working till 12, when I lunch. Then I write for my Persian till 1.30, or so, when I ride or walk out. Come in at 5, and work till 7, when I dine. At 7.30 my Persian comes and stays till 10, and at 10.30 I go to bed. You see I have not much leisure time! And the whole day long I talk Arabic.

To F. B.   *Tuesday, 22nd April, 1902.*

On Monday I went to lunch with my Persians. A young gentleman was invited to meet me – he's a carpenter – and he and I and Mirza Abdullah lunched together solemnly while the wife and sisters waited on us. We had a very good lunch, rice and pillau and sugared dates and kabobs. It was all spread on the table at once and we helped ourselves with our forks at will, dilating the while on the absurdity of the European custom of serving one dish after another so that you never knew what you were going to have, also of whipping away your plate every moment and giving you another! The conversation was carried on in Persian which I speak worse than anyone was ever known to do. I told you that there were 2 American Professors of Divinity in the Hotel? One whose name I don't know is a particularly attractive man, oldish, very intelligent and with a sweet goodness of face and I am sure of character which is very loveable. I was telling Mirza Abdullah about him last night and he said he would like to see him and ask him a question. So I went out and fetched my old American, telling him the sort of person he

had to deal with, and Mirza Abdullah (I being interpreter)
asked him what he considered were the proofs of Christ's
being God. The American answered in the most charming
manner, but of course could give no proofs except a personal
conviction. Mirza A. said, 'He speaks as a lover, but I want
the answer of the learned.' I felt as I interpreted between
them how much the philosophic inquiring eastern mind dif-
fered from ours. The value my professor attached to the
vivifying qualities of Christ's teaching was certainly lost on
the Oriental, and on the other hand Abdullah's dialectics
were incomprehensible to the western – at least the starting
point was incomprehensible. They talked for about an hour
and at the end Abdullah was quite as much at a loss as before
to understand why the Professor accepted one prophet and
rejected the others and I'm bound to say I quite sympathized
with him. He said to me after the Professor had gone: 'You
must reject all or accept all, but he chooses and can give no
reason. He believes what his fathers have taught him.' It was
a very curious evening. The professor was a perfect old
angel all the time. One could not help being immensely impressed with the quality of his faith.

She returns to England at the end of May. She has a pleasant
month at home, and early in July we find her in Switzerland again.

To F. B.   ROSENLAUI, *July 11, 1902.*

. . . Between the two Wellhorns there is an arête of rock
which has never been attempted – it is indeed one of the 4
impossibles of the Oberland – and we intend to do it, and
we think we can.

To F. B.   VORDER WELLHORN, *July 14, 1902.*

We have done the first of the impossibles, the Wellhorn
arête, and are much elated.

To H. B.   KURHAUS ROSENLAUI, BERNER OBERLAND,
                                          July 20, 1902.

This morning I started out at 5.30 to – well, Ulrich calls it
examining the movement of rocks, it means that you go up

and see if a stone falls on you and if it doesn't you know you can go up that way. It's a new ascent of the Wetterhorn – a mad scheme I'm inclined to think, but still we'll see how it goes. We went up the steep slopes and up rocks and under a glacier fall, where I examined the movement of a stone on my knee – fortunately a small one, but it hurt for it fell from a long way up – and then we hastily turned back. However, on examination we thought we could get up another way and we intend to try it seriously....

To H. B.   MEIRINGEN, *Sunday, August 3, 1902.*

For once I must begin by acknowledging that Domnul's gloomy forebodings came very near to being realised, and I am now feeling some satisfaction in the thought that my bones are not lying scattered on the Alpine mountains cold. Don't be alarmed, however, they are all quite safe and sound in the Grimsel and if it were not for a little touch of frostbite in the feet I should be merrily on my way to fresh adventures.... On Monday it rained and we could do nothing. On Tuesday we set out at 1 a.m. and made for a crack high up on the Wetterhorn rocks which we had observed through glasses. We got up to it after about 3 hours' climbing only to find to our sorrow that the séracs were tumbling continually down it from all directions. We concluded that it was far too risky – indeed it would have been madness to attempt it for we could see from the broken ice on the rocks that the great blocks were thrown from side to side as they fell and swept the whole passage and it was the only place where the cliffs could be climbed at all; we turned sadly back. I record this piece of prudence with pleasure.... Next day I came up here. It was a most delicious morning. I left Meiringen at 6 and shared my coach with a dear little American couple who were making a walking tour in Switzerland – by coach mostly, I gathered. There was also a pleasant Englishman called Campbell who was coming up with a rope and an ice axe, a member of the A.C. as I found on talking to him at the halting places. He appears later in the story. Well, we lunched here and set off in the afternoon to the Pavillon Dol-

fuss, of ill omen, where we arrived at 6. But anything more
inviting than the little hut that evening it would be difficult
to imagine. It was perfect weather, the most lovely evening
I have ever seen in the Alps. Until the sun set at 7 behind
the Schreckhorn I sat out of doors without a coat and walked
over the tiny alp botanizing while my guides cooked the
soup.... Every sort of Alpine plant grows on the cultivated
alp; I found even very sweet pale violets under the big stones.
I had it all to myself; I was the lord of all mountains that
night and rejoiced exceedingly in my great possessions. The
matter we had in hand was the ascent of the face of the Finsteraarhorn: it is a well-known problem and the opinions of
the learned are divided as to its solution. Dr Wilson looked
at it this year and decided against it. We have looked at it
for 2 years and decided for it and other authorities agree
with us in what I still think is a right opinion. The mountain
on the side facing the Schreckhorn comes down in a series
of arches radiating from the extremely pointed top to the
Finsteraar glacier.... The arête, the one which has always
been discussed, rises from the glacier in a great series of gendarmes and towers, set at such an angle on the steep face of
the mountain that you wonder how they can stand at all
and indeed they can scarcely be said to stand, for the great
points of them are continually over-balancing and tumbling
down into the couloirs between the arêtes and they are all
capped with loosely poised stones, jutting out and hanging
over and ready to fall at any moment. But as long as you
keep pretty near to the top of the arête you are safe from
them because they fall into the couloirs on either side, the
difficulty is to get on to the arête because you have to cross
a couloir down which the stones fall, not to speak of avalanches; the game was beginning even when we crossed it an
hour after dawn. We left the hut at 1.35 a.m.

Thursday. Crossed the séracs just at dawn and by 6 found
ourselves comfortably established on the arête, beyond the
reach of the stones which the mountain had fired at us (fortunately with rather a bad aim) for the first half-hour on the

rock. We breakfasted then followed a difficult and dangerous climb. It was difficult because the rocks were exceedingly steep, every now and then we had to creep up and out of the common hard chimney – one in particular about mid-day, I remember, because we subsequently had the very deuce of a time coming down it, or round the face of a tower or cut our way across an ice couloir between two gendarmes and it was dangerous because the whole rock was so treacherous. I found this out very early in the morning by putting my hand into the crack of a rock which looked as if it went into the very foundations of things. About 2 feet square of rock tumbled out upon me and knocked me a little way down the hill till I managed to part company with it on a tiny ledge. I got back on to my feet without being pulled up by the rope, which was as well for a little later I happened to pass the rope through my hands and found that it had been cut half through about a yard from my waist when the rock had fallen on it. This was rather a nuisance as it shortened a rope we often wanted long to allow of our going up difficult chimneys in turn. So on and on we went up the arête and the towers multiplied like rabbits above and grew steeper and steeper and about 2 o'clock I looked round and saw great black clouds rolling up from the west. But by this time looking up we also saw the topmost tower of the arête far above us still, and the summit of the mountain further still and though we could not yet see what the top of the arête was like we were cheered and pushed on steadily for another hour while the weather signs got worse and worse. At 3 just as the first snow flakes began to fall, we got into full view of the last two gendarmes – and the first one was quite impossible. The ridge had been growing narrow, its sides steeper as we mounted, so that we had been obliged for some time to stick quite to the backbone of it; then it threw itself up into a great tower leaning over to the right and made of slabs set like slates on the top with a steep drop of some 20 feet below them on to the col. We were then 1000 feet below the summit I should guess, perhaps rather less, anyway we could see our way up, not easy but possible, above this tower and once on the top we could get down the other side in any weather. It had to be tried: we sat down to eat a few mouthfuls, the snow falling fast, driven by a strong wind, and a thick mist marching up the valley below, over the Finsteraarjoch, then we crept along the knife edge of a col, fastened a rope firmly round a rock and let Ulrich down on to a ledge below the overhang of the tower. He tried it for a few moments and then gave it up. The ledge was very narrow, sloped outwards and was quite rotten. Anything was better than that. So we tried the left side of the tower: there was a very steep iced couloir running up at the foot of the rock on that side for about 50 feet, after which all would be well. Again we let ourselves down on the extra rope to the foot of the tower, again to find that this way also was impossible. A month later in the year I believe this couloir would go; after a warm August there would be no ice in it, and though it is very steep the rocks, so far as one could see under the ice, looked climbable. But even with the alternative before us of the descent down the terrible arête, we decided to turn back; already the snow was blowing down the couloir in a small avalanche, small but blinding, and the wind rushed down upon us carrying the mists with it. If it had been fine weather we should have tried down the arête a little and then a traverse so as to get at the upper rocks by another road. I am not sure that it could be done but we should have tried anything – but by the time we had been going down for half-an-hour we could see nothing of the mountain side to the right or to the left except an occasional glimpse as one cloud rolled off and another rolled over. The snow fell fast and covered the rocks with incredible speed. Difficult as they had been to go up, you may imagine what they were like going down when we could no longer so much as see them. There was one corner in particular where we had to get round the face of a tower.

We came round the corner, down a very steep chimney, got on to a sloping out rock ledge with an inch of new snow on it; there was a crack in which you could stand and with one hand hold in the rock face, from whence you had to drop down about 8 feet on to steep snow. We fixed the extra rope and tumbled down one after the other on to the snow; it was really more or less safe because one had the fixed rope to hold on to, but it felt awful: I shall remember every inch of that rock face for the rest of my life. It was now near 6. Our one idea was to get down to the chimney – the mid-day chimney which was so very difficult – so as to do it while there was still only a little snow on it. We toiled on till 8, by which time a furious thunderstorm was raging. We were standing by a great upright on the top of a tower when suddenly it gave a crack and a blue flame sat on it for a second, just like the one we saw when we were driving, you remember, only nearer. My ice axe jumped in my hand and I thought the steel felt hot through my woollen glove – was that possible? I didn't take my glove off to see! Before we knew where we were the rock flashed again – it was a great sticking out stone and I expect it attracted the lightning, but we didn't stop to consider this theory but tumbled down a chimney as hard as ever we could, one on top of the other, buried our ice axe heads in some shale at the bottom of it and hurriedly retreated from them. It's not nice to carry a private lightning conductor in your hand in the thick of a thunderstorm. It was clear we could go no further that night, the question was to find the best lodging while there was still light enough to see. We hit upon a tiny crack sheltered from the wind, even the snow did not fall into it. There was just room for me to sit in the extreme back of it on a very pointed bit of rock; by doubling up I could even get my head into it. Ulrich sat on my feet to keep them warm and Heinrich just below him. They each of them put their feet into a knapsack which is the golden rule of bivouac. The other golden rule is to take no brandy because you feel the reaction more after. I knew this and insisted on it. It was really not so bad; we shivered all night but our hands and feet were warm and climbers are like Pobbles in the matter of toes. I went to sleep quite often and was wakened up every hour or so by the intolerable discomfort of my position, which I then changed by an inch or two into another which was bearable for an hour more. At first the thunderstorm made things

rather exciting. The claps followed the flashes so close that
there seemed no interval between them. We tied ourselves
firmly on to the rock above lest as Ulrich philosophically
said one of us should be struck and fall out. The rocks were
all crackling round us and fizzing like damp wood which is
just beginning to burn – have you ever heard that? It's a
curious exciting sound rather exhilarating – and as there
was no further precaution possible I enjoyed the extraordinary magnificence of the storm with a free mind: it was
worth seeing. Gradually the night cleared and became
beautifully starry. Between 2 and 3 the moon rose, a tiny
crescent, and we spoke of the joy it would be when the sun
rose full on to us and stopped our shivering. But the sun
never rose at all – at least for all practical purposes. The day
came wrapped in a blinding mist and heralded by a cutting,
snow-laden wind – this day was Friday; we never saw the
sun in it. It must have snowed a good deal during the
thunderstorm for when we stepped out of our crack in the
first grey light about 4 (too stiff to bear it a moment longer)
everything was deep in it. I can scarcely describe to you
what that day was like. We were from 4 a.m. to 8 p.m. on
the arête; during that time we ate for a minute or two 3
times and my fare I know was 5 ginger bread biscuits, 2
sticks of chocolate, a slice of bread, a scrap of cheese and a
handful of raisins. We had nothing to drink but about two
tablespoonfuls of brandy in the bottom of my flask and a
mouthful of wine in the guides' wine skin, but it was too cold
to feel thirsty. There was scarcely a yard which we could come
down without the extra rope; you can imagine the labour of
finding a rock at every 50 feet round which to sling it, then
of pulling it down behind us and slinging it again. We had
our bit of good luck – it never caught all day. But both the
ropes were thoroughly iced and terribly difficult to manage,
and the weather was appalling. It snowed all day sometimes softly as decent snow should fall, sometimes driven by
a furious bitter wind which enveloped us not only in the
falling snow, but lifted all the light powdery snow from the
rocks and sent it whirling down the precipices and into the

couloirs and on to us indifferently. It was rather interesting to see the way a mountain behaves in a snowstorm and how avalanches are born and all the wonderful and terrible things that happen in high places. The couloirs were all running with snow rivers – we had to cross one and a nasty uncomfortable process it was. As soon as you cut a step it was filled up before you could put your foot into it. But I think that when things are as bad as ever they can be you cease to mind them much. You set your teeth and battle with the fates; we meant to get down whatever happened and it was such an exciting business that we had no time to think of the discomfort. I know I never thought of the danger except once and then quite calmly. I'll tell you about that presently. The first thing we had to tackle was the chimney. We had to fix our rope in it twice, the second time round a very unsafe nail. I stood in this place holding Heinrich, there was an overhang. He climbed a bit of the way and then fell on to soft snow and spun down the couloir till my rope brought him up with a jerk. Then he got up on to a bit of rock on the left about half as high as the overhang. Ulrich came down to me and I repeated Heinrich's process exactly, the iced extra rope slipping through my hands like butter. Then came Ulrich. He was held by Heinrich and me standing a good deal to the left but only half as high as he. He climbed down to the place we had both fallen from asking our advice at every step, then he called out 'Heinrich, Heinrich, ich bin verloren', and tumbled off just as we had done and we held him up in the couloir, more dead than alive with anxiety. We gave him some of our precious brandy on a piece of sugar and he soon recovered and went on as boldly as before. We thought the worst was over but there was a more dangerous place to come. It was a place that had been pretty difficult to go up, a steep but short slope of iced rock by which we had turned the base of a tower. The slope was now covered with about 4 inches of avalanche snow and the rocks were quite hidden. It was on the edge of a big couloir down which raced a snow river. We managed badly somehow; at any rate, Ulrich and I found ourselves on a place where there was not room for us both to stand, at the end of the extra rope. He was very insecure and could not hold me, Heinrich was below on the edge of the couloir, also very insecure. And here I had to refix the extra rope on a rock a little below me so that it was practically no good to me. But it was the only possible plan. The rock was too difficult for me, the stretches too big, I couldn't reach them: I handed my axe down to Heinrich and told him I could do nothing but fall, but he couldn't, or at any rate, didn't secure himself and in a second we were both tumbling head over heels down the couloir, which was, you understand, as steep as snow could lie. How Ulrich held us I don't know. He said himself he would not have believed it possible but hearing me say I was going to fall he had stuck the pointed end of the ice axe into a crack above and on this alone we all three held. I got on to my feet in the snow directly I came to the end of my leash of rope and held Heinrich and caught his ice axe and mine and we slowly cut ourselves back up the couloir to the foot of the rock. But it was a near thing and I felt rather ashamed of my part in it. This was the time when I thought it on the cards we should not get down alive. Rather a comforting example, however, of how little can hold a party up. About 2 in the afternoon we all began to feel tired. I had a pain through my shoulder and down my back which was due, I think to nothing but the exertion of rock climbing and the nervous fatigue of shivering – for we never stopped shivering all day, it was impossible to control one's tired muscles in that bitter cold. And so we went on for 6 hours more of which only the last hour was easy and at 8 found ourselves at the top of the Finsteraar glacier and in the dark, with a good guess and good luck, happened on the right place in the Bergschrund and let ourselves down over it. It was now quite dark, the snow had turned into pouring rain, and we sank 6 inches into the soft glacier with every step. Moreover we were wet through: we had to cross several big crevasses and get down the sérac before we could reach the Unteraar glacier and safety. For this we had felt no anxiety having relied upon our lantern but not a single match would light. We had every kind with us in metal match boxes but the boxes were wet and we had not a dry rag of any kind to rub them with. We tried to make a tent out of my skirt and to light a match under it, but our fingers were dripping wet and numb with cold – one could scarcely feel anything smaller than an ice axe – and the match heads dropped off limply into the snow without so much as a spark. Then we tried to go on and after a few steps Heinrich fell into a soft place almost up to his neck and Ulrich and I had to pull him out with the greatest difficulty and the mists swept up over the glacier and hid everything; that was the only moment of despair. We had so looked forward to dry blankets in the Pavillon Dollfuss and here we were with another night out before us. And a much worse one than the first, for we were on the shelterless glacier and in driving drenching rain. We laid our three axes together and sat on them side by side. Ulrich and I put our feet into a sack but Heinrich refused to use the other and gave it to me to lie on. My shoulders ached and ached. I insisted on our all eating something even the smallest scrap, and then I put a wet pocket handkerchief over my face to keep the rain from beating on it and went to sleep. It sounds incredible but I think we all slept more or less and woke up to the horrible discomfort and went to sleep again. I consoled myself by thinking of Maurice in S. Africa and how he had slept out in the pouring rain and been none the worse. We couldn't see the time but long before we expected it a sort of grey light came over the snow and when at last I could read my watch, behold it was 4. We gathered ourselves up; at first we could scarcely stand but after a few steps we began to walk quite creditably. About 6 we got to where we could unrope – having been 48 hours on the rope – and we reached here at 10 on Saturday.

They had all been in a great state of anxiety about us, seeing the weather, and had telegraphed to Meiringen, to Grindelwald, to know whether we had turned up. So I got into a warm bath and then discovered to my great surprise that my feet were ice cold and without any sensation. But having eaten a great many boiled eggs and drunk jugs of hot milk I went to bed and woke about dinner time to find my toes swollen and stiff. Frau Lieseguay then appeared and said that a S. American doctor had passed through in the afternoon and had seen Ulrich and Heinrich and had bound up their hands and feet in cotton wool and told them to keep very warm; so she bound up my feet too – my hands are nearly all right but I think my feet are worse than theirs. Still they seem better now and I don't expect I shall be toeless. They are not nearly as bad as my hands were in the Dauphiné, but the worst of it is that with swollen toes bound up in cotton wool one can't walk at all and I shall just have to wait till they get better. I slept for about 24 hours only waking up to eat, and it's now 4 in the afternoon and I'm just going to get up and have tea with Mr Campbell, who has, I hear, been an angel of kindness to my guides. They seem to be none the worse except that Ulrich had a touch of rheumatism this morning, and as for me, I am perfectly absolutely well except for my toes – not so much as a cold in the head. Isn't it remarkable! I do wonder where mother is and whether she is anywhere near at hand; if she were I should like to have nursed my toes in her company but I expect I shall be all right in a day or two. I don't mean to move till I am. Isn't that an awful dreffful adventure! It makes me laugh to think of it, but seriously now that I am comfortably indoors, I do rather wonder that we ever got down the Finsteraarhorn and that we were not frozen at the bottom of it. What do you think?

Captain Farrar of the Alpine Club writes as follows respecting this ascent:

'The vertical height of the rock face measured from the glacier to the summit of the mountain is about 3,000 feet. There can be in the whole Alps few places so steep and so high. The climb has only been done three times, including your daughter's attempt, and is still considered one of the greatest expeditions in the whole Alps.'

The following In Memoriam notice of Gertrude, written by Colonel E. L. Strutt, later editor of the *Alpine Journal*, appeared in the *A. J.* for November, 1926, at which time Captain Farrar was the editor:

'I do not know when Miss Bell commenced her mountaineering career. It was, however, in the first years of this century that her ascents attracted attention, and about the period 1901–1903 there was no more prominent lady mountaineer. Everything that she undertook, physical or mental, was accomplished so superlatively well, that it would indeed have been strange if she had not shone on a mountain as she did in the hunting-field or in the desert. Her strength, incredible in that slim frame, her endurance, above all her courage, were so great that even to this day her guide and companion Ulrich Fuhrer – and there could be few more competent judges – speaks with an admiration of her that amounts to veneration. He told the writer, some years ago, that of all the amateurs, men or women, that he had travelled with, he had seen but very few to surpass her in technical skill and none to equal her in coolness, bravery, and judgment.

'Fuhrer's generous tribute on what was probably the most terrible adventure in the lives of all those concerned…. "You who have made the climb will perhaps be able to correctly appreciate our work. But the honour belongs to Miss Bell. Had she not been full of courage and determination, we must have perished. She was the one who insisted on our eating from time to time…." The scene was high up on the then unclimbed N.E. face of the Finsteraarhorn, when the party was caught in a blizzard on that difficult and exposed face and were out for fifty-seven hours, of which fifty-three were spent on the rope. "Retreat under such conditions, and retreating safely, was a tremendous performance which does credit to all." The date was July 31 to August 2, 1902; the occasion was a defeat greater than many a victory. "When the freezing wind beats you almost to the ground, when the blizzard nearly blinds you, half paralyzing your senses … when the cold is so intense that the snow freezes on you as it falls, clothing you in a sheet of ice, till life becomes insupportable…" then, indeed, was Miss Bell preeminent.

'The Lauteraarhorn-Schreckhorn traverse was probably Miss Bell's most important first ascent, July 24, 1902. It is related that she and her guides, meeting on the ridge another lady with her guides making the same ascent from the opposite direction, were not greeted with enthusiasm. In the seasons 1901–1902 Miss Bell was the first to explore systematically the Engelhorner group, making with Fuhrer many new routes and several first ascents. An extract from a letter of the chief Alpine authority, dated December 10, 1911, may be quoted.... "You ask me for some notes on Miss Bell's ascents, and I send all I have ... she was not one to advertise, and yet, or probably because of it, they tell me that she was the best of all lady mountaineers.... (Signed) W. A. B. Coolidge."

'The notes contain the following, all relating to the different Engelhorner and all new routes or first ascents:

Similistock, August 30, 1901.

King's Peak
Gerard's Peak } August 31, 1901.

Vorderspitze
Gertrude's Peak
Ulrich's Peak } September 3, 1901.
Mittelspitze

Klein Engelhorn
Gemsenspitze
Urbachthaler Engelhorn } September 7, 1901.

Klein Similistock, July 8, 1902.

'For the reasons stated above, it is difficult to name her other expeditions in the Alps, but a well-known climber has stated that his most vivid recollection of an ascent of Mont Blanc was the effort required to follow Miss Bell.

'Such, briefly and inadequately rendered, are some of the Alpine qualifications of her who must ever be regarded as one of the greatest women of all time. – E. L. S.'

CHAPTER 8

1902 – 1903

Round the World the Second Time

AT the end of 1902 Gertrude and Hugo started off to go round the world together, their route being India (including the Delhi Durbar), Burma, Java, China, and America.

Shortly before their departure the Rev. Michael Furse, later Bishop of St Albans, came to stay with us at Redcar. He was a don at Trinity College, Oxford, when Hugo was an undergraduate there, and they became great friends. Hugo was devoted to him for ever afterwards. The Bishop now sends us these notes of a talk he had with Gertrude at that time.

'I remember well a walk which I took one evening on the sands at Redcar with his very remarkable and charming sister Gertrude; it was just before she and Hugo were going off round the world together. In her delightfully blunt and provocative way, she turned on me suddenly and said in a very defiant voice, "I suppose you don't approve of this plan of Hugo going round the world with me?" "Why shouldn't I?" I said. "Well, you may be pretty sure he won't come back a Christian." "Why do you say that?" I asked. "Oh, because I've got a much better brain than Hugo, and a year in my company will be bound to upset his faith." "Oh, will it?" I said. "Don't you be too sure about that. If I was a betting man I'd give you a hundred to one against it. But even if things do pan out as you think, I am tremendously glad Hugo is going with you, for I would much rather he came to the conclusion that the whole thing was nonsense *before* he took Orders than afterwards! You do your hardest" (which I fear was not the actual word I used, but something much stronger!) "and see what happens." '

The Bishop was right. Hugo returned unchanged, and in due course he was ordained in 1908.

In 1909 Mr Furse became Bishop of Pretoria. Hugo followed him to South Africa in 1912 and was with him as his chaplain until the Bishop came back to England for good in 1920.

To F. B.   *December 4th, 1902.*

... Hugo is the most delightful of travelling companions. We spend a lot of time making plans with maps in front of us. We are chiefly exercised as to how many of the Pacific Islands we shall visit. It is immensely amusing to have the world before us....

So many descriptions have been written of the Delhi Durbar, and of the well-trodden route which Gertrude and Hugo took afterwards, that it is not worth while giving her letters in extenso.

To F. B.   DELHI DURBAR, *Dec. 31.*

The function began with the entrance of the Delhi siege veterans – this was the great moment of all, a body of old men, white and native, and every soul in that great arena rose and cheered. At the end came some twenty or thirty Gurkhas, little old men in bottle green, some bent double with years, some lame and stumbling with Mutiny wounds. And last of all came an old blind man in a white turban, leaning on a stick. As he passed us, he turned his blind eyes towards the shouting and raised a trembling hand to salute the unseen thousands of the race to which he had stood true. After that Viceroys and Kings went by almost without a thrill. But still it was a great show....

IN THE TRAIN FROM ALWAR TO DELHI.

To F. B.   *January 18th, 1903.*

My thrice blessed Hindustani, though it doesn't reach to any flowers of speech, carries us through our travels admirably and here we were able to stop where no one has a word of English, without any inconvenience.

Aligarh. And here we are safely installed in the Morisons' house. He is one of the most charming of men – a son of Cotter Morison.

... Then follows a description of the Muhammadan College, the only residential college in India.

To H. B.   IN THE TRAIN–AS USUAL! *February 2, 1903.*

... I liked Mrs Morison on further acquaintance. They swear by her in the College and she was very kind to us. Mr Morison is without doubt the most charming of men. We had an early tea to which he had invited an old Nawab who is a great personage in the College. He was a delightful old man; we conversed in Persian, though I found I could quite well follow him when he spoke Urdu with Mr M. and Mr M. can understand, though he cannot speak Persian.... Hugo's attitude to his friends is too comic. We heard that one X. was at Hong-Kong. 'Good old X.' said Hugo, 'I must look him up.' I asked who he was. 'Oh, he was at Oxford with me.' 'Did you know him well?' 'No.' I asked him whether he liked him. 'No – no, I didn't like him. He's not at all an attractive person. Good old X.! I'll tell you what – I'll write and let him know we are coming.'... I got two lovely gowns of Madras muslin, embroidered from the foot to the knee, for 23 rupees, and an old man with a white beard is making them up for me at 4 rupees apiece. I think I shall go to him in future, he is so much cheaper than Denise. Hugo meantime bought stocks of white ducks and a silk coat of which he is very proud.... I wrote letters to all the people in the Straits Settlements, to tell them we're coming – lucky dogs!

To F. B.   BATAVIA, *March 16, 1903.*

We have at last got out of England and are now travelling on the Continent. No one knows what comfort on the sea can be till he travels by a Dutch boat....

They go to Singapore, where they stay with Sir Frank Swettenham. Hugo was very ill with some sort of malaria. Sir Frank Swettenham was endlessly kind to him, and kept him and looked after him until he was well enough to go away.

To F. B.   ASTOR HOUSE, SHANGHAI, *April 4th, 1903.*

We landed on Easter Sunday and had to do all our own getting ashore. The Chinese natives surrounded us and offered to carry our luggage, to carry us, to carry the ship, I fancy, if we would give them a long enough bamboo pole. I adore Chinamen with a passion that amounts to mania. They are the most delightful people in the world. They do everything to perfection. They'll make you a shirt in three

hours, a petticoat in two, wash your clothes before you can
wink, forestall your every wish at table, fan you day and
night when you have the fever – you should have seen the
Chinese boys sitting by Hugo's bedside at Singapore and
fanning him all day long....

So we went to a silk shop, and the most delightful gentleman in China showed us for two hours the loveliest stuffs I
have ever seen. Kings will leave their thrones in the hope of
catching sight of me when I wear a brocade I bought there,
and crown princes will flock after Elsa and Moll when they
are clothed in some Chinese crêpe I design for them. Hugo
addresses all Chinamen as Gnome, but as they don't understand they aren't offended. I like travelling in China. Hugo
nods and becks to everyone he meets and they nod back delighted.

They travel northward through China, sight-seeing on the way
and being much interested all the time.

To F. B.   PEKING, *26th April, 1903.*

You can't conceive what the horrible fascinating streets of
Peking are like. Full full of people, a high mud causeway
down the middle, crowded booths on either side and a strait
and uneven way between them and the shops. Your rickshaw
dashes in and out, bumps over boulders, subsides into ditches,
runs over dogs and toes and the outlying parts of booths and
shops, upsets an occasional wheelbarrow, locks itself with
rickshaws coming in the opposite direction and at a hand
gallop conveys you, breathless, through dust and noise and
smells unspeakable to where you would be.

To H. B.   TAIREN MARU, *May 20th, 1903.*

We may as well back out. I've seen Dalny and I know. We
may just as well back out. Five years old and a European
town. Roads – you don't know what that means in China –
fine streets of solid brick houses, a great port, destitute of
shipping as yet, but that will come, law courts, two hotels,
factories in plenty, six lines of rails at the station, a botanical

garden in embryo, but still there. It contains some deer, an eagle and two black bears – note the symbolism! Do you remember a story of Kipling's in which a Russian officer is well entertained by an English Regiment? He gets up after dinner to make a speech. 'Go away, you old peoples,' he says. 'Go away you – old – peoples!' and falls drunk under the table. That's the speech Dalny is making and I feel inclined to take its advice. In fact there is no alternative. We arrived at 7 a.m. on Thursday, went ashore and breakfasted at the Gastinnea Dalny where the proprietor fortunately spoke German. They take nothing but roubles, being in Russia, and we had to go to the renowned Russo-Chinese bank to change our notes. Having paid for our breakfast, our friend, the proprietor, put us into a droschky – a pukka droschky – and we drove round the town. Our driver was a cheerful Kurlander who spoke a little German too. He came out last autumn and meant to stay 2 years. 'Business is good?' said I, observing his fat and smiling face. 'Recht gut,' said he, 'sometimes one earns 18 roubles a day.' No wonder he smiled and grew fat. The railway cutting is being widened, the station is not yet finished. Both were black with thousands of Chinese coolies working for dear life. How long is it, therefore, between project and completion in Russian hands? Hugo gnashed his teeth, but I did nothing but admire. They deserve to rule Asia – and they mean to rule Asia. Go away, you old peoples!

They sail for Japan.

To H. B.   TOKYO, *May 23rd, 1903.*

I spent my time in the train learning Japanese so that when we arrived at Miyajima I was able to explain that we wanted to leave our heavy baggage at the station! (At this moment came in a gnome with a most exquisite grey alpaca gown he has just made me, an exact copy of one of Denise's but that cost £6 and this £3! I am glad to have it, for Peking dust put a final touch to my dilapidated toilette.)

They arrive in Canada.

LAKE LOUISE, ROCKY MOUNTAINS, *June 30, 1903.*

Need I tell you that I am now climbing the Rocky Mountains! We arrived at Glacier after a wonderful morning through the great cañons of the Selkirks. And at Glacier whom do you think I found, pray? 3 Swiss guides from the Oberland, ropes and ice-axes and everything complete. So we fell into one another's arms, and they said, 'Ach wass! it was Fraulein Bell! how did the Gracious Fraulein enjoy the Finsteraarhorn?' We discussed politics at dinner with our waiter at Vancouver. Says he: 'There's only one man understands the Colonies: that's Chamberlain.' G. B. loq.: 'I think you'll have to pay some of the piper if you want to call so much of the tune.' Waiter, loq.: 'I guess that's so, but they don't seem to think so out here.' And he handed me the potatoes.

Gertrude and Hugo landed at Liverpool on July 26th of this year. She was then in England until the following February, when we find her and her father staying at the Embassy in Berlin, after which she returned home.

CHAPTER 9

1903 – 1905

England – Switzerland – Paris

Our youngest daughter Molly was married to Charles Trevelyan on January 6th, 1904. As Gertrude was then at home with us and also during most of the preceding year, there are no letters to us concerning Molly's engagement in the previous November, or her marriage.

In August 1904 she again went to Switzerland, then returned to England till November, when she went to Paris to study with Reinach again.

To F. B.   PARIS, *November 8th, 1904.*

I had the most enchanting evening with Reinach. I got there at 7.30 and left at 11.30 and we talked without ceasing all the time. After dinner we sat in his library while he showed me books and books of engravings and photographs and discoursed in the most delightful manner. He does nothing but work – never goes out, never takes a holiday except to go and see a far away museum. And the consequence is he knows everything. I like him so much. This morning, I went to the Bibliothéque Nationale. Reinach had given me a letter to one of the directors and I was received with open arms. They are most kind. I looked at 2 wonderful Greek MSS. – illuminated – from 12 to 3.30! and I am going back there tomorrow to see ivories and more precious MSS. which they will have out for me. It is perfectly delightful. I should like to do nothing else for 6 months....

To F. B.   *Friday, November 11, 1904.*

I have spent the whole day seeing ivories at various museums. As far as Paris is concerned I've seen all the ivories that concern me, and I find to my joy that I'm beginning to be able to place them, so that this afternoon at Cluny I knew a good deal more than the catalogue – which I'm bound to add was very bad. They have some wonderful things here.

This happy result is a good deal caused by having looked through such masses of picture books with Reinach. Last night he set me guessing what things were – even Greek beads – it was a sort of examination – I really think I passed. Reinach was much pleased but then he loves me so dearly that perhaps he is not a good judge. He has simply set all his boundless knowledge at my disposal and I have learnt more in these few days than I should have learnt by myself in a year.

But you can't think what odd things they made about the 3rd and 4th centuries in Gaul. It's a most fascinating study.

CHAPTER 10

1905

Syria – Asia Minor

To F. B.   LONDON, *January 4, 1905.*

I have given Smith & Sons the following addresses – British Consulate, Jerusalem, for 3 weeks beginning from next week, British Consulate, Damascus, for the 3 weeks following; but I will let you know from Jerusalem by telegram....

Aren't I going a long way off? It is not nice at the beginning.

HAIFA, *Wednesday, 25th.*

... Oh, I've had such a day! I've lunched with my Persians, I've drunk tea with my horse-dealer, I've spent hours in conversation with my landlord, I've visited everyone I know in Haifa. I'm off tomorrow morning. I doubt if it will be very nice in tents tomorrow, but still!

To F. B.   *February 1, 1905.*

I had a ride full of vicissitudes from Haifa. The first day was extremely and unavoidably long, 31 miles which is more than one can comfortably take one's animals. Moreover the road lay all across the Plain of Esdraelon (which is without doubt the widest plain in the world) and the mud was incredible. We waded sometimes for an hour at a time knee deep in clinging mud, the mules fell down, the donkeys almost disappeared ('By God!' said one of the muleteers, 'you could see nothing but his ears') and the horses grew wearier and wearier. I got in to camp after dark, at a place called Jenin it was, feeling very tired and head-achy and wondering why. Next day I was worse and by the time I had ridden for an hour I realised that I had a sharp attack of Acre fever, a thing I invariably catch here. It was extremely disagreeable, but I rode on for 6 hours through the most beautiful

114

country – not that I paid much attention to it! – till I got to Samaria and then I determined I could go no further. The mules and baggage had gone by another road straight to Nablus and I had only my cook with me. At the entrance of the town is a great ruined Crusader church, one corner of which has been built up into a mosque. A single bay of the aisle is converted into a room, and hard by in a sort of lean-to there lives the Imam of the mosque. He hurried out and said he could put me up in the aisle room for the night, there was a bed of sorts in it and a few quilts, more or less clean, and then I dropped down and went to sleep. I wish you could have seen the Imam.... He was dressed in a long blue robe and had a white turban round his tarbush. He bustled about softly in his ragged socks and made me tea and filled a bottle with hot water to make me warm, and finally left me to an uneasy repose. However, next day I was almost well.

To F. B.   RAMELEH, *Friday, February 3, 1905.*

As regards the children's books: it is a pity to send them all away, I think. I remember what a joy ours were to us. Could not they be stored on a shelf in the long gallery? There are not so very many and I think they would be a joy to future children.

The books were kept, and as Gertrude foresaw, have been a great joy to the successive children of the family.

I have had a few very busy days in Jerusalem. First I have engaged a new cook. The last was not capable enough for me. I was forced to fall back on my muleteers for all service. (One of them, Habib, who is about 25, is turning out an admirable servant, trustworthy and willing and intelligent. He is a Christian from the Lebanon. I have also his father, Ibrahim, who is a good old soul, and a Druze, Mahmud, who knows the country into which I am going. They are all good men and I am keeping them on.) The question of a cook was very serious and I had to set about looking for one with great care. Finally I hit on one who seemed satisfactory and learnt from him that he had accompanied Lord

Sykes into Asia Minor. So I went off to Lord Sykes and lunched with him and heard a very good account from him. He said he was trustworthy and extremely brave, and on these qualifications I engaged him at once. Mark Sykes also says he can't cook, but it's 5 years since he was with him and we will hope he has learnt. So far I am very well satisfied with him.

To F. B.   *February 7th, 1905.*

I passed the funniest evening yesterday. My host was a well to do inhabitant of Salt, Yusef Succur by name (upon him be peace!). He established me in his reception room, which was well carpeted and cushioned but lacking in window panes, and therefore somewhat draughty. He and his nephew and his small boys held it a point of hospitality not to leave me for a moment, and they assisted with much interest while I changed my boots and gaiters and even my petticoat, for I was deeply coated in mud. That being accomplished they brought me an excellent dinner, meat and rice and Arab bread and oranges. When I had finished it was placed before my cook who had joined the party. Then I held an audience. Paulina, the daughter of the old man at Haifa who used to teach me Arabic, her brother-in-law, Habib Effendi Faris, the schoolmaster and the doctor all 'honoured themselves' ('God forbid! the honour is mine!' is the answer). We drank lots of bitter Bedouin coffee, and at last settled down to business, which was this: How am I to get into the Jebel ed Druze? Finally, Habib Effendi, who was kindness itself, arranged to send me out to his brother-in-law Namoud, who inhabits a ruin on a tiny hill called Tneib three hours east of Madeba. Now Madeba is east of the Dead Sea, and you will find it on a map. At 9.30 they left me, and my host, who was a magnificent looking old man, began to lay down the quilts for my bed. Then came my hostess, though they are Christians, her husband keeps her more strictly than any Muslim woman, and she sees no men. She was a very beautiful woman, dressed in the dark blue Bedouin clothes, the long robe falling from her head and bound round the forehead with a dark striped silk scarf.

Moreover, her chin and neck were closely tattooed with indigo after the Bedouin fashion. At 10 they left me, and I went to bed and slept like a top till 6. The only drawback to my comfort was that I could not wash at all. You see, I was lodged in the drawing room, and naturally there were no appliances for washing there – if there were anywhere. This morning Yusef gave me a very good breakfast of milk and eggs and bread and honey. Habib provided me with a guide and I set off about 8.30 for a long day's ride. It was fortunately heavenly weather. It had rained last night and rained itself out, we had a perfectly clear sky all day.

Wednesday, 8th.

All is well. At 10 last night came Namoud. We fell on each other's necks, metaphorically speaking, and swore friendship and he left with the prospect of good talks next day.

Thursday, 9th.

To-day we are weather-bound. The rain began this morning on a strong south wind which turned into a real storm – such rain as we seldom have in England and it was absolutely impossible to move. This afternoon there arrived half a dozen Bedouins or more, of the tribe of the Beni Sakhr, the biggest tribe hereabouts, driven out of their black tents by the rain. N.B. They had left their women behind in the black tents. They came to Namoud for hospitality, and he has lodged them in the big cave in which he and all his people live. I went in for an hour or two this evening and sat with them talking and drinking the bitter black coffee of the Bedouin. The dark fell and we were lighted by the fire over which two women were cooking the guests' meal. ('They eat little when they feed themselves, but when they are guests, much – they and their horses,' said Namoud.)

We sat round the embers of another fire by which stood the regulation three coffee pots and smoked and told tales, and behind us, with a barrier of bags of chopped straw and corn between, some twenty-three cows moved and munched. We made great friends, the Beni Sakhr and I. 'Mashallah!

Bint Arab,' said they: 'As God has willed: a daughter of the desert.'

Saturday, 11th.

And I am still at Tneib. Yesterday it stopped raining, but the weather was still so very doubtful that we decided not to risk matters by setting out for the desert. So I sent into Madeba for more corn, and myself employed the afternoon in riding out across the plain to a Roman camp called Kartal. On my way home I stopped at the tents of the Beni Sakhr and dined with them. It was a charming party. We sat round the fire and drank tea and coffee and were presently joined by three of the Sherarat, raggeder and dirtier even than most Arabs. They had come from a day or two out in the desert to buy corn from Namoud, much as Joseph and his brethren must have come down into Egypt. The Sherarat are a very big and powerful tribe, but of base blood. The high born Arabs like the Sakhrs won't intermarry with them; but their camels are the best in Arabia. They were very cold – it was a bitter evening – and crouched round the fire of desert scrub. Then came dinner, rice and meat and sour milk, very good. Namoud and I ate out of one dish, and all the others out of another. While we were eating we were joined by a fair and handsome young man whom all the Sakhrs rose to salute, kissing him on both cheeks. He was Gabtan, son of one of the Sheikhs of the Daja, the tribe to which I am going as soon as the weather clears. He had heard that Namoud was looking for a guide for me and had come in to take me to his uncle who is the head of all the tribe. To-day it has poured nearly all day and is still at it. So we were obliged to remain here. We laid plans for my journey and Gabtan asked me whether I thought I should have to fight the Turkish soldiery, as if so he would take his rifle. I assured him I did not intend to come into open conflict with the Sultan and I hoped to avoid the soldiers altogether. But he has decided to take his rifle, which I daresay is as well. There was a gleam of fine weather and I went out to watch the Sherarat buying corn. The corn lives in an ancient well, a very big deep cave underground, and is drawn out in buckets like water – only the buckets are of camels' hair. Then it has to be sifted for it is stored with the chaff to protect it from the damp. This is a mightily long business and entails an immense amount of swearing and pious ejaculations. We all sat round on stones and from time to time we said 'Allah! Allah!' 'Praise be to God the Almighty.' Not infrequently the unsifted corn was poured in among the chaff. Namoud loq.: 'Upon Thee, upon Thee, oh boy! may thy dwelling be destroyed! may thy life come to harm!' Beni Sakhr: 'By the face of the Prophet of God, may he be exalted!' Sherarat (in suppressed chorus): 'God! God! and Muhammad the Prophet of God, upon him be peace!' A party in bare legs and a sheepskin: 'Cold! cold! wallah! rain and cold.' Namoud: 'Silence, oh brother! Yallah! descend into the well and work.'

At four I went into the servants' tent to have tea over their charcoal fire. Namoud joined us and remained till seven telling us bloodcurdling tales of the desert. The muleteers and I listened breathless and Mikhail cooked our dinner, and put in an occasional comment. He is a most cheerful travelling companion is Mikhail. Namoud gave us a warning which I will tell you as it is an indication of the country we are travelling in. Between the Beni Sakhrs and the Druzes there is always blood. There is no mercy between them. If a Druze meets an Ibn Sakhr, one of them kills the other. Now one of my muleteers is a Druze. He has to pass for a Christian till we reach the Jebel Druze, 'for,' said Namoud, 'if the Sakhr here' (my hosts of last night, you understand) 'knew that he was a Druze, they would not only kill him, but they would burn him alive.' Accordingly, we have re-baptised him, for the moment, and given him a Christian name.

Sunday, 12th.

It was still rather stormy, but I decided to start whatever happened. We got off a little before nine, Namoud, Gabtan and I riding together. In about half an hour we crossed the Mecca railway which is the true boundary between towns and tents. We rode for some two hours across the open plain till we reached the foot of a low circle of hills, and here we found Gabtan's people, the Daja, a group of six or seven black tents, and were made welcome by his uncle, Fellah Isa, who is a very great man in these parts and a charming person. We went into his tent and coffee making began. It takes near an hour from the roasting of the beans onwards. By this time the mules had arrived, I lunched hastily and rode off with Namoud and Gabtan to see a ruin in the hills.... I came back to tea in my own tent and at six o'clock Gabtan summoned me to dine with the Sheikh Fellah. I hope you realise what an Arab tent is like. It's made of black goats' hair, long and wide, with a division in the middle to separate the women from the men. The lee side of it is always open and this is most necessary, for light and warmth all come from a fire of desert scrub burning in a shallow square hole in the ground and smoking abominably; we had had a discussion as we rode as to the proper word for the traces of former encampments, and at dinner I produced the MuaHakat (pre-Muhammadan poems) and found three or four examples for the use of various words. This excited much interest, and we bent over the fire to read the text which was passed from hand to hand, then came dinner, meat and sour milk, and flaps of bread, all very good. All my servants were 'guests' too, but their meal was spread for them outside the tent. I had left one of the muleteers to look after our tents in my absence, and to him too was sent a bowl of meat and bread 'for the guest who has remained behind'. Dinner over, we drank coffee and smoked cigarettes round the fire, and I spent a most enjoyable evening listening to tales of the desert and of Turkish oppression, and telling them how things are in Egypt. Egypt is a sort of Promised Land, you have no idea what an impression our government there has made on the Oriental mind.

Monday, 13th.

To-day the weather has turned out lovely, so we were right to wait those tedious four days.

UMM ER RUMANIN, *Wednesday, 15th.*

(The Mother of Pomegranates – but there aren't any.) We are encamped in the first Druze village, where we have been warmly welcomed. We had a tedious six hours' ride across the endless stony plain, enlivened by a little rabbit shooting. They were asleep under the stones, the rabbits, it was not a gentlemanly sport, but it fills the pot. The Sheikh of this town is an old man called Muhammad and he is one of the great Druze family of Atrash, who are old friends of mine. I've just been drinking coffee with him and having a pleasant talk. The coffee was made and served by a charming boy, Muhammad's only son. His mother, too, was an Atrash, and he looks as if he came of a great race. It is very pleasant travelling in this weather, but the nights, after midnight, are bitter cold. This morning the water in my tent was frozen. It is no small matter, I assure you, to get oneself out of bed, and dress before the sunrise with the frost glistening inside one's tent.

Thursday, 16th.

Without doubt this is a wonderful world. Listen and I will tell you strange things. I began my day in a most peaceful manner by copying inscriptions and was rather fortunate for I found several Greek, one Cufic and one Nabathaean – Lord knows what it means, but I put it faithfully down and the learned shall read. Then I breakfasted with Sheikh Muhammad al Atrash. Then I rode off with a friend, name of Salih, and we had a most pleasant journey to Salkhad. He was a remarkably intelligent young man, and questioned me as to every English custom down to the laws of divorce which I duly explained. He was also very anxious to know what I thought about the creation of the world, but I found that a more difficult subject. So we reached Salkhad and I went straight to the house of the Sheikh, Nasib el Atrash – he is another of the great family – and was made very welcome. Now I must tell you that there is a Turkish garrison here and a Kaimmakam 'et tout le bataclan'. I have not yet had a word in private with Nasib for whenever we begin to talk a

Turkish official draws quietly near till he is well within ear-shot – and then we say how changeable is the weather. When I went to his house again I found the Turkish Mudir who lives side by side with Nasib and acts as a sort of spy upon him. The case is this – I want to go out east to a wild country called the Safah and under the protection of the Druzes I can go, but the Turks don't like this at all, and spend their time telling me how horribly dangerous it is, not a word of all which talk I believe. Salkhad is a little black lava town hanging on to the southern slope of a volcano, and in the crater of the volcano there is a great ruined castle, most grim and splendid. This evening as I dined, deeply engaged in thinking of the intrigue which I am about to develop, I heard a great sound of wild song, together with the letting off of guns, and going out I saw a fire burning on the topmost top of the castle walls. You who live in peace, what do you think this meant? It was a call to arms. I told you the Beni Sakhr and the Druzes were bitter foes. A month ago the Sakhr carried off 5,000 sheep from the Druze folds in the plain. To-morrow the Druzes are going forth, 2,000 horse-men, to recapture their flocks, and to kill every man, woman and child of the Sakhr that they may come across. The bon-fire was a signal to the countryside. To-morrow they will assemble here and Nasib rides at their head. There was a soldier sitting at my camp fire. He wears the Turkish uni-form, but he is a Druze from Salkhad, and he hates the Turk as a Druze knows how to hate. I said: 'Is there refusal to my going up?' He replied: 'There is no refusal, honour us.' And together under the moon we scrambled up the sandy side of the mountain. There at the top, on the edge of the castle moat we found a group of Druzes, men and boys, standing in a circle and singing a terrible song. They were all armed and most of them carried bare swords. 'Oh Lord our God! upon them! upon them!' – I too joined the circle with my guide. 'Let the child leave his mother's side, let the young man mount and be gone.' Over and over again they repeated a single phrase. Then half a dozen or so stepped into the circle, each shaking his club or his drawn sword in the face of those standing round. 'Are you a good man? are you a true man? Are you valiant?' they shouted. 'Ha! ha!' came the answer and the swords glistened and quivered in the moonlight. Then several came up to me and saluted me: 'Upon thee be peace!' they said, 'the English and the Druze are one.' I said: 'Praise be to God! we too are a fighting race.' And if you had listened to that song you would know that the finest thing in the world is to go out and kill your enemy. When it was over we ran down the hill together, the Druzes took up a commanding position on the roof of a house – we happened to be on it at the time, for one always walks for choice on the roofs and not in the streets to avoid the mud – and reformed their devilish circle. I listened for a little and then took my leave and departed, many blessings following me down the hill....

Friday, 17th.

I've spent an 'appy day with Nasib. The Ghazu is put off for a day or two by reason of some difficulties between various Druze Sheikhs, and I'm afraid I shall not see the assembling of the Druzes.... Nasib was going to ride out to a village to the south, and I wanted to visit a shrine on a neighbouring hill, so we rode part of the way together, he and I, and some twenty Druze horsemen, all armed to the teeth – including me!...

DAMASCUS, *Monday, 27th.*

Here we are. I arrived yesterday afternoon, alighted at the most fascinating hotel, with a courtyard.

I find the Government here has been in an agony of nervousness all the time I was in the Jebel Druze! They had three telegrams a day from Salkhad about me and they sat and wondered what I was going to do next. The governor here has sent me a message to say would I honour him by coming to see him, so I've answered graciously that I counted on the pleasure of making his acquaintance. An official lives in this hotel. He spent the evening talking to me and offering to place the whole of the organization of Syria at my disposal. He also tried to find out all my views on Druze and Bedouin affairs, but he did not get much forrader there. I have become a Person in Syria!

... Every afternoon I hold a reception and Damascus flocks to drink my coffee and converse with me. That day I lunched in the bazaars, in the fashionable restaurant, unknown to foreigners, and ate fallap and the delicious dishes for which Damascus is renowned. And in the afternoon came the Governor, returning my call, and the usual stream followed him, so that I sat in audience till dinner time. Yesterday I spent the whole morning in the house of the Emir Abdullah. The Abdul Kadir family has a traditional friendship with the Beni Rashid, which is kept up by yearly presents to and fro. They are going to help me in my journeys thither and perhaps I shall take one of them with me. And after dinner I went to an evening party. It was in the house of a corn merchant who is the agent of the Druzes of the Hauran. I found there a Druze of a famous Lebanon family, the Arslan; he is a poet – I had not been presented with his latest ode – and a man of education and standing. I wish I could picture the scene – some eight or ten of the corn merchants, dressed in blue silk robes and embroidered yellow turbans, my friend the poet in European dress, and me, all sitting on the divan in a room blessedly empty of everything but carpets and the brazier. And then coffee and talk and talk and talk till I got up and took my leave about ten o'clock, and went away laden with thanks and blessings.

This has been a visit to Damascus that I shall not easily forget. I begin to see dimly what the civilization of a great Eastern city means – how they live, what they think; and I have got on to terms with them.

To F. B.   HOMS, *March 9, 1905.*

I took a walk through the bazaars, but that was not as pleasant as it might have been on account of the interest my appearance excited. It was an interest purely benevolent but none the less tiresome, for I was never without the company of fifty or sixty people. When I returned, the Kaimmakam came to see me, and we had a long talk, his secretary piecing out his Arabic and my Turkish. One of the principal inhabitants of Homs, Doury Pasha, to whom I had a letter of introduction from Damascus, has also sent to ask if he may call to-morrow. Oh Merciful! what fun I am having! Don't you think so?

To F. B.   KALAAT EL HUSN, *March 12.*

I am now living in perhaps the largest castle known – no, it's not quite so large as Windsor Castle, but very nearly. It is Crusader – but I must tell you how it all came about. I left Homs at an early hour yesterday – not early enough, however, to prevent my having a large, eager crowd to watch my departure. It is one of the most difficult things I know to keep one's temper when one is constantly surrounded and mobbed. The aggravation is quite as great when they are friendly; it is the fact of not being able to move without hundreds of people on every side that is so irritating. Only a fixed determination not to afford more amusement than I could help to the inhabitants of Homs kept me outwardly calm. We had a very long day, $10\frac{1}{2}$ hours, but when we left the carriage road that goes to Tripoli our way lay through such delicious country that every step of it was delightful. It was beautiful weather. The great castle on the top of the hill was before us for five or six hours. The sun shone on it and the black clouds hung round it as we rode up and up through flowers and grass and across running streams. But it was a long way and the animals grew very tired. At sunset we came to the dark tower. I rode through a splendid Arab gateway into a vaulted corridor which covered a broad winding stair. It was almost pitch dark, lighted only by a few loop-holes; the horses stumbled and clanked over the stone steps – they were shallow and wide, but very much broken – and we turned corner after corner and passed under gateway after gateway until at length we came into the court in the centre of the keep. I felt as if I were somebody in the Faery Queen, and almost expected to see written upon the last arch, 'Be not too bold'. But there was no monster inside, only a crowd of people craning their necks to see me, and the Kaimmakam very smiling and friendly, announcing that he could not think of letting me pitch my tents, and had prepared my lodging for the night. So we went up into the round tower in which he lives and he took me into his guest room, which was commodiously fitted with carpets, a divan and a bed – I supplied the washing appliances and the table – and he offered me weak tea while he engaged me in conversation. He is a man of some distinction, a renowned poet, I believe – but his hospitality outweighs all his other qualities. My men and my horses and me, he has taken us all in and provided for us all. There were two other guests besides me, one an old Moslem woman and the other a Christian lady, the wife of a government official.... The old Moslem woman was a nice old thing. Her son has recently been murdered in the mountains by a casual robber, and our talk turned mostly upon similar incidents which are very common here. The old lady crouched over a charcoal brazier and murmured at intervals: 'Murder is like the drinking of milk here. God! there is none other but Thee!' The talk seemed to fit the surroundings. My tower room must have heard the like of it often. 'Murder is like the drinking of water,' muttered the old woman. 'Oh, Merciful!' At nine they all left me – and one offered to spend the night with me, but I declined, politely, but firmly. Today is devilish weather, a strong wind and hailstones and thunder storms.... I spent a very agreeable evening in the company of my host and hostess. We all dined together and he and I talked. We got on to such terms that he ended by producing his latest copy of verses – and reading it aloud to me. We then fell to discussing the poets with much satisfaction, and he forgot his sorrows, poor man, and became quite brisk and excited. As we have often remarked, there is no solace in misfortune like authorship, be it ever so modest. I could have laughed to find myself talking the same sort of enjoyable rubbish in Arabic that I have so frequently talked in English, and offering the same kind of sympathy and praise to my friend's efforts. Yes, it might just as well have been London, and the world is, after all, made of the same piece.

KALAAT EL MUDDIK, *Sunday, March 19, 1905.*

One of the difficulties of searching for antiquities is that most of the people don't recognize any sort of picture when they see it, so that if you ask a man if there are any stones with the portraits of men or animals on them, he replies, 'Wallahi! we do not know what the picture of a man is like.' And if you show him a bit of a relief, however good it is he hasn't the least idea what the carving represents. Isn't that curious?

EL BAREH, *Monday, 20th.*

I made a 'detour' with Mahmud and visited two villages, one more beautiful than the other. We had an 'impayable' conversation by the way. It began by my asking Yunis whether he ever went to Aleppo. 'Oh, yes,' he said, he was accustomed to go when his sons were in prison there. I edged away from what seemed to me delicate ground by asking how many sons he had. Eight; each of his 2 wives had borne him 4 sons and 2 daughters. I congratulated him warmly on this. Yes, he said, but Wallahi! his second wife had cost him a great deal of money. 'Yes?' said I. 'May God make it Yes upon thee, oh lady! I took her from her husband and by God (May His name be praised and exalted!) I had to pay him 1,000 piasters (about 10 Napoleons) and to the judge 1,500.' This was too much for Mahmud's sense of decency. 'Wallahi!' said he, 'that was the deed of a Nosairiyeh or an Ismailiyeh!' 'Does a Muslim take away a man's wife? It is forbidden.' 'He was my enemy' replied Yunis in explanation. 'By God and the Prophet of God! there was enmity between him and me even unto death.' 'Had she children?' said Mahmud. 'Ey wallah' (i.e. of course), said Yunis, a little put out by Mahmud's disapproval. 'By the face of God!' exclaimed Mahmud, still more outraged, 'it was the deed of a heathen.' 'I paid 1,000 piasters to the man, and 1,500 to the judge,' objected Yunis – and here I put an end to the further discussion of the merits of the case by asking whether the woman had liked being carried off. 'Without doubt,' said Yunis, 'it was her wish.'

After this Gertrude goes to Aleppo (calling on the Governor) and then again into the desert and over rocky mountainous country to Konia. In April she is at Antioch, and then into Asia Minor. 'And I have to talk Turkish. There's nothing else for it' – back to Konia, and on to Binbirklisse.

To H. B.   BINBIRKLISSE, *May 13th, 1905.*

If you had read (and who knows? Perhaps you have!) the very latest German archaeology books you would be wild with excitement at seeing where I am. I must begin at the beginning and tell you about Konia. I stayed 4 days. My friend the German Consul (name of Loytved) is extremely intelligent and his wife very agreeable.

Then follow descriptions of splendid Seljouk Mosques in ruins.

Konia contains the mother house of the Dervishes and the founder of the order, Jelal ed Din Rumi the great Persian, is buried there. My visit to his tomb was a real pilgrimage for I know some of his poems and there are things in them that are not to be surpassed. He lies under a dome tiled with blue, bluer than heaven or the sea, and adorned inside with rich and sombre Persian enamel and lacquer and on either side of him are rows and rows of the graves of the Chelebis, the Dervish high priests and his direct descendants – all the Chelebis who have been ministers and over each is the high felt hat of the order with a white turban wrapped round it. Beyond the tomb are two great dancing halls with polished floors and the whole is enclosed in a peaceful garden, fountains and flowers set round with the monastic cells of the order, so he lies, Jelal ed din Rumi, and to my mind the whole quiet air was full of the music of his verses: 'Ah listen to the reed as it tells its tale: Listen, ah, listen, to the plaint of the reed.' 'They reft me from the rushes of my home, my voice is sad with longing, sad and low.' (But the Persian is the very pipe, the plaintive pipe of the reed, put into words and there is nothing so invades the soul.) I dined or lunched with the Loytveds daily, and he invited selections of banished Pashas daily to meet me. The result was some most interesting talks, for the best intelligence of Turkey is in exile and being in

exile speaks out. Some day I will tell you some curious tales.
So I have now an enormous circle of acquaintances in Konia
and I spent my last afternoon there sitting in the Ottoman
Bank and receiving the town. It was almost like Damascus
over again. And my clothes arrived from Smyrna! If you
had roughed it for 4 months with 2 tiny mule trunks you
would realise what that meant. All things are by comparison
and one evening when I put on a skirt that originally came
from Paris I felt almost too smart to move. I sent my horses
on 3 stations down the line and next day took train myself
with my camp furniture and some food and Fattuh. We
joined the horses on a blazing hot morning and packed our
single load on to a hired beast and set off across the plain to
Binbirklisse. The name means *The Thousand and one Churches*
and the learned have tried to identify it with the classic
Barata, but as then the learned knew nothing of Barata but
the name, it doesn't seem to me to matter much whether the
identification is correct or no. It lies at the foot of the Kara
Dagh, a great isolated mountain arising abruptly out of the
plain and whatever it was in classic times, it must have been
a very important early Christian city for it is full of churches
dating back Strzygowski thinks to pre-Constantine times.

May 16th.

I was up at 4 to-day and at 5 I rode off to the hills to see
one of the great sights of Asia Minor, the Hittite sculptures
at Loriz. I rode back to Eregli – blazing hot it was – and
took the train and came back to Konia. The consul and his
wife met me at the station and dined with me at the hotel
and I found there besides Professor Ramsay, who knows
more about this country than any other man, and we fell
into each other's arms and made great friends....

This was Gertrude's first meeting with Sir William Ramsay, and
it led to their interesting partnership in Asia Minor two years later.

*Extract from Sir William Ramsay's Preface to 'The Thousand and One
Churches'.*

'In 1905 Miss Gertrude Bell was impelled by Strzygowski's book
to visit Bin Bir Kilisse; and, when I met her at Konia on her return,

she asked me to copy an inscription on one of the churches, in letters so worn that she could not decipher it, which she believed to contain a date for the building. Her belief proved well founded, and the chronology of the Thousand and One Churches centres round this text. I sent her a copy of the text, the imperfect result of four hours' work, but giving the date with certainty; longer study was prevented by a great storm; and I printed in the *Athenaeum* the impression made on me by a hurried inspection of the ruins, mainly in order to reiterate in more precise form my old hope that an important architectural and historical investigation might be performed by an architect and an epigraphist, combining their work for a month or two on the site. This letter attracted her attention; she wrote suggesting that we should undertake the task; and as no one else seemed likely to do so, my wife and I arranged to join her in 1907....'

Sir William Ramsay, once more home from Asia Minor in 1927, writes me this further letter of appreciation of her work with him.

13 Greenhill Terrace,
Edinburgh.
24 June, 1927.

Dear Lady Bell,

...I should be glad if you would add an expression of my admiration for the thoroughness and alertness of Miss Gertrude Bell's examination of Bin Bir Kilisse on her first short visit. The important inscription was almost totally concealed in a little cave. During our work in 1907 I spent about a fortnight on that inscription and finally succeeded in deciphering it completely, and it appears in our joint work with the help of her eyes....

I am, Yours faithfully,
W. M. Ramsay.

CHAPTER II

1905 – 1909
London – Asia Minor – London

IN the following June Gertrude was in London again, enjoying herself there as usual. She spent the summer at Rounton. She was extremely keen about the garden and especially greatly absorbed in starting a rock garden which afterwards became one of the show gardens of the North Riding. It was exquisitely situated, formed round a lake, from the shores of which was a view of the wide amphitheatre of the Cleveland Hills.

In the autumn she went to Paris to study with Reinach again.

We have no letters from Gertrude in 1906. That year she seems to have spent between London and Rounton, enjoying mightily having people to stay during the summer, seeing the rock garden grow and writing her book of travels – *The Desert and the Sown* – which came out the following year. Early in April 1907 she is in Asia Minor again.

The technical results of Gertrude's work with Sir William Ramsay were shown in the book they wrote together, *The Thousand and One Churches*, published in 1909, in which the plans and measurements of the more important churches and architectural remains were given.

From her letters from Asia Minor in 1907, therefore, I have taken extracts relating to her personal experiences only, on the road. Although travel in Asia Minor is not so adventurous as crossing the deserts of Arabia, it has an adventurous and picturesque side of its own.

To F. B.   SMYRNA, *April 4th, 1907.*

I hope I shall get off on Monday. My preparations are really all finished but I have to wait and hear about the head man for my diggings whom Mr Richard Whittall is engaging for me. As this is the most important matter of all I cannot leave without settling it. Then to call on all my Whittall friends. They have the bulk of the English trade in their hands, branch offices all down the southern coast, mines and shooting boxes and properties scattered up and down the S.W. coast of Asia Minor and yachts on the seas. They all have immense quantities of children. The sons, young men now in the various Whittall businesses, the daughters very charming, very gay. The big gardens touch one another and they walk in and out of one another's houses all day long gossiping and laughing. I should think life presents itself nowhere under such easy and pleasant conditions.

The head man engaged by Mr Whittall was Fattuh, who was to be Gertrude's faithful servant for many subsequent years.

To F. B.   MILETUS, *April 12, 1907.*

In this sort of travel one goes on very short commons. One starts early and one gets in late; there is no time to cook, and there is no meat to be had if one could cook it. So I have lived mostly on eggs and rice and sour milk, not a bad diet of its kind if you have enough of it, and to-night's dinner (soup and a chicken) was the best meal I have had for some days....

I gave up thinking ... for the crossing of that river was in itself sufficient matter for thought. There was no bridge – if there had been one it would have been broken – the water was deep and the ferry-boat was a buffalo cart. The river came nearly over the buffaloes' backs; we had to take every-thing off the horses and lead them behind us – the buffaloes didn't care, they plodded steadily on and held up their noses to keep them out of the water. Now a buffalo can't hold up his nose very far; a little more and they would have been drowned, but they did not think of that. At the other side we changed horses and rode 25 miles into Aidin, all good going till we came to the Meander valley where it was the very devil. Before we reached it, as we rode along the high road there came a sound of crying and presently we saw a heap of something on the broad road. It was a dead man, lying as he had fallen with a tattered coat thrown over his face, and be-side him a ragged child, a little girl sitting all alone in the sun, and wailing, wailing – you have never heard the East mourning, it is always the same and always more melancholy than any other sound. A man passed just before we reached the child, he merely drew his horse aside and rode on. Eh! a man more or less in the world, and a gypsy at that. We stopped and questioned her. They had sent on news to Aidin, her brother had gone, she didn't know when they would come. And so she took up her dirge again. We rode on to the ferry over the Meander and tried to hire a cart to bring in the dead man's body, but no one would go – no, he must stay there till his people came, that was the custom. The girl? She would stay too to keep the dogs off and if night fell and she was afraid she would come in to the nearest village. Yes, someone would go and watch with her if I would give him two mejidis. But I knew that was no good as he would come away the moment my back was turned. So I rode on too; the child will come into the village at nightfall and the man is dead and does not care how long he lies alone. But I felt a beast, all the same. We crossed the Meander in a ferry – the bridge was broken, I need scarcely say, and the high road beyond was all under water. So we splashed for an hour along a narrow cobbled path running between bottomless swamps. We came to Aidin about 5, it is against the hills and all shining in the sun. But what makes it chiefly memorable is that I got Elsa's telegram here saying she was engaged to Herbert Richmond.

Several weeks of travel in Asia Minor followed, finding, photographing and planning ruined sites.

To F. B.   MADEN SHEHER, *Saturday, May 25, 1907.*

I really must begin a diary to you. The Ramsays arrived yesterday. I was in the middle of digging up a church when suddenly 2 carts hove into sight and there they were. It was about 3 in the afternoon. They instantly got out, refused to think of going to the tents, Lady R. made tea (for they were starving) in the open and R. oblivious of all other considerations was at once lost in the problems the church presented. It was too delightful to have someone as much excited about it as I was!... They have brought their son Louis with them, who is deeply learned on birds and beasts and has a commission from the British Museum to collect the small mammalia of these parts.

Now I must tell you something very very striking. The church on the extreme point of the Kara D., at which I worked for 2 days before R. came, has near it some great rocks and on the rocks I found a very queer inscription. The more I looked at it the queerer it became and the less I thought it could be Christian or anything that I knew, so I took it down with great care, curious rabbit-headed things and winged sort of crosses and arms and circles, and with some trembling I showed it to R. The moment he looked at it he said, 'It's a Hittite inscription. This is the very thing I hoped most to find here.' I think I've never been so elated. We now think of nothing but Hittites all the time.

Now this is the manner of Asia Minor: there is never a shrine of Christian or Moslem but if you look long enough you will find it has been a holy place from the beginning of history, and every church on the top of the hill stands on a site where the Hittites worshipped. We began to find queer things, a tower of a very ancient sort of fortification, and then we found cuttings in the rocks which puzzled us for a long time till I, who had seen the same before in Syria, discovered that they were winepresses, and the long and the short of it is that we think we have a Hittite settlement at Maden Sheher and that this was the entrance fort. Of course we may get no more evidence and the thing will have to remain as a supposition, but the inscription on the top of the Kara D. is a fixed point.

Then followed excited days of visiting churches, planning, deciphering, guessing.

... I haven't told you half enough what gorgeous fun it's being! You should see me directing the labours of 20 Turks and 4 Kurds! We are going to get something out of it, you'll see.

To F. B. YAILE, *June 8, 1907.*

Today we have had the greatest exodus known since the days of the Jews. We have moved all our camp up to the yaila, the summer quarters. It took 11 camels and 4 donkeys to transport us. Now this is the place that I first came to two years ago. It is on a shoulder of the Karadagh, 1000 ft. above Maden Sheher and it is entirely composed of churches, chapels and monastic foundations. A few Turkish hovels are accommodated in the ruins – in one of them I stayed two years ago. The people are overjoyed at my return and gave me a most cordial welcome. They sent down to me while I was at Maden Sheher to say they hoped I was coming up and I hired from them all the camels for the transport. One of the most interesting parts of our job has been the tracing of the first settlement of the mountain. It began with my Hittite High Place; there we found several vestiges of an ancient town at Maden Sheher and today Sir W. has seen 3 Hittite inscriptions on an outlying spur of the mountain – he went there while we were moving camp. Of these and of the High Place we are going to take casts so as to have absolutely perfect impressions of them. Isn't it a good thing I learnt to take casts, by the way! Without that we could not have got perfect impressions of these things for the stone is so rough that it is extremely difficult to get anything like a good rubbing. We are getting so much material that it will certainly make a book. Our plan is that Sir W. shall write the historic and epigraphic part and I the architectural. I think it will be well worth doing, for this is the first time that an accurate study has been made of any one district in these parts, hitherto people have only travelled through and seen what they could see and gone on. We shall certainly be able to contribute a great deal to the knowledge of such settlements as this must have been. I look forward to a delightful winter at home drawing my plans and writing my part of the book. I should have been helpless here without Sir W. and the more I work with him the more I like him and respect his knowledge. In fact, it's being a magnificent success, quite everything I hoped it would be.

It will be a very dull book, you understand, but I intend it to be magnificently illustrated. I wonder if Heinemann will do it for me!

To F. B.   KARADAGH, *June 17, 1907.*

Of course you can't write to me much. I'm busy too in a modest way.... I believe this is the very first time anyone has set about to explore thoroughly a single district in central Asia Minor. See what we have got out of it! Two great Hittite sites and a vast amount of unexpected Byzantine remains. We spend much time discussing our book, which is to be a great work, please God! Oh, it's delightful, delightful! I only do so hope you think I was right to stay out here. I could scarcely bear it if you didn't – at a breath from you I would come back by the next train. I hate being away, you understand, but I am deeply absorbed by this work. It grows more and more exciting as one gets further into it.

To F. B.   KARA PUNAR, *June 30, 1907.*

Yesterday I took the road again. A great plain is a wonderfully beautiful thing. It stretched away and away from my tent door as far as the eye could see, as level to the horizon as it was level under my feet. It looked like an immensely wide floor made ready for some splendid spectacle. To-day we rode over it again for 3 hours to Karabanar, a small town lying at the foot of the Karajadagh. There lives on the plateau the largest beetle I have been privileged to see. Black and green is his colour and he is the size of a mouse.

I lunched in the khan, waiting for my luggage cart. They gave me quite a nice bare room to myself; publicity, however, was ensured by a window which opened into the room next me. Then the Kaimmakam and another came to call. Thank Heaven I can now talk enough Turkish not to be left speechless with Kaimmakams and the rest. We were in the thick of making arrangements to go straight on into the hills.

When I arrived I had asked if there were pack horses. 'As many as you like can be found,' said the innkeeper. Presently he returned to say there were none. 'Then,' said I, 'I will take a cart to the village at the edge of the hills.' 'Most excellent,' said the surrounding company, 'the cart will draw you to the hills and then you will get camels.' 'Camels are to be found, then?' said I. 'Many,' said they. Then arrived the Kaimmakam and the Other, and I explained that I was leaving at once for Salur with my luggage in a cart. They heartily approved this plan. Over the coffee the Other let fall a remark to the effect that I should find no people at all as they had all gone up to yaila. 'Then how shall I find camels?' said I. 'Effendim,' said he, 'there will be no camels.' Finally I resolved to take camels from him and after waiting for 4 hours the camels have appeared. An incident similar to this occurs daily when travelling in Asia Minor; the wonder is that one gets through at all.... There go the camels with a 'Haidé! father! pull, my soul! hasten, hasten!' from all on-lookers.

IKIKOYU.

They pulled very well and we got in here at 5.30....

OUAJEK, July 1.

I must tell you that this expedition into the Karajadagh is rather an adventure. No one has as yet explored the mountain. We have come into the heart of it and pitched tents and so far all is well. The whole of the upper part of the mountain is entirely deserted. It's extraordinarily lonely. There are said to be robbers about.

I have no less than 6 men here, including the 2 camel drivers, so I don't feel at all anxious even if they should be still in these parts.

Saturday, July 6th.

An aged man appeared this morning at the tents and professed to know all the ruins round about, so Fattuh engaged him as guide-in-chief for the day. His name was Ali as I had presently cause to know. After breakfast I went down to the village and drew the church and by dint of wading about in dark and horrible stables and poking into the dark and horrible houses that had been built in the aisles and apse I got it out all complete and it proved extremely interesting. Then I came in and changed all my things, for the houses and the stables were, as always, alive with fleas. Very great travellers would no doubt think nothing of this, but I find it an almost intolerable vexation, yet one can't leave a church unplanned because there are fleas in it. Then I questioned the aged man as to what I should ride out and see. He said: 'Many churches there are, a very great many.' 'Where?' said I. 'Over there,' said he, 'that side,' waving his hand vaguely round the mountains, 'there is one.' 'What is his name?' said I (there's no neuter in Turkish). 'Ali,' said he. 'Not your name, the church's name.' 'Chanderlik,' said he. 'Aren't there any in the other direction?' said I, for the way he seemed to be pointing was my route for to-morrow. 'Not any at all,' said he. A bystander, 'Many, a great many; over there there is one.' 'What is his name?' said I. The bystander: 'Ali.' 'Not *his* name, the church's name?' 'Uleuren there is, and Karneuren, and Yazlikisle a...' so on and so on. (Euren means ruin and kisle means church.) Ali indignantly, 'No, churches! ruins, muins' (you repeat the word changing the first letter to '*m*' when you want to say 'and so forth'), 'euren meuren' said he louder and louder, 'all destroyed, mestroyed, pulled down, broken, all ruins.' 'It's ruins I want to see,' said I. 'All ruins,' he said, 'all broken, moken, no marble churches, all marble and so forth, not any at all.' 'My soul,' expostulated a fellow townsman, 'there are two at Uleuren.' 'No marble churches' said he (there aren't any anywhere, I may mention), 'all ruins, all broken.' However, we went to Uleuren and I found two churches and a long inscription. Ali was not a success as an archaeologist and I declined to employ him further. Nor did he want to come.

We are now going round to the north side of the mountain where I am told there are a million if not a billion churches – or something of the kind. I hope there may be one or two. I know how you are spending this Sunday – how I wish I were with you! I also wish so many flies were not spending Sunday with me.

Wednesday, July 10th.

I thought of you a great deal on Monday and very much longed to see Elsa looking as pretty and as happy as I am sure she did look. I shall love to see the wedding photographs and hear all the tales. Now that it is all over I am glad I did not come back, for you see I should have been landed with my work half done and a horrible feeling that I could not go ahead properly for want of knowledge.

The long-expected robber turned up in the night and I was awakened by my servants' firing at him. They missed him, but he missed our horses.

The following preposterous conversation has just occurred:

G.B. loq: Oh! Fattuh, to whom does this poplar garden belong?

F. – To a priest, my lady.

G.B. – Doesn't he mind our camping in it?

F. – He didn't say anything.

G.B. – Did you ask him?

F. – No, my lady.

G.B. – We must give him some backshish.

F. – At your Excellency's command.

A pause.

F. – My lady.

G.B. – Yes?

F. – That priest is dead.

G.B. – !!! Then I don't think we need bother about the backshish.

F. – No, my lady.

The trouble is they don't use speech for the same purpose in the East as we do in the West.

Sunday, 14 July.

From Akserai we had 3 days of absolutely uninteresting travel across the great plains to Konia.

Tuesday, 16 July.

Everything comes to an end, even the road from Akserai to Konia. We got in at 10 o'clock this morning.

ON BOARD THE 'IMOGEN', OFF CONSTANTINOPLE,
To F. B.   *July 27, 1907.*

I'm having a mighty fine time, I must tell you. The Ambassador was more than cordial. Then he insisted on carrying me off to Therapia with him – the Embassy is there now.

So I flew back to my Hotel and packed and went down to the quay. Up came Huguenin, the Director of the German Rly. So I introduced myself to him, and he pushed me and my box into his launch and steamed up the Bosphorus till we met Sir Nicholas coming down to fetch me. This morning I went into C'ple and did a lot of business and then came back to Therapia to lunch. Now I have gone off with the O'Conors on their yacht to sail about these waters till Monday. It is perfectly delightful and they are both extraordinarily kind.

PERA PALACE, CONSTANTINOPLE,

To H. B.   *Thursday, August 4, 1907.*

Today I accomplished the most important object of my visit here – I saw the Grand Vizier. He is a very great man, is Ferid Pasha....

There are troops of professors and people of that kind here who have all been to see me. I find it vastly entertaining.

I expect I shall be in London about the 7th or 8th and I should be most grateful if Marie could be sent up to meet me there. I shall have to stay a day or two to get some clothes.

To F. B.   LONDON, *Friday, August 9, 1907.*

Today I lunched with Sir Edward [Grey] and Mr Haldane – Willie [Tyrell] told Sir E. I was here and he quickly asked me to lunch. It was most interesting and delightful. I'll tell you about it.

Sir Henry C. B. hasn't sent for me yet – I'm a little surprised, aren't you? So different from my habits in Constantinople.

CAMBO, NORTHUMBERLAND,

To F. B.   *Wednesday, September 4, 1907.*

I don't think I ever saw anything more adorable than Moll's children. There's no question about Pauline's being pretty, I think she's quite charming. We have just been spending an hour with them in their garden trying to photograph them. I don't know that it will be a great success for there was no sun and one of them was always crawling busily out of the picture so that all you saw was the end of its legs. Then I photographed Moll with them, she looks so beautiful with them hanging about her. Now we are going to take Pauline with us and look at the Wallington garden.

All the following year, 1908, she was at home absorbed in writing *A Thousand and One Churches*, the work she wrote in collaboration with Sir William Ramsay, recording their architectural experiences in Asia Minor.

Early in 1909 she made one of her most important desert expeditions, to the castle of Ukhaidir. It is deplorable that there are no letters from her to be found about her very important undertaking of the reconstruction by plans and measurements of this immense castle. She subsequently wrote a book published by the Clarendon Press in 1914. The book is a quarto volume 13 inches by 10 inches of 168 pages of letterpress, two maps and 93 plates which included 15 ground plans of her own planning and 166 photographs taken by herself, besides photographs and plans from other sources. It is dedicated to Dr Walther Andrae.

She was in England during the latter half of 1909, and again enjoyed at Rounton the company of a succession of congenial visitors.

She writes from Ardgowan, Greenock, in September, where she was staying with Sir Hugh and Lady Alice Shaw Stewart.

To F. B.   ARDGOWAN, *September 15th, 1909.*

There is an amusing party, the Gerald Balfours, Rayleighs Bear Warre and others. The men go shooting every day. As for Lord Rayleigh I think he is very alarming, but he took me into dinner yesterday and told me most exciting things suited to my understanding about radium. He opens doors into a wonderful unknown world which I shall never be able to walk in however. My hostess is delightful....

Hugo was ordained at Ripon on September 19th, 1909.

I don't think I shall go to Ripon. I do feel so entirely out of that atmosphere. Of course don't say that to Hugo, I would not wound his feelings for the world, and if you think I shall do so by not going, I will.

To F. B. LONDON, *October 5th, 1909.*

... I went straight to the office and had an interview with a very capable lady who used to be the organising secretary of one of the Suffrage societies and has seen the error of her ways and wants to work for us. I fancy she will make an excellent and very sensible speaker and I intend to follow the matter up.

During this year the women's suffrage agitation took greater proportions. Gertrude was strongly opposed to it. I have found no letters from herself about it, but Lady Jersey who was Chairman of the Women's Anti-Suffrage Committee sends me the following note respecting Gertrude's connection with it.

From the Dowager Countess of Jersey.

'In the summer of 1908 Gertrude became interested in the movement against the extension of the Parliamentary Franchise to Women, and joined Mrs Humphry Ward, myself and others in the formation of a Women's Anti-suffrage League. The women received throughout practical assistance from men, among whom Mr John Massie was the able adviser and Hon. Treasurer. After two or three years Lord Curzon and Lord Cromer formed a larger League into which the Women's Society was ultimately merged.

'In the initial steps and until her departure for her great Arabian journey, Gertrude displayed her usual delightful energy and powers of organization.... It is impossible here to name the many keen women who rendered devoted assistance. It was soon realized that defence was harder than attack.... But in Gertrude at least there was never any want of spirit, and her unfailing good temper and direct common sense encouraged and inspired those who sometimes felt the task of opposition a hard one.

'In the Great War Gertrude's unrivalled experience of the East immediately marked her out for important spheres of action and her colleagues in the Anti-Suffrage cause had regretfully to abandon the hope of welcoming her back to their counsels; they however are among the many who, while mourning her death, are proud of her life of achievement.'

CHAPTER 12

1910 – 1911

Italy – Across the Syrian Desert

In these letters from Rome, Gertrude is again in places too well known to make it worth while to give her descriptions of them. I quote however some personal extracts, which show her keenness and thoroughness of study.

She goes from Rome to Spalato.

She goes to Dalmatia and then back to Spalato, where she is shown the palace of Diocletian by Monsignor Bulic, Director of Antiquities, 'the most charming old man imaginable'.

To F. B.   ROME, *February 28th, 1910.*

I have decided to stay on here another week with Eugénie. [Mrs Arthur Strong.] I have got a very nice room in her pension. But I shall miss Father dreadfully. We have had the most interesting ten days together and I hope he has enjoyed them as much as I have. He is such an ideal companion. With the archaeologists he is in his element, and he disconcerts the learned by extremely pertinent questions! but they are all delighted with him and I think he puts them upon their mettle and that they are far more interesting when he is there.

To F. B.   ROME, *March, 1910.*

When my literary remains come to be published the letters from Rome will not occupy an important place. I have not a minute to write but I must seize spaces between archaeologists to tell you what I am doing.... Yesterday morning I spent three hours with Delbrück who gave me the most wonderful disquisition I have ever heard on the history of architecture. It was a regular lecture. He had prepared all his notes and all his books to illustrate what he was saying. He is a very remarkable man and as he talked I got the hang of things that had always remained mysteries to me. He

ended by saying that it was absurd that I should be so ig-
norant of the Roman monuments and by telling me that I
ought to come here for 6 weeks to study. He is perfectly right
and I'm contemplating quite seriously whether I will not
come in Oct. and Nov. and study. I would like to do it before I go back to the East. It is a bore but after all 2 months
is a short time in one's life. If it would give one a real hold
of Roman problems it would be infinitely well spent. We'll
talk of this when I come home.

This project was not carried out and Gertrude was in England
working at her book, *Amurath to Amurath,* during the summer and
autumn of 1910. She goes to the East again in January 1911.

To F. B.   BEYROUT, *Jan. 16th, 1911.*

You remember I told you that my delightful Sheikh —
was in prison on a charge of murder. Fattuh tells me they
succeeded in getting him out, by a free use of my testimony
to his character! I'm delighted. He'll be able to murder
someone else now. What a country! Already I feel my standards of virtue entirely changed.

To F. B.   DAMASCUS, *January 27th, 1911.*

I shall not be able to post a letter to you for a long time
because I shall not be in the way of a post-office, but when
I get to Hit I will send word to our consul in Bagdad and
ask him to telegraph to you, 'Arrived Hit'; then you will
know that all is well and that I shall be in Bagdad about a
fortnight later.

To F. B.   DUMIER, *February 9th.*

We're off. And now I must tell you the course of the negotiations which preceded this journey. First as you know I
went to the sons of Abdul Kadir and they called up Sheikh
Muhammad Bassam and asked him to help me. I called on
him the following evening. He said it was too early, the
desert camels had not come in to Damascus, there was not a

dulul (riding camel) to be had and I must send out to a
village a few hours away and buy. This was discouraging as
I could not hope to get them for less than £15 apiece, I
wanted five and I should probably have to sell them for an
old song at Hit. Next day Fattuh went down into the bazaar
and came back with the news that he and Bassam between
them had found an owner of camels ready to hire for £7
apiece. It was dear but I closed with the offer. All the arrangements were made and I dispatched the caravan by the
Palmyra road. Then followed misfortune. The snow closed
down upon us, the desert post did not come in for three weeks
and till it came we were without a guide. Then Bassam invented another scheme. The old sheikh of Kubeisa near Hit
(you know the place) was in Damascus and wanted to return
home; he would journey with us and guide us. So all was
settled again.

SYRIAN DESERT, *February 10th.*

Three hours from Dumeir we came to some water pools
which are dry in summer and here we filled our skins, for
where we are camping there is no water. There was a keen
wind, rising sometimes into a violent storm which brought
gusts of hail upon us, but fortunately it was behind us so that
it did not do us much harm. Late in the afternoon another
hail storm broke over us and clearing away le t the distant
hills white with snow. We had come to a place where there
was a little scrub which would serve as firewood, and here
we camped under the lee of some rising ground. Our companions have three big Arab tents, open in front, and we our
two English tents, and oddly enough we are quite warm in
spite of the rain and cold wind. I don't know why it is that
one seldom feels cold in the desert; perhaps because of the
absence of damp. The stony, sandy ground never becomes
muddy. A little grass is beginning to grow and as you look
over the wide expanse in front of you it is almost green. The
old sheikh is lamenting that we are not in a house in Damascus (but I think one's first camp in the Hamad is worth a
street full of houses); 'By the head of your father!' he said,

'how can you leave the garden of the world and come out into this wilderness?' Perhaps it does require explanation.

February 13th.

Don't think for a moment that it is warm weather yet. At 5.30 to-day (which was the hour of my breakfast) the thermometer stood at 26°, but there was no wind. We were off soon after six. The sun rose gloriously half an hour later and we began to unfreeze. It is very cold riding on a camel, I don't know why unless it has to do with her extreme height. We rode on talking cheerfully of our various adventures till after ten which is the time when my companions lunch, so I lunch too. The camels were going rather languidly for they were thirsty, not having drunk since they left Damascus. They won't drink when it is very cold. But our guide, Ali, promised us some pools ahead, good water, he said. When we got there we found that some Arabs had camped not far off and nothing remained of the pools but trampled mud. The extraordinary folly of Bedouin habits is almost past belief. They know that the pools collect only under a sloping face of rock; if they would clear out the earth below they would have good clear water that would last them for weeks; not only do they neglect to do that but they don't even clear out the mud which gets deeper and deeper till there is no pool at all. So we had to go searching round for another pool and at last we found one about a mile away with a very little water in it, but enough for the riding camels, my mare and our water skins. It is exceedingly muddy however. We got into camp about four not far from some Arab tents. This is our plan of action: first of all we all set to work to put up our tents, my part of the proceeding being to unpack and set up my camp furniture. By the time I have done that and taken off my boots Fattuh has tea ready. My companions scatter over the plain with axes to gather firewood which is a little dry plant called Shih, six inches high at the highest. We speak of it as the trees. A few strokes with the pick makes the square hearth in the tents and in a moment a bundle of shih is blazing in it, the sheikh has settled down to his narghileh

and coffee making has begun. We never stop for five minutes but we pile up a heap of shih and warm our hands at
the bonfire. We seek out for our camping place a bit of low
ground. When we get near the place Ali purposes to camp
in, the old sheikh is all for stopping. 'This room is fair,' says
he looking at a little curve in the bank. 'Wallahi oh sheikh,'
says Ali 'the next room is better; there are more trees.' So
we go on to the next afforested chamber. It is a wonderfully
interesting experience this. Last night they all sat up half
the night because my mare pricked her ears and they
thought she heard robbers. They ran up the banks and
cried out, 'Don't come near! we have soldiers with us and
camels.' It seemed to me when I heard of it (I was asleep at
the time), a very open deceit, but it seems to have served the
purpose for the thief retired. As we rode this morning Ali
detected hoof marks on the hard ground and was satisfied
that it was the mare of our enemy.

February 14th.

We got into camp at three, near some Arab tents. The
sheikh, a charming old man, has just paid us a long visit.
We sat round Muhammad's coffee fire and talked. It was
all the more cheerful because the temperature is now 46° –
a blessed change from 26°. My sponges have unfrozen for the
first time. We have got up into the high flat plain which is
the true Hamad, the Smooth, and the horizon from my tent
door is as round as the horizon of the sea. The sharp dry air
is wonderfully delicious: I think every day of the Syrian
desert must prolong your life by two years. Sheikh Muhammad has confided to me that he has three wives, one in
Damascus, one in Kubeisa and one in Bagdad, but the last
he has not seen for twenty-three years. 'She has grown old,
oh lady – by the truth of God! and she never bore but one
daughter.'

February 15th.

We were off at five this morning in bitter frost. Can you
picture the singular beauty of these moonlit departures! the
frail Arab tents falling one by one, leaving the camp fires

blazing into the night; the dark masses of the kneeling camels; the shrouded figures binding up the loads, shaking the ice from the water skins, or crouched over the hearth for a moment's warmth before mounting. 'Yallah, yallah, oh children!' cries the old sheikh, knocking the ashes out of his narghileh. 'Are we ready?' So we set out across the dim wilderness, Sheikh Muhammad leading on his white dulul. The sky ahead reddens, and fades, the moon pales and in sudden splendour the sun rushes up over the rim of the world. To see with the eyes is good, but while I wonder and rejoice to look upon this primeval existence, it does not seem to be a new thing; it is familiar, it is a part of inherited memory. After an hour and a half of marching we came to the pool of Khafiyeh and since there is no water for three days ahead we had to fill all our empty skins. But the pool was a sheet of ice, the water skins were frozen and needed careful handling – for if you unfold them they crack and break – and we lighted a fire and set to work to thaw them and ourselves. I sent the slow baggage camels on, and with much labour we softened the skins and contrived to fill them. The sun was now up and a more barren prospect than it revealed you cannot imagine. The Hamad stretched in front of us, flat and almost absolutely bare; for several hours we rode over a wilderness of flints on which nothing grew. It was also the coldest day we have had, for the keen frosty wind blew straight into our faces. We stopped once to wait for the baggage camels and warmed ourselves at a bonfire meanwhile, and again we stopped for half an hour to lunch. We watched our shadows catch us up and march ahead of us as the sun sank westward and at three o'clock we pitched camp in the stony waste. Yet I can only tell you that we have spent a very pleasant day. The old sheikh never stops talking, bless him, he orders us all about when we pitch and break up camp, but as Fattuh and I know much more about the pitching of our tents than he does, we pay no attention. 'Oh Fattuh' said I this evening when he had given us endless advice, 'do you pity the wife in Bagdad?' 'Effendim,' said Fattuh, 'she must be exceedingly at rest.' Still for my part I should be sorry not to see Sheikh Muhammad for twenty-three years.

A week of travelling followed. Long days of 12 and 13 hours, often in great difficulties for lack of water.

February 22nd.

An hour's ride from our camp this morning brought us to the small desert fortress of Amej.... But Muhiyyed Din and the other sheep merchants found that their sheikhs were close at hand and we parted with much regret and a plentiful exchange of blessings. So we rode on till at four o'clock we reached the fortress of Khubbaz and here we have camped beneath the walls where Fattuh and I camped two years ago. It feels almost like returning home. It blew all day; I must own that the desert would be nicer if it were not so plagued with wind.

February 23rd.

The morning came grey and cheerless with an occasional scud of rain. We set off about six and took the familiar path across barren watercourses to Ain Zaza. The rain fell upon us and made heavy and sticky going, but it cleared before we reached the Ain and we lunched there and waited for the baggage camels till eleven. Kubeisa was only an hour and a half away, and it being so early I determined to refuse all the Sheikh's pressing invitations that we should spend the night with him, and push on to Hit, three and a half hours further. The baggage camels were informed of the change of plan and Fattuh and I rode on in high spirits at the thought of rejoining our caravan that evening. For you remember the caravan which we despatched from Damascus was to wait for us at Hit. But before we reached Kubeisa the rain came down again in torrents. Now the ground here is what the Arabs called 'sabkha', soft, crumbly salt marsh, sandy when it is dry and ready at a moment's notice to turn into a world of glutinous paste. This is what it did, and since camels cannot walk in mud I was presently aware of a stupendous downfall and found myself and my camel prostrate in the sticky glue. It feels like the end of the universe when your camel falls down. However we both rolled up unhurt and made the best of our way to the gates of Kubeisa. And here another misfortune awaited us. The rain was still falling heavy, Abdullah, Father of Camels, declared that his beasts could not go on to Hit across a road all sabkha and even Fattuh admitted that, tired and hungry as they were, it would be impossible. So in great triumph and with much praising of God, the Sheikh conducted us to his house where I was seized by a pack of beautiful and very inquisitive women ('They are shameless!' said Fattuh indignantly) and conducted into the pitch dark room on the ground floor which is the living room. But the sheikh rescued me and took me upstairs to the reception room on the roof. Everyone we met fell on his neck and greeted him with a kiss on either cheek and no sooner were we seated upstairs and a bonfire of trees lighted in the middle of the room, than all the worthies of Kubeisa began to assemble to greet him and hear the news. At the end they numbered at least fifty. Now this was the room in which I was supposed to eat and sleep – there was no other. I took Fattuh aside – or rather outside, for the room was packed to overflowing – and said 'The night will be troublesome'. Fattuh knitted his brows and without a word strode down the stairs. I returned to the company and when the room grew too smoky with trees and tobacco sat outside talking to the sheikh's charming son, Namân. The rain had stopped. My old acquaintances in Kubeisa had all been up to salute me and I sat by the fire and listened to the talk and prayed that Fattuh might find some means of escape. He was as resourceful as usual. After a couple of hours he returned and said 'With your permission, oh Muhammad. We are ready.' He had found a couple of camels and a donkey and we were off. So we took a most affectionate leave of the Sheikh and left him to his narghileh. Half the town of Kubeisa, the female half, followed us through the streets, and we turned our faces to Hit. The two camels carried our diminished loads, Fattuh rode the donkey (it was so small that his feet touched the ground and he pres-

ently abandoned it in favour of one of the baggage camels
and sent it back) and I was supposed to ride my mare. But
she had a sore heel, poor little thing, and kept stumbling in
the mud, so I walked most of the way. We left at 2.30 and
had two and a half hours before sunset. The first part of our
way was hard and dry; presently we saw the smoke of the
Hit pitch fires upon the horizon and when we had passed
between some low hills, there was the great mound of Hit
and its single minaret in front of us. There remained an hour
and a half of journey, the sun had set and our road was all
sabkha. The camels slipped and slithered and tumbled
down: 'Their legs are like soap,' explained the camel boy.
If the rain had fallen again we should have been done. But
it kept off till just as we reached Hit. The mound still loomed
through the night and we could just see enough to keep more
or less to our road – less rather than more – but not enough
to make out whether stone or mud or sulphur pools lay in
front of us. So we three great travellers, Fattuh, the mare
and I, came into Hit, wet and weary, trudging through the
dark, and looking, I make no doubt, like so many vagabonds,
and thus ingloriously ended our fine adventure. The khan
stands outside the town; the khanji is an old friend. 'Ya
Abud!' shouted Fattuh, 'the caravan, our caravan, is it here?'
'Kinship and welcome and may the earth be wide to you!
They are here!' The muleteers hurried out, seized my bridle,
seized my hand in theirs and laid it upon their forehead. All
was safe and well, we and they and the animals and the
packs. Praise God! there is no other but He. The khanji
brought me tea, and various friends came to call. I dined
and washed and went to bed.

And so you see, we have crossed the Syrian desert as easily
as if it had been the Sultan's high road, and we have made
many friends and seen the ruins we went out to see, and over
and above all I have conceived quite a new theory about the
mediaeval roads through the desert which I will prove some
day by another journey. And all that remains is the hope
that this letter, which is the true history of all, will not be
lost in the post.

To F. B.   RAMADI, *February 25th.*

We bought a wild duck of a man in Rakkahyyeh marsh, the same appeared for dinner to-night. I said: 'Oh, Fattuh, this duck is very good. May God conquer her women!' He replied: 'How much we laboured with her! She would not cook.' 'She has turned out well,' said I. 'A double health!' said Fattuh, 'May God destroy her dwelling!'

UKHAIDIR, *March 1st.*

I have had a hard day's work correcting a few details in my old plan and beginning the measurements for an elevation. We have three men to watch over us to-night and being within the castle walls I think we are safe from attack – at least I hope so; one is never very safe at Ukhaidir. My friends of last time have left and the castle is empty of all but us. I wish they had cleaned up a little before they went away; it is very dirty.

March 3rd.

I worked for eleven hours yesterday at elevations and had therefore little time to think of anything else.

March 4th.

We left Ukhaidir this morning. I wonder whether I shall ever see it again and whether I shall ever again come upon any building as interesting or work at anything with a keener pleasure. We are now bound for Nejef, but you are not to think that we are taking any common road to it. On the contrary we have cut straight across the desert, for I had heard of a couple of ruins, one at least unvisited, which I longed to see, Sheikh Sukheil and Nasir.

Another week of long and often difficult days followed, mapping and planning ruins as she went, and they arrive at Bagdad.

Sunday, 12th.

Bagdad lies on the east side of the river but the bridge had been swept away by the floods, so Fattuh and I having left our horses at the khan with the baggage horses (which had come in hours before) stepped into a 'guffa' and floated down the Tigris to the Residency. The Lorimers were most friendly and gave me a large and very welcome tea.

To H. B.   BAGDAD, *March 18, 1911.*

(This for the private ear of my family.) Mr Lorimer says that he has never met anyone who is in the confidence of the natives in the way I am, and Mr Lorimer, I should wish you to understand, is an exceptionally able man!

To F. B.   *21st March, 1911.*

... Mr Lorimer and I steamed up the river in the launch and called on Sir William Willcocks. He is a twentieth century Don Quixote, erratic, illusive, maddening – and entirely loveable.... I left Bagdad early on Sunday morning. I do owe an immense debt of gratitude to the Lorimers. No two people could have been kinder. The road to Khanikin, which I am now following, is the quickest way to the Persian frontier.

Tuesday, March 28th.

Most wonderful of all were the mountains of Persia, range beyond range and white with snow. So we rode gaily along the broad road scattered with tiny mud-built huts where you can drink tea and buy bread and dates and hard-boiled eggs, and towards noon we came to Khanikin which lies on either bank of the Heliwan river. The storks had arrived before us; they were nesting on every house top. Sami Pasha's relations in Bagdad had given me a letter to a Kurdish chief of high repute, Mustafa Pasha, and to his house I went. I accepted his invitation – there was nothing else to be done – and was lodged in a tiny room at the top of the house side by side with a pair of storks. Mustafa Pasha was sitting in his reception room when I arrived, with a number of friends. They most of them spoke Arabic, but between themselves they spoke Kurdish, which bored me, for I wanted to hear what they were saying. We spent a couple of hours in this fashion, the Pasha transacting business from time to time and receiving innumerable letters. This is also typically oriental. Every man would appear to carry on an unlimited correspondence with the other inhabitants of his town or village, which is the more surprising as they all seem to visit each other every day. I was beginning to feel rather hungry when fortunately the Pasha called out to his servants to bring food. Some 8 of us went into the next room where we found a table spread bountifully with a variety of meats and we ate from the dishes with our fingers as best we might. It was all very good, if messy.

Towards sunset the Pasha invited me to come into the harem and I spent some time with his two wives and his other female relations. They were extremely pleasant and I don't doubt that they were glad to see me, for they never go out of the house. 'We are imprisoned in the courtyard,' they said. Their furthest excursion is to take their air on the roof. When the Pasha was exiled he left them behind and they spent all those years alone in Khanikin. Next day I was talking to one of my muleteers, a Moslem, and I told him how Mustafa Pasha's ladies never went beyond the courtyard. 'Wallahi!' said he, 'that is how it should be.' And then he told me that his mother (his father is also a muleteer) had never been outside their house in Aleppo until last year, when she went to Mecca with her husband. What a great adventure the Hajj must seem to them, who see the world for the first time !...

She then rides north again with a man Mustafa Pasha had sent to them with directions to see to their safety.

... About 1 o'clock we reached Kasr-i-Shirin which stands most beautifully on the river Helwan, a straggling street climbing the hill side, the great fort of Kerim Khan standing on top. It was to Kerim Khan that I was specially recommended, and I took a short cut up to his fortress, forgetting that I ought to pass through the Persian custom house which is managed by a Belgian. You see I had become so accustomed to neglecting custom houses. I interviewed the Khans (there were a great many of them) and told them I was going to work in the ruins. They bade me very welcome and I galloped after my caravan. The ruins, I must tell you, are a couple of great Sassanian palaces and it was these that I had come all this way to see. I found my servants camping near the first palace and a little upset because two bullets had whizzed past their ears while they were riding up to it. However, I told them that Kerim Khan would look after us, and after that I forgot all else in the excitement of working at the palace. A good many people came out to see me in the course of the afternoon and they all assured me that we should be greatly troubled by thieves if we spent the night there. I remained sceptical as to the thieves, but there was no doubt about the rifle bullets, and it is almost as annoying to be shot by accident as on purpose. The last incident of this eventful evening was the arrival of a mild-looking man with a message from Kerim Khan. He said that the Serkar had heard that I had had some dispute with the head of the Custom House and desired to know whether I was in any difficulty, for he would be glad to settle it by having all the Custom House people shot. It was merely a complimentary expression of good will, though so picturesquely couched. I sent back my salaams and thanks and said there was no need for extreme measures as I had made it up with the head of the Custom House. I worked for the next two days at the palaces without so much as turning round. I went out to the ruins at 6 a.m. and remained there till 9 p.m. and I never stopped for a moment drawing, measuring and photographing except when Fattuh sent or brought me lunch and tea. It is almost more than the human frame can bear when you have got to struggle through such an undertaking single-handed and I wished several times that the Sassanians had never been born....

I'm glad I've seen Kasri Shirin; it is one of the most beautiful places I have ever been in and I shall never forget the exquisite look of it all as I worked from dawn till dusk....

Next morning we had a difficult job to tackle, the crossing of the Diala, bridgeless and in flood. We rode through the first arm of it; it was not very deep, up to a tall man's waist; but it was very swift. In the middle I heard shouting above the turmoil of the waters and looking round caught the terrified eye of my donkey who had been swept off his feet, thought his last hour was come. One of the ferrymen with us rescued him, as well as the muleteer whom he had spilt in mid stream, and they were both brought safely over. The second arm was too deep to ford. We crossed in a craft called a kelek, 19 inflated skins tied together and floored over with reeds. It looked very frail in those swift waters but it served our purpose and in 4 journeys took us and our loads over. The last kelek load was the donkey, bound hand and foot, with Fattuh sitting on his head and one of the muleteers on his tail. The horses had to swim. Two of the ferrymen stripped naked and got on to the 2 bare-backed mares – the others were driven behind them and I watched, with my heart in my mouth, while the rushing water swept them down. May God be praised and exalted! they all clambered out safely on the other side....

She crosses the Zab again, where she changes Zaptiehs and buys provisions.

... We rode off with our new Zaptieh, but once outside the town I found that he was heading for Mosul, whereas I wanted to go to Kalat Shergat. I protested and he declared that he knew no other road to K. Shergat. So I rode back to the mayor and with the aid of a very imperfect map (War Office!) explained that I did not wish to go a day's journey out of my way. He came with me, good man, to the Mudir, and I restated my case. The Mudir was much perplexed; one day more or less seemed to him a small matter to fuss about. He asked to see the map, but since he looked at it upside down we were not much further forward. He got more satisfaction out of my permit from Kerkuk which was the next thing he asked to see. It stated in the clearest language that I was to do anything I liked – the officials treat me with unparalleled generosity and kindness – and that everyone was to help me to that end. I then suggested that I should take the Zaptieh and add to him a man of the town as guide. The Mudir agreed with relief and told the mayor to find a guide. The mayor and I went down into the street and there met an aged party whom the mayor clapped on the back and taking him by the hand ticked off on his fingers all the places to which he was to lead me, ending with Shergat. The old man did not seem to be the least surprised – it is a two days' journey, you must realize. He tucked up his skirts, made a suitable reply in Turkish and marched off down the street, I following: 'In the peace of God! and give him two mejidehs (7s.) when you get to Shergat,' said the mayor. 'Upon my head!' said I, 'we salute you,' and rode triumphantly away.

Sunday, April 2nd.

My old guide is a great source of satisfaction to me. He has no visible means of support: he does any odd job that turns up and if someone happens to need a guide he is always ready to meet their wishes. 'Khanum Effendi' (we talk Turkish), 'I had not a penny left. And then you came. God is merciful; you came! There is no God but God!' When we began our march this morning he repeated the profession of faith uninterruptedly under his breath for an hour, and he never neglects the appointed hours for prayer, though he has to run with all his might to catch us up afterwards. I make the caravan go slowly while he prays, so that he has not to run so far. He has a wife and two small children. How they live is not stated. We had a 9 hours' march to-day and it was hot, but he walked all the way with unceasing cheerfulness, except when my kind muleteers mounted him on their animals for an occasional half hour. He takes special pride in telling me the names of all the villages. 'Khanum Effendi, that is so-and-so – write, write!' So I get out my map and put it in.

Monday, April 3rd.

Safely arrived at Kalat Shergat where Dr Andrae and his colleagues have given me a very warm reception.

To F. B.   *April 14, 1911.*

I spent three enchanting days at K. Shergat and would gladly have stayed longer. Three of the four who were there:

two years ago I found this year and two others whom I had not seen before. One of them, Herr Preusser, had visited two of my Tur Abdin churches and is publishing them, so we had a great time comparing plans. But chiefly I found this year, as I found two years ago, great profit from endless talks with Dr Andrae. His knowledge of Mesopotamian problems is so great and his views so brilliant and comprehensive. We went over the whole ground again with such additional matters as I had brought from Kasri Shirin, and as he had derived from two more years of digging. He put everything at my disposal, photographs and unpublished plans, and his own unpublished ideas. I don't think that many people are so generous. The only drawback of my visit was that I was so reluctant to go away, and I carried a heavy heart over the high desert to Hatra – which is a long way! But one can't be heavy-hearted at Hatra; it is too wonderfully interesting. It was (perhaps you know?) the capital city of the Parthian kings about whom we know so little. The Parthians were an eclectic folk; their arts sprang up on ground that had already been strongly Hellenised by the Alexandrids; and they learnt, no doubt, from the Romans, with whom they were always at war. They worked out these new ideas upon old oriental foundations, and the palace at Hatra is the one building left out of all their cities where you can see the results at which they arrived, for it stands to this day. We arrived late on a grey and stormy afternoon and were received with acclamations by the Turkish army. I shall write a long article for some leading journal when I get home, and call it 'The Pacification of the Desert', for it should be known how well and wisely the Turks are handling matters here.

We had a difficult journey next day. Fattuh was very ill and we had a march of nearly 11 hours which we could not shorten because there was no fresh water. We passed a rain pool in the morning, watered our horses and took a skinful with us, but the day was hot and the men thirsty, and by five o'clock there was scarcely any left. At last we saw Arab tents ahead and knew that there must be drinkable water near at hand. We put up our tents near them, boiled water

and made hot compresses for Fattuh and forced him to lie
down while the muleteers made shift to cook some sort of
dinner. The Arabs were very sympathetic and brought us
some curds and milk, but the water they had was next to
undrinkable, drawn from standing rain pools. We joined
company with a body of the Shammar who were on their
way northwards from Riza Bey's gathering of the clan at
Hatra. They were moving camp when I came up to them
and the whole world was alive with their camels. Now the
Shammar are *Bedu;* only the Shammar and Anazeh are real
Bedawin, the others are just Arabs. Akh-el bair we call the
Bedu, the People of the Camel. They never cultivate the soil
or stay more than a night or two in one place, but wander
ceaselessly over the inner desert. It was delightful to see their
women and children travelling in the camel howdahs and
their men carrying the long spears that are planted before
the tent door.

Fattuh having called in a native doctor who bled him
copiously he rather surprisingly recovered....

Monday, April 17.

There is a charming passage in Sir Edward Grey's book
on flyfishing in which he praises the various moods of Nature.
'Rain,' says he, 'is delightful,' and I remember when I read
it, thinking of warm May rain on our opening beech leaves
at home and thoroughly agreeing with him. But one begins
to feel rather differently about it when one is camping in
pitiless torrents. It rained like the devil on Saturday night
and like ten thousand devils on Sunday. The wind howled
through my tent ropes till it sounded like a hurricane on
board ship and the rain thundered against the canvas. I
thought my tent would go down more than once, but my
excellent servants kept the pegs firm by piling stones on to
them. The storks were less fortunate: their house was blown
away....

She goes on by Nisibin to Mardin, and so into the mountainous
region of the Tur Abdin, exploring ruins, planning, photographing,

over the rocky ridges of the Tur Abdin across the valley and down into a rocky gorge.

... And at the foot of the cliff rolled the Tigris, in full flood, between the broken piers of a huge stone bridge. The first thing we learned was that there could be no crossing of the Tigris till it had run down. The ferry boat is a raft on skins, on which you can't put horses, and neither raft nor the horses could cross in that flood. We were delayed for two days, but they were not wasted days....

More photographing of inscriptions in fifteenth-century mosques and minarets.

On the afternoon of the second day the river had dropped so far that I gave the order to cross – but I shall long remember the rather too exhilarating sensations of that ferrying, the raft darting down the flood and the two horses panting and groaning in the water beside it....

After 12 hours' ride she reaches Mayafarkin, where she makes a day's halt.

... I found, first, the most splendid ruined mosque I have ever seen, secondly, the remains of a huge basilica of the fifth century and thirdly, a great domed church of the sixth or seventh century. I have had two days' hard work at these three. I feel very triumphant over them. They have not been published, and no one knew any more than I did when I arrived, what a wealth of material there was at Mayafarkin.

Saturday, May 6th.

When the 1st of May came I had a great 'sehnsucht' for the daffodils and the opening beech leaves at Rounton – it's not all beer and skittles travelling, you know. The splendid finds at Mayafarkin consoled me a little, but I still have an overpowering desire to see my family. However the work here must be done first – one does not pledge oneself to ancient buildings for nothing. I feel out here more like the Heathen than ever, for the passion for stocks and stones becomes a positive worship.... Poor Maurice! his collar bone is really too brittle. I have the most delicious post-card from Pauline – angel!

To F. B.   *Sunday, May 14, 1911.*

It has become really hot and this morning we set out before sunrise, while it was still cool. But we did not avoid heat and it is still at 6 p.m. 87° in the shade. I do not mind it, but it makes the horses languid. Birejik is one of the most famous of the Euphrates passages. Here Crassus passed over the river to his defeat at Harran: the eagles of the 5th Legion turned backwards from the bridge of boats, but he would not heed the omen. To-morrow I go to Carchemish in the hope of finding Mr Hogarth there.

Just after I had written to you the Kaimmakam came over to call on me and told me that Mr Hogarth had left but that Mr Thompson was still at Carchemish. Accordingly I went there – it was only 5 hours' ride – and found Mr Thompson and a young man called Lawrence (he is going to make a traveller) who had for some time been expecting that I would appear. They showed me their diggings and their finds and I spent a pleasant day with them.

This is Gertrude's first meeting with T. E. Lawrence. She then returns to Aleppo and is back in England in June.

CHAPTER 13

1913 – 1914

The Journey to Hayil

To H. B.   LONDON, *October 28th, 1913.*

Last night I went to a delightful party at the Glenconners' and just before I arrived (as usual) 4 suffragettes set on Asquith and seized hold of him. Whereupon Alec Laurence in fury seized two of them, twisted their arms until they shrieked. Then one of them bit him in the hand till he bled. And when he told me the tale he was steeped in his own gore. I had a great triumph on Monday. I got Edwin Montagu to lunch to meet Major O'Connor and the latter talked for 1½ hours of all the frontier questions – admirably E.M. sat and listened for 1½ hours and then summed up the whole question with complete comprehension. I was enchanted. He is not only able, E.M., he is the real thing – he's a statesman....

On November 13th she starts for the East via Marseilles.

To F. B.   ALEXANDRIA, *November 20, 1913.*

Alexandria is not much of a place but it makes me feel as if I were dropping back into the East. Oh my East! My cab-driver yesterday showed all the solicitude of one's oriental servants, took me for a drive along a very smelly canal because I was tired of looking at catacombs and insisted on my drinking a cup of coffee under the trees to fortify me before I went to the museum! It did fortify me, or else he did.

To H. B.   DAMASCUS, *November 29th, 1913.*

I sent you to-day a telegram which I fear will rather surprise you asking you to make the National Bank telegraph £400 to my credit through the Ottoman Bank London to the Ottoman Bank here. I telegraphed to you because I did not know whether if I telegraphed straight to the National Bank they would think the request sufficient without receiv-

ing it in writing, but I hasten to explain to you (which I
could not do in the telegram) that this is not a gift for which
I am asking. I wish to borrow the money from the N. Bank.
The position is this: As far as I can make out, and I have
now had a good deal of information from many sides, there
never was a year more favourable for a journey into Arabia
than this. The desert is absolutely tranquil and there should
be no difficulty whatever in getting to Hayil, that is Ibn al
Rashid's capital and even much further. Moreover I have
got to-day exactly the right man as a guide. He was with Mr
Carruthers 3 years ago. I heard of him with the highest
praise from him. To-day he turned up at Bassams and Bassam
at once told me that I could not have one who is better acquainted than he with all the Arab tribes. To have got him
is a piece of extraordinary good luck. He is the man of all
others who I should have chosen. So much for the chances
of success in this business. As for the expenses, you see this
time I have to begin by buying everything I shall need here.
As far as I can make out we shall need 17 camels (we have
bought one or two already) and they cost an average of £13
apiece including their gear. Bassam says I must reckon to
spend £50 on food to take with us, £50 more for presents
such as cloaks, keffeyehs for the head, cotton cloth, etc. It is
obvious that this is wise advice because the things are worth
much more there than they are here and a kerchief which
costs only 5s. here is a respectable present in the desert. That
comes altogether to £321. Bassam says I ought to take £80
with me and to give £200 to the Nejd merchant who lives
here in return for a letter of credit which will permit me to
draw the sum in Hayil. I think both these sums are reckoned
very liberally but I don't like to provide myself with less
money lest when I get into the heart of Arabia (Inshallah) I
should not be able to do anything for want of funds. You
will see that I have now come to a total of £601. I could not
possibly explain all this in my telegram so I attempted to
explain nothing but I hope you will not say No. It is unlikely
that you will because you are such a beloved father that you
never say No to the most outrageous demands – perhaps it is

a pity that you don't. I am practically using all my next year's income for this journey, but if I sit very quiet and write the book of it the year after I don't see why I shouldn't be able to pay it all back. And the book ought to be worth something if I really get to Nejd and beyond.

Dearest beloved Father don't think me very mad or very unreasonable and remember always that I love you more than words can say, you and Mother.

To F. B. *December 15th, 1913.*

A misfortune has befallen us. Fattuh fell sick a week ago and we fear it is typhoid. Fortunately his wife is here. I have put off my departure from day to day and now I'm going – my camels left to-day and I sleep with the Mackinnons and start to-morrow. I still hope that in three weeks or so when I near the railway F. may be able to join me and he of course never doubts for a moment that he is coming. But it is a horrible bore. I've got a boy to take his place – take his place indeed! He seems bright and quick, I like him and I do not doubt that after a day or two my camp will fall into order....

To F. B. *20th December, 1913.*

I got off safely on the 16th from the kind Mackinnons, drove out a couple of hours, picked up my camels, loaded water and went off into the desert. We camped early about an hour or more S. of Dumeir and it was as well we did so, for the first night in camp always means a good deal of sorting out, and when you have no single man with you who has ever travelled with a European you can guess what it is like. I had to show them everything, and find everything myself, Fattuh not being there, who had packed all. They did not even know how my English tents went up, nor how to boil an egg. But they are all most anxious to please me and most willing to learn, and by dint of patience and timely instruction I am getting things into shape. It rained and blew all the night of the 16th and all the day of the 17th, impossible to travel if the devil had been behind us (and I was a little afraid that the Damascean authorities might look for us), so there we sat and shivered and overhauled our packs. I have learnt by now to bear rainy days in camp when you are never for one moment warm or dry and the hours seem endless. We sent to Dumeir for firewood for the men, chopped straw for the camels and cotton cloth for me, with which I sat at my needle and made bags for all our provisions. It is long since I have sewed so diligently. Next day was fine, but what with wet tents and unaccustomed men we took $2\frac{1}{2}$ hours to break camp – I despaired, but kept silence until later, and the second morning we were under $1\frac{1}{2}$ hours from the time I woke till the time we marched and that is as good as anybody can expect. I have good servants, you see, and besides I know the job and they soon find that out. We struggled on the 18th for an hour through the mud and irrigation canals of the Dumeir husbandry – a horrible business with the camels slipping and falling. At last we were out in the open desert, with the rising ground of the stony volcanic country, the region of Tells, under our feet, and mud forgotten. We marched through it all yesterday and all to-day, a barren region of volcanic stones and tells. We have sighted but one camp of Arabs in all our way. A man rode out from it to see who we were and we found them to be one of the half-cultivator tribes from near Damascus. For water we have an occasional rain pool, very muddy, but I still have drinking water with me from Damascus, and bread and meat and eggs and butter, so that hardships have not yet begun. It was bitter cold last night; the temperature fell to 28° and I woke up several times shivering. When we set off to-day in a dense mist the sparse grass and shrubs were all white with frost and we ourselves blue with it. But one takes no harm. The mist did not lift till near mid-day, which made mapping most tedious as I could take no long bearings, but we came into camp early in the afternoon (having started early) in glorious sunshine and I am now writing in the long afterglow of a cloudless sunset. Already I have dropped back into the desert as if it were my own place; silence and solitude fall round you like an impenetrable veil; there is no reality but the long hours of riding, shivering in the morning and drowsy in the afternoon, the bustle of getting into camp, the talk round Muhammad's coffee fire after dinner, profounder sleep than civilization contrives, and then the road again. And as usual one feels as secure and confident in this lawless country as one does in one's own village. We have a Rafiq, a comrade of the Ghiyatah with us – we fetched him from Dumeir to stand surety for us if we met his tribe. We ought by rights to have a man of the Beni Hassan, with whom our Ghiyatah is useless since they are deadly foes and if we come across the B. Hassan we will take one along. Good, please God! the earth is ours and theirs and I do not think we shall trouble one another. Such good mushrooms grow here. I have them fried for dinner.

December 22nd.

A preposterous and provoking episode has delayed us to-day. We had marched about 2 hours when we sighted camels and the smoke of tents. We took them to be (as indeed they were) Arabs of the Mountain, the Jebel Druze, with flocks. I told you that we tried in Dumeir to get one of the Jebel Druze Arabs as a companion and failed – and we suffered for it. Presently a horseman came galloping over the plain, shooting as he came, into the air only. He wheeled round us, shouting that we were foes, that we should not approach with weapons, and then while he aimed his rifle at one or other of us Muhammad and Ali tried to pacify him, but in vain. He demanded of Ali his rifle and fur cloak, which were thrown to him, and by this time a dozen or more men had come galloping or running up, some shooting, all shouting, half dressed – one of them had neglected to put on any clothes at all – with matted black locks falling about their faces. They shrieked and leapt at us like men insane. One of them seized Muhammad's camel and drew the sword which hangs behind his saddle with which he danced round us, slashing the air and hitting my camel on the neck to make her kneel. Next they proceeded to strip my men of their revolvers, cartridge belts and cloaks. My camel got up again and as there was nothing to be done but to sit quiet and watch events that's what I did. Things looked rather black, but they took a turn for the better when my camel herd, a negro, was recognized by our assailants, and in a minute or two some sheikhs came up, knew Ali and Muhammad, and greeted us with friendship. Our possessions were returned and we rode on together in quiet and serenity. But to avoid the occurrence of such events, or worse, we are to take with us a man from their tents, and to that end we have been obliged to camp near them that a suitable companion may be found. The sheikhs have drunk coffee with me, enjoyed a long conversation with all of us and been so good as to accept my backsheesh in token of our gratitude in being rescued from the hands of the shepherds. And they have given us a comprehensive letter to all the Arabs of the Mountain. Good, please God, but I feel not a little impatient at the delay.

BURQA, *December 25.*

What sort of Xmas Day have you been spending? I have thought of you all unwrapping presents in the Common Room and playing with the children. But you were certainly not breakfasting out of doors in a temperature of 28°, which was what I was doing at 7 a.m. It was so cold that I could not take rubbings of my inscriptions till late in the morning, because it was impossible to keep the water liquid. I have worked hard all day, planned, photographed, taken a latitude. Late in the afternoon I discovered that the boulders were covered with Safaitic inscriptions and I copied them till night fell. They are pre-Muhammadan, the rude inscriptions of nomad tribes who inhabited these deserts and wrote their names upon the stones in a script peculiar to this region. So you can picture the history of Burqa – the Byzantine outpost with Safaitic tribes camping round it; the Muhammadan garrison of the 7th century; then a gentleman who passed along in the 8th century of the Hejira and wrote his name and the date upon the walls; then the Bedouin laying their dead in the courtyard of the fort (it is full of graves) and scratching their tribe-marks on the stones; and lastly we to read the meagre tale. Well, I have had a profitable day. I have not had time to think whether it has been merry. Bless you all.

December 31st.

Yesterday we rode all day over stones. At noon we reached a Roman outpost, a little fort on a hill top. I sent my camels on and keeping two men with me planned and photographed the place. We got into camp late, but since we were without the baggage camels we trotted our camels wherever the ground permitted. It was a nice camp by some springs – the joy of clean water! This morning we moved into Qasr Azraq, which stands among palm trees, surrounded by a multitude of springs. I had ridden on with one man, whom I left with my camels while I went into the castle alone. It is inhabited by Arabs, but in the front room I found a Druze who greeted me with the utmost cordiality and gave me coffee. I then began to plan the castle when immediately I was surrounded by Arabs all shouting at the top of their voices that if I wrote a line they would burn my book. I took them all down to my Agent, Ali, the postman of 3 years ago (they had shut the great stone gate of the castle to keep me prisoner the better while they haggled with me). We sat down under the palm trees and I smoked and left Ali to explain, with the result that before long they declared themselves to be entirely at my service. I've worked at this place all day and shall have another day at it to-morrow. I really don't know if it was worth the trouble, but I dislike leaving things undone in far away places. I rather think I have got one new Greek inscription. I must take a rubbing of it to-morrow and see what can be made of it. So the year ends.

January 2, 1914.

They were all outlaws and outcasts at Azraq and, as Ali observed, as we rode away this morning, 'The world would be more restful if they were all dead.'

To H. B.   *January 9th, 1914.*

As I said before, paf! I'm caught. I was an idiot to come in so close to the railway, but I was like an ostrich with its head in the sand and didn't know all the fuss there had been about me. Besides I wanted my letters and Fattuh. Well, I've got both. Fattuh turned up yesterday morning, just arrived from Damascus, still looking pale and thin (and no wonder), but with a clean bill of health from Dr Mackinnon. And do you know I really believe that his coming makes up for all the misadventure? I have missed him dreadfully, my faithful travelling companion. Never in the world was anybody given more devoted friendship and service than he gives me. He was in the seventh heaven at being with us. Well, meantime none of the 4 men whom I had sent into Madeba and Ziza to buy stores had returned. In the middle of the morning one of the camel drivers arrived with chopped straw, and after the camels and I had lunched (I on all the luxuries Fattuh had brought from Damascus) I rode off to Mshetta, which is only an hour from my camp. As we came back Ali, the camel driver, looked up and said 'Are those horsemen or camel riders going to our tents?' I looked, and they were horsemen and, what is more, they were soldiers, and when we rode in they were sitting round our camp fire. More and more came, to the number of 10, and last of all a very angry, rude (and rather drunken) little Jack-in-Office of a Chaowish, who said they had been looking for me ever since I left Damascus. There it was. We put on a good countenance and when the Chaowish stormed we held our tongue. I sent off at once telegrams to Beyrout and Damascus to the two Consuls, but I had to send a man with them to Madeba and the Chaowish intercepted them and put the man, one of my camel drivers, into the Ziza castle, practically a prisoner. Thither he presently sent Fattuh also, on some imaginary insult (F. had said nothing) and then he ransacked our baggage, took possession of our arms, and posted men all round my tent. All this which he had not the slightest right to do I met with an icy calmness for which God give me the reward;

and later in the evening he began to feel a little alarmed himself and sent to ask me whether I would like Fattuh back. But I refused to have Fattuh routed out again for the night was as icy as my demeanour and I, shivering in bed, had some satisfaction in thinking of how much those unwelcome guardians of ours were shivering outside. The temperature was 22°. There was a frozen fog. To-day we have waited for the Kaimmakam of Salt to turn up or send permission for us to go elsewhere. He is the nearest authority and I only wish he would come. The Chaowish left us in the early morning to the care of 6 or 7 soldiers and turned up in the evening very affable. We have spent the day not unpleasantly, gossiping with the soldiers, mending a broken tent pole, and also in very long periods of gossip in Fattuh's tent, one member of the expedition or another dropping in to share in the talk. And I am busy forging new plans for I am not beaten yet. But I fancy this road is closed and I shall probably have to go up to Damascus and start afresh via Palmyra. The Bagdad Residency is the best address for me. It's all rather comic. I don't much care. It's a laughable episode in the adventure, but I do not think the adventure is ended, only it must take another turn. I have done some interesting work in the last 3 weeks – just what I meant to do, but I have not enjoyed the thing much up to now and my impression is that this is not the right road. I think I can do better. Anyhow I will try. God ordains. Fattuh observes cheerfully 'I spent the first night of the journey in the railway station, and the second in prison, and now where?'

To F. B.   AMMAN, *January 14, 1914.*

My troubles are over. I have to-day permission from the Vali to go when I like. The permission comes just in time for all my plans were laid and I was going to run away to-morrow night. They could not have caught me. However, I am now saved the trouble – and amusement! of this last resource. The delay has had the advantage of giving Fattuh a few days to pick up strength. He looks and is much better than when he joined me but one does not recover from typhoid in a twinkling of an eye. Now I think he will be able to travel without fatigue. To-morrow I camp again at Ziza in order to pick up two rafiqs – one of the Beni Sakhr and one of the Sherarat who will serve us as guarantors when we meet their tribes as we probably shall in a few days.

To H. B.　　　　　　　　　　　*January 19th, 1914.*

I must begin a chronicle, though Heaven knows when it will be sent off. We left Amman on the 15th, I have given the authorities at Amman an assurance that the Ott. Government was not responsible for me. This amounted to little, for wherever I went without gendarmes the government had the right to wash its hands of me. And I could not take gendarmes into the desert. I rode up that day to the farm of some Christians in the hill above Lina, where I was given a regal entertainment. Also Nimrud, the man who helped me in 1909, came up and spent the night there. I was delighted to see him.

I must tell you that I was in some trouble about my muleteers. The three men I had brought from Damascus were very uncertain as to whether they would come on with me. – I think they really dreaded the perils of the road. While we were at Amman we had fetched another man from Damascus, a nephew of my old guide, Muhammad, his name is Said. It was as well we did so, for on the 16th, just as I was starting, the three Agail threw down their camel sticks and declared that they would not come. I had Said and my negro camel herd, Fellah, an excellent boy. My hosts pressed into my service a fellah, a peasant, on their farm (his name is Mustafa), and I engaged as third man an Agaili, who had followed us from Amman in hope of getting work. His name is Ali, not to be confused with Ali Mausar, the postman guide of 1911, who is still with me and will never, I think, leave me. Besides these, I have Salim, another nephew of Muhammad's, whom I took at first in Fattuh's place; he is an admirable servant and a very nice, well-educated man. I like

him immensely. And finally, I have Fattuh, the lynch pin o₁
the whole party.

So we set out. My hosts provided me with two Rafiqs, a
man of the Sherarat of whom I have not seen much, and a man
of the Beni Sakhr, Sayyah, who is a delightful companion.

January 21st.

We rode all day across flint strewn desert on the 20th.
About mid-day two camel riders came up behind us and
proved to be Jadan, the great Sheikh of the Agaili, and one
of his men. They had spied us as we passed under the
Thlaithuwât and, taking us for a raiding party, had followed
us to see where we were going.

'We took you for foes,' said he.

'No, praise be to God,' said I, 'we are friends.'

So he rode on with us for an hour, for company, and then
turned back to reassure his people. And we came at two
o'clock to the last of the castles, Baîr, as yet unplanned and
unphotographed. The plan is a very old type and the place
may be 8th century. It is very famous on account of its wells,
and in summer and autumn, if the Sukhur are not camped
here, all the ghazus pass this way. I have therefore heard
more raiding stories here than ever before, and I will tell
you one:

Muhammad, Sayyâh (my rafiq) and I were sitting on the
top of the biggest well, which is about twenty metres deep,
and M. observed that when he first knew Baîr this well was
filled up. A party of the Isa had fallen here on the Sukhur
and killed a horseman. The Sukhur killed of the Isa two
camel riders. The Isa were thirsting and the Sukhur, before
they made off, threw the two dead men and their camels
into the well and rolled in a few big stones on top, so that
the Isa might not drink and follow them.

'Haram,' said I, 'it is forbidden.'

'No,' said Sayyâh, 'their thought was good.'

'The Arabs are devils,' observed Muhammad.

'Devils,' said Sayyâh.

'They are the very devil,' said I, and with such conviction

that Sayyâh looked up and laughed. You may take that as an example of our usual conversation.

Sunday 25th.

To-day we set off in a frosty dawn and marched on down the valley. Ali and I walked on for an hour and waited in a sandy hollow for the camels, and the foot-prints were all round us in the sand. 'They are fresh,' said Ali. The valley ended in a wide, open plain, set round with fantastically riven hills black and rusty red as the volcanic stone had weathered. The light crept round them as we marched across the plain. They stood in companies watching us, and in the silence and emptiness were extraordinarily sinister. Suddenly Sayyâh called out, 'There is smoke.' A tall spire of smoke wavered up against a black hillock. I must tell you that we were waterless and thirsty – the camels had not drunk for four days. We were not at all sure when we should find water, neither did we know in the least what Arabs had kindled the fire whose smoke we watched, but the consensus of opinion was that it was a ghazu – raiders. These are the interesting moments of desert travel. We decided that it was best to go up and see who was there; if they were enemies, they would be certain to see us and follow us anyway; if they were friends they would give us news of the tribes and water. The latter question, however, we solved for ourselves – we found the pool for which we had been looking. We watered the camels, leaving the men to fill the water skins, Muhammad, Ali, Sayyâh and I went on to examine that questionable smoke; we crossed a little ridge, and on the farther side saw flocks of sheep, and the shepherds of the Howaitât who came up and greeted us and gave us news of their sheikhs. All was safe and we went on into the hills and camped.

Tuesday, 27th.

Yesterday we rode into the hills. On our way back we met a camel rider who told us that a very regrettable incident had occurred the night before. A man who was camping with the Sukhur had attacked a small camp of the Howaitât

– he had an old grudge against the dwellers in it – and carried off sheep. The Howaitât pursued him and killed him; in revenge his brother shot three of the pursuers and fled to the tents of the Sukhur. This news caused my Sukhur rafiq, Sayyâh, to feel very anxious as to the reception he might meet with in the tents of the Howaitât and I tried to comfort him (with some success) by assuring him that under no circumstances would I desert him. But all turned out well. We reached the tents of Harb, one of the sheikhs of the Howaitât, and were received with all kindness, Sayyâh included. Harb killed a sheep for us and we all dined with him that night. Towards the end of dinner another guest arrived, who proved to be Muhammad Abu Tayyi – the Abu Tayyi are the great sheikhs of the Howaitât. He is a magnificent person, tall and big, with a flashing look – not like the slender Beduin sitting round Harb's fire. He carried the Howaitât reputation for dare-devilry written on his face – I should not like to meet him in anger.

To H. B.   *February 4, 1914.*

I have really delayed too long in beginning my next letter to you. Since I sent off the last by Sayyâh (I wonder if you will get it?) we have changed our plans several times and I still hesitate to pronounce that we are really on the road to Nejd, though I think we are. At any rate we are in Arabia, in the very desert and no doubt about it. But you must hear. When it came to the point of leaving Harb's tents I found that the question of who was to come as our new rafiq was by no means settled. On the contrary, all the Arabs and all my men were gathered round the camp fire with faces the one longer than the other. It seemed that the desert before us – the way to Taimah – was 'khala', empty, i.e., there were no tribes camping in it. It would be, they all assured me, infested by ghazus who would fall upon us by night and undoubtedly rob us, if not worse. Whether this were true or no I had no means of judging, but I take it to be against the rules of the game to persist in taking a road against which I am warned by all, and moreover there was the conclusive

difficulty that we could get no rafiq to lead us along it. Therefore, after prolonged consultations, it was decided that we
should strike east, go to Jof, throw ourselves on the kindness
of the Ruwalla and make our way south, if possible, and, if
not possible, east to Bagdad. We set out next morning with
Harb's brother, Awwad, as rafiq, for Jof and the Wadi Sirhan in pursuance of this plan. I did not add anything to my
letter, though Sayyâh was not yet gone, because the future
seemed so doubtful, and it was as well I did not. I should
have said we were going to Jof and it would have been no truer
than that our way lay to Taimah. Riding over the last hills
– they were very delicious, full of herds of camels – we came
presently to the big tent of Audah, the great sheikh of the
Howaitât. Audah was away, as we knew, raiding the Shammar, but we stopped for coffee and photographs and then
rode on east. But it happened that a man who was among
the coffee drinkers had given Awwad the information that
some of the Ruwalla were camped in the Wady Sirhan. Now
as any man of the Ruwalla whom he might chance to meet
would cut his throat at sight it was clear that he could not
conduct us to the Wadi Sirhan and I was again rafiq-less. I
sent him off to the tents of Muhammad, Audah's brother (he
turned up in Harb's tents the first night we were there – a
formidable personage) to fetch a Sherari of repute who had
no blood feud with the Ruwalla, and we came into camp
and waited results. He returned in an hour accompanied by
Muhammad himself and several others who all stayed to dine
and sleep. Muhammad brought in a lamb and a very beautiful ostrich skin, and further, over the coffee cups, he told me
of a ruin in the Jebel Tubaiq which, if I would come back
with him to his camp, he would take me to see. Now I was
very reluctant to turn back, but a ruin is a ruin, and moreover it is my job to determine what kind of ruin it may be.
So next day we rode back with Muhammad, my men inclined to grumble and I not a little inclined to doubt my
own wisdom. We had got our Sherari guide, Musrud, and
might have gone on if we wanted. But after all I was right.
In the first place the ruin was worth seeing. It has a Kufic

graffito and all complete and to get to it I rode five hours across the Jebel Tubaiq, saw and photographed a pre-Muhammadan High Place (so I take it to be) and got a far better idea of these exceedingly interesting hills. They are full of wild beauty and full of legend; they deserve a good month's study which I may perhaps give to them some day, and me such friends with the Howaitât. For I made great friends with Muhammad. He is a good fellow and I like him and trust him. In the 3 days I spent with him – one, indeed, a very long one, was spent in riding over the hills and back – I saw him dealing out justice and hospitality to his tribe and found both to be good. Of an evening we sat in his big tent – he is an important person, you understand – and I listened to the tales and the songs of the desert, the exploits of Audah, who is one of the most famous raiders of these days, and romantic adventures of the princes of Nejd. Muhammad sat beside me on the rugs which were spread upon the clean soft sand, his great figure wrapped in a sheepskin cloak, and sometimes he puffed at his narghile and listened to the talk and sometimes he joined in, his black eyes flashing in question and answer. I watched it all and found much to look at. And then, long after dark, the 'nagas', the camel mothers, would come home with their calves and crouch down in the sand outside the open tent. Muhammad got up, drew his robes about him, and went out into the night with a huge wooden bowl, which he brought back to me full to the brim of camel's milk, a most delectable drink. And I fancy that when you have drunk the milk of the naga over the camp fire of Abu Tayyi you are baptised of the desert and there is no other salvation for you. I saw something of the women, too – Muhammad's wives and sister.

February 7th.

Three days' journey have not brought us along very far. There is such abundance of green shrubs and flowering weeds that the camels stop and graze as we go, and yesterday we came into camp very early so as to give them a good feed. A day or two more of this sort of country will make a won-

derful difference to them. Yet it is nothing but sand and
sandstone, long barren hills and broken sandstone tells. But
the early rains have been good and to-day there were places
where the bare desert was like a garden. It is very delightful
to see. Also the rain which fell upon us the day we left the
J. Tubaiq was very heavy over all this land. We find the
sandstone hollows full of clear, fresh rain water and scarcely
trouble to fill our water skins, so plentiful is the supply each
night. It is wonderfully fortunate. Yesterday we had an absurd adventure. Besides the Shammar family we have a
couple of Sherarat tents with us, the people miserably poor
(they seem to be kept from the ultimate starvation which
must overtake them by small gifts of flour from us) possessing
nothing but a few goats and the camels which carry them.
These goats had gone on with their herd before dawn; just
before the sun rose the Shammar and Sherarat followed on
their camels and I went behind them on foot for I wanted
to take bearings from a little ridge ahead. We had been
camping in a very shallow valley. Musrud was with me. We
may have walked about 100 yards when all those in front of
us turned round and hurried back to us. 'They are afraid,'
said Musrud. 'They have seen an enemy.' Ghadi, the chief
Shammari came riding up. 'What is it?' I asked. 'Gom,' he
answered, 'foes.' 'How many?' said I. 'Twenty camel riders,'
he answered, and shouted to my men 'To the valley, to the
valley!' We crouched all the camels behind the sand heaps
and tamarisk bushes, got out our arms and waited. Nothing
happened. Presently Ghadi crept back to the ridge to scout.
Still nothing happened. Then Fattuh, Musrud and I went
across to the ridge and swept the world with my glasses.
There was nothing. We waved to the others to come on and
marching down the hills in complete security, came to the
conclusion that the 20 camel riders could have been nothing
but the Father of goats who was found presently pasturing
his innocent flock ahead of us. At night I announced that I
intended to take a rafiq of the Beni Maaz, the Goat Tribe,
and this not very brilliant witticism threw the whole company round the coffee fire into convulsions of laughter.

February 10th.

On Feb. 8 we fell among thieves – worse than the goats. An hour or two after we had struck camp we met some of the Howaitât who told us that Sayyâh, Sheikh of the Walad Sulaiman was camped a few hours to the east. Since it was pretty certain that he would hear of our presence we thought it wiser to camp with him that night and take a rafiq from him – otherwise, you understand, he would probably have sent after us in the night and robbed us. He received us with all courtesy, but it was only pretence. Presently the one-eyed ruffian came into our camp, examined all our possessions and asked for everything in turn. We thought at first to get off with the loss of a revolver, but it ended by my having to surrender my Zeiss glass also to my infinite annoyance. He swore that no Christian had ever visited this country and none should go, that he would send no rafiq with us so that he might be free to rob us, and finally he proposed to Said and Fattuh that they should aid him to kill us and share the spoil. He got no encouragement from them and I do not know that any of the threats were more than words. I clung to my glass as long as I could, but when at last Said, who knows the Arabs, advised me to yield lest things should take a worse turn I gave way. We got our rafiq, Sayyâh's cousin, and are therefore assured against 'the accursed of both parents'. We took also two men of the Faqir, another tribe whom we may meet. They are said to be still more unfortunate in their ancestry than the Walad Sulaiman. One of their sheikhs was camping with Sayyâh and he sent his brother and another with us.

February 12th.

We rode yesterday over a barren pebbly waste and came down through sandhills to a desolate low lying region wherein we found water pools. We watered our camels and filled our water skins and then turned our faces S.E. into the Nefûd which lay but an hour from us. The Nefûd is a great stretch of sandhills, 7 or 8 days' journey across.

February 19th.

Marching through the Nefûd is like marching through the Labyrinth. You are for ever winding round deep sand pits, sometimes half a mile long, with banks so steep that you cannot descend. They are mostly shaped like horseshoes and you wander along until you come to the end and then drop down into low ground, only to climb up anew. How one bears it I don't know. I should think that as the crow flies we barely covered a mile in an hour. But there is something pleasant about it too; the safe camping grounds among the sands, the abundance of pasture, the somnolent monotony. But we have done with it. We came out of it to-day.

February 24th.

We are camped within sight of Hayil and I might have ridden in to-day, but I thought it better to announce my coming and therefore I sent on Muhammad and Ali and have camped in the plain a couple of hours or so from the town. We finished with the Nefûd for good and all yesterday, and to-day we have been through a charming country – charming for Arabia – of great granite rocks and little plains with thorny acacia trees growing in them and very sweet scented desert plants. We passed a small village or two, mud houses set in palm gardens and all set round with a mud wall. I hope the Hayil people will be polite. The Amir is away raiding and an uncle of his is left in charge.

March 7th.

And now I must relate to you the strange tale of my visit to Hayil. I broke up camp at sunrise on the 25th and rode towards the town. When we had been on the road for about an hour we met Ali on his camel, all smiles. They had seen Ibrahim, the uncle in charge. He was most polite, said I was very welcome and ha! ha! there were three slaves of his household come out to receive me. With that he pointed to 3 horsemen riding towards us, one of whom carried a long lance. So we came up to the walls of Hayil in state, skirted round them, and entered the town by the S. gate. At the doorway of the first house stood Muhammad al Murawi. ... I walked up a long sloping passage – not a stair, a ramp – to an open court and so into a great room with a roof borne on columns and divans and carpets round the walls. It was the Roshan, the reception room. Here I sat and one of the slaves with me. These slaves, you must understand, are often very important personages. Their masters treat them like brothers and give them their full confidence. Also when one of the Rashids removes the reigning prince and takes his place (which frequently happens) he is careful to murder his slaves also, lest they should revenge the slain. The men then went away to see to the lodging of the camels and the pitching of the tents in the wide courts below. (There are five courts to my domain, all mud-walled and towered. It was here that in the old days, before the Mecca railway, the Persian Hajj used to lodge.) Thereupon there appeared upon the scenery two women. One was an old widow, Lu-lu-ah, who is the caretaker here, as you might say. The other was a Circassian, who was sent to Muhammad al Rashid by the Sultan as a gift. Her name is Turkiyyeh. Under her dark purple cloak – all the women are closely veiled here – she was dressed in brilliant red and purple cotton robes and she wore ropes of bright pearls round her neck. And she is worth her weight in gold, as I have come to know. She is a chatter-box of the first order and I passed an exceedingly amusing hour in her company. She had been sent here to spend the day and welcome me. After lunch Ibrahim paid me a state visit, slaves walking before him and slaves behind. He is an intelligent and (for an Arab) well educated man. He was clothed in Indian silks and carried a gold mounted sword. He stayed talking till one of the slaves announced that the call to afternoon prayer had sounded. Then he rose and took his leave. But as he went he whispered to old M. al Murawi that as the Amir was away and as there was some talk in the town about my coming, a stranger and so on, he was bound to be careful and so on and so on – in short, I was not to leave the house without permission. I spent most of the afternoon sitting in the women's court and talking to Turkiyyeh who was excellent company. My camels badly wanted rest; there is no pasturage near Hayil and we decided to send them away to the Nefûd with one of my men and a couple of Hayil men whom Ibrahim had provided. I sold 6 camels – the Amir being away raiding and with him all available camels, they are fortunately much in request at this moment – 6 which were badly knocked up by the journey, and sent the remaining 13 away next morning. And then I sat still in honourable captivity and the days were weary long. On the 27th Ibrahim invited me to come and see him in the evening – I had expressed a wish to return his call. After dark he sent a man and a couple of slaves and I rode through the silent empty town to the Qasr, the fortress palace of the Amirs. I rode in at the gate and was conducted by troops of slaves to the Roshan, the great columned reception room, where I found Ibrahim and a large company sitting on carpets round the walls. They all rose at my entrance. I sat at Ibrahim's right hand and we talked for an hour or more while the slaves served us first with tea and then with coffee. Finally they brought censers and swung them before each one of us three times and this is the sign that the reception is ended. So I rode home, tipping each of the many doorkeepers as I left. I had sent gifts of silken robes to all these people – Ibrahim and the chief slaves and the absent Amir – to him a Zeiss glass and a revolver also. I was now living upon the money which I had received for my six camels and it became necessary to ask for the £200 which I had deposited with the Amir's agent in Damascus. It was met by the reply that the Letter of Credit was made out to the Amir's treasurer who was away raiding with him and that the money could not be paid to me till he returned. Now the Amir will in all probability be away for another month. I did not contemplate remaining in Hayil for a month, even if I had been free to go and come as I chose. Moreover I was persuaded that the Amir's grandmother, Fatima, who is a very powerful person in his court, had been left in charge of the treasury and could give (or withhold) as she pleased. But I could not risk being left here penniless. I had just £40. I told my men that it must suffice, that I should call in my camels, take the 8 best and go with Fattuh, Ali and Fellah to Bagdad, while the rest of the men would wait another week till the camels were rested and return to Damascus via Medina and the railway. The money I had would just suffice for all of us and for the tips in the house here. So it was agreed and after two more days I asked for a private audience with Ibrahim, went again to the Qasr at night, saw him and again heard from him that no disbursement could take place in the Amir's absence. I replied that if that were so, I much regretted that I should have to leave at once and I must ask him for a rafiq. He said the rafiq was ready and anything I wished should be given. That morning I must tell you, he had returned the gifts I had sent to him and to his brother Zamil, who is away with the Amir. Whether he did not think them sufficient or what was the reason I do not know. I took them back with me that evening, said I had been much hurt and must request him to receive them, which he did. He had lent me a man in the morning and I had ridden out with one of his slaves to a garden belonging to him and beyond the town. For this I thanked him and we parted on the best of terms. Next day I sent a messenger out for my camels – they proved to be two days away – and again I sat still amusing myself as best I might and the best was not good. I had no idea what was in their dark minds concerning me. I sat imprisoned and my men brought me in rumours from the town. Ali, in particular, has two uncles here who are persons of consideration; they did not care to come and see me, but they sent me news. The general opinion was that the whole business was the work of Fatima, but why, or how it would end, God alone knew. If they did not intend to let me go I was in their hands. It was all like a story in the Arabian Nights, but I did not find it particularly enjoyable to be one of the 'dramatis personae'. Turkiyyeh came again and spent the day with me and next day there appeared the chief eunuch Said – none more powerful than he. He came to tell me that I could not leave without permission from the Amir. I replied that I had no money and go I must and would, and sent this message to Ibrahim and Fatima. But he answered that going and not going was not in our hands. I sent hasty messages to Ali's uncles and in the afternoon one of their nephews came to see me – an encouraging sign. That night I was invited to the Qasr by the women. The Amir's mother, Mudi, received me and Turkiyyeh was there to serve as introducer of ambassadors. It was more like the Arabian Nights than ever. The women in their Indian brocades and jewels, the slaves and eunuchs, and the great columned rooms, the children heavy with jewels – there was nothing but me myself which did not belong to medieval Asia. We sat on the floor and drank tea and ate fruits – vide, as I say, the Arabian Nights passim. Thereupon passed another long day. At night came Turkiyyeh – the women only go out after dark. We sat in the big Roshan here and drank tea, served by one of my slaves – for I also have two or three. A single lamp lighted us and the night wind blew through the chinks of the shutters. No windows are glazed. I told her all my difficulties, that I had no money and could get none, that I sat here day after day and that they would not let me go. Next day I was invited by two boys of the sheikhly house – I won't tell you all the relationships, though I heard them all – to spend the afternoon in a garden near at hand. I went and there were the two boys and all the other Rashid male babies – all that have not been murdered by successive usurping Amirs, and of course many slaves and the eunuch Said. We sat on carpets in a garden pavilion, as you may see in any Persian miniature you choose to look at, and I again put forward my requests, which were again met by the same replies on the part of Said. I ended by declaring that I wished to leave the next day and asked for a rafiq. Thereat we wandered through the gardens and my hosts, the two boys, carefully told me the names of all the fruit trees (which of course I knew) and the little children walked solemnly hand in hand in their long brocade robes. And then we drank more coffee and at the afternoon prayer I left. After prayers came Said and told Muhammad al Murawi that I must understand that nothing could be done till permission came from the Amir. I went to the men's tent and spoke my mind to Said without any Oriental paraphrases and, having done so, I rose abruptly and left them sitting – a thing which is only done by great sheikhs, you understand. The camels came in at dusk and I, thinking that in the end I should have to stay here for another indefinite time, was already beginning to plan where to send them out to graze, when after dark came Said and another with £200 in a bag and full permission to go where and when I liked. The rafiq was ready. I replied with great dignity that I was much obliged and that I did not intend to leave till the next day for I wished to see the Qasr and the town by daylight. And to-day I have been shown everything, have been allowed to photograph everything and do exactly as I pleased. I gave £10 in backshish in the Qasr. As I was returning I was given an invitation from Turkiyyeh and I went to her house. She says she explained the whole position to Fatima and I think that the 'volte-face' is due to her, but however it may be I am profoundly thankful. I go to Bagdad. After careful enquiries I feel sure that the road south is not possible this year. The tribes are up and there is an expedition pending from here. They would not, therefore, give me a rafiq south and I should have considerable difficulty in going without their leave. So Hayil must suffice for this year. Moreover I have learnt a good deal about travel in this country and I know that none of the southern country can be travelled 'à la Franca'. If ever I go there I must go with no more baggage than I can carry on my own camel.

Sunday, March 22nd.

We are within sight of Nejef. I have camped an hour from the town because I know there is no camping ground near it and I should probably have to put up in the Government sarai, which is tiresome. Also I very much want to get through to Bagdad without questions or telegrams. Oh, but it is a long dull way from Nejd! I wanted to come up by the old pilgrim road, which has a certain historic interest and is also the shortest, but the morning I left Hayil came a slave with a message to say I was to travel by the western road as the eastern was not safe. As I did not much mind the one way or the other I acquiesced. Two days out we met the Amir's messengers bringing in a tale (which they served up to us) of a highly successful raid, the flight of all the Anazeh before the Amir and the capture of Jof. They said the Amir was a few days further on. But when we had crossed the Nefûd for 4 days and come near the place where he was reported to have been he had left and crossed over to the eastern road and was said to be off raiding some tribes further east. I did not intend to turn back for him and it would have been useless for I might have taken days to find him, so I went on my way in all tranquillity. We rode for ever over immense levels, not a valley or a hill to be seen and so little water that we were almost always too short of it to spend it in washing. As long as we were with the Shammar and that was for the first 10 days, we were perfectly safe with a rafiq from Hayil. He rode with us for 8 days and we took on another Shammari for the next 2 days. Then the fun began. We had to get through the Shia tribes of Iraq, all out in the desert now for the spring pasture and all accursed of their two parents. The first we reached were the Beni Hasan and we spent a very delicate hour, during which it was not apparent whether they meant to strip us or to treat us as guests. Ultimately they decided on the latter course. We camped with them, they killed a lamb for us and gave us two rafiqs next day. That day luckily we saw no one and camped in solitude. Early on the following morning we sighted tents and our rafiqs were reduced to a state of quivering alarm for they will kill each other just as gaily as they kill you. One of them, however, was induced to ride up to the tents, which he found to be those of an allied tribe. He brought back two new rafiqs for he and his companion flatly refused to go on. So we rode on for 6 hours or so and then again we sighted tents and – 'même jeu!' The rafiqs even talked of turning back and leaving us. But again we made one of them go up and enquire what Arabs they were and as great good luck would have it they were the Ghazâlat who are the only people of any real importance and authority in these parts. We camped with them and took on an excellent rafiq – a well-known man – his name is Dâwi. With him we have felt comparatively safe, but if we had not had him with us we should have been stripped to the skin twice in these last two days. The first morning we came down to water at some horribly stagnant pools we found a large company of the Madan filling their water skins there. The Madan are possibly the worst devils known. The offered Dâwi £30 if he would abandon us for they could not touch us as long as we had a sheikh of the Ghazâlat with us for fear of the Ghazâlat, you understand. And yesterday afternoon we met a large caravan of Madan coming up from Meshed and in a moment we were surrounded by stalwart armed men who laid hold of our camels and would have made them kneel. But Dawi called out to them and when they saw him they let go and drew off. This morning a casual person who was tending flocks sent a rifle bullet between the legs of our camels. Dâwi ran out and expostulated with him before he sent another and we protested loudly at the treatment he had accorded us. 'An enemy does not come riding across the top of the plain in full daylight,' said Ali, 'and if you feared us the custom is to send a bullet over the heads of the riders till you have found out whether they are friends or foes.' He admitted that he had broken the rules and, for my part, I rejoiced that he had broken none of the camels' legs. Even to-night I don't upon my honour know whether we are safe camping out here two hours from the town, but the men seem to think it is all right, and anyhow here we are! The edges of the desert are always stormy and difficult. The tribes are not Bedu but Arab, a very important distinction, for they have not the code and the rules of the Beduin. But these Shia people are a great deal worse than any one we have met upon our whole way. Having penned these lines it occurred to me to go and ask Ali whether he thought we were safe for the night. He replied that he did not and that his mind was far from being at rest. (He had chosen the camping ground himself, I must mention.) I enquired what he thought we

had better do. He thought we had better go on to a village.
It was then two hours before sunset. We packed the dinner,
which was cooked, into our good camp saucepans, struck
camp and loaded all in half an hour and off we set! It was a
most absurd proceeding, but I thought it would be still more
absurd to have a regrettable incident on this last night of
our desert journey. Just at sunset we reached a small village
of wattle huts and here we have camped. The villagers have
received us with much courtesy and to the best of our belief
we are in security at last.

To H. B.   BAGDAD, *March 29th.*

Yes, we were safe and we got here without further incident.
I drove from Meshhed to Kerbela – Nejef and Meshhed are
the same – dined and spent the evening with our vice-consul,
and drove into Bagdad next day. I have fallen on my feet
with some new acquaintances, Mr Tod, the head man of
Lynch's company and his darling little Italian wife.

It's queer and rather enjoyable at first, the sense of being
in perfect security, but one soon loses the realization of it.

To H. B.   *23rd April, 1914.*

Behold I'm 11 days out from Bagdad and I have not begun to tell you my tale. I have been put to it to get through
the long days and I have been too tired at the end of them
to write. I drove out from Bagdad to Feluja, on the Euphrates, having arranged that my camels were to leave Bagdad
the previous day and meet me at Feluja. The day they left
Ali made an unjustifiable request – that I should take a
cousin of his with us, the cousin wishing to escape military
service. I refused and Ali struck. Fattuh got him and the
camels off with great difficulty late at night; in consequence
they had not arrived when I reached Feluja – and when they
came Ali had brought the cousin with him! I was very angry,
Ali was in the Devil's own temper and I dismissed him on
the spot to find his way back to Bagdad with the cousin. He
has given me a great deal of trouble. I have put up with a
great deal for the sake of long acquaintance, but gross in-

subordination I won't stand and there is an end of him. My party therefore was Fattuh, Sayyif and Fellah (the negro) and I was left without a guide for the Syrian desert. I am travelling very light with two small native tents, a bed on the ground, no furniture, no nothing – for speed's sake. We pitched our tiny camp half-an-hour out of Feluja in the desert by some Dulaim tents – it was blazing hot, and what with the heat and the hardness of the ground (to which I have now grown accustomed) I did not sleep much. Next day we rode along the high road to Ramadi on the Euphrates, where lives the chief Sheikh of the Dulaim. I went straight to him. He received me most cordially, lodged me in his palm garden, gave me a great feast and a rafiq from his own household, Adwan, a charming man. It was blazing hot again and noisy, dogs and people talking, and I slept less than ever. We were off before dawn and struck south west into the desert to the pitch springs of Abu Jir. We arrived in a dust storm, the temperature was 91° and it was perfectly disgusting. The following day was better, as hot as ever, but no dust storms. We rode on west into the desert. Two days more, west and slightly north, with the temperature falling, thank Heaven, brought us up on to the post road and here we fell in with the sheikh of the Anazeh and I took a new rafiq from him, Assaf is his name, and very reluctantly said good-bye to Adwan. We rode down the following day to Muhaiwir in the Wadi Hauran, where I had been 3 years ago. The world was full of Anazeh tents and camels – a wonderful sight. It meant, too, that with my Anazeh rafiq I was perfectly safe. And in two more days we came to the great sheikh of all these eastern Anazeh, Fahad Bey, and I alighted at his tents and claimed his hospitality. He treated me with fatherly kindness, fed me, entertained me, and advised me to take a second rafiq, a man of the Ruwalla, who are the western Anazeh. I spent the afternoon planning a ruin near him – a town, actually a town in the heart of the Syrian desert! Only the fortified gate was planable, the rest was mere stone heaps, but it throws a most unexpected light on the history of the desert. There was most certainly a settled population at one time in these eastern parts. We had violent thunderstorms all night and yesterday, when I left Fahad, a horrible day's journey in the teeth of a violent wind and through great scuds of rain. To-day, however, it has been very pleasant. I have been following the old road which I came out to find and am well content to have my anticipations justified. We came to a small ruin in the middle of the day which I stopped to plan. Fahad told me that the desert from the camp to Bukhara is 'Khala', empty, i.e., there are no Beduin camped in it. I like solitary camps and the desert all to myself, but it has the drawback of not being very safe. With our two rafiqs no Anazeh of any kind will touch us, but there is always the chance of a ghazu. Very likely they would do us no harm, but one can't be sure. However, so far I have run my own show quite satisfactorily and it amuses me to be tongue and voice for myself, as I have been these days. But I am tired, and being anxious to get through and be done with travel, we are making long marches, 9 and 10 hours. Oh, but they are long hours, day after day in the open wilderness! I have come in sometimes more dead than alive, too tired to eat and with just enough energy to write my diary. We are now up nearly a couple of thousand feet and I am beginning to feel better.

On the 24th we began the day by sighting something lying in the desert with an ominous flutter of great wings over it. Assaf observed that it was 3 dead camels and 2 dead men, killed ten nights ago – ghazu met ghazu, said he.

May 2nd.

We rode through the mountains, a beautiful road but I was too tired to enjoy it much. Also we made very long hours, ten and twelve a day. On the 30th we went into Adra and camped there, on the very spot where I mounted my camel the day I set out from Damascus, four months and a half ago. Next morning, yesterday, through gardens and orchards to Damascus. I rather think I shall catch a boat to C'ple on the 8th, getting there on the 12th, stay there a week or less and come on by train, getting to London about the 24th.

This arrival at Damascus on her return journey marks the end of Gertrude's travels in the desert with her caravan.

Dr David Hogarth, President of the Royal Geographical Society, gave an account on April 14th, 1927, before the Society, of Gertrude's adventurous expedition to Hayil from which I quote the following:

'Her journey was a pioneer venture which not only put on the map a line of wells, before unplaced or unknown, but also cast much new light on the history of the Syrian desert frontiers under Roman, Palmyrene, and Ummayad domination.... But perhaps the most valuable result consists in the mass of information that she accumulated about the tribal elements ranging between the Hejaz Railway on the one flank and the Sirhan and Nefûd on the other, particularly about the Howaitât group, of which Lawrence, relying on her reports, made signal use in the Arab campaigns of 1917 and 1918.

'Her stay in Hayil was fruitful of political information especially concerning both the recent history and the actual state of the Rashid house, and also its actual and probable relations with the rival power of the Ibn Sauds. Her information proved of great value during the war, when Hayil had ranged itself with the enemy and was menacing our Euphratean flank. Miss Bell became, from 1915 onwards, the interpreter of all reports received from Central Arabia.'

Dr Hogarth also said in reference to her return across the Hamad to Damascus from Bagdad:

'To another European woman, in the days before desert motor services had been thought of, such a journey would have seemed adventurous enough. But to Miss Bell, who had been into Nejd, the crossing of the Hamad seemed something of an anti-climax.

'... The jaded traveller, writing in April 1914, her diary and letters at Bagdad, had no suspicion that, in little more than a year, the knowledge and experience acquired during the past four months would become of national value. Nor could she foresee that, even after the war, Northern Nejd would return to the obscurity from which she had rescued it. Up to this year of grace, 1927, her visit to Hayil, thirteen years ago, remains the last that has been put on scientific record by a European traveller....'

CHAPTER 14

1914 – 1915 – 1916

War Work, Boulogne, London, Cairo

GERTRUDE was then in England for the rest of the summer. At the outbreak of war she was at Rounton. During September 1914 she went round to various places in the North Riding of Yorkshire giving addresses on the war, and cheering people on. She was an admirable speaker, and her addresses always roused enthusiasm.

After this she went for a time to Lord Onslow's Hospital at Clandon, and afterwards, by the initiative of Lord Robert Cecil (afterwards Lord Cecil), to Boulogne, where she worked with Flora and Diana Russell in the office for tracing the Missing and Wounded.

To F. B.   BOULOGNE, *December 1, 1914.*

In time I think we ought to have one of the best run offices in France. We are already scheming to get into closer touch with the front which is our weak point. Lord Robert asked the Adj. General to let us have a representative and he refused categorically. Now we have a great plan for getting lots of Army Chaplains for it is quite clear we shall have to make our own channels for ourselves. Also I have several other ideas in my head to put into execution gradually. I'll tell you about them as they evolve.

We have had the most pitiful letters and we see the most pitiful people.

To H. B.   BOULOGNE, *December 30, 1914.*

... Do you mind my being here, dearest father. I feel as if I had flown to this work as one might take to drink, for some kind of forgetting that it brings, but, you know it, there's no real forgetting and care rides behind one all the day. I sometimes wonder if we shall ever know again what it was like to be happy. You sound terribly overworked....

To F. B.   BOULOGNE, *January 1, 1915.*

A happier New Year. What else can I wish you? Diana
and I caught ourselves wondering last night whether the next
31st Dec. would find us still sitting at our desks here. We saw
the New Year in after all. It happened this way. Yesterday
morning there 'débouchéd' in our office Mr Cazalet, who is
working with Fabian Ware out at the Front. Mr Cazalet
brought a tangled bundle of letters and lists from which we
had been working to compare with ours and to be put
straight for him. We had 24 hours for the work before he returned to the front. It was just like a fairy story only we
hadn't the ants and the bees to help us in a mountain work.
Diana ran out got a great ledger and proceeded to make it
into an indexed ledger which we couldn't find here.

We had two hours off from 7 to 9 to dine with her cousin
who has come out to look for a missing son – dead I much
fear. At 9 we went back to the office. By 9.30 everything was
sorted out and I began to fill the ledger Diana keeping me
supplied, we could not have done it if I had not prepared all
that was possible beforehand. At midnight we broke off for
a few minutes, wished each other a better year and ate some
chocolates. At 1 a.m. a young man of our acquaintance seeing our lights burning came up to know if he could help us
but he could not and so sent him away with thanks. By 2
a.m. we were within an hour or two of the end so we came
home to bed. I was back at 8.15 prepared the ordinary day's
work, shortened it a little, the rest will stand over for to-
morrow got through my part with the men when they came
in and leaving Diana to clear up the rest returned to the
ledger. By 12.30 it was finished with just an hour to spare
and I took it to Mr Cazalet. It had been an exciting time
but we won it and now this really important thing is set
going. There now remains a card index of names to write
for him but we have a week for that.

From Boulogne Gertrude was summoned back to London by
Lord Robert Cecil. The office in London for tracing the wounded
and missing was in a state of chaotic confusion and Lord Robert

opined that Gertrude would be the best person to put it straight –
which she did, and succeeded in organising it on efficient lines.

In November she was sent for to Cairo. Dr David Hogarth, then
in close connection with Col. T. E. Lawrence, who was later to take
an active part in the Revolt in the Desert, felt that Gertrude's
knowledge of the tribes of Northern Arabia would be invaluable.
Through his intervention therefore and that of Capt. Hall (afterwards Vice-Admiral Sir Reginald Hall) in London, it was proposed to Gertrude that she should go to Cairo at once. She went
there in November 1915.

To F. B.   CAIRO, *November 30th, 1915.*

I telegraphed to you this morning after my arrival and
asked you to send me by Lady B. another gown and skirt.

I have not yet been to see the MacMahons but I must
leave a card on them to-day. For the moment I am helping
Mr Hogarth to fill in the intelligence files with information
as to the tribes and sheikhs. It's great fun and delightful to
be working with him.

Capt. Woolley [now Sir Leonard Woolley], ex-digger at
Carchemish and head in the Intelligence Dept. at P. Said
came on board to meet me. Next morning I came up here.
Mr Hogarth and Mr Lawrence (you don't know him, he
is also of Carchemish exceedingly intelligent) met me and
brought me to this hotel where they are both staying.

To F. B.   CAIRO, *December 6th, 1915.*

Mr Hogarth leaves tomorrow, to my great sorrow. He has
been a most friendly support and I have scarcely yet found
my own feet yet. They have given me some work to do on
Arab Tribes their numbers and lineage. It is a vague and
difficult subject which would take a lifetime to do properly.
I should think it will be about a month before I can get it
into any sort of shape, but it rather depends on what information one can collect. I haven't begun yet for I have
been doing odds and ends of jobs for Mr Hogarth which have
taken all my time. Far the nicest people who I have met are
the MacMahons with whom I dined last night. They are
both charming, so pleasant and agreeable. They gave me a

standing invitation to come in whenever I liked and I am going to have a long talk with him one of these days.

To F. B.   CAIRO, *December 13th, 1915.*

... The days pass quickly here. I am quite happy and beginning to feel a little more as if I were getting hold of things. I do the same thing every day all pleasant but not matter for good letter writing. I have an Arabic lesson from 8.15 to 9.30 then I walk up to the office and work at tribes or annotate telegrams – the latter is great fun. Back to lunch and then to the office again and I seldom get home much before 7... but usually I dine here with Col. Wright, Mr Lawrence and a party of people, we all share the same table. And it is not till after dinner that I go back to Arabic and do a little work for next morning. I wonder if you sent me out a purple evening chiffon gown by Lady Brassey – I telegraphed for it, but I haven't heard anything of it or her yet. Also a new white skirt from Ospovat which I found I hadn't got. I am rather short of clothes for a prolonged stay in Cairo. It is heavenly weather – almost too nice for wartime I feel. Still I think I'm right to be here....

She stayed in Cairo for 6 weeks, during which time she met one person after another who interested her, either old friends or new acquaintances.

To F. B.   ON THE NILE, *December 25th, 1915.*

You don't mind my staying, do you? as long as they have a job for me. Of course if you want me I will come home. I rather wish I had brought more clothes. Could you possibly send out to me the blue shot silk gown with a little coat and its own hat trimmed with feathers? And if you are sending anything I should like too the purple satin day gown with a cape – Marie knows which I mean – and a mauve parasol, I have lots I know. I don't know whether things sent by parcel post would be likely to reach me. Both gowns would fold up so small that they could almost be sent by letter post – not a hat however. Perhaps if you were to ask the kind

Captain Hall he could contrive to send out a small box for me, by bag even. I should be very grateful – and the sooner the better.

To F. B. CAIRO, *January 1, 1916.*

A second year of war – and I can only wish you as I wished you last first of January that we may not see another. Never another year like the last. It's probable that I may go on for a few days to India towards the end of the month. I have had long and very interesting letters from Domnul and an invitation from the Viceroy [Lord Harding] who wants to see me.

Domnul, the Rumanian word for 'gentleman', is an affectionate nickname for Sir Valentine Chirol, dating from Bucarest days.

To H. B. CAIRO, *January 24th, 1916.*

I can't write through censors and I must therefore send you a private word by bag enclosed to the Hogarths to tell you what I'm doing – it is of course only for you Mother and Maurice.... When I got Lord H's message through Domnul I suggested that it might be a good plan if I, a quite unimportant and unofficial person were to take advantage of the Viceroy's invitation and go out to see what could be done by putting this side of the case before them and hearing that. My chief has approved. I cabled to Domnul and received from him an enthusiastic reply. So I'm going. I don't suppose I shall be in India more than ten days or a fortnight. I shall go straight up to Delhi to Lord H. If they will let me I would very much like to go to Basrah for a week or two on my way back. I shall very probably spend a few days at Aden before I return here as there is a good deal of information about tribes and the people which we want from them and don't seem to get. I feel a little anxious about it, but take refuge in my own extreme obscurity and the general kindness I find everywhere. I shall find Domnul at Delhi which will make everything easy, otherwise I don't think I should have the face to set out on a political mission.

To H. B. CAIRO, *January 28, 1916.*

I'm off finally at a moment's notice to catch a troop ship at Suez. I really do the oddest things. I learnt at 3 p.m. that I could catch it if I left at 6 p.m. which did not allow much time for thought. I'm charged with much negotiation – and I hope I may be well inspired.

An officer who was at Cairo at the time said afterwards that he 'never saw anyone mobilize as quickly as Miss Bell'.

CHAPTER 15

1916 – 1917

Delhi – Basrah

To F. B.   VICE-REGAL LODGE, DELHI, *February 11th, 1916.*

... But in order properly to appreciate dust you must go by train across the desert of Sinde. We reached Delhi at 7.30 a.m. I hadn't an idea what was to happen to me, nor whether anyone knew I was coming and behold when I got out, coated in dust on an icy cold morning, there was Domnul on the platform and a Vice-Regal motor waiting outside. You may imagine my joy.

Then followed some very interesting days at the Vice-Regal Lodge discussing the situation with the Viceroy, seeing Mr Baker and Mr Lutyens, hearing of the new Delhi.

To H. B.   VICE-REGAL LODGE, DELHI, *February 18th, 1916.*

... No one has helped another as you helped me, and to tell you what your love and sympathy meant is more than I know how to do.

... As at present arranged I leave Delhi on the 23rd, spend a day or two at Lahore and start from Karachi on the 27th. What will happen after that I have no idea. The V. is anxious that I should stay at Basrah and lend a hand with the Intell. Dept there, but all depends on what their views are and whether I can be of any use. That hangs on me, I feel – as we have often said, all you can do for people is to give them the opportunity of making a place for themselves. The V. has done that amply.

To F. B.   VICE-REGAL LODGE, DELHI, *February 18th, 1916.*

... The Viceroy took me one afternoon, to see the new Delhi. It was very wonderful seeing it with him who had invented it all, and though I knew the plans and drawings I didn't realise how gigantic it was till I walked over it. They have blasted away hills and filled up valleys, but the great town itself is as yet little more than foundations. The roads are laid out that lead from it to the four corners of India, and down each vista you see the ruins of some older imperial Delhi. A landscape made up of empires is something to conjure with.

Extract from letter written to Captain R. Hall (afterwards Vice-Admiral Sir Reginald Hall, G.C.B.) from the Vice-Regal Lodge, Delhi, Feb. 20th, 1916.

DEAR CAPT. HALL,

... Before I went to Basrah I remember your putting your finger on the Bagdad corner of the map and saying that the ultimate success of the war depended on what we did there. You are one of the people who realized how serious are the questions we have to face.

To H. B.   *March 3rd, 1916.*

We are within half an hour of Basrah. I've come on a transport. It interests me immensely coming into this country from this direction, which I have never done before. We have been steaming up the river all the morning through a familiar landscape of palm groves and Arab huts, with apricot trees blooming here and there in untidy mud-walled gardens – I'm so glad to see it all again and I feel as if I were in my own country once more and welcome it, ugly though it is. Now it remains to be seen whether they find a job for me or send me away without delay.

I wish I knew how Maurice is and were certain that he is not going back to France yet.

To F. B.   BASRAH, *March 9, 1916.*

I wish I ever knew how long I was going to stay in any place or what I were likely to do next. But that is just the kind of thing which one never can know when one is engaged in the indefinite sort of job which I am doing. There is, however, a great deal of work to be done here. I have al-

ready begun to classify the very valuable tribal material
which I find in the files at the Intel. Dept, and I think there
are pretty wide possibilities of adding to what has been collected already. It is extraordinarily interesting; my own previous knowledge, though there was little enough of it, comes
in very handy in many ways – as a check upon, and a frame
to the new stuff I am handling. And I can't tell you how
wonderful it is to be in at the birth, so to speak, of a new
administration. To-day I lunched with all the Generals – Sir
Percy Lake, General Cowper, General Offley Shaw and
General Money, and as an immediate result they moved me
and my maps and books on to a splendid great verandah
with a cool room behind it where I sit and work all day long.
My companion here is Captain Campbell Thompson, ex-
archaeologist – very pleasant and obliging and delighted to
benefit with me by the change of workshop, for we were
lodged by day in Col. Beach's bedroom (he is the head of the
I.D.), a plan which was not very convenient either for us or
for him. The whole of Basrah is packed full, as you may
understand when it has had suddenly to expand into the
base of a large army. Finally I have got an Arab boy as a
servant. His name is Mikhail. Sir Percy Cox came back last
night – he has been away at Bushire – and he also is going to
help me to get all the information I want by sending on to
me any Arabs whom he thinks will interest me. Therefore if
I don't make something of it, it will be entirely my own fault.
I'm thankful to think that M. won't be back in France at
any rate till the end of April. The relief it is to know that he
is not fighting.

To H. B.   BASRAH, *March 24, 1916.*

... I sometimes try to picture what it will be like when we
are all at home together again and daren't think of it lest the
Gods should be taking heed. We are now on the edge of important things and we hold our breath. If we don't succeed
– it will be uncommonly awkward. I don't know that there is
much point in my being here, but I'm glad I came because
one inevitably understands much more about it. And I'm

glad I have got to know Sir Percy Cox. He is a very remarkable person, not the least remarkable thing about him being his entire absence of any thought about himself. He does his job – a gigantic job – and thinks no more about it.

I wonder if Elsa is back at Rounton yet. Very soon the wild daffodils by the little pond will come out and nod their heads to the east wind. It is 3 years since I saw them.

To F. B.   BASRAH, *April 9, 1916.*

... This week has been greatly enlivened by the appearance of Mr Lawrence, sent out as liaison officer from Egypt. We have had great talks and made vast schemes for the government of the universe. He goes up river to-morrow, where the battle is raging these days....

I have nearly finished my tribe handbook, but I want to go up to Nasariyeh before it is put into its final form, for I know it needs checking from there. For that I must wait to see the result of Kut.

To F. B.   G.H.Q., BASRAH, *April 27, 1916.*

Nothing happens and nothing seems likely to happen at Kut – it's a desperate business, Heaven knows how it will end. Meantime I have been having some very interesting work and as long as it goes on, I shall remain. One is up against the raw material here, which one is not in Egypt, and it is really worth while doing all these first hand things. I don't mind the heat – there has been nothing to speak of so far, the thermometer seldom above 90°, and I rather like it. But I wish I had some clothes; my things are beginning to drop to pieces; I wonder if you are sending me out any, and if they will ever arrive. I think I shall write to Domnul in Bombay for some cotton skirts and some shirts. One wears almost nothing, fortunately, still it's all the more essential that that nothing should not be in holes.

I was also much obliged to Father for his very interesting statistics about the falling mark, and for the article on the Mesop. campaign in the Economist. I fear the latter is nothing short of the truth, but the blame needs a good deal of distribution. I don't hold a brief for the Govt of India, but it is only fair to remember that K. drained India white of troops and of all military requirements, including hospitals and doctors, at the beginning of the war, that the campaign was forced on them *from England*, and that when it developed into a very serious matter – far too big a matter for India to handle if she had had command of all her resources – neither troops, nor artillery, nor hospital units, nor flying corps, nor anything were sent back in time to be of use. And what was perhaps still more serious was that all their best generals had gone to France or Gallipoli many of them never to return.

Politically, too, we rushed into the business with our usual disregard for a comprehensive political scheme. We treated Mesop. as if it were an isolated unit, instead of which it is part of Arabia, its politics indissolubly connected with the great and far reaching Arab question, which presents indeed different facets as you regard it from different aspects, and is yet always and always one and the same indivisible block. The co-ordinating of Arabian politics and the creation of an Arabian policy should have been done at home – it could only have been done successfully at home. There was no one to do it, no one who had ever thought of it, and it was left to our people in Egypt to thrash out, in the face of strenuous opposition, from India and London, some sort of wide scheme, which will, I am persuaded, ultimately form the basis of our relations with the Arabs. Well, that is enough of politics. But when people talk of our muddling through it throws me into a passion. Muddle through! why yes so we do – wading through blood and tears that need never have been shed.

To H. B.   G.H.Q., BASRAH, *May 4th, 1916.*

For some days before it actually happened it was clear that Kut must fall. The Admiral has just come down here; I have not seen him yet. And to-day the Army Commander and all G.H.Q. staff return from up river. I must then find out what they wish me to do. If they will let me, I shall stay for the work is extremely interesting and I think I can make a good deal more of the sort of jobs I have been doing if they will give me a free hand to re-cast a lot of their Intelligence publications. I am now engaged in getting into communication with Ibn Rashid, whom it is rather important to preserve as a neutral if we can do no more. He is only about 4 days off and Sir Percy Cox has approved warmly of my sending him a letter. A curious game, isn't it, but you can understand that it is exciting to have a hand in it. The climate is, of course, infernal, but oddly enough I don't mind it.

To H. B.   G.H.Q., BASRAH, *May 14, 1916.*

You will tell me, won't you, if you think I ought to come home. I will do exactly what you think right and what you wish, but if you do not send for me I shall stay here as long as they will let me – I might be recalled to Egypt, where they are fussing to have me back, but I am persuaded that for the moment I am much more useful here and indeed I am beginning to feel that I am being really useful. I should have to go a long way back to tell you how many gaps there were to fill. I have got hold of the maps and am now bringing them out in an intelligible form, but that is only one among the many odd jobs which I do. Also the natives here are beginning to know me and drop in with news and gossip. Finally, and I think most important of all, there is the difficult gap between Mesop. and Egypt to bridge and I hope I am going to be the person who is charged with the task. Sir P. Cox wants me and as I have a great respect and admiration for him and get on with him excellently I believe I can keep the matter going without friction. There is so much, oh so much to be thought of and considered – so many ways of going irretrievably wrong at the beginning, and some of them are being taken and must be set right before matters grow worse. I do know these people, the Arabs; I have been in contact with them in a way which is possible for no official, and it is that intimacy and friendship which makes me useful here now. That is why I want to stay; but when I have letters from home telling of sickness and sorrow I can scarcely bear to be away from you.

To F. B.   G.H.Q., BASRAH, *May 26th, 1916.*

... I have a lace evening gown, a white crêpe gown, a stripy blue muslin gown, two shirts and a stripy silk gown, all most suitable, and the last superlatively right. Thank you so very much. I ride pretty regularly in the mornings for an hour and a half, setting out at 5.30, and feel much better for plenty of hard exercise. One comes in wet through, has a bath and breakfast, and begins work at 8 or a little before. After that you can't with any comfort go out in the sun till towards evening. The shade temp. is not much over 100°. You keep all doors and windows shut and electric fans spinning, and except for about an hour in the afternoon you don't feel it. One sleeps on the roof. The temp. drops to a little above 90 and probably to 80° or so before dawn. It is quite comfortable.

To H. B.   G.H.Q., BASRAH, *June 25th.*

I'm delighted to hear that M. doesn't go back to France yet, but how will he like a Welsh regiment, I wonder. Your encouragement to me to remain here came just at the right moment and I have decided to let them appoint me official Correspondent to Cairo. A routine order is now to be issued making me part of I.E.F.'D', the Indian Expeditionary Force 'D', and I believe I'm to have pay, but fortunately I need not wear uniform! I ought to have white tabs, for I am under the Political Department. It's rather comic isn't it. It has its disadvantages, but I think it's the right thing to do.

But I feel rather detached from you – I wish I could sit somewhere midway and have a talk with you once or twice a week.

To H. B.   BASRAH, *July 3, 1916.*

I have entered on my new duties, to my great satisfaction and amusement. I go every morning at 9 to the Political Office – it's about 10 minutes' walk – and work there till 12.30. They give me a cup of coffee in the middle of the morning. Then I have a cab to fetch me and come back to lunch, after which I rest for half-an-hour and go to G.H.Q., where I either find some job waiting for me, or I write things from the notes I have made during the morning. I hope that it will all work out very well and that it will be satisfactory to the Egyptians. There's no denying that the weather is confoundedly hot. We have had some bad days, temperature over 111, and very damp. Hot nights, too. One swears at it, but I'm perfectly well so I haven't any business to complain. There is a terrible amount of sickness, however, among people who have to be out of doors and who are not luxuriously lodged and fed. To carry on a campaign under these conditions is no small matter, for not only are your soldiers enduring more casualties than in the worst battle, but your staff vanishes like sand before the sun – clerks, typists, servants, they go down before you can wink, and you are left to do the things for yourself.

G.H.Q., *July 16.*

Don't forget, Father, to let me have your paper on Trade Unions. I've always time and the greatest interest for your observations on these matters.

To H. B. & F. B.   G.H.Q., BASRAH, *July 23rd.*

I had a letter from Maurice besides the one enclosed by Father. Thank Heaven he's out of it for the moment. And still more thanks that he is not out here. It's Hell at the front and nothing short of it. Sir Victor Horsley's death will make people realize perhaps that the climate is warm whereas the daily death from heatstroke of people who are not 'de connaissance' doesn't filter through.

Goodbye, my dearest parents. I'm liking my work with Sir Percy very much and indeed I like it all, as well as I should like anything. But I shan't be sorry when the temp. drops 20°.

To F. B.   G.H.Q., BASRAH, *August 9th, 1916.*

I've been, I'm ashamed to say, on the shelf with fever this week. I'm all right again but feeling like a limp rag. The stiffening will come back in a day or two. I shall not let this happen again if I can help it. A small daily dose of quinine ought to keep it off. We really have got the north wind at last, which means cool nights even if it doesn't much alter the temperature of the days. Cool nights make a world of difference; the temp. before dawn drops sometimes to 77°. One feels deliciously frozen! A fall of 30° from the daytime temperature isn't bad. The dates are all yellow; they will be ripe very shortly. I'm a great deal too woolly to write.

To F. B. BASRAH, *September 20th, 1916.*

I didn't write last week because I was having jaundice and truly miserable. It was a mild bout and I'm better but I am going this afternoon for change of air to a sort of big rest house attached to our officers' hospital a few miles down river. It seems a sensible thing to do and I hope a few days will set me on my feet again and restore me to my usual complexion.

It's so provoking to be laid up when there's such a lot of work to do. The thing is growing and this week came a letter from the W.O., to whom I send articles through the Intell. Dept, saying I was sending just what they wanted and would I send more. So that's all right. It makes me want to be back more than ever. Everyone is immensely kind; the Consulting Physician of the Force comes to see me and the woman who is Inspector General of all the hospitals looks after me. I'm ashamed of bothering them about such a silly little ailment.

Will you please send me a winter hat. Something of this kind in dark violet. Either of these would do. Also I would immensely like a soft black satin gown which I could wear either by day or night – crossed over in front, skirt down to the ground. I would like Marte (Conduit St) to make it because she will make me something pretty. She doesn't usually make anything but evening gowns, but if you told her it's for me and where I am I know she would do it for me.

To H. B. BAIT NAMAH, *20 September, 1916.*

I'm still in hospital but I've made a very rapid cure (I was pretty bad when I came) and I hope they will let me go back to Basrah in a day or two. I've been quite extraordinarily comfortable and the kindness of everyone is past belief. It really was very pleasant to find oneself here with all the trouble of looking after one's own self lifted off one's shoulders.

Do you know I've never been so ill as this before. I hadn't an idea what it was like to feel so deadly weak that you couldn't move your body much nor hold your mind at all. When once I began to mend and to eat I didn't mind it....

Would you give Bain the bookseller an order for me. He is to send me every month from 4 to 6 new books, novels and poetry, nothing very serious, he knows exactly the kind of thing I like. Tell him I left England last November and have read nothing that has come out since so he will have plenty to go on with. He might send one or two regularly every week. New poetry I love to have and Bain knows perfectly well the sort of novel I like – Anthony Hope at one end of the scale and the Crock of Gold at the other!

To H. B.   BASRAH, *November 23rd, 1916.*

As a fact I am not writing from Basrah but from somewhere on the Shatt al Arab below Qurnah after what seems to me, looking back on it, to have been an immense journey – but I'll begin at the beginning. I left Basrah on a Saturday night – the I.G.C. motored me down to what we call the terminus station. I found the night train making itself ready, with a small guard's van hitched on to it for me. This I furnished with a camp bed, a chair and the station master's lantern and off we started about 6 into the desert. If ever years hence I come back into this country and travel to Bagdad by the Basrah express, I shall remember, while I eat my luxurious meal in the dining car, how first I travelled along the line in a guard's van and dined on tinned tongue, tinned butter and tinned pears by the light of the station master's lantern. What happened after that I don't know, for I went to bed and except for an occasional vague consciousness of halts in a wide desert dim with starlight, I didn't take note of anything in particular till the dawn crept in at my windowless window and I woke to find my van standing outside rail head camp in the middle of Arabia, so to speak.

At 8 o'clock there rolled in General Brooking's motor car and a motor lorry and we bumped over the grass tufts and over the sun-split mud of what had been flood water in the spring, to Khamiseyeh, where we have had troops ever since Ibn Rashid came filibustering round last summer. For Khamiseyeh is one of the markets of Central Arabia and he who holds these holds the tribes, as Ibn Rashid found to his cost and perhaps has related by now in Hayil. A mud-built, dirty little place is Khamiseyeh, watered by a small and evil looking canal from the Euphrates which runs into the town up to the walled square where the caravans lodge when they come up from Jebel Shammay. I drove straight into our camp, picked up General Tidswell, who is in command, and made him take me round the town. And there we met the Sheikh of Khamiseyeh, who is a friend of mine and on his pressing invitation went to his house and drank a cup of tea. He had a guest, Sheikh Hamud of the Dhafir, one of our friendly Beduin, and we sat for a while listening to the latest desert news, which I translated for the General. I hadn't met Hamud before, though he was one of the Sheikhs of whom I had heard much talk when I was riding up from Hail. And so on, over the desert, some 25 miles to Nasariyeh, putting up gazelle and sand grouse as we went. I never thought to watch them from a motor.

To F. B.   BASRAH, *December 9, 1916.*

The winter isn't really very nice here. One is usually sneezing, when not coughing, and one wishes one had a nice warm comfortable place to sit in. To think that I was once clean and tidy—! However, these are things of the past. I've been busy with a long memorandum about the whole of our central Arabian relations, which I've just finished. It will now go to all the High and Mighty in every part. One can't do much more than sit and record if one is of my sex, devil take it; one can get the things recorded in the right way and that means, I hope, that unconsciously people will judge events as you think they ought to be judged. But it's small change for doing things, very small change I feel at times.

To H. B.   BASRAH, *December 15, 1916.*

... Do you know I was thinking yesterday what I would pick out as the happiest things I've done in all my life, and I came to the conclusion that I should choose the old Italian journeys with you, those long ago journeys which were so delicious ... except only in that very big thing, complete love and confidence in my family – I've had that always and can't lose it. And you are the pivot of it. But for that I don't care much one way or the other what happens, except that sometimes I should very much like to see you. But I'm quite content here, interested by the work and very conscious that I couldn't anywhere be doing things that would interest me so much.

The world continues to look autumnal – scarcely wintry yet – in spite of the eternal green of the palms. There is a yellow mimosa in flower, fluffy, sweet-smelling balls, a very heavenly little tree, albeit thorny. Yes, there's always plenty of small change, isn't there!

To H. B.   AMARAH, *January 1, 1917.*

I will begin the New Year before breakfast by writing to you and sending to you and all my dear family all the best of good wishes.

I must tell you I felt dreadfully depressed on Xmas Day thinking of other Xmas Days when we were together and used to be so absurdly happy a long time ago. I hope Maurice has been with you this year.

I spend my time in seeing local people and getting lots of information about tribes and families which had baffled me in Basrah, a satisfactory occupation.

To F. B.   BASRAH, *January 13th, 1917.*

I came back to find the most delightful pile of letters.... If you have no time to die, as Maurice says, I wonder you have time to write me such splendid long letters! You really must not do it when you feel dreadfully run. Still, I won't deny that I do enjoy having news from you both.

I've just drawn up a little memorandum about administrative progress, which I think ought to give satisfaction to the High and Mighty at home. (Happy to tell you that I hear my utterances receive a truly preposterous attention in London.) Just at this moment, this is the only theatre of the war where things look rather bright.

The only thing that keeps one going is to have lots of work. At times I feel as if I wasn't worth my keep here, and then at other times I think I'm doing a certain amount of good, but fundamentally, I am sure it is no good bothering as to whether one is or isn't useful, and the only plan is to apply oneself steadfastly to what lies before one and ask no questions.

To F. B.   BASRAH, *January 20th, 1917.*

A box has just arrived from Marte, through T. Cook & Sons – it ought to have contained a black satin gown, but it has been opened (probably in Bombay, it was sent by Cook to his agents in Bombay) and the gown has been abstracted. Isn't it infuriating? All that was left was a small cardboard box inside, containing the little black satin coat Marte sent with the gown, some net, and a gold flower. These, by reason of their being in the small box, the thief couldn't get out, for he only opened a part of the nailed-down lid, and made a small hole in the interior cardboard lining, through which he pulled the gown. I hope Marte insured it so that Cook will have to pay – but that thought does not console me much at this moment! Marte had better repeat the gown as quickly as possible and send it in a small box by post. That is the only way of getting things. If it can't possibly go by post it must go through the military forwarding officer, but it takes 6 months! Will you tell Marte.

To H. B.   BASRAH, *February 16th, 1917.*

It was the finger of Providence that led me to get into my new abode, for we have had five days of rain and Basrah is a unique spectacle. It is almost impossible to go out. I put on a riding skirt and a pair of india rubber top boots – which I had fortunately procured from India – and stagger through the swamp for half-an-hour after tea and it's all one can do. Yesterday the sun shone, and the I.O.C. and I managed to get down to the desert in a motor and walked along the top of some mounds on the edge of the palm gardens, which so much encouraged me that I jumped up at sunrise to-day hoping to be able to ride. But no sooner was I donned than down came the rain again, through the mud roof of my room too and there was nothing for it but to change sadly into ordinary clothes – and write to you.

To F. B.   BASRAH, *February 17th, 1917.*

... The box and the umbrella have come too! Isn't it great. I am so thankful for shoes, skirts, umbrella (we are in the middle of rain) silk coat and everything. If only that rogue hadn't stolen my black gown I should be well supplied till the hot weather comes.

You have taken such a lot of trouble – thank you so very much.

To H. B.   BASRAH, *March 2, 1917.*

I had a grand post at the beginning of the week with 2 letters from you (Jan. 11th and 18th) and 3 from Mother. I really was starved for letters from home and consequently fattened on them.... We really have got the Turks shifted this time, how far shifted we don't yet know. If they make a stand before Bagdad I suppose we shan't go on; in any case, I don't know that we shall go on – the line of communication is immensely long. But no matter; what we have already accomplished will make a difference and we may expect developments in other directions. Congratulatory effusions are coming in from Basrah – I wonder what the real thought is at the bottom of most of them. But up country the people who have come in to us will be content, for they will feel greater security; and the people who haven't come in will have grave doubts as to whether they 'backed the right horse' – they're having them already. The Turks thought the crossing of the Tigris in the face of opposition a sheer impossibility. We have that from the prisoners. Let's hope, in consequence, that they are not so well prepared for the achievement as they should be – indeed their headlong flight seems to indicate as much. My own belief is that they won't be able to hold Bagdad for long if we are close up.

To H. B.   BASRAH, *March 10th, 1917.*

We are now hourly awaiting the news of our entrance into Bagdad. I had a letter from Sir Percy to-day, from the Front, full of exultation and confidence. I do hope I may be called up there before very long. It's a wonderful thing to be at the top of the war after all these months of marking time, and say what you will, it's the first big success of the war, and I think it is going to have varied and remarkable consequences.

We shall, I trust, make it a great centre of Arab civilization, a prosperity; that will be my job partly, I hope, and I never lose sight of it.

I had one foot in the grave for five days with a shocking cold in the head – it's now better, and I'm riding again before breakfast.... I never saw anything so beautiful as the kingfishers – flocks of them whistling through the palm groves, two kinds, a big and a little blue kind, and I rather think a third brown, but I have not been able quite to spot him yet.

To H. B.   BASRAH, *March 17th, 1917.*

Since last I wrote the goal has been reached; we have been a week in Bagdad. I've had no news actually from Bagdad, but I hope I shall get letters this week. I need not tell you how much I long to hear exactly what it is all like. Just 3 years ago I was arriving there from Arabia – 3 lifetimes they seem as I look back on them. I went to tea last week with the Matron-in-Chief, the notable Miss Jones, whom I like, and afterwards she took me to see the wounded Turkish prisoners. I stammered into Turkish, which I haven't spoken for 7 years, and they were only too delighted to hear even a few words of Turkish spoken. There they were, the round-faced Anatolian peasants – I could have laughed and wept to see them – from Konia, from Angora, from Caesarea, even from C'ple, and we talked of their houses and what far country they lay in. Most of them were well content to be done with war for ever.

I long to go up to Bagdad, but it is no good bothering yet.

To F. B.   BASRAH, *March 30th, 1917.*

I'm sitting with my hands in front of me, practically, and shall remain in that attitude till I go up to Bagdad. It is the first time I have been idle since the war began. However, it is not my desire, and Heaven knows that marking time is far worse than working.

Before this letter arrived we had a telegram from Gertrude saying 'address Bagdad', and knew that her ardent wish to go there had been gratified.

CHAPTER 16

1917

Bagdad

To F. B. & H. B.   *April 15th, 1917.*

We are within two hours of Bagdad and I'm free to admit that coming up this river gives one a wholesome respect for our lines of communication. This is the 9th day we've been at it, tying up for a few hours at night but steaming 17 or 18 hours a day notwithstanding. It's well that it wasn't a month later for already the temperature is 90 and on a crowded ship it's hot. We passed Kut before sunrise, but I got up to see it – poor tragic little place – its shelled walls and shattered palm trees catching the first flash of day.

To H. B.   BAGDAD, *April 20th.*

Such an arrival! Sir Percy made me most welcome and said a house had been allotted to me. I went off to see it and found a tiny stifling box of a place in a dirty little bazaar. It was absolutely empty – what furniture I had was with my heavy luggage and not yet landed, and I hadn't even a boy, as I had left my servant to look after the heavy luggage. Fortunately, like a good traveller, I had not parted from my bed and bath. These I proceeded to set up and further unpacked my box which had been dropped into the Tigris, and hung all the things to dry on the railings of the court. It was breathlessly hot. I hadn't so much as a chair to put anything on, and when I wanted water for washing I had to open my front door and call in the help of the bazaar. Fortunately they responded with alacrity. I dined with Sir Percy, armed myself with a loaf of bread for breakfast and returned to my empty house to sleep. By good luck my servant turned up late that night, so that there was someone to water tea for me next morning.

I confess, however, that after having done my hair and breakfasted on the floor I felt a little discouraged. It was clear that something must be done at once, and I proceeded to hunt for one. The first thing I tumbled on to was a rose garden with three summer houses in it, quite close to the Political Office and belonging, forby, to an old friend of mine, Musa Chalabi. I decided at once that this was the thing, but a kitchen had to be built and a bath room, and sunblinds to be put up – a thousand things. I got Musa Chalabi to help me and summoned in an old man, a servant whom I've known for ages, and after five days' work I'm in – 'tant bien que mal' and it promises very well. My old man Shamao has engaged me a cook and the Englishman who runs all the supplies Col. Dixon is my faithful friend, having been charged by the I.G.C. to look after me. And my roses I must tell you are glorious. Oh, but it is hot! I'm longing for my thin summer clothes. I wonder when they will reach me here.

Meantime all my acquaintances and friends have flocked in to see me. I've visited the Naqib, the head religious man and an ally of many years' standing, and have been received with open arms. And it is all wildly interesting – War Office telegraphing for signed articles from me, etc., etc. I'm going to have an exciting summer. Sir P. gives me lots of thrilling things to do and is the kindest of chiefs. Bagdad is a mass of roses and congratulations. They are genuinely delighted at being free of the Turks. The rest for another time, I am so busy.

To H. B. & F. B.   BAGDAD, *April 27th, 1917.*

My duties are of the most diverse kinds. We are very short-handed. I take on everything I can to spare Sir Percy – interview representatives of innumerable creeds, keep an open door for tribal sheikhs and messengers from the desert whose business I discover and send up in brief to Sir Percy, and then behind all this there's my real job, the gathering and sorting of information. Already the new tribal maps and tribe lists are getting into shape, and the first big batch of confidential notes on Bagdad personalities will be issued to our Political Officers to-morrow – that's not bad going. Presently

all the new surveys will begin to come in and I shall have
the revision and correction of the place names, a thing I like
doing because in the first place it's so nice to get them right,
and in the second it teaches me so much geography. The
head survey man is an enthusiast, and gives me a free hand.
And then I'm going to be Curator of Antiquities or at least
I'm going to show the Revenue Commissioner all the old
buildings and scraps of buildings that are left here, and he
has promised to keep guard over them.... It's a thousand
times more interesting than Basrah, you understand. To-day
there arrived by miracle two charming black satin gowns
from Marte which makes me hope that my new cotton
gowns may presently arrive also. I'm very badly in need of
them. It's almost too hot already for unwashable clothes,
even in the evening. I shall rejoice when I hear that muslin
gowns are on their way....

Oh if it were as near the end in France! Is Maurice still
out of it? Every time a post comes in I dread to hear that he
has gone back.

Maurice (now Colonel Bell, C.M.G.) had gone to the front in
the beginning of 1915 in command of the 4th Battalion, Green
Howards. He was invalided home the following year and then had
a command in England.

To H. B.   BAGDAD, *May 3rd, 1917.*

The days melt like snow in the sun. But it's just as well for
I've been realizing this evening that if I weren't so very busy
I should be very lonely. To-day I was in the office from 8.30
to 8, and had scarcely anything to show for it by reason of
the reams of odds and ends that take up all the time.

To F. B.   BAGDAD, *May 11th, 1917.*

This week's post is drifting in – a very welcome one from
Moll announcing the sending off of my summer clothes. The
patterns are charming – it's to be hoped they'll wash. But
Lord how glad I shall be to have them. My present appearance is that of a hobbledehoy in straitened circumstances
who has outgrown her wardrobe – only it's my gowns which

have diminished (from much washing) not I who have increased. The event of the week has been the arrival of Mr Storrs [afterwards Sir Ronald Storrs] from Egypt. He's here for a fortnight. He brings a perfect hurricane of fresh air from outside and I'm jiggered if we shan't send him back on the wings of a similar storm which will blow open their eastern-facing doors and windows.

... I'm getting to be rather a dab at Arab politics – but it doesn't make them seem the easier. We've shouldered a gigantic task, but I can't see what alternative there was.

This is how I pass my days: I'm out riding before 6, sometimes through the gardens by the river bank, sometimes round the old line of the city wall, a gallop in the desert and home through the bazaars. Occasionally I inspect an ancient monument on the way back – I did so this morning. A bath and breakfast and so to the office before 9. I'm there till after 7. I have a cup of coffee and a bowl of sour curds at 12.30 and tea with Sir Percy at 4 – it's the only time I peaceably see him. People drop in all day. Occasionally one has a clear hour or two – generally there's a lull between 12 and 2 and one tries to straighten out all the information one has acquired. But the end of the day finds me with two or three unfinished things and no hope of getting at them the day after. They are piling and piling up and I can't think when I shall be able to clear them off. That's the only bother – there's always just a bit too much to do. I come back to dinner in my garden at 8 and I generally go to bed at 9.30, at which time I begin to fall asleep. It's gloriously cool still but that must certainly end in a day or two.

I must tell you I love Bagdad, and the people are so outgoing – partly propitiatory no doubt, but they are glad to have us.

To H. B.   BAGDAD, *May 18th, 1917.*

... I couldn't possibly come away from here at this moment. It's an immense opportunity, just at this time when the atmosphere is so emotional; one catches hold of people as one will never do again, and establishes relations which won't dissolve. It is not for my own sake, but because it greases the wheels of administration – it really does, and I want to watch it all very carefully almost from day to day, so as to be able to take what I hope may be something like a decisive hand in final disposition. I shall be able to do that, I shall indeed, with the knowledge I'm gaining. It's so intimate. They are beyond words outgoing to me. What does anything else matter when the job is such a big one? Incidentally I may tell you – so that you won't be surprised when you see me – that this summer will turn my hair quite white. It is one of the results of this climate. However, that won't matter to gentlemen like one I had in to-day, who was so holy that he couldn't look an unveiled woman in the face! It didn't prevent him from desiring to have a long talk with me on his private affairs, and at the end I'll admit he tipped me a casual wink or two, just enough to know me again. General Wauchope has been here, Mr Philby has come up from Amarah, he's so quick and intelligent.... There never was anything quite like this before, you must understand that – it's amazing. It's the making of a new world. You see I couldn't come away. The W.O. has telegraphed for a series of signed articles on Mesop. and Asia Minor. I shall have to set about them, but it's a wide order.

To H. B. & F. B.   BAGDAD, *May 26, 1917.*

... The post brought me a letter from Mother this week – and also, what do you think? Two muslin gowns! I hope they are swallows, so to speak, announcing all my summer clothes.

The great event in our circles is the arrival of Fahad Bey, paramount sheikh of the Amarah, an almighty swell and an old friend of mine. I stayed with him in the desert three years ago on my way back to Damascus. I hope that with his help we shall get a move in among the tribes. Anyhow, it's a great 'coup' getting him to burn his boats and come in to us. We had the most tenderly affectionate meeting I assure you. Now I'll tell you a sweet story. There came in a couple of old sheikhs, hopelessly ragged and very sorry for themselves, for their tribe happens to be just in the borderland and first they had been harried by the Turks and then by us, and finally making the best of a bad business, they had sought refuge with us, and we, after our truly idiotic manner, had clapped half their followers into gaol, and they couldn't find them, so they came to me and I said I would ask Sir Percy what could be done. At that they almost wept with gratitude and declared that they would forthwith send me a beautiful mare. But I said no, it was a kind thought, but I could not take presents and therewith I went down to talk to Sir Percy. When I came back I found them with their two old heads together and as soon as they saw me they said, 'Khatun – if you won't take the horse we're going to send you – a gazelle!' The gazelle hasn't materialised yet, and I rather hope it won't, for gazelles eat everything including all your most important papers, but wasn't it nice of them to hit on such small change for mares. The great pleasure in this country is that I do love the people so much.

I told you about Fahad Bey, didn't I. We had a conference with him one morning, in which he ended by describing the powerful effect produced by a letter from me last autumn – I wrote to him from Basrah. 'I summoned my sheikhs' he wound up (I feeling more and more of a person as he proceeded), 'I read them your letter and I said to them, Oh Sheikhs,' – we hung upon his words – 'This is a woman – what must the men be like!' This delicious peroration restored me to my true place in the twinkling of an eye. We took him to see an exhibition of flying yesterday to his immense delight. He said he had never enjoyed anything so much: He even ventured into an aeroplane – so that he might tell the Arabs, he explained; but once there he turned to me anxiously and said 'Don't let it go away!'

Oh my dearest ones it's so wonderful here – I can't tell you how much I'm loving it.

To H. B.   BAGDAD, *June 8, 1917.*

I must write to you because I've been reading with profit your papers on dumping and the future of trade. The former appears to me to be unanswerable and the latter both brilliant and moderate. My compliments.

I'm completely recovered – no further bulletins will be issued. But I've retained the excellent habit of sleeping for an hour after lunch, which, though a terrible waste of time, brings a remarkable increase of energy. I'm busy at spare moments with the W.O. articles of which I told you. I've written 4 and I think they will run to 7. It's no light task in the midst of so many other things. They are as good a plea as I can make for the Arab race and I want people to listen. Frankly, who knows if I don't? Life has been 'égayée' by the coming of a harmless old lunatic from the Syrian side of the desert. The motive of his journey was as follows: he met in the desert a woman of stupendous stature and luminous countenance. On being questioned she declared that she was the sun, but this reply did not, apparently, satisfy our friend and pressing her further she admitted that she was the British Government. Thereat he resolved to come straight to Kokus (Sir Percy Cox) seeking the sun, as he reasonably explained. The word Kokus is rapidly passing into the Arabic language, not as a name but as a title. You are a Kokus, just as once upon a time you were a Chosroes or a Pharaoh. I'm currently described as a Kokusah, i.e., a female Chosroes. Isn't it delicious!

To F. B.   *June 1917.*

... I've been dining out frequently. Sir Percy and I dined with General Cobbe. Next evening I dined with General Gunning. The matron of the hospitals was of the party, a nice woman. And it's so pleasant to meet a woman. My chief female friend is the Mother Superior of the Dominican Convent, a charming French woman from Touraine. She comes in often to the office to see me on business of one sort and another, and I have often, to my great pleasure, been able to help her. It's something to be a 'Kokusah' you see. Last night – to continue – I dined with the head of the police, Major Gregson, and spent the evening talking to a General called Edwardes. Let me announce to you the arrival of 2 charming hats – for which many thanks to Moll – your chiffon veils, brown stockings. Of the gowns 2 arrived a fortnight ago and no more since.

The gazelle has materialised and now inhabits my garden. It lives chiefly on the little wizened dates which fall at this season from the unripe bunches on my date trees, and on cucumbers both of which for a child of the desert must be acquired taste. But it seems to flourish on them. It is a darling little animal. I'm on the look out now for a mongoose.

To F. B.   BAGDAD, *June 22nd, 1917.*

Ramadhan began last night and everyone is fasting. We keep Ramadhan in state here with big guns at sunset and an hour before dawn. I was awakened to-day by the latter. It is to warn people that they must hasten with their last possible meal. And as I lay wondering over it all I was aware of a bright light through my garden. I sleep on the roof of my Central Summer House, and looked up to see a blazing palm leaf fire in the still hot air near my gardener's tent. It was his wife cooking the last meal which must be eaten while it is light enough to distinguish a white thread from a black. Strange isn't it? to be so much in the midst of it all – strange and delightful for I love it.

It has become to me more than a second home now – it's a new life, a new possibility of carrying on existence. Only I'm afraid of my personal perspective melting. I'm so flattered, so absurdly over-estimated by my chiefs in England, by my colleagues, and of course the Arabs. – If I become too egregious do call me smartly to attention. It is so immensely difficult to preserve the values....

The sand flies are outrageous to-night. I stop in every sentence to engage them in mortal combat but they carry out a strategic retirement after inflicting some casualties. The flying ants are as numerous but they don't bite Heaven be praised. Still I hate the way they cock their tails in the air.

July 6, 1917.

We've got our treaty settled with my friend Fahad of the Anazeh.

To H. B.   BAGDAD, *July 13th, 1917.*

We have had a week of fierce heat which still continues, temperature 122 odd and therewith a burning wind which has to be felt to be believed. It usually blows all night as well as all day and makes sleep very difficult. I have invented a scheme which I practise on the worst nights. I drop a sheet in water and without wringing it out lay it in a pile along my bed between me and the wind. I put one end over my feet and draw the other under and over my head and leave the rest a few inches from my body. The sharp evaporation makes it icy cold and interposes a little wall of cold air between me and the fierce wind. When it dries I wake up and repeat the process. This evening Sir Percy and I went out motoring at 7 but it was too hot. The wind shrivelled you and burnt your eyeballs. They say it does not last very long like this – inshallah! at last the sand-flies have given up the ghost. Also you get an immense satisfaction out of iced lime juice and soda, usually rather an anaemic drink. There is a pleasant hour just after dawn when I usually ride. My room in the office I shut up all day long and have it sluiced out with water two or three times a day. By these means I keep the temperature just under 100. Yes, that's what it is like.

To H. B.   BAGDAD, *July 20th, 1917.*

There came in the other day a tribesman who had been my guide on the last four days into Najaf when I came up from Hayil. They were the worst days of all the road, and he served me well. He is a grave silent man, well known in the desert. Twice to my knowledge he saved me from being stripped to the skin – on one occasion, though accursed of their two parents, the Iraq tribes had surrounded my caravan and couched the camels before they saw him. On his rebuke they left us. I had sent word to him that I was here and bidden him to come. Besides the usual present from Sir Percy which they all get when they come for the first time, I gave him Rs. 100, and clothed him. He stood solemnly while I flung round him a thick cloak, heavily woven with gold – such wear in this heat! – and draped an orange coloured silk kerchief over his head. I owed him a costume in return for that which remained on my back thanks to him. Another nice thing happened this week. One of my Damascenes who came down with me to Nejd, has turned up here. He heard I was at Basrah, 'and I come to your service', he said. Sir Percy is delighted to have him; we shall put him to use.

The hot silence has been broken by 20 big gun shots, which announce the end of Ramadhan. Even I hear them with thankfulness.

To H. B.   BAGDAD, *August 3, 1917.*

I must tell you I've been on the sick list this week and am not off it yet. Having survived the heat I caught cold with the first chill morning and a cold in this country reduces me at once to a state of maddening and unconquerable feebleness. It's no good forgetting it; one has to knock under. So for 4 days I've done absolutely nothing and am still much as before, confound it. But the first day when I was lying in my comparatively cool room in the office and cursing, in came Col. Willcox to pay me a friendly call – I could have embraced him, his visit was so opportune. So now he comes regularly to see if I have pneumonia or consumption – but I never have. Well, he told me some interesting things about the heat wave and its consequences. (It began on July 10 quite suddenly with a temperature of 122 and ended on July 20 with a temperature of 122·8. In between it was frequently over 120). He notes that 115 is the limit of human endurance. The moment the temp. rises above that point, heat strokes begin, and when it drops below, they end. We could have saved many lives if after the crisis was over there had been any cool place to put the men in. But there wasn't and after fighting through the heatstroke they died of heat exhaustion.

To H. B.   BAGDAD, *August 31st, 1917.*

I am coming out of hospital to-morrow. I am perfectly sound but very slack. I don't suppose I shall be much better till the weather begins to cool down, which it ought to do in the latter half of Sep. It is still damnably hot.

To H. B.   BAGDAD, *September 5, 1917.*

I didn't go to Samarra after all. Doom struck out, as the poet says, like a blind camel and he caught me straight and full. For with my box and bedding packed, my dinner almost carried to General Lubbock's hospitable board – I was going to dine with the Father of Railways on my way to the train – I began to feel curiouser and curiouser and anyhow very certain that I had fever. And then Col. Willcox drifted in (Providence always directs the angelic man to my door just when I want him) took my temperature and shattered my plans. I held out for two miserable days in my own house, too achy and above all too headachy to stir, and then came into hospital with a temperature of 102. Sandfly fever. Everyone has it. I don't know how I've escaped it so long. They don't know what it is really; they haven't caught its microbe yet. But you get your money's worth out of it, if only from the intolerable headache. Quinine is no good. They give you febrifuges and phenacetin and feed you only on slops, all of which things being unfit, so to speak, for human consumption, you find yourself pretty ragged when at last the devil thing goes.

I'm really over the thing – it's gone. But there's no doubt I shall feel cheap for a bit and as soon as I can I shall go away for a fortnight. Col. Willcox is very keen that I should do this and I think it will be salvation. It's so beautifully cool now that one can go anywhere. They are extremely kind to me in this hospital. They treat me as if I were a Major General.

Damnable as sandfly fever is it isn't a matter for the smallest anxiety so please feel none, you and Mother. I feel ashamed of behaving like this.

To F. B.   BAGDAD, *September 6, 1917.*

There's one thing I forgot to answer in some old letters from you and Father. Please, please don't supply information about me or photographs of me to newspaper correspondents. I've said this so often before that I thought you understood how much I hate the whole advertisement business. I always throw all letters (fortunately they're not many in number) asking for an interview or a photograph straight into the waste paper basket and I beg you to do the same on my behalf....

It's still very hot, but the temperature is falling, though very slowly. The nights are quite pleasant, but in the middle of the afternoon it's usually about 112°. I won't deny that when you come to September here you feel you've reached about the limit of human endurance. I shan't stay through the whole of next summer.

To F. B.   BAGDAD, *September 25, 1917.*

To think that I've been nearly two years without a maid! but I'm exceedingly tidy, thanks to your good supply of clothes. Oh would you please send me a pair of plain tortoiseshell combs. There's a lizard walking about my walk and catching, I suppose, sand flies. God prolong its existence!

To H. B. & F. B.   *October 18th, 1917.*

Yesterday came your telegram through Admiral Hall enquiring after my health. I'm afraid you will be rather agitated when you come to hear that I've been ill again which I haven't told you in my present reply. But I'm now very nearly well of my fever which I don't suppose I should have had if I hadn't been rather run down before. I've been for the last 6 days at the Convalescent Hospital, a delicious place on the river about 2 miles below Bagdad. They have taken immense care of me and I've got well with great rapidity. In 3 days' time I'm going up to Samarra for a week to stay with Gen. Cobbe.

I might be able to see Mrs Taggart's grandson if he's at Bagdad. I'll try anyhow.

Mrs Taggart was a woman at the Clarence Ironworks, a very old friend.

You don't seem to be aware – indeed I only knew of it by letters of congratulation received this mail from Sir Reginald Wingate and others – that I'm a C.B.E. I am, however. Its rather absurd....

To H. B.   BAGDAD, *October, 1917.*

You know your friendship is more to me than anything. What a thing it is to be able to talk of friendship with one's parents. Those who haven't got it don't know what it means.

I'm much better. Even after my racketty morning in Bagdad I don't feel a bit tired, and I've been writing letters all this afternoon. But oh, I do long to be back at work! However, I'll be patient this time and take the Samarra time to get really well in.

To F. B.   BAGDAD, *October 26th, 1917.*

Thank you for your congratulations – I don't really care a button about these things. As for Samarra, I've no luck with it, for just as I was starting – actually stepping into the launch to go and dine with General Lubbock on my way to the station, came a telegram from General Cobbe putting me off. Turks had heaved into sight and there was a possibility of active operations. They've since heaved out of it again, and I may after all go up presently, but I've ceased to believe it. I'm very much enjoying being back in the office though I'm not much more than a half timer as yet. Still I'm getting better every day. The weather is delicious but it is extraordinary how one feels the cold. My room at the office is now under 70°, but after sunset I sit wrapped up in a thick coat and add to it a woollen comforter to walk home in. It's a way the human frame has of showing resentment for having been called upon to endure a temperature of 122°. I find that this is the season for gardening operations; I've some vegetables, peas, lettuce, onions and a local sort of mustard and cress – the latter I've not only sown but eaten. And in order not to be too utilitarian, I've bought 7 pots of geraniums and

4 of carnations besides sowing carnations and eschscholtzia. I wish I had snapdragon seeds. A clump of chrysanthemums is coming into bloom, and my rose trees are flowering. Everything comes to life when the summer is over, even the washed-out European. And one forgets at once how infernal it was. I hope my bijou residence won't prove too damp in winter; it's so nice being quite away by oneself. Anyhow it's particularly pleasant now.

The shirts haven't arrived but I expect they'll turn up and I've enough to go on with for the moment. And oh I'm so sorry to bother you, but would you send me 8 pairs of white thread stockings – they will go by letter post at the worst, and they'll arrive just about the time the warm weather begins again. Those I have are worn out beyond mending.

To H. B.   BAGDAD, *November 2, 1917.*

You sent me a lot of interesting pieces which I read with much satisfaction and agreement. I always feel when I read your works such an admiration for your style as well as your matter. It's so lucid and so pointed, so entirely unstrained. I hand on some of your works to Sir Percy who reads them with grave attention, not unmixed with surprise. It is all new to him.

To H. B.   BAGDAD, *November 9th, 1917.*

No mail as yet this week. Happy to tell you I'm much better and have felt to-day quite a zest in life – for the first time. I am beginning some nice new jobs. One is the taking over of the editorship of Al Arab, the vernacular paper we publish. I'm full of schemes for making it more alive by getting provincial correspondents and a local news-writer. I feel certain my public will take more interest in hearing that Ibn so and so was fined for being out without a lantern after dark than in the news that an obscure village in Flanders has been bombed. Père Anastase, the sub-editor comes weekly to read our leading articles, which I censor. He's an Arab from the Lebanon, straight out of Chaucer all the same; very learned in his own tongue, he speaks and writes French like a Frenchman....

To F. B.   SAMARRA, *November 22nd, 1917.*

I wrote to you last week the day before I was to come up here with the I.G.C. We all dined that evening with Col. Dixon, the Director of Local Resources; the C. in C. was to have been there also but sent a message at the last moment to say he wasn't well. At the beginning of dinner Colonel Willcox was called away – an urgent case of illness, it didn't occur to anyone to ask who it was. Next morning before breakfast the I.G.C. came to my house and said that our departure must be postponed, the C. in C. was dangerously ill of cholera and was not expected to live. I flew round to Sir Percy – it was still very early – and found that he had not yet been informed. It was almost incredible to us all. There had been a little cholera in the town for some weeks past, nothing very serious but very widely distributed – where he got the infection it is impossible to say. He rallied in the afternoon and was distinctly better next morning, well enough to receive a telegram from his wife and dictate an answer. Then his heart failed, he became unconscious and died in the evening. The I.G.C. came in after dinner and told me. It has had for him a tragic ending, the conquest of Bagdad, and yet how fortunate it is when the man dies before the name. There is a splendid sentence in Ammianus Marcellinus' history of that other conqueror who was mortally wounded, N.E. of Ctesiphon, the Emperor Julian, and 'praised the Almighty God that he should die in the midst of glory fairly earned'. General Maude was, I should think, a greater Commander, but the epitaph might be his....

To her family.   SAMARRA, *November 30th, 1917.*

I'm still here though I wanted to go back a day or two ago. The Corps Commander (my kind host) insisted however on my staying till the end of the week to 'complete the cure'. I'm really most briskly well and longing to get back to work. I'm going back to Bagdad the day after to-morrow.

To H. B. & F. B.   BAGDAD, *December 13th, 1917.*

... My only news of the outer world is derived from the egregious Reuter and that not good, and one begins to consider what the end will be. Till the Americans can bring in great reinforcements – and *can* they across all the seas? – it's clear that we shall be put to it to hold our own. It's like the first year of the war over again. Well, it's no good guessing, and we know too little even to guess. Here War is at an end, but administration goes on apace. We are taking hold of the Euphrates valley to the S.W. and getting into lands unmapped and tribes little known. I want to go down there at the end of the month. I went one afternoon to see the Remount establishment outside the town. Capt. Lupton presides over it. A clearing place with the horses playing about in great paddocks under the palm trees, and a model farm attached where they grow their own maize and barley and vegetables. Capt. Lupton offered me a very handsome Arab mare if the General (Holdsworth) consented. I met the latter next day in the Street and he approved the suggestion. So, in the official phrase, I'm issued with her – Heaven prosper me for writing such horrible English.

To H. B.   BAGDAD, *December 29, 1917.*

I am very glad to hear that Maurice is better and congratulate Mother on her pleasant nights with Zeppelins....

On Xmas Day I dined with General Stuart Wortley, a Ladies' Dinner, the other guests being matrons and nurses, a quite agreeable evening, but I've crept, on the whole, into a very long shell and seldom care to be pricked out of it by anybody's pin. Also I've got a temporary (let's hope) anaemia of the brain which makes me work so slowly that I never get through my jobs and bring work home every night to finish after dinner. Incessant interruption at the office adds immensely to the fatigue of putting together reports or compiling information. I've no sooner got hold of the thread than it's broken by someone with a petition or a complaint or what not, and my slow mind must laboriously gather it up again. Perhaps a fortnight's absence in the Euphrates will make me a little less imbecile. There are times when I can scarcely find words to talk or write in French, much less in Arabic. And memory is a lost art. Though half-witted I'm physically well. I've liked this cold weather and not felt cold as I did last year, though it's much colder here than in Basrah. But it's the general sense of being too much driven through not working quickly enough – because I can't – which is tiresome. I would like to take a month off, learn Arabic and see people – but the awful amount one would have to catch up at the end of it deters me. I'm almost reluctant to go away, because I know what a task it will be to write the next fortnightly report when I have to look everything up instead of jotting it down as it happens. But I very much like doing the fortnightly reports, which are the record of our work here, and though I haven't leisure to do them as well as they should be done, they will still be valuable.

Did I tell you of a visit I paid to the home for Armenian girls? Over 100 of them have been collected here, from all places and of all ages. There's an American fund to provide for them. Some had lived for months with the Arabs and were tattooed like Beduin women, some had just borne children and some were such children themselves that they could not remember whence they came. The Beduin coming down to our frontiers from the north bring hundreds of these girls with them. One woman when she first saw the Tigris burst into tears. 'Ah,' she cried, 'the mass of water here! and my sister died in the desert of thirst.' And ah! the rivers of tears, the floods of human misery that these waifs represent. What is life worth in this age of violence?

I write every week and if you don't get letters it is not because I don't send them.

CHAPTER 17

1918 – 1919

Bagdad

To F. B.   KARBALA, *January 3rd, 1918.*

I'm having a little holiday which is very pleasant and beneficial. I was beginning to feel terribly caged and stale and, though I haven't stepped out of the cage very far, or for very long, it's agreeable to be knocking about a tiny corner of the world again. It's a corner so full of associations. So many times I've come over the Bagdad–Karbala road after long desert expeditions, with a sense of accomplishment, and, at the same time, with that curious sense of disappointment which one nearly always feels with the accomplished thing. The best time, I think, was when I came back with the plan of Ukhaidir in my pocket – the worst when I came up from Arabia. I find myself forever stepping back into a former atmosphere – knowing with my real self that it has all melted away and yet half drugged with the lingering savour of it, and chiefly what I miss is the friendly presence of my good Fattuh, who smoothed all the way of travel and is now where? dead, I fear. I hear there are no men left in Aleppo; all have been taken for the War and Turkish soldiers have a poor chance.

The fortnight's holiday takes her motoring through familiar places full of memories.

Yesterday, I motored out along the sandy road, the very familiar road, to Karbala, and reached Major Pulley's house about midday. He had put me up close at hand in Col. Leachman's house, the latter being out in the desert with the Arabs, my very own Arabs, Fahad Bey's tribe, but I can't go to them. And then out through mud and swamp on to the edge of the Syrian Desert, which lifted its yellow shoulder in front of me in a manner so inviting that I could scarcely bear to turn away from it.... I had tea in my own house before a wood fire and afterwards received a visit from

one of the desert merchants, one of the Agail who had somehow heard I was here. I knew one of his brothers in Damascus and another in Bagdad. They come, like all Agail, from
Central Arabia, and we sat talking desert gossip for a long
time – until I felt again that I could scarcely bear to be so
close and not go in to the tribes. What a welcome Fahad
Bey would give me! He's about 2 days away.

To H. B. HILLAH, *January 16th, 1918.*

On my way home yesterday I stopped at Babylon, having
been asked by Sir Percy to advise about the preservation of
antiquities. 'Tempi passati' weigh very heavy there – not
that I was thinking of Nebuchadnezzar, nor yet of Alexander, but of the warm welcome I used to find, the good
company, the pleasant days spent with dear Koldewey – it's
no good trying to think of him as an alien and my heart
ached when I stood in the empty dusty little room where
Fattuh used to put up my camp furniture and the Germans
and I held eager conversation over plans of Babylon or
Ukhaidir. What a dreadful world of broken friendships we
have created between us.

To F. B. BAGDAD, *January 25th, 1918.*

Yesterday I went all over the Civil Hospital with the Muni-
cipal doctor, Capt. Carey Evans – he is a son-in-law of Mr
Lloyd George. He is doing his work with real intelligence
and is full of schemes for the future.... Medical organization
is of the very first importance, not only because there is so
much to be done but also because it is so deeply appreciated.
It is an invaluable political asset if you choose to look at it
from that point of view. Hospitals and dispensaries are the
first things the people ask for, and they flock to them, men
and women, and don't hesitate to undergo operations or any
treatment you please. Capt. C. E. says the standard of vitality is much higher than in Europe; the people here pull
through operations which he would not dare to attempt at
home. Their nervous system is much more solid. They don't
suffer from shock....

To H. B.   BAGDAD, *February 8th, 1918.*

It is getting quite perceptibly, but pleasantly warmer. I've begun to discard some of the innumerable wraps I wear by day and coverings by night. To-day, with the soft air blowing into my room, I thought of R'ton in February and wondered whether by chance it were snowing with you.... It is curious to find how many of the Bagdad notables are tribesmen, often only settled in the town for the last generation or two. Some sheikh builds himself a town house, sends his sons to school and starts them in a learned profession leading to Government employment. And at once they settle down into citizens. But the tribal links are unbroken. Any sheikh with business in the town looks by right to his kinsman's house for entertainment in the matter of daily meals – a pretty expensive duty it is – and if a member of the town family gets into trouble he will seek sanctuary with the tribe, safe in the assurance that he would never be given up. Several men I know fled to their tribe during the year before the Occupation, when the Ottoman hand was heavy on the Arabs of Bagdad. Most of these are now in our service and their tribal connection makes them all the more useful. We have a few really first-class Arab officials, just as we have found a few really first-class sheikhs who will assume responsibility and preserve order. There are not many of them, but such as there are, are invaluable. And we in our turn have an immense responsibility towards them.... We are pledged here. It would be an unthinkable crime to abandon those who have loyally served us. But there! if I write of Arabs I shall write all night.

To H. B.   BAGDAD, *February 15th, 1918.*

... All the telegrams prepare me for a terrific assault in France. I've also got your address at the Horden meeting which is *excellent*. It is so full of ideas and of wise appreciations. When I feel stale I think of your wonderfully fresh mind. There's no doubt you are a very remarkable person and I say it quite without prejudice....

However many native lands I may have I've only one

father and mother anyway and I'm therefore ever your devoted daughter.

March 1, 1918.

Yesterday afternoon I went to see one of our new primary schools where the headmaster is a friend of mine. There wasn't a very large attendance. I went round the 3 classes and asked them questions. In the smallest class we held a kind of general intelligence examination and I began by asking who was king of England. One student of history (aged about 7) replied unhesitatingly Chosroes, and another with a better grasp of modern politics amended with Lloyd George. (I don't know whether Father will be able to bear that story!).... The roses in my garden will be out in a week or two and I'm eating my own lettuces, but I'm sorry to say the cabbages have burst into luxuriant yellow flower before they ever became cabbages, so to speak.

To F. B.   BAGDAD, *March 28th, 1918.*

... A terrible cloud has fallen on our work here in the murder at Najaf of one of our Army Political Officers [this was Captain Marshall]. He was a brilliant creature – I personally was very fond of him, and spent a delightful afternoon with him three weeks ago when I was at Kufah. He had I thought a great future, and I do most bitterly regret him....

This tragedy cast a great storm over the end of my journey, but I must tell you the remainder of my tale. I wrote to you from Samawah the day before I left. I came up the Hillah branch of the Euphrates in a motor launch from Samawah to Diwaniyah. Capt. Goldsmith, a young Surrey officer, came with me for the first couple of hours, with a party of 19 mounted police – for honour you understand, not for safety, I could have done with less but in spite of them all the ride over the desert green with aromatic plants was delicious. The smell of a desert in spring is like nothing in this world. Each night I held a levy of notables after dinner. The second night when I had listened to the praises of myself, my government and my host, I was fortunately relieved by the entrance of an aged worthy whose appearance and conversation I must describe to you. His face was black with age, his beard scarlet with henna; the black and red were enfolded in a gigantic white turban. As he entered we all gave him salutations which were repeated when he had sat down. Talk then flagged until he took up his tale. 'As I came in,' said he, 'As I entered the very door, without a pen I composed a verse.' 'Without a pen!' – ejaculations of surprise and admiration fell from the company and we begged to be acquainted with the production. He raised his ancient bony hand as though he would bid the world listen, and in a cracked voice recited three times running, an egregious couplet to the effect that all had learned humanity from the high Government, and that the coming of the Khatun (me) had filled the universe with joy. After the third recital I felt it my duty to write it down – seeing that he had no pen. The rest of the hearers overflowed with praise and a general hope was expressed that 'Please God' and with His help the Haji would that night be able to complete the ode so felicitously begun. But whether he did or not I don't know, for I fled from Diwaniyah in a motor very early before the notables were awake.

The I.G.C. has been up for a couple of days cheerful and cheering as ever. Also whom do you think I have seen? Driver Woodcock, Mrs Taggart's grandson. I gave him some cigarettes and a book of mine, which he asked me for, and to-day I've got him some razors and things from the Red Cross.

To her family. BAGDAD, *April 5th, 1918.*

Mr Bullard and I rode miles up the Tigris and dropped in to call on a charming old gentleman who owns a large garden by the river bank. My other gardener host, Haji Naji, came in to see me this week. He was dressed in beautiful purple cloth and looked very imposing. 'Do you sit here all day and work?' said he, inscribing imaginary epistles in the air with his forefinger. 'Very laborious!' and he tapped his forehead to indicate his sense of my mental effort. 'You must come out again to my garden and be happy among the fruit trees.'

Behind all one's doings lies the terrible sense of these days in France. The first assault seems to have spent itself – at what cost! – and we now, with deep anxiety, await news of the second.

Goodbye, my beloved family....

April 18, 1918.

My own feeling is that it's no good attempting to make plans while everything in France hangs in the balance. While things are very critical I don't want to leave this country for, naturally, it will make people here extremely jumpy as to their future – and I, in a small way, am one of the people who can help to comfort them. If I went, I fear they might think I was deserting them, and that would make them more nervous still.

We've just had the Willingdons here. I saw a great deal of them and loved them both. The Chief insisted on my coming with them to Babylon. We had a delightful two days. We motored to Hillah, where we lunched.... We went to Babylon; this wonderful spring had clothed the ruin mounds in flowering weeds and cast a fresh beauty over the dust of palaces. I took them on to a high place, spread out a map, and told them all the long tale, down to Nebuchadnezzar, and then down to Alexander, who died there in the palace on the northern mound. The Willingdons were the most enchanting audience, so was the Chief, and one of the staff said that though he hated ruins (i.e., the staff man hated them) he really had liked Babylon. Lady W. and I agreed that I really had slung quite a good scalp on to my belt!...

April 19, 1918.

The nuns are making me a muslin gown – it will be a monument of love and care, for I really believe they lie awake at night thinking what new stitches they can put into it. I often go in to see them after tea; we sit on the balcony in their courtyard and talk of France and Bagdad. And then they all troop down in a body to the door to wave me farewell down their narrow, curling street – it's not 6 feet wide, nor are any streets wider in the heart of Bagdad.

Goodbye, darling Father. I think and think of you. However long I'm away from you, your love and Mother's is like the solid foundation on which all life rests. But I don't feel as if I could bear not seeing you for very much longer.

To H. B.   BAGDAD, *May 4th, 1918*. Received *June 2nd, 1918*.

The event of the week was a tea party which I gave to the ladies of Bagdad in Sir Percy's house. I asked no one but the big people, mainly Moslems, and to my surprise they came in flocks. An Armenian family (Madame Sevian and her daughters, whom I liked very much), the Mother Superior and some of the nuns came to help and it was an immense success. I've heard that the ladies said that not even in a Mohammedan house would so much care have been taken to exclude all males – it's odd, isn't it, that the success of a party should depend on the absence of that element! One woman, the wife of the Director of Religious Bequests (Moslem of the Moslem), said as she went away that if only they could see one another and meet more in company life would be quite different. So now I'm concocting a scheme to hire the cinematograph for an evening, and have a ladies' night. They never see anything or go anywhere, think of it!

To her family.   BAGDAD, *June 14, 1918*.

I've now got a Persian cook, who, besides being able to cook (an art none of my former cooks have possessed), knows no Arabic, so I'm forced to do my housekeeping in Persian, which amuses me – doubtless amuses the cook also at times. The nuns have made me some muslin gowns which are really quite nice – also cheap. The 'essayages' are not like any other dressmaking I've ever known. I go in after riding before breakfast and stand in practically nothing but breeches and boots (for it's hot) while the Mother Superior and the darling dressmaking sister, Sœur Renée, hover around ecstatically and pin on bits of muslin. At our elbows a native lay sister bearing cups of coffee. We pause often while the Mother Superior and Sœur Renée discuss gravely what really is the fashion. The result is quite satisfactory. Sœur Renée isn't a Frenchwoman for nothing.

My roses are flowering anew, rather dusty in the face, poor little things, but very sweet.

To H. B.   BAGDAD, *July 5th, 1918.*

... Two splendid long ones from you.

And the first and most interesting thing in them is your suggestion that you might come here next spring. I can't imagine greater pleasure than showing you this world of mine. I hate your not knowing what has meant so much to me.

I'm going to Persia on Tuesday night. I really feel as if a judgment ought to fall on me for doing anything so nice. It has been very hot this week. The temp. danced up one day to 118 and I can't keep my office under 100. I'm still very well, but I don't feel as if I could bear 3 uninterrupted months of it.

The holiday in Persia was all that she had meant it to be.
She goes to Kirmanshah, then to Gulahek, full of memories of her youth – and so back to Bagdad.

To F. B.   BAGDAD, *August 30th, 1918.*

If Sir Percy had been here this winter I think they could have done quite well without me, but the moment I got back Capt. Wilson told me the staggering news that he had been appointed to Teheran. But his absence makes me feel that it wouldn't have been right for me to have been away this winter. But it is a disappointment, isn't it! I was looking forward so much to having him here after all these months. However, Capt. Wilson and I are excellent colleagues and the best of friends and I know I can do a good deal to help him by seeing people.

To F. B.   BAGDAD, *September 5th, 1918.*

Why, yes, of course I wrote all the Arab of Mesopotamia. I've loved the reviews which speak of the practical men who were the anonymous authors, etc. It's fun being practical men, isn't it. Oh, I do so agree with you as to the great luck of having something to do during the war – no matter if it's much too much to do. It would be far greater suffering to stand outside it all. Father sends me the most delightful accounts of the Geographical Society meeting and dinner. How glad I am that it was he not I – firstly because he did it much better than I should have done it, thereby keeping up the credit of the family, and secondly because he liked it much better. I really should have been ashamed to receive that medal; it's far too great an honour.

To H. B.   BAGDAD, *November 28th, 1918.*

I am having by far the most interesting time of my life and thank Heaven I am now well and can grapple with it adequately. The Franco-British Declaration has thrown the whole town into a ferment. It doesn't happen often that people are told that their future as a State is in their hands and asked what they would like. They are all talking and mercifully they all come in to me with the greatest eagerness to discuss what they think. On two points they are practically all agreed, they want us to control their affairs and they want Sir Percy as High Commissioner. Beyond that all is divergence. Most of the town people want an Arab Amir but they can't fix upon the individual. My belief is (but I don't yet know) that the tribal people in the rural districts will not want any Amir as long as they can have Sir Percy – he has an immense name among them – and personally I think that would be best. It's an immense business setting up a court and a power. The whole situation requires very delicate handling. We can't be too wary at this moment when the public mind is so fluid that anything serves to divert it in one direction or another. I always speak quite frankly and they believe me, I think. They know I have their interests more deeply at heart than anything else and they trust me in the same sort of way that they trust Sir Percy. I'm so thankful to be here at this time, whatever happens I must remain till Sir Percy is brought back. We've telegraphed very fully, A. T. Wilson and I, and I think we have given a just view of the state of things....

... I'm quite sure that I prefer Generals to Bps.

BAGDAD, *January 17th, 1919.*

I flew with a young man last week – literally not figuratively. We flew for about three-quarters of an hour up and over the Tigris. For the first quarter of an hour I thought it the most alarming thing I had ever done and eagerly wished that that good young man would return to the ground. It was a windy day, the aeroplane wobbled a good deal. However, I presently became accustomed to it and was much interested and excited. I shall go up whenever I have an opportunity so as to grow quite used to it.

January 31st, 1919.

I'm sorry I shall not see the country here this spring, it will be wonderful after such a winter of rain.

But I shall see you and I'm immensely looking forward to it. I can't quite believe yet that in 6 weeks or so I shall be in England.

And do you know what I look forward to very much? A leg of mutton! That's not poetic, is it, but you should see and try to eat the meat I live on. I can't think what part of an animal it grows on. I must learn to cook mutton chops while I'm at home – and then see if I can't get them here.

She goes to the Conference in Paris.

To H. B. HOTEL MAJESTIC, PARIS, *March 7th, 1919.*

You must have been surprised at not hearing from me before, but I've dropped into a world so amazing that up to now I've done nothing but gape at it without being able to put a word on to paper. Our Eastern affairs are complex beyond all words, and until I came there was no one to get the Mesopotamian side of the question at first hand. The magnates have been extremely kind.... They have all urged me to stay and I think for the moment that's my business. I'm filling up the time by getting in touch with the French and finding out for myself what their views are....

Her father joins her in Paris.

We had a very delightful lunch to-day with Lord Robert and T. E. Lawrence – just we four. Lord Robert is I think the salient figure of the Conference and T. E. Lawrence the most picturesque. I spend most of my time with the latter and the former is unfailingly helpful.

Gertrude is in England for the rest of the summer and leaves again for the East in July.

To H. B.   *26th September, 1919.*

.... We reach Port Said on the 28th so I'll begin to write to you. The weather beautiful, the ship excellent. And Marie [Delaère, her devoted maid] is proving an admirable traveller, and wonders why everyone who can doesn't do this all the time. For my part I've never been so well dressed on a ship for she digs into the boxes and produces a fresh costume daily....

To her family.   ALEPPO, *October 17th, 1919.*

I've been doing the usual thing here, seeing people, but the chief person I've seen is Fattuh. He looks older and as if he had been through an awful time, as indeed he has. He has lost everything he had – he was beginning to be quite a well-to-do man and now he has only a horse and a small cart with which he brings in wood to sell in Aleppo. He was chiefly suspect because he was known to have been my servant. I went to see his wife – they live now in a tiny house which they have hired. He used to have two big houses of his own, poor Fattuh. I was very very glad to see him. He is preparing food for me to take on my motor journey and he still has some of my camp kit, cups and plates and things, so that I need not buy anything. We have had such happy times together – I called to mind joyous departures from Aleppo, and looking at his haggard face I said, 'Oh Fattuh before the war our hearts were so light when we travelled, now they are so heavy that a camel could not carry us.' He smiled and said, 'Big lady, no, a camel couldn't carry you.' My poor Fattuh.

To F. B. BAGDAD, *November 2, 1919.*

I have been to pay a visit of condolence on one of the big families, the head of which, an old friend of mine has died. I'm very sorry he's dead but I'm glad he won't have the opportunity of dying again so that I shall not have to pay another visit of condolence.... All the women of the family met me on the threshold of the harem, dressed in the blackest black, their hair cut short, and tears streaming down their cheeks. N.B. He has been dead a month. They cried uninterruptedly for ten minutes and again at intervals whenever they remembered to do so....

To F. B. *Sunday, November 30th, 1919.*

Another thing came in to-day, quite as important as the post – two most beautiful Arab greyhounds sent to me by my old friend the paramount chief of the Anazeh, Fahad Beg. They had walked ten days down the Euphrates with two tribesmen to conduct them, and came in half starved. They are sitting beside me on my sofa as I write, after wandering about the room for half an hour whining. They are very gentle and friendly and I hope they will soon get accustomed to living in a garden instead of a tent. They are perfectly lovely and of course of the finest Arab breed. We have named them Rishan and Najmah – the feathered (that's because of his feathered tail) and the star....

BAGDAD, *December 7th, 1919.*

I'm gradually getting my house furnished and it's going to be very nice. Maple writes that my things were sent off in October. I ordered them in July! In the meantime I've bought a charming black cupboard and chest in the bazaar, very cheap too. Marie has been invaluable in making curtains and generally seeing to things. She is the greatest comfort – I don't know how I did without her. Also my new cook – Oh father you'll love to see him. When he trails about in an abba he gives 'cachet' to my garden, I can tell you! Only, though he can cook a good deal and makes excellent cakes, he can't read or write and as his memory is deficient the morning accounts are a trial. They run as follows:

G.B. Yallah! Mahdi! the accounts. I must go to the office.

M. Oh Your servant, Khatun. I bought what's its name.

G.B. Well, what is its name.

M. Rice. Two krans.

G.B. Eight annas. What next?

M. Then I bought what's its name.

G.B. What? Yallah!

M. Bread, 6 annas.

G.B. Go on.

M. And then I bought what's its name.

G.B. Merciful God! What?

M. Sugar, two rupees.

G.B. Two rupees. Yallah!

M. And then – Khatun, I forgot the eggs yesterday, one rupee.

G.B. All right go on.

M. And then I bought meat, one rupee.

G.B. What next?

M. Wallah, I bought – Khatun shall I prepare for your Excellency this evening ester? (stew).

G.B. What you like. Finish the accounts.

M. On my head. And then what's its name.

and so on, and so on till I'm hysterical between impatience and laughter....

Do you know what they call me here? Umm al Muminin, the Mother of the Faithful, and the last person who bore that name was Ayishah the wife of the prophet. But you see why I can't leave.

Sunday, December 20th, 1919.

Who so angelic as my two dogs who are curled up beside me on the carpets as I write. I'm beginning to persuade them that sofas and chairs are not meant for greyhounds....

Bagdad

To H. B.   BAGDAD, *January 4th, 1920.*

... And this country, which way will it go with all these agents of unrest to tempt it? I pray that the people at home may be rightly guided and realize that the only chance here is to recognize political ambitions from the first, not to try to squeeze the Arabs into our mould and have our hands forced in a year – who knows? perhaps less, the world is moving so fast – with the result that the chaos to north and east overwhelms Mesopotamia also. I wish I carried more weight. I've written to Edwin [Montagu] and this week I'm writing to Sir A. Hirtzel. I'm so sure I'm right that I would go to the stake for it – or perhaps just a little less painful form of testimony if they wish for it!

To F. B.   BAGDAD, *January 25th, 1920.*

I had an interesting day on Monday. First of all we had the formal opening of the Girls' School – our first. I had invited the important native ladies and to my pleasure the Mohammedans turned up better than I expected. Miss Kelly, the Directress of Education, had made the school look very nice.... I made a long speech in Arabic explaining the arrangements of the school and the way the children would be educated. The Muhammadan ladies took their share in it, chiming in with assent and approval. It was most exhilarating. Then Mrs Howell declared the school open after which we showed them round and then gave them tea. A most successful performance. That evening I had two young Arabs to dinner and a very interesting officer in the police service, Captain Morgan, to meet them. They came at 7 and stayed till 10.30 talking as hard as they could go, about education and the reform of religious endowments and all sorts of things. We were all on the most cordial terms when they left. I'm going to repeat the entertainment weekly, with different couples of my young men, the Arab young men I mean. I feel certain it's a good plan.

To F. B.   BAGDAD, *February 14th, 1920.*

I had a really delightful 3 days in Hillah, where I arrived feeling half dead and recovered steadily. I was staying with the Political Officer, Major Tyler, and all his staff, some 10 young men; great fun it was.... Our job was to inspect the first beginnings of the land survey, the agrarian settlement which lies at the root of all our tribal problems – a gigantic task it's going to be, but if we get it done right it will mean agrarian peace for ever and a day. So we met the surveyors and looked at maps and boundary marks – heaps of earth in this country, not stones, for there are none. And then we rode back and half-way stopped and lunched at the mudhif of the chief sheikh of the district. He had gathered in representatives of all neighbouring tribes concerned in the settlement, but being a poor man he had let it be understood that he intended to provide only for us and the Bani Hasan, his nearest neighbours. So when our great tray of foods had been set before us, another was laid in the end of the mudhif and the Bani Hasan summoned to it. The rest of the company contented themselves with cigarettes and coffee. After lunch there was a great talk – this is how business is conducted in the provinces, and there's no better council chamber than a sheikh's mudhif.... It was a delightful scene. Our host had fought against us at Kut, having mobilized his tribe at the order of the Turks. 'What was it like,' I asked, 'when you fought with the Turks?' 'Khatun,' he replied solemnly (that's what they call me – Madam), 'we had nothing to eat. Mind you, they had plenty, but they gave us nothing.' 'Did you fight hungry?' I asked. 'Wallahi no,' he answered. 'We returned home.'

To F. B.   BAGDAD, *February 29th, 1920.*

It's too exciting to think that Father is already on his way here. It's also the first spring day after bitter cold and drenching rain, and being Sunday I'm not going to the office. I've installed myself in the verandah of my garden having brought all my work here for a good morning, which I shall begin by writing to you.

I'm very busy trying to get a private hospital for women of the better classes – they have already organized an excellent ward in the Civil Hospital for poor women. It was when we showed them this that the well born women asked if they would collect the money to pay for the building. It will cost, 'tout compris' Rs. 45,000, and they must pay for it if they want it – an 8 bed hospital of 4 rooms with a bath room and nurses' room, 6 rooms in all. We had an immense tea party at Aurelia Tod's whose house is more convenient than mine, being in the middle of the town. She did it beautifully for us. I explained the matter of the hospital to the ladies and they were all very enthusiastic. I am now sending a personal letter to 10 of the richest men in this town asking them each to give Rs. 3,000. The rest I think we should have no difficulty in collecting in small subscriptions.

To F. B.   *March 14, 1920.*

It's a problem here how to get into touch with the Shiahs, not the tribal people in the country; we're on intimate terms with all of them, but the grimly devout citizens of the holy towns and more especially the leaders of religious opinion, the Mujtahids, who can loose and bind with a word by authority which rests on an intimate acquaintance with accumulated knowledge entirely irrelevant to human affairs and worthless in any branch of human activity. There they sit in an atmosphere which reeks of antiquity and is so thick with the dust of ages that you can't see through it – nor can they. And for the most part they are very hostile to us, a feeling we can't alter because it's so difficult to get at them. I'm speaking of the extremists among them; there are a few with whom we are on cordial relations. Until quite recently I've been wholly cut off from them because their tenets forbid them to look upon an unveiled woman and my tenets don't permit me to veil – I think I'm right there, for it would be a tacit admission of inferiority which would put our intercourse from the first out of focus. Nor is it any good trying to make friends through the women – if the women were allowed to see me they would veil before me as if I were a man. So you see I appear to be too female for one sex and too male for the other.

There's a group of these worthies in Kadhimain, the holy city, 8 miles from Bagdad, bitterly pan-Islamic, anti-British 'et tout le bataclan'. Chief among them are a family called Sadr, possibly more distinguished for religious learning than any other family in the whole Shiah world. A series of accidents led them to make advances to me to which I replied that if they would like me to visit them I should be delighted to honour myself.... The upshot was that I went yesterday, accompanied by an advanced Shiah of Bagdad whom I knew well. I rather fancy he is secretly a free-thinker. We walked through the narrow crooked streets of Kadhimain and stopped before a small dark archway. He led the way along 50 yards of pitch-dark vaulted passage – what was over our heads I can't think – which landed us in the courtyard of the Saiyid's house. It was old, at least a hundred years old, with beautiful old latticework of wood closing the diwan on the upper floor. The rooms all opened on to the court – no windows on to the outer world – and the court was a pool of silence separated from the street by the 50 yards of mysterious masonry under which we had passed. Saiyid Hassan's son, Saiyid Muhammad, stood on the balcony to welcome us, black robed, black bearded and on his head the huge dark blue turban of the Mujtahid class. Saiyid Hassan sat inside, an imposing, even a formidable figure, with a white beard reaching half way down his chest, and a turban a size larger than Saiyid Muhammad's. I sat down beside him on the carpet and after formal greetings he began to talk in the rolling periods of the learned man, the book-language, which you never hear on the lips of others. Mujtahids usually have plenty to say – talking is their job; it saves the visitor trouble. We talked of the Sadr family in all its branches, Persian, Syrian and Mesopotamian; and then of books and of collections of Arabic books in Cairo, London, Paris and Rome – he had all the library catalogues; and then of the climate of Samarra which he explained to me was much better than that of Bagdad because Samarra lies in the third climatic zone of the geographers. He talked with such vigour that his turban kept slipping forward on to his eyebrows and he had to push it back impatiently on to the top of his head.... And I was acutely conscious of the fact that no woman before me had ever been invited to drink coffee with a mujtahid and listen to his discourse, and really anxious lest I shouldn't make a good impression.

So after about three-quarters of an hour I said I feared I must be troubling him and I would ask permission to take my leave. 'No, no,' he boomed out, 'we have set aside this afternoon for you.' I felt pretty sure then that the visit was being a success and I stayed another hour. But I tackled this next hour with much more confidence. I said I wanted to tell him about Syria and told him all I knew down to the latest telegram which was that Faisal was to be crowned. 'Over the whole of Syria to the sea?' he asked, with sudden interest. 'No,' I answered, 'the French stay in Beyrout.' 'Then it's no good,' he replied, and we discussed the matter in all its bearings. Then we talked of Bolshevism. He agreed that it was the child of poverty and hunger, 'but,' he added, 'all the world's poor and hungry since this war.' I said that as far as I made out the Bolshevist idea was to sweep away all that ever had been and build afresh. I feared they didn't know the art of building. He approved that. Then as I made signs of going, he said, 'It is well known that you are the most learned woman of your time, and if any proof were needed it would be found in the fact that you wish to frequent the society of the learned. That's why you're here to-day.' I murmured profound thanks for the privilege (with a backward glance at the third climatic zone), and took my leave in the midst of a shower of invitations to come again as often as I liked.

To F. B.   BAGDAD, *Sunday, April 10, 1920.*

I'm leaving it to Father to describe an experience which I'm sure he'll do at length. This is only a word to tell you that it's wonderful having him. It is most interesting to see him sizing up our problems and he happens to have arrived at a very crucial time. I think we're on the edge of a pretty considerable Arab nationalist demonstration with which I'm a good deal in sympathy. It will, however, force our hand and we shall have to see whether it will leave us with enough hold to carry on here....

What I do feel pretty sure of is that if we leave this country to go to the dogs it will mean that we shall have to reconsider our whole position in Asia. If Mesopotamia goes Persia goes inevitably, and then India. And the place which we leave empty will be occupied by seven devils a good deal worse than any which existed before we came.

With these few words, I remain your affectionate daughter.

To H. B.   BAGDAD, *Thursday, 6th May, 1920.*

It was a delightful surprise to have a letter from you this morning. I wonder how anyone can complain about anything when they have a father like you. I can't tell you what it was like to have you here. One takes for granted where you are concerned that no matter how unfamiliar or complex the things may be that you're seeing and hearing, you'll grasp the whole lie of them at once, and it's only when I come to think of it that I realise what it is to have your quickness of intelligence. Anyhow, I feel certain that you know the general structure here as well as we know it ourselves and I'm enchanted that you should, not only because it makes my job so much more interesting knowing that you understand it, but also because it's good for us all that you should be able to put in a word for us at home....

To H. B.   BAGDAD, *Sunday, 9th May, 1920.*

With what different feelings I write to you now that you've been here! All the news seems to be of the utmost moment now you know all about it. The first and chief is Frank's [Balfour] engagement to Phyllis Goschen. I'm very very glad about it. I like her.

Captain A. L. Smith [Lionel] came to dine. We had a long

and satisfactory talk about the education of Arabs. I'm not quite happy about what we're doing; nor is he. It's all very well to say we mustn't start secondary schools till we have really first-rate material, both in teachers and pupils, but we can't wait for that. We must get a move on and be content with second best, for the people here are so immensely keen to be provided with higher education and if we hold back they will think we are doing it on purpose to keep them back. You have to look at it from the point of politics as well as of education.

To F. B. *Sunday, May 23, 1920.*

Another very nice thing has happened this week – Fattuh has turned up, driving a man down from Aleppo....

I am so glad to have my dear Fattuh. He wants to go back to Aleppo as soon as we can devise a safe way to get him back. His first words when he came in were, 'Is His Excellency the Progenitor still with you?' I said, 'How did you know he had been here?' 'Oh,' said Fattuh, 'one of the Beduins in the desert told me that the Khatun was well and her Father was with her.'

So I suppose it's the talk of Arabia....

To H. B. BAGDAD, *June 14th, 1920.*

We have had a stormy week. The Nationalist propaganda increases. There are constant meetings in mosques where the mental temp. rises a great deal above 113. The extremists are out for independence, without a mandate. They play for all they are worth on the passions of the mob and what with the Unity of Islam and the Rights of the Arab Race they make a fine figure. They have created a reign of terror; if anyone says boo in the bazaar it shuts like an oyster. There has been practically no business done for the last fortnight....

To H. B. BAGDAD, *Sunday, June 20th, 1920.*

Ramadhan ended.... On Friday morning I rode out before breakfast round the suburbs of Bagdad where I knew people would congregate, and saw the whole world making merry over the great feast of Islam, 'Id-al-Fitr', the festival of fast breaking. There were numberless booths of sweet-meat sellers, merry-go-rounds with children swinging in them, groups of women all in their best clothes, and the whole as little revolutionary as anything you can imagine. The East making holiday....

On Sat. morning when I got to the office, Ghallal (head Kavass, you remember) met me with beaming smiles and told me Sir Percy had come. I went to the Mess and found him breakfasting with Lady Cox and Major Murray, and I felt as if a load of care had been lifted. To-day, according to my custom, I didn't go to the office. Sir Percy sent me a note in the afternoon saying that he wanted to come and have a talk. He came after tea. We talked a great deal about how to bridge over the next 4 crucial months till he comes back. H.M.G. have telegraphed to him to return to England at once and he leaves to-morrow. Though, of course, I hate his going, I'm thankful that he will be there to appeal to. For I can write everything to him as I can do to no one else, he being my real Chief, and he will be able to take direct action. At 7 he went to see the Naqib taking me with him. It was touching to see the Naqib's joy. We sat in the court-yard – it was fearfully hot and stuffy – and had an hour's talk....

BAGDAD, *June 27th, 1920.*

Don't forget to go on loving me.

To H. B. BAGDAD, *Sunday, July 4th, 1920.*

The political tide ebbs and flows and we don't get much further. The mayor dropped in while I was breakfasting a few days ago, as his habit is, and told me that several of the leaders had approached him and asked whether if they accepted the mandate they could be sure that we really meant to set up an Arab Govt. He replied that they might be certain of it and that he was ready to go further into the matter with them at any time, but so far they have done nothing more....

This morning I rode out before breakfast to see H. Naji and found a large party of people with him. We talked long about the political situation, they pointing out a good many of our errors, more of omission than of commission. They were extremely reasonable and had my full sympathy. We all agreed that there was no reason why the mandate shouldn't work with goodwill on both sides. Haji Naji, who is heart and soul with us, took a wise part in this conversation....

I'm quite well and it's not particularly hot, seldom up to 110. As long as I don't have fever or something silly I shall be all right, and I see no reason why I should have anything....

BAGDAD, *August 16th, 1920.*

And now I'll tell you about the revolution. The committee of ex-deputies co-opted at the beginning of the week a number of people among whom were 4 of the leading extremists. On Wed. these 4 all refused the invitation and at the same time the police gave warning that there was to be a monster meeting in the big mosque next day, after which a procession through the town was to be organized. It would undoubtedly have led to disturbances and that was the object desired. For the extremists have seen the ground cut under their feet by the formation of a moderate constitutional party round the committee of ex-deputies and they have no card left but an appeal to the mob. The police were therefore ordered to arrest the 4 leaders. I think they must have bungled the matter for they only got one, the others got away to Kadhimain and are now, I hear, in Najaf. Orders were then issued forbidding the holding of meetings in Mosques, together with a curfew – no one to be out in the streets after 10 p.m. The combined effect has been excellent as far as Bagdad is concerned. The town has returned to its normal life and I think there is scarcely anyone who doesn't breathe a sigh of relief. Most of them asked why it wasn't done sooner but I think that A.T. has behaved with great wisdom in the matter. He has waited until it was clear that if the agitation was allowed to continue the town would be given over to rioters – most of those who attended the mosque meetings were riffraff of the worst sort – and there he has struck for the protection of public security. And everyone knows that it isn't an attempt on his part to suppress Arab nationalist sentiment.

The worst news is that Col. Leachman has been ambushed and killed on his way from Bagdad to Ramadi. He was holding the whole Euphrates up to Anak single handed by means of the tribes, troops having all been withdrawn, and we don't know what will happen in those regions....

Mr Humphrey Bowman was Director of Education in Iraq. He sends me the following striking account of Gertrude as seen in the midst of an Arab circle, not in the desert, but in Bagdad:

'Sir Edgar Bonham Carter was giving an At Home to a number of Arab notables in Bagdad in 1919. Only one or two British were there, Cooke and myself, possibly another. We were all sitting on chairs round the room as we do in the East, getting up whenever some special guest entered. At last the door opened and Gertrude came in. She was beautifully dressed, as always, and looked very queenly. Everyone rose, and then she walked round the room, shaking hands with each Arab in turn and then saying a few appropriate words to each. Not only did she know them all by name – there must have been 40 or 50 in the room – but she knew what to say to each....'

To H. B.   BAGDAD, *August 30th, 1920.*

Gertrude visits the Naqib.

... While I was sitting with him this morning listening to his explanation of his neutral attitude throughout Ramadhan I was overcome – as I not infrequently am – with the sense of being as much an Asiatic as a European. For if I'm not too Asiatic to form a clear opinion, he made a pretty good case....

To be able to exchange the frankest views with the Ancient East, as I do with the Naqib, is both amazing and delightful.

To F. B.   BAGDAD, *September 5, 1920.*

The truth is I'm very tired of being so hot. One always feels in September as if one could not bear it any longer. We had some bad days this week with a blazing wind, but really it's beginning to cool off a little. One doesn't need a fan till about 10 a.m., but fan or not my office nears 100° every afternoon....

The problem is the future. The tribes don't want to form part of a unified state; the towns can't do without it. How are we going to support and protect the elements of stability and at the same time conform to the just demand for economy from home? For you can't have a central government if no one will pay taxes and the bulk of the population won't pay taxes unless they are constrained to do so. Nor will they preserve a sufficient amount of order to permit of trade....

We are now in the middle of a full-blown Jihad, that is to say we have against us the fiercest prejudices of a people in a primeval state of civilization. Which means that it's no longer a question of reason. And it has on its side the tendency to anarchy which is all over the world, I think, the salient result of the war. When one considers it, it's very comprehensible that the thinking people should revolt at an organization of the universe which could produce anything so destructive to civilization as the war. The unthinking people, who form the great mass of the world, follow suit in a blind revolt against the accepted order. They don't know how to substitute anything better, but it's clear that few things can be worse. We're near to a complete collapse of society – the end of the Roman empire is a very close historical parallel. We've practically come to the collapse of society here and there's little on which you can depend for its reconstruction. The credit of European civilization is gone. Over and over again people have said to me that it has been a shock and a surprise to them to see Europe relapse into barbarism. I had no reply – what else can you call the war? How can we, who have managed our own affairs so badly, claim to teach others to manage theirs better? It may be that the world has need to sink back into the dark ages of chaos, out of which it will evolve something, perhaps no better than what it had.

To H. B.   BAGDAD, *September 19th, 1920.*

... Sir Percy knows what complete confidence there is between us and that I should always tell you exactly what I think or do. That I should be able to do so is to me the foundation of existence and it is entirely owing to you that you are to me not only a father but also the closest and most intimate friend. You have been the only person to whom I have related fully the ups and downs of these extremely difficult months and as far as anyone can relate without prejudice circumstances in which they have played a part, I have done so to you. You will therefore believe me when I tell you that it is only quite recently that I have realized how prominent a place I have occupied in the public mind here as the pro-Arab member of the administration. Over and over again lately I have heard from the frequenters of the coffee shops, my own servants and casual people up and down the bazaars, that I am always quoted in the coffee-shop talk as the up-holder of the rights of the Arabs. I have invariably replied that the talk is incorrect; it is H.M.G. which upholds the rights of the Arabs and we are all of us the servants of H.M.G.

To H. B.   *October 3rd, 1920.*

This morning being Sunday I rode out before breakfast to see Haji Naji. He had a party of guests sitting in his arbor and he was showing off the 'sécateur' you sent him. 'The first,' he said, 'that has been seen in the Iraq,' and he proudly snipped off the branches of an adjacent mulberry tree to show how well it worked. I wished you had been there to see. I've been very agricultural this week. I attended a demonstration at the cotton farm where experiments are being made in various kinds of cotton and various treatments. About a dozen Bagdad landowners were present and were deeply interested. So was I. On an average of 3 years, a certain long-stapled American variety seems to be the most promising. There seems every reason to believe that we shall produce as good cotton as is grown anywhere in the world, and their yield is very large....

To H. B. and F. B.   BAGDAD, *October 10th, 1920.*

I don't know what I should do without your weekly. letters, they are the only link I have with the outer world. I do sometimes feel dreadfully isolated.

I had a long talk with Sasun Eff: the other day – I went to call on his sister-in-law and found all the men there eager to embark on talk. Sasun Eff said he felt sure that no local man would be acceptable as head of the state because every other local man would be jealous of him. He went on to throw out feelers in different directions – one might think of a son of the Sharif, or a member of the family of the Sultan of Egypt, if there was a suitable individual, or of the family of the Sultan of Turkey? I said that I for my part felt sure that Sir Percy didn't and couldn't mind whom they selected except that I thought the Turkish family was ruled out – it ought to be an Arab Prince.... Anyone they think we are backing they will agree to, and then intrigue against him without intermission. It is not an easy furrow to plough! These reflections will throw an illumination on what is being said in the English papers, from which it would appear that Sir Percy has only to say 'Hey Presto' for an Arab Government to leap on to the stage, like another Athene springing from the forehead of Zeus. You may say if you like that Sir Percy will play the role of Zeus but his Athene will find the stage encumbered by such trifles as the Shiah problem, the tribal problem and other matters, over which even a goddess might easily stumble. But if he's not a Zeus he is a very skilful physician and one in whom his patient has implicit confidence. The last item is our chief asset and it's clear to me that whatever line he may decide to pursue, it's up to us to follow him with all the strength and ability we may individually possess. The underlying truth of all criticism is however – and it's what makes the critics so difficult to answer – that we had promised self-governing institutions, and not only made no step towards them but were busily setting up something entirely different. One of the papers says, quite rightly, that we had promised an Arab Government with British Advisers, and had set up a British Government with Arab Advisers. That's a perfectly fair statement.

...

Tuesday, 12th October.

A word to say that Sir Percy arrived yesterday, thank Heaven. The Office is in rather a turmoil with no one knowing exactly what they ought to do next, so I can't write at length about his reception – I will next week. I'm taking on a sort of temporary Oriental Secretary job till people find their feet.

*

I include here two historical summaries, written by Sir Percy Cox and Sir Henry Dobbs respectively, of the years during which Gertrude worked under them in the East. I am most grateful to them for this very valuable help.

By Major-General Sir Percy Cox, G.C.M.G., etc.:

I first met Gertrude Bell at the house of mutual friends, the late Sir Richmond and Lady Ritchie, during the winter of 1909.

... After this brief intercourse, I did not meet her again until the spring of 1916, when after a period of some months spent in our Arab Intelligence Bureau at Cairo, working up Arab questions and more particularly inter-tribal relations, she was sent on deputation to G.H.Q. Intelligence in Mesopotamia and reported herself at General Sir Percy Lake's Headquarters at Basrah. The intention was that, having thoroughly mastered on the record the intricacies of Arab politics in the Hejaz, she should now work up tribal questions from the Iraq side and maintain liaison in regard to these matters with her late comrades of the Arab Bureau at Cairo. After she had spent some weeks at her task, the military authorities decided that the particular service for which she had been deputed to Basrah had been completed as far as it could be for the time being, and finding a member of her sex a little difficult to place as a permanency in a military G.H.Q. in the field, they offered her services to me in my capacity of Chief Political Officer – services which were gladly accepted. Thus began the 10 years of devoted service to myself and my successors, which were only terminated by her untimely death in harness on 11th of July 1926.

My duties as Chief Political Officer to the G.O.C.-in-Chief at the period when she joined me were partly military and partly civil. In the first place I was the medium of communication between the Military Commander and the civil population, and his adviser in his political dealings with them. For this purpose I worked as a member of his G.H.Q. Intelligence and was always in close touch with that branch, assisting in the examination of prisoners and spies, the sifting of information, the provision of informers and interpreters and so on. On the purely civil side it devolved on me, under the G.O.C.'s supreme control, to implement as far as the fluctuating tide of war allowed, the assurances which we had given to the Arabs at the beginning of the campaign, both in the Persian Gulf and in lower Mesopotamia – assurances which it may be well to emphasise here.

As regards the Persian Gulf, our self-imposed task of maintaining Pax Britannica had inevitably created for us in the course of several generations a series of treaties and obligations of responsibility towards the Arab rulers on its shores which there could now be no question of our disregarding. We had treaties of old standing with the Sultan of Muscat; with the Sheikhs of the Pirate (now the Trucial) coast of Oman, with Bahrein, and with the Sheikh of Qatar. We were on intimate terms with Ibn Saud, the Wahabi chieftain of southern Nejd, who in 1913 had succeeded in extending his independent authority to the coast of the Persian Gulf, and whose future prosperity and success depended mainly on our recognition and sympathetic co-operation in his plans of progress and reform. At the head of the Gulf the Sheikh of Koweit had been assured of our support against any Turkish encroachment on his independence; and finally, on the banks of the Shatt-el-Arab was the Sheikh of Mohammerah, Arab by race though subject to Persia, who looked to us in view of the commercial stake we enjoyed in his territory to secure fair play for him in his relations alike with Persia and with Turkey.

These close connections of treaty and friendship were an invaluable asset to us when the time came to contemplate the lively probability of Turkey's entry into the war against us; but if full advantage was to be taken of them it was clearly of primary importance that we should demonstrate to our friends at the outset the circumstances in which war had been forced upon us and should take such prompt action as would convince them that we

were alive to the danger in which they would be placed, as friends
of ours, and intended to take adequate steps to safeguard their interests as well as our own. Accordingly, the moment news of the
outbreak of war with Turkey was received I was instructed to
issue a proclamation in the above sense, assuring our Arab friends
at the same time that their liberty and religion would be scrupu-
lously respected, and that all we asked of them was that they
should preserve order in their own territories and ensure that their
subjects indulged in no action calculated to injure British interests....

In furtherance of this policy it was our duty as far as military
exigencies permitted, to enable the peaceable inhabitants of the
territory gradually falling under our occupation, to carry on their
normal vocations; but the initial difficulties involved in setting up
a civil administration with war in lively progress were naturally
considerable and were greatly enhanced in this case by the fact
that, the Turkish regime having been almost entirely alien, all
Turkish officials and those non-Turks who had been employed in
the administration, fled with the retreating armies as each centre
was evacuated, and we found no local material with which to re-
place them. Nevertheless, as soon as we had settled down in Basrah
a beginning was made towards the establishment of a system of
government which would be consonant with the spirit of our an-
nouncements. For this branch of my duties I had separate Offices
and Staff and divided my working hours between the Army
G.H.Q., whether at the Base or in the Field, and my Civil Headquarters at Basrah. It was here that Gertrude Bell joined me, as
also did Captain Arnold Wilson (afterwards Lieut.-Colonel Sir
Arnold Wilson, K.C.I.E., etc.)....

Steady progress continued to be made with the creation of administrative machinery in all its branches throughout the Basrah
Vilayet, and Gertrude Bell worked devotedly as Oriental Secretary to myself or my deputy, Captain Wilson, in the Basrah Secretariat. During the late summer of 1915, I had arranged to rendez-
vous at Ojair with the Sultan of Nejd for the purpose of concluding
the Treaty negotiations, and a year later, after the final signing of
the documents, His Highness was invited first to a durbar at
Koweit and afterwards to Basrah for a short visit, in the belief that
it would be of interest and value to him to see the working, and the
immense proportions, of a great military base and port such as
Basrah had now become, and would also be a useful means of
demonstrating to the inhabitants of the Basrah Vilayet the very

close relations existing between us and the great Arab Chiefs of the principalities on their borders. I remember well with what delight and enthusiasm Gertrude Bell entered at this time into all the arrangements for Sultan Ibn Saud's visit, looking forward keenly as she did to making the acquaintance of this great and attractive actor on the Arabian stage. Ibn Saud, who had heard me speak of Gertrude Bell and her pre-war expedition to Hayil, had never before come in contact with any European woman, and the phenomenon of one of the gentler sex occupying an official position with a British Expeditionary Force was one quite outside his bedouin comprehension. Nevertheless, when the time came he met Miss Bell with complete frankness and sangfroid as if he had been associated with European ladies all his life.

Except for the interruption of this 'royal visit' and an occasional week-end trip to Basrah to enable me to keep in touch with passing events in the sphere of the civil administration and to see to the welfare of my wife, who at this time was engaged in good works among the troops in Basrah, I was able to remain with Sir Stanley Maude's Headquarters on the Tigris front throughout the winter campaign, which saw the recovery of Kut, the sudden crossing of the Tigris at Shimran and the subsequent advance on Bagdad, ending in its occupation on the 11th of March 1917.

The fall of Bagdad was an event full of significance and pregnant with possibilities both for ourselves and for the enemy. Throughout the Empire and among our allies the brilliant success of General Maude's campaign aroused the utmost enthusiasm, so that the tragedy of Kut seemed almost effaced in the public mind; while for the Turks the loss of Bagdad not only deprived them of their base of operations in Mesopotamia but laid them open to an Anglo-Russian offensive in the Mosul Vilayet.

... We found the pre-war British Residency in use as a Hospital, in which the Turks had left us an unwelcome legacy in the shape of their worst cases of wounds and disease. Its sanitary condition was indescribable, but other hospital accommodation was gradually found for the inmates, and the Residency after a thorough cleansing and overhaul was fitted up as Army Headquarters. I was allotted a house on the river bank below the Residency which had before our entry been the Austrian Consulate, and there I began to form a Secretariat.

Directly the news of our occupation of Bagdad got abroad I was perforce overwhelmed with visitors; first the notables of Bagdad and then the tribal Sheikhs from near and far, many of whom had never submitted to the authority of the Turkish Government and were complete strangers to Bagdad. Some attempt had to be made to determine and record from whence these visitors came, what their relations were to one another and what was their relative importance among themselves, matters not at all easy for newcomers to diagnose. It was in connection with this task that I began to feel the want of Gertrude Bell's indefatigable assistance and decided to bring her and one or two others up from the Basrah office to form a nucleus for my Secretariat at Bagdad. I remember that when I told him that some of my staff were coming up from Basrah, including Miss Bell, the G.O.C.-in-Chief expressed considerable misgiving at the news, as he feared her arrival might form an inconvenient precedent for appeals from other ladies, but I reminded him that her services had been specifically offered to me by his predecessor as an ordinary member of my Secretariat; that I regarded and treated her no differently from any male officer of my Staff, and that her particular abilities could be very useful to me at the present moment.

These first six months of our occupation of Bagdad were indeed no easy period of the Civil Administration. The Army was fully occupied consolidating its position round Bagdad and needed to husband its strength to the utmost for the coming winter campaign, and so detachments for outlying places could not be spared; nor, for fear of inconvenient incidents, could civil officers be allowed to go far afield. In these circumstances it was naturally difficult for tribesmen to believe, especially in the face of the violent Turko-German propaganda which was rife at the time, that the existing regime at Bagdad was at all secure or that the Turks would not eventually return.

Those who prided themselves on their intimate acquaintance with world politics declared that Iraq would undoubtedly be handed back to Turkey in exchange for the liberation of Belgium. Such rumours found their echo among the Sheikhs in general, causing many of our firmest friends to waver, or at least to wait on events.

From the beginning of July 1917 my designation was altered to that of 'Civil Commissioner', and while I still, of course, remained subject to the supreme authority of the Army Commander, I was given the right henceforth of direct communication with the Secretary of State for India.

During the period of which I am speaking, the summer of 1917, the limits of our occupation beyond Bagdad were roughly: on the right flank, Baquba, on the river Diyala; in the centre, Samarra, on the Tigris line; and on the Euphrates west of Bagdad, Falluja; and thence back to the Hindiyeh barrage on the same river.

On the Diyala the process of consolidation was necessarily slow, for not only had the country suffered greatly from long devastation by Turkish troops, but until the autumn of 1917 the canal-heads were still in the enemy's control.

The Tigris gave us no further trouble; those tribal leaders who had joined the Turks again on our retirement from Ctesiphon had thought it safest to remain with them when they in turn retreated towards Mosul; meanwhile their sons, or other suitable kinsmen, had been installed for the time being in their holdings along the river and were now occupied in the cultivation of their lands, much as in time of peace. A most favourable impression was created at this time in the Tigris area by our decision to rebuild Kut-al-Amara. The work of reconstruction was supervised with much skill and judgment by the District Political Officer, and the countryside saw in the regeneration of the town not only profit and advantage to themselves but also some pledge that a new order of things so solidly established must have come to stay.

On the Euphrates west of Bagdad there was little to be done for the moment, and it was not until Sir Harry Brooking's successful push in November 1917 had brought about the capture of Ramadi that the tribal Sheikhs of that area began to come in.

On the middle Euphrates, from the Hindiyeh barrage to Samarra, the position was a curious one. Not a single British soldier was located south of that barrage until December 1917; nevertheless, that area being the centre of an important grain-growing district, irrigated by the Euphrates canals, could not in the interests of the Army be altogether neglected and a Political Officer had accordingly been sent to Hillah in May 1917. His authority however did not extend to Diwaniyeh and southward thereof, where the local Sheikhs, after their visit to me on our first entry into Bagdad, had to be left pretty much to their own devices.

But the most thorny problem on the Euphrates at that time was not so much the tribes as the Holy Cities of Islam, Karbala and Najaf. As in other cases on the lower Euphrates the Sheikhs of these towns, after their visit to me at Bagdad, had been sent back to their homes with pious instructions from me to maintain law and order themselves; and in order to strengthen their hands and give them some official recognition, small monthly allowances were provided for them; but before many weeks had passed it became evident that the arrangement was working unsatisfactorily both for the towns and for us. On the one hand the Sheikhs were found to be abusing their positions and making hay while the sun shone; while, worse still, the existence of a brisk trade in supplies to the enemy, both on the Iraq front and in Syria, was brought to light. If further trouble was to be avoided, closer control had clearly become essential, and British Political Officers were accordingly posted at Karbala, and at Kufa in the Shamiyeh district on the border of which lies Najaf. These officers for the time being had to rely entirely on their own judgment and force of character and were often placed in positions of great difficulty and no little personal risk. Karbala it is true gave no serious trouble, but Najaf, where the town was in the hands of a lawless crew of local Sheikhs, remained a thorn in our side for some time to come.

Unfortunately, affairs here culminated in the murder of a most promising young officer, Captain W. L. Marshall, who after serving with much credit in a similar post in the Holy City of Kadhimain was selected for the difficult charge at Najaf on account of his special qualifications and experience.

At the time of this tragedy I myself was on my way to Cairo to attend a conference regarding Arab affairs. Our deliberations ranged over all the problems in which we in Mesopotamia and they in the Hejaz were mutually interested. While there I received a summons to proceed on to London for the discussion of various current questions connected with Mesopotamia, and again, while en route back to Bagdad, I was directed to make a further diversion to Simla to confer with the Government of India. On arrival there I learnt that His Majesty's Minister at Teheran, Sir Charles Marling, who for months past had been having an extremely harassing time in the endeavour to combat Turko-German activities in Persia and the lively pressure which they were exercising upon the Persian Government, had been ordered home on sick leave and that it was desired that I should relieve him.

During the 20-odd months that I spent as British representative at Teheran events had continued to move apace in Mesopotamia. In fact, at the time I left Bagdad both General Allenby and General Marshall were on the point of launching their respective autumn campaigns. In Palestine the former's forces were concentrating in the coastal plain and on September 19th commenced those brilliant operations which resulted in the destruction of the Turkish Army, and the occupation of Damascus and Aleppo.

In Iraq, Sir William Marshall opened his campaign on the 23rd

October, determining to combine a frontal attack on the Turkish position across the Tigris at the Fatha Gorge with the advance of a column simultaneously from Kifri, with the object of threatening the Turkish communications. With such success were his plans crowned that by the 30th October the greater part of the opposing force had surrendered and the pursuit of the remainder was in active progress; we were within 12 miles of Mosul the following day when news of the Armistice reached the Commander-in-Chief. Two days later Mosul itself was occupied.

There has been a disposition in some quarters to suggest that having regard to the pronouncement made to the inhabitants by Sir Stanley Maude on our entry into Bagdad, under instructions from home, and to the Anglo-French declaration promulgated by his successor Sir William Marshall in November 1918, alluding respectively to the realisation of the 'natural aspirations of the noble Arabs' and 'the establishment of national government' that, on the conclusion of the Armistice, some prompt nationalization of the administration should have been attempted.

This argument is plausible in theory, and had the settlement of the Peace terms followed closely on the heels of the Armistice it might have been feasible in practice; but the actual course of events was far otherwise.

The work of peace proceeded very slowly; six months had already elapsed before the Terms to be imposed on Turkey were even discussed. It was not until May 1920 that, as the result of the San Remo Conference, the allocation of the Mandate for Mesopotamia to Great Britain was made known, and even this announcement remained inoperative until confirmed in August 1920 by the Treaty of Sévres, destined in turn never to be ratified.

A vast tract of country from Mosul to the Persian Gulf now lay under our civil administration and it would have been nothing short of dangerous, apart from the mere loss of efficiency involved, to embark upon any drastic change in the structure of that administration while the situation was so fluid. I emphasize this aspect of the question because when disturbances arose later there was a disposition, as is so often the case when arrangements do not work quite 'according to plan', to confuse incidental phases of the unrest with its fundamental causes.

By the end of the war the people of Mesopotamia had come to accept the fact of our occupation and were resigned to the prospect of a permanent British administration; some, especially in Basrah and the neighbourhood, even looked forward with satisfaction to a future in which they would be able to pursue their commerce and agriculture with a strong central authority to preserve peace and order. Throughout the country there was a conviction, which frequently found open expression, that the British meant well by the Arabs and this was accompanied by a frank appreciation of the increased prosperity which had followed in the track of our armies and, no doubt, by a lively sense of favours to come, in the way of progress and reform. But with the Armistice, and the Anglo-French declaration by which it was immediately followed, a new turn was given to the native mind. In Bagdad, where political ambitions are more highly developed than elsewhere in Iraq, within a week of the publication of the Declaration the idea of an Arab Amir for Iraq was everywhere being discussed and in Mohammedan circles met with universal approval, though there was no consensus of opinion as to who should fill the role.

Meanwhile, as acting Minister in Persia, I was naturally absorbed in the heavy duties of my own sphere and had not fully realised the turn which matters were taking in Iraq. I was the more surprised therefore to receive a telegram one morning from H.M.'s Foreign Office informing me that it was desired that I should return to my post in Mesopotamia; but that I was to come first to London. On 10th June my wife and I left Teheran, reaching Bagdad four days later. There we stayed with Colonel Wilson for two days and I was able to learn from him and from Gertrude Bell the latest developments of the situation. A few days previously, on the 2nd June, Colonel Wilson had interviewed a self-appointed Committee of 15 Bagdadis, which had been formed to voice opposition to the Mandate and had asked to be allowed to lay their views before the Civil Commissioner. An announcement was accordingly drafted and was sent to the leading delegates on the 20th June. It stated that Mesopotamia was to be constituted an independent state under the guarantee of the League of Nations and subject to the Mandate of Great Britain, and that Sir Percy Cox was to return in the autumn to establish a provisional Arab Government, pending preparation of a permanent organic law. But alas, by now the fuse of disaffection had burnt too close to the powder, and probably nothing could have prevented the explosion. On 2nd July the tribesmen at Rumaithah, in the lower Euphrates area, broke into open revolt.

By the time I reached London a few days later, the public at home were thoroughly disturbed at the turn things were taking in Iraq.

Asked for my opinion as the officer on the spot, I replied that to my mind evacuation was unthinkable; it would mean the abandonment of the Mandate and of the seven or eight millions' worth of capital assets which we had in the country; the complete violation of all the promises we had made to the Arabs during the war, and their inevitable re-subjection to chaos and the hated yoke of the Turk as soon as we left; and lastly that an evacuation, which would arouse the active resentment of the betrayed inhabitants, could only be carried out without bloodshed if at least another division were sent to see it safely through. As to whether the alternative policy of establishing forthwith a national Government had a reasonable chance of success, I replied that without being too confident, I thought it had, and that the risk was at any rate worth taking if regarded as the only alternative to evacuation. Considerable discussion followed, but ultimately I was asked whether if this course was decided upon I was prepared to undertake the task. I replied in the affirmative and left for Bagdad with my instructions by the next mail. The task before me was by no means an easy or attractive one. The new line of policy which I had come to inaugurate involved a complete and necessarily rapid transformation of the façade of the existing administration from British to Arab and, in the process, a wholesale reduction in the numbers of British and British-Indian personnel employed. But fortifying myself with the conviction that the project had at least an even chance of success, and was at any rate the only alternative to evacuation, I took heart of grace. My position, however, was a very solitary one to begin with, and the presence of Gertrude Bell and of Mr Philby and Mr C. C. Garbett, both of the I.C.S., whom I had brought out with me from home, was a great asset to me at this time. A year later I had to part company with Mr Philby because at the stage of development at which we had then arrived his conception of the policy of H.M.'s Government began to diverge too much from mine, but I none the less readily recognize the great value he was to me in the early days.

Though the back of the rebellion was practically broken by the time I reached Basrah, a good many sections of the tribes in the Basrah Vilayet were still 'out', and it was not until February that the rising could be said to have been finally cleared up. Meanwhile, it did not take me long after my arrival at Bagdad to realize that I was being confronted at every turn with questions of policy affecting the future of Iraq which I did not feel justified in disposing of myself without consultation with the representatives of the people. As an immediate expedient, therefore, I determined to institute at once a Provisional Government which, under my control and supervision, should be responsible for the administration and political guidance of the country until the general situation had returned to normal and a start could be made with the creation of national institutions. It was here that I felt that my venerable friend the Naqib, or Chief Noble, of Bagdad, who had given me such friendly co-operation on our first occupation of Bagdad, could now – if he would – render great and patriotic service, and I decided to appeal to him to preside over the proposed Council of State. Age and failing health might well have excused him from emerging from the studious seclusion of a Darwish in which he had preferred to spend the latter years of his life, but on 23rd October when I appealed to him, in the interests of his country, to shoulder the task, he courageously rose to the occasion, though with no little hesitation, and agreed to undertake the formation of a Cabinet.

In the meanwhile, in connection with the new departure of policy in Iraq, the control of its destinies had been transferred from the India Office to the Colonial Office, of which Mr Winston Churchill had now assumed the portfolio on transfer from the War Office. He determined to summon a conference at Cairo early in March, which I, among other British representatives in this region, was bidden to attend.

It was clear that the main questions which would have to be threshed out at the conference would be the reduction of the present heavy expenditure; the qualifications of the various possible candidates for the throne of Iraq; the treatment of the Kurdish provinces; and the nature and composition of the force to be created for the defence of the new State in the future.

As regards the question of expenditure, if my memory serves me right, the figure for the past year had been 37 millions sterling, whereas the Commander-in-Chief and I had come prepared with a draft scheme providing for reduction forthwith to 20 millions, with a progressive annual reduction thereafter, until the irreducible minimum should be reached.

As to the second question, it was easiest to arrive at a result by the process of elimination. My experience of public feeling on the question in Iraq had convinced me that among the several local candidates whose names had been suggested from time to time there was no individual who would be accepted or even tolerated by all parties in Iraq, while among the non-Iraqi possibilities there was no doubt whatever that one of the family of the Sherif of Mecca (King Hussein of the Hejaz) would command the most general if not the universal support of the inhabitants. It is common knowledge that the Amir Faisal won the ballot.

On 18th August the Ministry of the Interior informed His Highness the Naqib, as President of the Council, that an overwhelming majority of the people supported the Amir Faisal's election, and accordingly on 23rd August in the presence of representatives of all local communities and deputations from every Liwa in Iraq, except Sulaimaniyeh and Kirkuk, I proclaimed His Highness the Amir Faisal to have been duly elected King of Iraq and at the same time announced his recognition as King by His Britannic Majesty's Government.

But it was an insecure and troubled heritage on which the new King of Iraq had entered. On the north the Turks, though theoretically the position was one of prolonged armistice, pending conclusion of peace, were in fact clearly hostile. On the desert frontier of Iraq to the south-west, the bedouin tribes had since the early part of 1921 been in a continual state of unrest as the result of the operations of the Sultan of Nejd against his enemy Ibn Rashid and the Shammar tribes of Hayil. In the following March a serious attack took place by a strong raiding party of Ibn Saud's 'Akhwan', as the Wahabis now style themselves, upon a harmless encampment of pastoral nomads guarded by a detachment of the Iraq Camel Corps, some 30 miles south of the railway line and near the provisional frontier.

Unfortunately the episode took place at a moment when a serious divergence of view already existed between the British and the Iraq Governments as to the precise nature of their relations with one another. It was extraordinary with what aversion the mandatory idea had always been regarded in Iraq. The mere terms 'Mandatory' and 'Mandate' were anathema to them from the first.

The anti-mandate agitation gained impetus and continued throughout the summer. In June, a vigorous campaign started in the Arab Press; symptoms of disorder again began to appear on the Euphrates, while the collection of revenue dropped to vanishing point, and though at the end of June the Council of Ministers accepted the treaty, it was with the characteristic reservation that it should not be ratified until agreed to by the forthcoming Constituent Assembly. The month of August was marked by the formation of two extremist political parties, and on the 16th of that month the whole of the existing moderate Cabinet, unable to keep the extremist elements within bounds, resigned, with the exception of the Naqib, who retained his post as Prime Minister in the hope of preventing a landslide.

Meanwhile the extremist elements proclaimed that a new Cabinet was to be formed out of their number, under the presidency of a certain religious firebrand, and a joint manifesto was published in the vernacular papers demanding that the British element in the administration should be entirely eliminated.

It was in such a highly charged atmosphere that on a stifling day in August I proceeded officially to the Palace to offer my congratulations to His Majesty on this the first anniversary of his accession, and just before entering the building was treated to an anti-mandate demonstration by what proved to be a small packed crowd. I took immediate steps to demand an apology, which was accorded, but at the same moment it was announced that King Faisal had been struck down by a sudden and dangerous attack of appendicitis, necessitating an immediate operation and involving his complete insulation from the affairs of State for some time to come. I was thus faced with a unique if critical situation. The Cabinet had resigned; the King was incapacitated; the Bagdad Vilayet and the Euphrates tribes were on the verge of rebellion to all appearances likely to be not less serious than that of 1920 and organized by the same elements. The Turks at the same moment, with their prestige greatly increased by their defeat of the Greeks, were in Rowandus and Rania and were threatening Sulaimaniyeh. No authority was in fact left in the country except my own as High Commissioner and I felt bound to use it to the full. Accordingly a proclamation was at once issued explaining the situation and stating that the emergent measures which were being taken did not portend any change in the settled policy of H.M.'s Government. At the same time all friendly and moderate persons who had the welfare of their country at heart were called upon to rally to the side of the High Commissioner and resist irresponsible agitators. The ringleaders were forthwith arrested, the two new extremist parties closed down and certain mischievous papers suppressed. At the same time the two Persian divines who had been responsible for the anti-foreign manifestoes were advised to repair to their own homeland for the benefit of their health, while some of the Arab officials on the Lower Euphrates who by their intrigues had fostered the disaffection were dismissed or transferred.

The effect of these measures was instantaneous; and except for a few isolated acts of defiance and the chronic unrest in the Kurdish districts which continued for some time to respond to Turkish propaganda and incitement, the whole of Iraq proper was quiet by 10th September. On that date King Faisal was reported strong enough to give me an interview, whereat he thanked me cordially for the action taken during the interregnum.

With the restoration of the King's health, the moment had come for the instalment of a new Cabinet, which the Naqib had succeeded in forming by the end of September 1922. Difficulties with regard to the Treaty and the Mandate had by now been cleared away in correspondence with the Secretary of State, and on 10th October His Highness the Naqib and I signed the Treaty of Alliance between Great Britain and Iraq, which was published on 13th October, together with a proclamation by His Majesty King Faisal to his people expressing this profound satisfaction with the event. The period for which this, the original Treaty, was to run was twenty years, and during the long negotiations which led up to it, nothing less than fifteen years was ever discussed, but, as the sequel shows, the period was destined to be considerably curtailed.

With the near approach of the first Lausanne Conference, Turkish propaganda, suggesting the intended restoration of Iraq to Turkey, grew stronger and stronger and had considerable effect both on the Sheikhs of the Euphrates and the inhabitants of northern Iraq. The King's Irade on 21st October ordering elections for the Constituent Assembly, which was to accept the Treaty and pass an Organic Law laying down the Constitution, was countered by a 'fatwah' or religious decree countersigned by some disaffected divines of Karbala and Kadhimain, forbidding participation in the elections.

It was now realized that a more vigorous line of action on the part of the Iraq Government was needed to cope with these adverse forces, and the venerable Naqib who had remained at the helm of affairs so gallantly through so many changes of weather felt that the time had come when he could resign the ship of state to the command of a younger man, and he was succeeded by Abdul Muhsin Bey, who reconstructed the Cabinet.

At this juncture a change of Government took place in England which profoundly affected the future in Iraq. The Coalition Government under which the Iraq Treaty had been framed and signed had resigned on 23rd October, ten days after its signature, and the question of Iraq became a prominent plank in the course of the General Election which followed; a fierce newspaper campaign being conducted against the expenditure of British money in the country and several members of the new House of Commons pledging themselves to work for its evacuation by the British at the earliest moment. As a consequence, a Cabinet Committee was set up in London in December 1922 to decide upon the future of Iraq. Meanwhile the Treaty lately signed, with its twenty years' duration clause, had not been ratified, while at the first Lausanne Conference the Turkish delegates had resolutely refused to entertain any idea of the Mosul Vilayet remaining with Iraq, or to refer the Turco-Iraq frontier question to the League.

It was of course open to Great Britain to refuse to ratify the Treaty, and thus for four months Iraq remained in dire suspense (flooded all the time with Turkish propaganda) as to whether she would not after all be handed back to Turkey.

I was called home to attend the deliberations of this conference, and Sir Henry Dobbs, having in the meanwhile arrived, on appointment as Counsellor to the High Commissioner, with the prospect of succeeding me at the end of my term, I left for London on 19th January 1923, leaving him in charge.

I returned from my mission on 31st March, bringing with me the results of the deliberations of H.M.'s new Government.

In compiling this condensed narrative of the period of our association, it has not been possible for me to allude repeatedly to the great degree to which Gertrude Bell enjoyed my confidence and I her devoted co-operation, a co-operation which I know from my successor she rendered with the same singleness of purpose to him. Her letters will tell their own story.

P. Z. C.

By H.E. Sir Henry Dobbs, K.C.S.I., etc., High Commissioner for the Iraq.

On taking up the work of High Commissioner in January 1923, I found that all hope of holding an early election for the Constituent Assembly had vanished, while the Turkish threat on the north was growing more insistent. The first Lausanne Conference was on the verge of collapse. In Sulaimaniyeh the newly restored Sheikh Mahmud was already showing signs of revolt.

Sir Percy Cox returned on the 31st March 1923, bringing with him the result of the deliberations of the British Government in the shape of a draft protocol to the Treaty of Alliance. The Protocol cut down the period of the Treaty from twenty years to a maximum of four years from the date of ratification of peace with Turkey, and provided that, if before the lapse of that maximum period, Iraq became a member of the League of Nations, the Treaty should terminate immediately. The Protocol was signed on 20th April 1923. The more far-seeing people feared that the reduced period was too short to enable Iraq to stand upon her own feet, and the so-called pro-British sections of the population, especially some of the Euphrates tribes, the inhabitants of Basrah and the Assyrians of Mosul, professed to regard this reduction as a betrayal of their interests. But the politicians of Bagdad and Mosul welcomed it with enthusiasm, and even King Faisal and his Ministers, while expressing constant gratitude for the support and favours received in the past, were undisguisedly delighted that a near term had been put to authoritative control by Great Britain of their affairs.

Sir Percy Cox left Iraq at the beginning of May 1923 amid spontaneous demonstrations of affection and regret from all classes of the population. During his absence in London I had in January 1923 taken steps to restore general confidence in the face of Turkish threats. For this purpose a force, composed partly of British and partly of Iraq troops, moved up to Mosul. His Highness the Amir Zaid, the brother of King Faisal, who had arrived in Iraq in November 1922, took up his residence at Mosul to initiate political measures for winning over Kurdish sentiment to the Iraq side. He also superintended the formation of a force of Arab tribal irregulars to operate, if need be, against invaders of the plains to the west of Mosul. Plans for a Kurdish rising with the co-operation of Sheikh Mahmud of Sulaimaniyeh came to light. To forestall such a combination, Sheikh Mahmud's headquarters were bombed from the air, and he took to the mountains.

The frontiers having been strengthened and the Turkish menace for the time staved off, the field was free to deal with the agitation of the reactionary Shiah divines against the election for the Constituent Assembly. By July 1923 their demeanour towards King Faisal and towards the Iraq Government had become intolerably arrogant, and King Faisal saw no other way than to authorize the deportation of their leader, Sheikh Mahdi at Khalisi.

King Faisal had during this period made a progress throughout the whole country for the purpose of explaining his policy and exhorting the people to take part in the elections, and I followed shortly afterwards in his steps, so that the people were left in no doubt as to the identity of purpose of the British and Iraq Governments. The registration of primary electors was finally completed by 16th December 1923, secondary elections began on 25th February 1924, and all results were declared by the middle of March 1924.

The late summer and autumn of 1923 were marked by the growing tension between Iraq and Ibn Saud, consequent partly on raids carried out upon Nejd territory by the Shammar who had taken refuge in Iraq when Ibn Saud took Hail in 1921. Finally a conference was arranged at Kuwait under the Presidency of Colonel Knox, lately Acting Resident in the Persian Gulf, to decide outstanding questions not only between Nejd and Iraq, but also between Nejd and Hejaz and Trans-Jordan. It met on 17th December 1923 and was in a fair way to achieve some settlement, at all events between Iraq and Nejd, when on 14th March 1924 a very serious raid by Akhwan, not less than 2,000 strong, was carried out upon the Iraq frontier nomads, 186 persons, men, women and children being killed, and 26,000 sheep and 3,700 donkeys being captured. This aroused such indignation in Iraq that the conference had to be abandoned.

In the meantime the Cabinet of Abdul Mushin Beg had resigned on 16th November 1923 as a consequence of differences of opinion with His Majesty King Faisal, leaving the subsidiary agreements incomplete. Jafar Pasha had succeeded him as Prime Minister and concluded the discussion of the Agreements subsidiary to the Treaty. They were signed on the 25th March 1924. The whole Instrument of Alliance was thus ready for submission to the Constituent Assembly, which was opened by His Majesty King Faisal on 27th March 1924.

On the 20th April 1924 the Committee of the Assembly, appointed to study the Treaty and Agreements, presented a report containing some able criticism. Agitation against the Treaty, which had already led to the attempted assassination of two pro-Treaty deputies, increased, and it became clear that, without some assurance regarding future financial treatment, there was little hope of passing the Treaty. Finally, His Britannic Majesty's Government gave an undertaking that, after ratification, they would reconsider the financial obligations of Iraq. This somewhat eased the situation, but also in some quarters increased the expectation of further British concessions and the anti-Treaty agitation continued. His Britannic Majesty's Government therefore resolved to put an end to a tension which was becoming dangerous by bringing the Iraq Mandate before the League of Nations at the session of June 1924, and announced that, if the Iraq Assembly had reached no decision by 10th June, this would be taken as a rejection of the Treaty. As a result the Constituent Assembly accepted the Treaty and Agreements shortly before midnight on the 10th June, stating in a rider to their resolution that they did so in reliance on the assurance that, after ratification, the British Government would 'amend with all possible speed the Financial Agreement in the spirit of generosity and sympathy for which the British people are famous'.

After disposing of the Treaty the Constituent Assembly proceeded to the consideration of the Organic Law and the Electoral Law, which were passed, the first on 10th July and the second on 2nd August 1924.

In Article 3 of the Treaty of Lausanne it had been provided that the frontier between Turkey and Iraq should be laid down in friendly agreement to be concluded between Turkey and Great Britain within nine months, and that, in the event of no agreement being reached, the dispute should be referred to the Council of the League of Nations. Pending the decision, the two Governments had undertaken that no military or other movement should take place which might modify in any way the present state of the territories in question. During May and the first week of June 1924, Sir Percy Cox had carried on in Constantinople fruitless negotiations with the Turkish Government on the frontier question. The Turks had been adamant in their demand for the whole Mosul Vilayet, and their intransigence had probably been encouraged by the reports from Bagdad that the Iraq Constituent Assembly was about to reject the Treaty with Great Britain. On 9th June 1924, the day before the Iraq Assembly accepted the Anglo-Iraq treaty, the Constantinople negotiations had broken down.

At the beginning of September 1924 the Turks concentrated troops for the invasion of the Assyrian area, and on the 14th they crossed the River Haizil into what was undoubtedly Iraq territory. They were met by an attack from the air and driven back and thereafter diverted their march to the north through the territory of the Sindi Guli Kurds (still Iraq territory), through which they moved and laid waste the Assyrian country, driving the Assyrians, some 8,000 in number, down into the valley of Amadia, where they had to be supported by the Iraq Government.

Ultimately the Turks agreed before the League to preserve the *status quo* until the frontier was decided. A preliminary dispute as to the line of the *status quo* was settled by a special meeting of the League at Brussels in October 1924, and this provisional line has since been known as the 'Brussels line'.

The Frontier Commission, consisting of three Commissioners, eminent subjects of Sweden, Belgium, and Hungary, reached Bagdad in January 1925, and spent three months in examining the frontier.

One of the chief matters of concern to the Frontier Commission appeared to be the future of the Christians of Mosul, and especially of the Nestorians or Assyrians who, as narrated above, were at the time of the visit of the Commission refugees in Iraq territory. They had revolted against Turkey in 1916, at the instigation of Russia, and then, being deserted by the Russians after the revolution, had fought their way through Persian territory to a junction with the British troops, losing two-thirds of their number in the process.

They were united in a determination never again to submit themselves to Turkish rule. In order to reassure them as to their future, two successive Iraq Cabinets, those of Jafar Pasha and of Yasin Pasha, officially pledged the Government of Iraq to provide lands in Iraq for those Assyrians who might be dispossessed of their original homes by the decision of the League of Nations. It can hardly be doubted that this liberal attitude on the part of the Government of Iraq had its influence on the deliberations of the Frontier Commission. The Commission terminated its labours in the third week of March 1925.

On 21st March 1925, on the eve of the departure of the Commission, the Organic Law was officially promulgated amid widespread rejoicings, and orders were given for the completion of the new lists of primary electors and for the commencement of the parliamentary elections.

While the elections were in progress the Secretary of State for the Colonies despatched to Iraq a Financial Mission to enquire into the financial position and prospects of Iraq. Another factor in the favourable situation was the visit to Iraq in the first half of April 1925 of the Right Honourable L. S. Amery, Secretary of State for the Colonies, and of the Right Honourable Sir Samuel Hoare, Secretary of State for Air.

The First Iraq Parliament met on 16th July 1925, and was opened by King Faisal. Thus Iraq had in July 1925 attained the first stage of her development. She had accepted, through her representatives, a Treaty of Alliance with Great Britain; she had passed an Organic Law and set up a stable and constitutional

Government under it. It only remained for her frontiers to be fixed according to the decision of the League of Nations before she could apply for admission to the League of Nations and take on the full status of an independent state.

In August 1925 the report of the Frontier Commission was published.

In January 1925 a protest had been lodged with the Turkish Government through His Britannic Majesty's representative in Constantinople, against violation of the *status quo* boundary line by a band under Turkish instigation, and in June enquiries were addressed by His Majesty's Government to the Turkish Government as to the reason for the large concentration of troops in the area north of the Iraq frontier, since it had been officially declared that the Kurdish rebellion had been suppressed. At the same time reports began to come in that the Turks were taking vengeance on the Christians and Kurds of Goyan, who had testified to the Frontier Commission their desire to be included in Iraq, and some 500 refugees arrived at Zakho. Early in September, reports began to be received of atrocities committed on Chaldean villages north and also south of the provisional frontier. The villagers, though they had never taken part against Turkey during the war, were being systematically removed from the neighbourhood of the frontier and transported into the interior, but many escaped, in a pitiable state of destitution, and reached Zakho with tales of massacre and violence. The Iraq Ministry of the Interior placed a sum of money at the disposal of the Mutasarrif of Mosul for the relief of these unfortunate people. Mr Amery brought the matter in strong terms before the Council of the League at the meeting in September 1925, the Turkish delegate equally hotly denied the accusations; and the Secretary of State requested the Council to send an impartial commission to report on the matter and also on charges and counter-charges as to the violation of the provisional frontier. The Council entrusted the task to a distinguished Estonian, General Laidoner, and the Commission arrived on 26th October. The Turkish Government refused to allow General Laidoner to pursue enquiries north of the 'Brussels' line, so that the Commission had access to such evidence only as could be gathered within Iraq territory. Immediately before its arrival the refugee camps were visited by the General Secretary of the Friends of Armenia Society, who satisfied himself that the Iraq authorities were diligent in their efforts to succour the refugees, but that owing to their number and their desperate plight, help from outside was required. He sent telegrams to various Christian societies and communities, and a committee was formed in London to collect funds, which were despatched to the High Commissioner and distributed through a committee of three British officers well acquainted with conditions on the frontier. In December, Colonel Fergusson, a member of the King's Bodyguard, was sent out by the British Committee to administer all monies collected.

In the League Council decision, which was published in Bagdad on 17th December 1925, the Council unanimously held that the Turco-Iraq frontier should be the 'Brussels' line on condition that Great Britain undertook by means of a new treaty with Iraq to continue her present relations with Iraq for a period of twenty-five years, unless before the expiry of that period Iraq were admitted to membership of the League. The Turkish delegate refused to recognize the arbitral authority of the League Council and was not present at the meeting. All through Iraq there was a general sense of deep relief, and of hope that the stability thus attained would be reflected in the prosperity which the country would now be able to achieve.

After considerable discussion, the text of the new Treaty as approved by the British Government reached Bagdad on 27th December 1925.

By a Treaty between Great Britain, Iraq, and Turkey in June 1926, Turkey recognized the existing frontier or 'Brussels' line, subject to one very slight variation, and Turkey and Iraq entered into mutual obligations of 'bon voisinage'. On the 14th June the two chambers of the Iraq Parliament accepted the Treaty and King Faisal immediately ratified it. On the 25th June the King gave a State banquet to celebrate the signing of the Treaty, at which His Majesty expressed his profound thanks to the British Government and its representatives for all that they had done for Iraq. Miss Gertrude Bell was one of the most prominent of the guests at this banquet, and shared conspicuously in the general atmosphere of congratulation which marked the close of the first stage in the existence of Iraq. It was the last State function which she attended.

CHAPTER 19

1920

Bagdad

To H. B.   *Sunday, 17th Oct., 1920.*

I must try and give you an account of this remarkable week. Sir Percy arrived on Monday, 11th, at Bagdad West. When we got to the station, about 4.30, his train being due at 5.30, we found a sort of reception room, flagged and carpeted, with the railed off approach to the line.... I was told to go into the reception room, where gradually there collected some 20 or 30 Magnates of Bagdad... the C. in C. with his staff, the heads of the departments and officers of Sir Percy's H.Q. here. The salute of 17 guns was fired outside the town, and the wind being contrary we didn't hear it, so that quite suddenly we were told the train was in sight, and we hurriedly took up our positions in the railed off space; on the right Sir Edgar with the heads of departments and me, next to us the consuls, then the religious heads, on the left the C. in C. with his staff, Saiyid Talib and the deputies, the mayor and one or two magnates, such as the eldest son of the Naqib. Outside the enclosure was a crowd of people, British officers and their wives and a lot of others whom I couldn't distinguish – more of these later. It was near sunset when the train drew up and the C. in C. went forward to greet Sir Percy. He came out dressed in white uniform, and after shaking hands with the C. in C. stood at the salute while the band played 'God save the King'. I thought as he stood there in his white and gold lace, with his air of fine and simple dignity that there had never been an arrival more momentous – never anyone on whom more conflicting emotions were centred, hopes and doubts and fears, but above all confidence in his personal integrity and wisdom.... When he came into the enclosure Sir Edgar presented me, while I made my curtsey, it was all I could do not to cry.

Lady Cox, Mr Philby and Captain Cheesman (the latter is Sir Percy's private secretary) had got out of the train by this time, and we had all exchanged warm greetings. Lady Cox stepped out after ten hours of dusty journey, looking as if she had emerged from the finest bandbox – a miracle, as we told her. Then we all drove to Sir Percy's house....

It is quite impossible to tell you the relief and comfort it is to serve under somebody in whose judgment one has complete confidence. To the extraordinarily difficult task which lies before him he brings a single-eyed desire to act in the interests of the people of the country....

With that we all dined with the C. in C. I sat by Sir Percy and had a most enjoyable dinner in spite of the fact that I was sitting in a raging draught. I forget if I told you that I've got bronchitis. Well, I have, and I don't see much chance of curing it. However, that's a minor consideration.

Next morning I went early to the office. Sir Percy called me up at once and we talked over some telegrams – I trying to conceal the fact that it was a wholly novel experience to be taken into confidence on matters of importance! No sooner had I got to my office than I began to receive letters and visitors, each more indignant than the last, saying that the whole town was in an uproar over the reception ceremony because the notables had been invited and were herded together, all but a very small number, in the dust outside the enclosure and hadn't even had the opportunity of shaking Sir Percy by the hand. 'We came in love and obedience,' said a really furious old sheikh of distinction, 'and when we tried to get near His Excellency we were pushed away.' Even the brothers of the Naqib had been treated with this same lack of ceremony....

So I decided at once to invest myself with the duties of Oriental secretary, there being no one else in the office who knows Bagdad, and calling in Mr Philby for help we drafted a form of invitation to all the notables of Bagdad for the following morning. It was almost lunch time before we got hold of Sir Percy, but meantime I had prepared the list of names – over 100 – and drawn up also a small list of people

to whom he ought to give private interviews. He approved
everything and gave me a free hand ... and we had the invitations out that evening. It still makes me hot and cold to
think what would have happened if we hadn't tackled the
situation promptly, for there wasn't a single person in
authority who was thinking of the Arab side of the matter
and of how supremely important it was that Sir Percy should
be put into immediate personal touch with the town.

Next morning we had our reception – a huge success. The
space in Sir Percy's room being rather limited I had sent
out the invitations in 3 batches, leaving half an hour between each batch. We seated about 30 people at a time in
Sir Percy's room and had them in 4 relays; those who were
waiting were entertained by Mr Philby and me in the waiting room next door to Sir Percy. But I went in with one of
the batches and saw how well it was going, with all the
people sitting round and being properly served with coffee
and cigarettes, while Sir Percy explained his programme
and asked their opinions.

On Thursday evening after Sir Percy had laid his definite
selection of Arab Ministers before Mr Philby and me, I got
him to meet the rest of our group – Major Murray, Major
Yetts and Capt. Clayton, and we had a most satisfactory
talk. I wanted him to realize that these were the men who
would work heart and soul with him, and it didn't take him
long to find it out. At the end he told Mr Philby to submit to
him a scheme for his own secretariat. This is the most thorny
of all questions, because it is the personal one. We think he
ought to have a complete secretariat at the Residency, Civil
Secretary, Political Secretary, Military Secretary and Private Secretary....

I have kept religiously out of the controversy, the more
readily because I feel perfectly certain that Sir Percy will go
his own way. They were as bitterly opposed to an Arab
Cabinet, but Sir Percy had gone straight through. He knows
there is no alternative, and having made up his mind, nothing moves him. His direct simplicity is beyond all wonder
... it's still like a dream to find all things one has thought

ought to be done, being done without question. I feel equally sure that when it comes to the difficult point of dealing with the tribal insurgents on the Euphrates he will drop all the silly ideas of revenge and punishment which have been current ... and be guided only by consideration for the future peace of the country under an Arab Govt. The first question is whom to call on to form a Cabinet? Most of the people he has seen have suggested the Naqib, and I think he will make an attempt in that direction to-morrow. I am convinced not only that the Naqib will refuse for himself, but that he will also refuse to recommend anyone....

The object of the provisional cabinet is merely that it should prepare for and hold the first general election. As soon as you get an elective body, that body chooses its own official representatives and the provisional govt. vanishes. While a good third of the country is still in open rebellion, it's obvious that you can't hold a general election, yet it's equally obvious, as Sir Percy sees, that you can't delay in setting up some form of native institutions. They all expect that he will do something at once, and if he doesn't the golden opportunity will be lost and confidence shaken.

To H. B.   BAGDAD, *Oct. 24th, 1920.*

I mentioned bronchitis last week – well, it's won and I've spent the last six days in my house and partly in bed. As a result of which I'm now very nearly all right. In a way I'm not sorry, tiresome as it was to be laid up, to have been removed from the fierce personal controversies of which the echoes have reached me, and the inhabitants of Bagdad have seen to it that I've not been removed from the political crisis. For they have been at all hours by my side.... On the plea of enquiring after my health they have sat on my sofa – the big Persian sofa in my dining-room which has arrived since you left – and poured out their hopes and fears. I made an attempt to close my doors up to 11 a.m. but it wasn't very successful. When the Mayor of Bagdad rolled up at 9 or the Naqib sent his son Saiyid Mahmud I was obliged to 'endosser' dressing-gown and go out to see them.

On Thursday Sir Percy sent round a message to say that he had called a council of state for that afternoon in my house, since I couldn't come to the office. They assembled at three o'clock, Sir Percy, Evelyn Howell, Mr Philby, Mr Bullard, Sir Edgar and Col. Slater. Then followed three hours of poignantly interesting discussion for Sir Percy produced his scheme for a provisional cabinet, Arab Ministers and British Advisors. ... Finally he carried his scheme through with unimportant alterations, and announced that he was now going to lay it before the Naqib.

Saturday began with a notable visit from Jafar Pasha. He is the Major-General of distinguished service first with the Turks and then with Faisal. Jafar is the first of the Mesopotamians to return from Syria, and on his attitude much will depend....

Saiyid Hussain Afnan came in. I had just embarked on a heart to heart talk with Saiyid Hussain about some leading articles which he proposed to publish in his paper, when in came Mr Philby and others, and on top of them Sir Percy. Everyone but Mr Philby melted away, and we two turned to Sir Percy, breathless with excitement. 'Well,' he said, 'he has accepted.' He had come straight from the Naqib who had agreed to undertake the formation of the provisional govt. So the first success is scored and no one but Sir Percy could have done it. Indeed, that even he should have induced the Naqib to take a hand in public affairs is nothing short of a miracle. Sir Percy's delight and satisfaction was only equal to ours and we all sat for half an hour bubbling over with joy and alternately glorifying the Naqib and the High Commissioner.

To H. B.   BAGDAD, *November 1st, 1920.*

We have had a very critical week, but on the whole things are going as well as could be hoped. On Monday night the Naqib's letters and telegrams to the 18 people whom he invited to form the Council of State were prepared. That night I dined with Capt. Clayton and Major Murray to meet Jafar Pasha. It was an amazing evening.

The man is an idealist with a high purpose, animated by fervour for his race and country…. When we parted that evening I did not think he would refuse the Naqib's invitation to join the Cabinet as Minister of Defence. Nor did he. … That day a number of acceptances came in. In the afternoon I gave a great tea-party in my garden to Fahad Bey and the Agail…. It was really splendid. Fahad Bey sat and told tales of the desert and ended by opening his robes and showing me a huge hole in his breast formed by a lance thrust into his back in a youthful raid. 'And I looked down and saw the head of the lance sticking out here.' No one but an Arab of the desert could have recovered…. On Wednesday morning all seemed to be going well. In the afternoon Major Yetts dropped in to tea with the Tods. Mr Tod sprang upon us that he had called on Sasun Eff. to congratulate him on his becoming Minister of Finance, and found him with Hamid Pasha Baban (who had been offered a seat in the Cabinet without portfolio) both in the act of refusing…. I left my cup of tea undrunk and rushed back to the office to tell Mr Philby. He wasn't there, but there was a light in Sir Percy's room. I went in and told him. He bade me go at once to Sasun Eff. and charged me to make him change his mind. I set off, feeling as if I carried the future of all Iraq in my hands, but when I got to Sasun's house, to my immense relief, I found Mr Philby and Capt. Clayton already there. The Naqib had got Sasun's letter and had sent Mr Philby off post haste. I arrived, however, in the nick of time. They had exhausted all their arguments, and Sasun still adhered to his decision. I think my immense anxiety must have inspired me, for after an hour of concentrated argument he was visibly shaken, in spite of the fact that his brother Shaul (whom also I admire and respect) came in and did his best against us…. We got Sasun Eff. to consent to think it over and see Sir Percy next day. I had an inner conviction that the game was won – partly, thank heaven, to the relations of trust and confidence which I had personally already established with Sasun – but we none of us could feel sure. I didn't sleep much that night. I turned and turned in my mind the arguments that I had used and wondered if I could not have done better.

Next morning, Thursday, Sasun Eff. came in at ten; I took him straight to Sir Percy and left them. Half an hour later he returned and told me that he had accepted. He asked me what he could now do to help and I sent him straight to the Naqib.

Oh, if we can pull this thing off; rope together the young hotheads and the Shiah obscurantists, and enthusiasts like Jafar, polished old statesmen like Sasun, and scholars like Shukri – if we can make them work together and find their own salvation for themselves, what a fine thing it would be. I see visions and dream dreams. I omitted to mention that the Council of State of the first Arab Govt. in Mesopotamia since the Abbassids meets to-morrow.

To H. B.   BAGDAD, *November 7th, 1920.*

This week has been comparatively uneventful. The Cabinet met for the first time on Tuesday.

After the Cabinet Meeting the Naqib sent for Fahad Bey and asked whether he would be prepared to take a message from the Cabinet to the Insurgent Tribes. Fahad came hotfoot in to me. 'Khatun,' he said, 'you I know and Kokus I know, but of Arab Governments I have no knowledge. Never will I give any answer to the Naqib till I'm assured that Kokus would approve.' I brought in Mr Philby and together we assured him. 'Oh, Khatun,' said he, 'Oh, Feelbi, on your heads you tell me that Kokus would approve.'

I couldn't help feeling that with such staunch allies as Fahad there was little fear that the influence of Kokus would not avail!

As soon as we can we must proceed to the election of a National Assembly. And I shall be very much mistaken (but then I often am) if they don't ask for the son of the Sharif as an Amir. I regard that as the only solution....

To H. B. and F. B.   BAGDAD, *November 22nd, 1920.*

My garden is a mass of chrysanthemums – brown and yellow and white and pink. It's very cold – the cold has come early – and the dogs have been obliged to wear last year's coats till Marie has time to make new ones, that will be after she has made a gown for me. They are disgracefully ragged and look like beggar dogs....

To H. B.   BAGDAD, *November 29th, 1920.*

We are greatly hampered by the tribal rising which has delayed the work of handing over to the Arab Govt. Sir Percy, I think rightly, decided that the tribes must be made to submit to force. In no other way was it possible to make them surrender their arms or teach them that you mustn't lightly engage in revolution, even when your holy men tell you to do so....

Yesterday Sir P. and I and Capt. Cheesman and Capt Pedder went out shooting on the river bank opposite Ctesiphon.... We had about 20 Arab beaters.

I love walking with the beaters and hearing what they say to each other in the broadest Iraq dialect which I'm proud to understand. Their clothes are amazingly unfitted for any job they're likely to undertake, especially struggling through thorns. They treat me with constant solicitous politeness, beat down the thorns with their bare feet so as to let me pass and bustle out of the way to give me the easiest place. You're not an Oriental for nothing....

To H. B.   BAGDAD, *December 12th, 1920.*

It is exactly three weeks since the last Mail came in. Do my letters arrive with any regularity? I write as you do every week. But this week there's not much to write about for I've been rather a poor thing with a chill. I stayed at home two days and then couldn't bear it any longer so I went back to the office.

The idea is to have 30 Tribal members in the election assembly, 20 being representatives of the 20 biggest tribes and the other ten one apiece for the small tribes grouped together in each of the new ten divisions. I have supplied the data to the Electoral Law Committee and selected the 20

Tribes. I don't think the Council will quarrel with my selection.

To H. B.   BAGDAD, *December 18th, 1920.*

The Council is aware and Sir Percy has constantly impressed upon them, the vital need of getting down to the formation of a native army to relieve ours. No Govt. in this country, whether ours or an Arab administration, can carry on without force behind it. The Arab Government has no force till its army is organized, therefore it can't exist unless we lend it troops. Mesopotamia is not a civilized state, it is largely composed of wild tribes who do not wish to shoulder the burden and expense of citizenship. That is why it needs force for the maintenance of internal order.

Meantime we've been busy with other matters. The early part of the week was devoted to the electoral law about which I wrote you last week. We were all agreed that it would be disastrous if the tribesmen were to swamp the townsmen, but I pressed upon them the consideration that whatever may have happened in Turkish times, an Arab National Govt. could not hope to succeed unless it ultimately contrived to associate the tribesmen with its endeavours. Jafar Pasha propounded the possible alternative of securing representation by divisions not by specified tribes. I said I thought that would meet the case excellently. Next morning he and Sasun returned with a revised scheme – 2 tribal representatives for each Division, but any tribesman who liked to register could vote in the ordinary way – first-rate proposal, for while it secures a minimum of ten tribal members in the assembly, it does not preclude tribesmen from taking part in elections like other registered electors – if they like.

This was finally carried in the afternoon's sitting.

To H. B.   BAGDAD, *December 25th, 1920.*

I must tell you a silly story, to understand which you must learn a little Turkish. There's an amusing idiom in Turkish by which you say 'such like' by repeating the original word, only changing its initial letter to 'M'.... We got recently an account of the conversation between the Sharif and an Arab of these parts – the latter told us the story. The Sharif was fuming against all and sundry: 'Who' he cried 'is this Kokus Mokus and this Philby Milby?' Sir Percy was delighted....

Bagdad

BAGDAD, *January 3rd, 1921.*

... Upon my soul I'm glad I don't know what this year is going to bring, I don't think I ever woke on a first of January with such feelings of apprehension. You can struggle through misfortune and failure, when they approach you slowly – you see them coming and gradually make up your mind to the inevitable. But if the future opened suddenly and you knew when you woke on the first of January all that lay before you it would be overwhelming. For the truth is there's little that promises well....

To H. B.   BAGDAD, *January 22nd, 1921.*

Talib seems to me to be doing very well. He put up to the Council the other day a long list of proposals for administration appointments in the provinces, Mutasarrifs and Kaimakams. It is very essential to get these appointments made so that people in the provinces may see Arab officials stepping in and realize that there is an Arab Government....

I've a feeling that we're making good progress. There's a greater sense of stability, the Arab Government is gaining ground and people begin to see that we really intend to do by it all we say.

We had to go to the funeral of the woman who was Matron in chief during the war and had come back here to help us with the organization of our civil hospital. I personally loved her for all her kindness to me, beginning from the time when I had jaundice in Basrah and not a soul to look after me. She was an angel of goodness, poor Miss Jones. And I hoped as I walked behind the Union Jack that covered her coffin that when people walked behind my coffin it would be with thoughts even dimly resembling those that I gave to her....

To H. B. BAGDAD, *Jan. 22nd, 1921.*

We have had a distracted week on account of the races. I didn't intend to go more than one day, but the first day, Thursday, Aurelia telephoned and said I must come so I went with them. There was a pretty good sprinkling of Bagdad Magnates and I thought it fairly amusing, so I went again to-day and was very much amused.... It was Cup Day, I must tell you; we didn't go till after lunch but the Coxes went in state at 11 a.m. and stayed the whole day. Sir Percy wore a frock coat and a grey top hat to the admiration of all beholders. I may mention that I was also very smart in a Paris hat and gown – it's really quite nice to dress up for once, a thing I haven't done for months....

To H. B. BAGDAD, *Jan. 30th, 1921.*

Do you know this is the eighth Xmas I've been away – 1913 Arabia, 1914 Boulogne, 1915 Egypt, 1916 Basrah and all the rest Bagdad. Extraordinary isn't it. . . .

The other event of the week besides the suppressing of the *Istiqbal*, is the arrival of an emissary from Ibn Saud. Ahmad Thanayan is a relation of the Imam and was with his son Faisal in England in 1919. He was brought up in Constantinople and even knows a little French. A very delicate ailing man of about 30, with the fine drawn Najd face, full of intelligence and drawn yet finer by ill health. He has with him Ibn Saud's doctor, Abdullah Ibn Said, a Mosuli by origin, educated in Constantinople ... and I had them to dinner to-night. It was the most interesting and curious dinner party I ever gave. Besides the two Najdis I had Major Eadie, Saiyid Muhi ud Din and Shukri Eff. al Arusi. The latter is one of the finest figures in Bagdad. An old scholar who comprises in himself all knowledge as such is understood by Islam – he teaches Mechanics, using the Hadith (traditions of the prophet) as text book and other sciences by like methods – a true Wahhabi, he neither drinks nor smokes, and he is the only known Mohammadan who has never married.... He found in Wahhabi Central Arabia the land of his dreams and looks upon it as the true source of all inspiration and learning. When he came in he fell on Ahmad Thanayan's neck while the latter fished among his beautiful embroidered cashmiri robes and produced from them a letter from Ibn Saud to Shukri. And to crown the cordiality of the gathering, Muhi ud Din discovered in the Doctor a former Constantinople acquaintance, and the embracing began afresh on their part. So we sat down to table – as queer a gathering as you could well see; Shukri, the unworldly old scholar, hanging on Ahmad Thanayan's words while the latter described the immense progress of the extreme Wahhabi sect, the Akhwan (brotherhood), in Najd; Mudi ud Din, the smooth politician and divine, ... and Ahmad with his long sunken face lighted up by the purest spirit of fanatical Islam. 'The Imam, God preserve him, under God has guided the tribes in the right way,' – 'Praise be to God,' ejaculated Shukri – 'They are learning wisdom and religion under the rules of the Brotherhood,' – Shukri Eff: 'God is great,' – 'Not that they show violence,' – 'Ahmed Effend. 'God forbid.' – 'No such things happen among us as happened in Europe with the Inquisition and with Calvins' – (I must tell you incidentally that the Akhwan when they do battle kill all wounded and then put the women and children of their enemies, who are also infidels else they wouldn't fight the Akhwan, to death...). After dinner my four Arab guests carried on a brisk conversation among themselves. They discussed medicines and the properties of herbs, the doctor, incidentally, stating that incense was a capital disinfectant, they discussed the climate and customs of Najd and other matters of importance. Major Eadie and I sat listening and I felt as if we were disembodied spirits playing audience to an Oriental symposium, so entirely did our presence fail to impede the flow of talk which the learned men of the East are accustomed to hold with one another. Muhi ud Din played the game with the perfection of courtesy, but when they all went away, he last, I whispered in his ear: 'For all that I shall not join the brotherhood.' 'Nor I!' he whispered back fervently. It's an interesting world I'm living in isn't it?...

In March 1921, Mr. Churchill, who had been moved from the War Office to the Colonial Office, summoned a conference in Cairo to consider affairs in the Middle East. It was attended by Sir Percy Cox with various members of his staff, including Gertrude. (Sir Percy gives some details about it in his historical summary, p. 266.)

To H. B.   [On the way to Cairo] *February 24th, 1921.*

On the Tigris boat and continued on the *Hardinge.*

The last week has seen the first arrival of a new element, the Mesopotamian officers who were in Syria are beginning to return, the first to come being Nuri Pasha Said, Jafar's brother-in-law. He came last week.

There are no letters from Gertrude during the Conference – Her father joined her in Cairo for a while.

To F. B.   BAGDAD, *April 16th, 1921.*

Will you send me some thick woollen tricotine of a blue as near as may be to the enclosed colour, enough for Marie to make me a winter everyday gown, jumper and skirt. Also some soft blue silk on which to mount the skirt, the same colour. Further will you give a pattern of the blue to my hat maker, Anne Marie in Sloane Street, and tell her to send me by parcel post a blue felt hat – she knows the kind of shape like the green felt she made for me last year trimmed with reddish brown wings, pheasant would do or a red brown feather trimming of some kind. Not ostrich feathers, that's too dear.

To H. B.   BAGDAD, *April 17th, 1921.*

... There was a rumour – that on the way down to Basrah when we went away, I had said to persons not named that the object of the conference was to declare Faisal King.... it was entirely untrue, but no doubt he knows that formerly when people pressed me to give my own opinion I have always said that Faisal would I thought be the best choice. I am therefore identified as a Sharifian, which I don't mind at all, but I have always been careful to say that the choice must rest with the people, and I am now careful to keep my private opinion for the present to myself....

Meantime the general attitude of the country with regard to ourselves has immensely improved. There's a consensus of opinion that whatever happens they can't do without our guidance and help. Being Sunday, I rode down early this morning to Haji Naji and had breakfast with him on native bread, fresh unsalted butter, sugared apples and coffee. He is hand in glove with the Sharifians, thinks Naji, Nuri, Jafar and Co., the best Mesopotamians he knows and is convinced that the overwhelming majority in the country is for Faisal. Said he with his customary wisdom, 'Let the people do it themselves; the British Government need not interfere.' It is so restful and delicious sitting with him under his fruit trees which were in flower when I left and are now loaded with green fruit. It was a heavenly morning and hot sun and a cool little north wind.... I'm happy in helping to forward what I profoundly believe to be the best thing for this country and the wish of the best of its people....

To H. B. BAGDAD, *Apl. 25th, 1921.*

Capt. Thomas, who is a musician, carried up a piano with him to Shatrah and invited his Sheikhs to come and listen to the Pathétique sonata. At the end he asked what they thought of it. 'Wallahi,' said one, 'khosh daqqah.' By God a good thumping.

To H. B. BAGDAD, *May 5th, 1921.*

Your weekly letters are the greatest joy, I don't know what I should do without them....

We are not having a very easy time. Persia is a doubtful quantity but so far remains quiescent.

In Angora, I think I told you, the extremists have got the upper hand, which from our point of view means that Turkish agitation continues on our northern frontier....

My young Nationalist friends are alarmed at the activity of the Turks on the frontier and the existence of a large body of pro-Turkish feeling in this country. Their fear is that the return of the Turks would kill or indefinitely postpone their dearest hopes – namely the setting up of an independent Arab State. This is the sentiment which we want to foster, and as it is held exclusively by Sharifians, they are the people for us to back, as we decided at Cairo. Unfortunately there must have been many delays and Faisal who should have been here in the middle of May has not yet left Mecca. The League of Nations is holding up the mandate in deference to American prejudice and Mr Churchill's statement in the House which ought to have taken place on June 2nd is again postponed. Sir Percy has urged that we should drop the mandate altogether and go for a treaty with the Arab State when it is constituted. It would be a magnificent move if we're bold enough to do it.

Meantime the amnesty is out and my friends are busying themselves in the constitution of a moderate Sharifian party with a definite programme – the latter was submitted to me....

To F. B.   BAGDAD, *May 8th, 1921.*

On Friday there was an immense tea party at the Persian Consul's in honour of the Shah's birthday – I wonder how many more birthdays the Shah will celebrate on his throne! Persian affairs seem fairly stable but there's a great pressure of opinion against the rich landlord class, most of whom are indeed in prison, the Shah only, who is the greatest landlord of them all, being spared....

May 15th, 1921.

It strikes me that not many people of the upper classes are fasting this year. Even the Naqib, for the first time in his life, is not keeping the fast – for reasons of health. He would have died of it.... I wonder how long the fast will hold Islam – like the veiling of women it might disappear, as a universal institution, pretty fast. The women who have come back from Syria or Constantinople find the Bagdad social observances very trying. They have been accustomed to much greater freedom. As soon as we get our local institutions firmly established they will be bolder. They and their husbands are afraid that any steps taken now would set all the prejudiced old tongues wagging and jeopardise their future. Nevertheless these new men bring their wives to see me, which is an unexpected departure from Bagdad customs according to which a man would never go about with his wife.

To H. B.   BAGDAD, *May 29th, 1921.*

The amnesty is out to-morrow, Heaven be praised. It will set free the hands of our Nationalists and they will get to work in earnest. Mr Churchill's statement to the House ought to clear the air further, for he must, I take it, say something about Faisal's being a candidate acceptable to H.M.G. which will be widely regarded as indicating that he is the most acceptable.

I'm thinking of going to Sulaimaniyah at the end of the week for a few days – to Kirkuk for a couple of nights and so on by motor. Sulaimaniyah has refused, on a plebiscite, to come in under the Arab Govt. and is going for the present to be a little Kurdish enclave administered directly under Sir Percy…. The population is wholly Kurdish and they say they don't want to be part of an Arab State.

To H. B.   BAGDAD, *June 12th, 1921.*

I don't for a moment hesitate about the rightness of our policy. We can't continue direct British control though the country would be better governed by it, but it's rather a comic position to be telling people over and over again that whether they like it or not they must have Arab not British Govt….

To H. B.   BAGDAD, *June 19th, 1921.*

We here are now launched on our perilous way. On Monday my old friend the Mayor came to my office and said that since Faisal was coming it was up to the notables of Bagdad to make a proper reception for him and not to leave it all to the young extremists.

His partisans were growing naturally impatient and anxious to get busy. Sir Percy realized this and unofficially approved the project presented through me – that they should summon the town to a big meeting on Friday, 6 days before Faisal's arrival. Thursday afternoon the Naqib … made a sound move. He informed the Council of Ministers that Faisal was coming and that they must make preparations to receive him properly and see that he was suitably lodged. Therefore they appointed a reception committee of 5 Ministers.

Next day Naji Suwaidi and the Mutasarrif came to my office after the meeting to report. It had been a great success, everyone had been present and 60 people had been chosen to go down to Basrah to welcome Faisal – would I kindly make arrangements with the Railway. There remained the question of his lodging here which they proposed to solve by putting him into some rooms in the Sarai (the Government offices) which were now under repair … if they could be got ready in time. Public Works declared that it couldn't be done. Jafar telephoned to me in despair on Saturday morning; I telephoned to Public Works, made suggestions for covering bare walls with hangings and finally the thing was arranged.

This morning, being Sunday, Mr Tod and I rode before breakfast to Haji Naji … Haji Naji presently drew me aside and told me he thought of going with the party to Basrah only he was rather afraid of being lost in the ruck. I said I would give him a letter of introduction to Mr Cornwallis, who is coming with Faisal, so that he might be treated with consideration.…

To H. B.   *June 23rd, 1921.*

Faisal arrives in Basrah today. His adherents anticipate that his coming will be the sign for a great popular ovation. Heaven send it may be so for it will immensely simplify matters for us. Meantime there can be no question that it is regarded with anxiety by the Magnates. On Monday we had a strong deputation from Basrah bringing a petition in which they asked for separate treatment for the Basrah area. They were ready to accept a common King but they asked that Basrah might have a separate Legislative Assembly, a separ-

ate Army, police service and raise and spend its own taxes,
making a suitable contribution to the central administration.
They came to me on their way to Sir Percy and asked me to
support their request. I said No; whatever H.M.G. decided
would have my loyal support as a Government servant, but
until that decision was given I must exercise my private
opinion which was that what they asked was not in the interests of the country as a whole and would not prove to be
permanently in their own interests.... I have been elected
President of the Bagdad Public Library....

The Reception Committee got their programme through
the Council on Monday. What they wanted to know was
what part Sir Percy was going to take and above all whether
he would provide a guard of honour. I promised to get the
reply as soon as possible. Meantime Nuri Said, who had been
in Basrah, had seen me the previous evening and told me
about the popular demonstration. He thought it might result
in an immediate acclamation of Faisal as King, and asked me
anxiously whether we should mind that. I answered in suitable terms that we only wanted to know the opinion of the
country.

Already the whole town is flying the Sharifian flag. I saw
it to-day flying on every other shop in the Bazaar. The intention is good but the flag heraldically bad. I don't know if
you know it. The red triangle colour comes over the black
and green colour on colour, and therefore wrong isn't it....

Yesterday we had news of Faisal's arrival in Basrah and
an excellent reception, heaven be praised....

I'm told that Naji Suwaidi is in favour of a mandate rather
than the proposed treaty, because a mandate gives us more
authority! Faisal wants a treaty I know, so probably that's
the way it will work out, and for my part I think it's quite
immaterial. You can't run a mandate without the goodwill
of the people, and if you've got that it doesn't matter whether
it is a mandate or a treaty, but what rejoices me is the fulfilment of my dream that we should sit by in an attitude of repose and have them coming up our front door steps to beg
us to be more active....

NOTICE

TO

ALL AUTHORS, PUBLISHERS AND BOOKSELLERS

The Salam Library, Bagdad, intends to issue a periodical publication – in Arabic and English – the object of which is to review books published in Oriental languages, Arabic, Persian, Turkish, Hebrew, Syriac, Hindustani, etc.; and also books published in European languages, English, French and German, etc.

This publication will deal only with books presented to the library with a request from the publisher or author asking for a review or notice of the book.

It will also give an account of such manuscripts as may be found in the library or are to be found in local bookshops. Thus the Salam Library's periodical publication will be the best means for introducing European books to Orientals and Oriental books to Europeans and will serve as a means to facilitate the sale of books.

The Committee of the Salam Library is composed of Arab and British members who will undertake the publication of the periodical.

(Signed) GERTRUDE BELL,
President, Salam Library.
BAGDAD.

Gertrude sent copies of this notice to be distributed in England, together with a circular, addressed to English publishers, asking if they would care to send books to the Salam Library.

CHAPTER 21

1921

Bagdad

To H. B. BAGDAD, *June 30th, 1921.*

It's being so frightfully interesting – there! there! Let me begin at the beginning. Where was I? It was Monday's vernacular paper which gave the first full account of Faisal's arrival at Basrah and the quite admirable speech which he made at a big function they had for him. On Wednesday Faisal was to arrive at 7 a.m. Col. Joyce and I motored to the station together, going all the way up the big street to the upper bridge. The whole town was decorated, triumphal arches, Arab flags, and packed with people, in the streets, on the housetops, everywhere. At the station immense crowds. It was very well arranged with seats for the magnates all round, and all filled with magnates. Sir Percy and Sir Aylmer and a guard of honour and all. But we learnt there had been an 'éboulement' on the line – he couldn't get through and might be here at mid-day! Sir Percy quickly took command. Noon at the end of June is not an hour at which you can hold a great reception out of doors.... He was accordingly asked to spend the day in the train and get in at 6 p.m. And so behold me at 5.30 again setting off for the station.... And this time the train arrived.

Sidi Faisal stood at the carriage door looking very splendid in full Arab dress, saluting the guard of honour. Sir Percy and Sir Aylmer went up to him as he got out and gave him a fine ceremonious greeting, and all the people clapped. He went down the line of the guard of honour, inspecting it.... Sir Percy began to present the Arab Magnates, representatives of the Naqib, etc. I hid behind Mr Cornwallis, but Faisal saw me and stepped across to shake hands with me. He looked excited and anxious – you're not a king on approbation without any tension of the spirit – but it only gave his natural dignity a more human charm.

This morning on my way to the office I went to the Saria and gave my card to Faisal's A.D.C. He said would I wait a minute, the Amir would like to see me; it was a little past seven, rather early for a morning call. I waited, talking to the A.D.C. and presently Faisal sent for me. They showed me into a big room and he came quickly across in his long white robes, took me by both hands and said 'I couldn't have believed that you could have given me so much help as you have given me.' So we sat down on a sofa. I assured him that Sir Percy was absolutely with him....

Mr Cornwallis came into the office later and I told him I had called on Faisal. He said (I must tell you because it pleased me so much) 'That was quite right. All the way up he had been hearing your praise and he gave me a message for you in case he didn't see you to speak to to-day. I was to tell you how grateful he was. And my private spy the man I sent to Basrah tells me the people constantly say, "Is the Khatun satisfied...." '

The next event was that evening's banquet in the Maude gardens. It was really beautifully done. The place lighted with electric lights looked lovely.

Faisal carried on a little conversation in French with Sir Aylmer, but mostly he and I and Sir Percy, and Abdul Majid and I talked across the table. Faisal looked very happy and I felt very happy and so did Sir Percy....

Then got up our great poet, of whom I've often told you, Jamil Zahawi, and recited a tremendous ode in which he repeatedly alluded to Faisal as King of the Iraq and everyone clapped and cheered.

But it's not all smooth yet. We get reports about the lower Euphrates tribes preparing monstrous petitions in favour of a republic and of Shiah Alim Mujtahids being all against Faisal. I don't believe half of them are true but they keep one in anxiety. To-day I sent for one of the principal Euphrates Sheikhs.... He is a strong Sharifian and we talked the whole matter over. In the afternoon Faisal sent for me and told me his ideas which were very sound. I also gave him a few suggestions to bring before Sir Percy.... With that Faisal went off to see Sir Percy, so I should think things will happen. I'm beginning to feel as if I couldn't stand it much longer! One is straining every nerve all the time to pull the matter forward; talking, persuading, writing, I find myself carrying on the argument even in my sleep.

To H. B. BAGDAD, *Thursday, July 7th, 1921.*

What helps everything is that Faisal's personality goes three quarters of the way. He has been roping in adherents; they most of them come round to me to be patted on the back at which I am getting to be an adept. It's a little more delicate when they are trembling on the brink but I then bring in the overwhelming arguments that Sir Percy and Faisal are working hand in hand – it's really remarkable how completely satisfied they are if they know that Sir Percy approves. He has an extraordinary hold on the country.

Friday, July 8th.

Last night the Naqib gave a dinner to Faisal in his house opposite his own mosque. The English guests were Sir Percy and his staff. All the rest were the Ministers and Notables of Bagdad. Sir Percy took me. The streets were crowded with people as we drove up; the Naqib's family received us at the door and we climbed up two flights of stairs into a roof overlooking the mosque, a sort of wide balcony. It was carpeted and lighted; the mosque door opposite was hung with lamps and the minarets ringed with them. The Naqib was sitting with the Ministers; he got up and faltered forward to meet Sir Percy, a touching and dignified figure. The rest of the guests, some 100 I should think, sat below us on the open gallery which runs round two sides of the courtyard on the first story of the house. A burning wind blew on us while we drank coffee and talked till the clapping of hands in the street announced the arrival of Faisal. Faisal, Sir Percy, the C. in C. and I went down: then the Naqib with a servant on each side of him to help him. The long dinner-table stood on the open gallery. Faisal sat in the place of honour opposite the Naqib with the C. in C. on one side of him and I on the other.... It was a wonderful sight that dinner party. The robes and their uniforms and the crowds of servants, all brought up in the Naqib's household, the ordered dignity, the real solid magnificence, the tension of spirit which one felt all round one, as one felt the burning heat of the night. For, after all, to the best of our ability, we were making history.

The Naqib, so much honoured and esteemed, died in May 1927.

But you may rely upon one thing – I'll never engage in creating kings again; it's too great a strain....

To H. B.   BAGDAD, *July 16th, 1921.*

The heat is terrific, day after day over 121 and the nights hot too.... Sir Percy and I think we ought to put at end of difficult telegrams home: N.B. temp. 121.8. On the other hand, politics are running on wheels greased with extremely well melted grease and Sir Percy and Faisal are scoring great triumphs. On Monday the 11th the Council, at the instance of the Naqib ... unanimously declared Faisal King, and charged the Ministry of the Interior with the necessary arrangements. I was dining alone that night and feeling anxious – the heat makes one not quite normal, I think. You may fancy what it was like to get to the office next morning and hear this news from Sir Percy, the moment I arrived. He added that he felt, good as this was, that it wasn't enough and that we must have an election by Referendum to be able to prove that Faisal really had the voice of the people. With that, one of Faisal's A.D.C.'s telephoned to me and asked me to go round. His ante-chamber was a sight to gladden one – full of Bagdad nobles and sheikhs from all parts of the Iraq. I went back to Sir Percy to report. The thing we have been looking for seems to be in a fair way to fulfilment. Sir Percy and Faisal between them are making a new Sharifian party composed of all the solid moderate people.... Faisal has played his part; he has handled his over-zealous adherents with admirable discretion....

To H. B.   *Wednesday, July 20th, 1921.*

Really these days are so packed with incident that I must
quickly record them before one impression overlays another.
In an atmosphere which has been uninterruptedly at a maximum of over 120 for the last three weeks – I may mention
that for the first time in my life I've got prickly heat – not
very bad however. Well – on Monday the Jewish community
gave a great reception to Faisal in the Grand Rabbi's official
house.... The Rabbi is a wonderful figure, stepped straight
out of a picture by Gentile Bellini. The speeches on this occasion are all set speeches.... But yet they were interesting
because one knew the tensions which underlay them, the
anxiety of the Jews lest an Arab government should mean
chaos, and their gradual reassurance, by reason of Faisal's
obviously enlightened attitude. Presently they brought the
Rolls of the Law in their gold cylinders, they were kissed by
the Grand Rabbi, and then by Faisal, and they presented
him with a small gold facsimile of the tables of the law and a
beautifully bound Talmud. I whispered to him that I hoped
he would make a speech. He said he hadn't meant to say
much but he thought he must, and added 'You know I don't
speak like they do. I just say what is in my thoughts.' Towards the end he got up and spoke really beautifully; it was
straight and good and eloquent.... He made an immense
impression.

The Jews were delighted at his insistence on their being of
one race with the Arabs, and all our friends ... were equally
delighted with his allusion to British support....

To H. B.   BAGDAD, *July 27th, 1921.*

I'm immensely happy over the way this thing is going. I
feel as if I were in a dream.... On our guarantee all the solid
people are coming in to Faisal and there is a general feeling
that we made the right choice in recommending him. If we
can bring some kind of order out of chaos, what a thing
worth doing it will be!

Our great heat is over, the temp. has fallen to about 115
more or less which is quite bearable, and I'm very well.

To H. B. BAGDAD, *July 31st, 1921.*

I must now give you an account of our doings. Over-shadowing all else was the display at Ramadi. Fakhri Jamil Zadah and I left at 4 a.m. but Faisal was a little in front of us. We caught him up at Naqtah, half way to the Euphrates and asked leave to go ahead so that I might photograph his arrival at Fallujah. Outside that village a couple of big tents were pitched in the desert and for several miles crowds of tribal horsemen gathered in and stood along the track as he passed.

Under the steep edge of the Syrian desert were drawn up the fighting men of the Anazeh, horsemen and camel riders, bearing the huge standard of the tribe. We stopped to salute it as we passed. Ali Sulaiman the Chief of the Dulaim and one of the most remarkable men in Iraq came out of the Ramadi to meet us. He has been strongly and consistently pro-British....

We drove to the Euphrates bank where Ali Sulaiman had pitched a huge tent about 200 ft. long with a dais at the upper end and roofed with tent cloth and walled with fresh green boughs. Outside were drawn up the camel riders of the Dulaim, their horsemen and their standard carried by a negro mounted on a gigantic white camel; inside the tribesmen lined the tent 5 or 6 deep from the dais to the very end. Faisal sat on the high diwan with Fahad on his right while Major Yetts and I brought up people to sit on his left – those we thought he ought to speak to. He was supremely happy, a great tribesman amongst famous tribes and, as I couldn't help feeling, a great Sunni among Sunnis.... Faisal was in his own country with the people he knew. I never saw him look so splendid. He wore his usual white robes with a fine black abba over them, flowing white headdress and silver bound Aqal. Then he began to speak, leaning forward over the small table in front of him, sitting with his hand raised and bringing it down on the table to emphasize his sentences. The people at the end of the tent were too far off to hear; he called them all up and they sat on the ground below the dais, rows and rows of them, 400 or 500 men. He spoke in the great tongue of the desert, sonorous, magnificent – no language like it. He spoke as a tribal chief to his feudatories. 'For four years,' he said, 'I have not found myself in a place like this or in such company' – you could see how he was loving it. Then he told them how Iraq was to rise to their endeavours with himself at their head. 'Oh Arabs are you at peace with one another?' They shouted 'Yes, yes, we are at peace.' 'From this day – what is the date? and what is the hour?' Someone answered him. 'From this day the 25th July (only he gave the Mohammedan date) and the hour of the morning 4 (it was 11 o'clock) any tribesman who lifts his hand against a tribesman is responsible to me – I will judge between you calling your Sheikhs in council. I have my rights over you as your Lord.' A grey bearded man interrupted, 'And our rights?' 'And you have your rights as subjects which it is my business to guard.' So it went on, the tribesmen interrupting him with shouts, 'Yes, yes,' 'We agree,' 'Yes, by God.' It was like descriptions of great tribal gatherings in the days of ignorance, before the prophet, when the poets recited verse which has come down to this day and the people shouted at the end of each phrase, 'The truth, by God the truth.'

To H. B.   BAGDAD, *August 6th, 1921.*

Faisal has promised me a regiment of the Arab Army – 'the Khatun's own'. I shall presently ask you to have their colours embroidered. Nuri proposes that I should have an Army Corps!

Oh Father, isn't it wonderful. I sometimes think I must be in a dream.

Sorry to say that it's desperately hot again. As regards climate this is being the devil's own summer.

To H. B.   BAGDAD, *Aug. 14th, 1921.*

The referendum is finished and we are only waiting for the last of the signed papers to come in from the Provinces, after which Faisal will be proclaimed King without delay. With one exception he has been elected unanimously....

To H. B.   BAGDAD, *August 21, 1921.*

I must tell you another nice tale about the Coxes. You know he is a great naturalist. He is making a collection of all Mesopotamian birds – sometimes they arrive dead and sometimes alive. The last one was alive. It's a huge eagle, not yet in its grown up plumage but for all that the largest fowl I've ever set eyes on. It lives on a perch on the shady side of the house and it eats bats, mainly. These bats are netted for it in the dusk when they obligingly fly across the river and over Sir Percy's garden wall. But the eagle likes to eat them in the morning, so the long suffering Lady Cox keeps them in a tin in her ice chest, and if ever you've heard before of an eagle that lives on iced bat you'll please inform me.

To H. B.   BAGDAD, *August 28th, 1921.*

We have had a terrific week but we've got our King crowned and Sir Percy and I agree that we're now half seas over, the remaining half is the Congress and the Organic Law.... The enthronement took place at 6 a.m. on Tuesday, admirably arranged. A dais about 2 ft. 6 in. high was set up in the middle of the big Sarai courtyard; behind it are the quarters Faisal is occupying, the big Government reception rooms; in front were seated in blocks, English, Arab officials, townsmen, Ministers, local deputations, to the number of 1,500.

Exactly at 6 we saw Faisal in uniform, Sir Percy in white diplomatic uniform with all his ribbons and stars, Sir Aylmer, Mr Cornwallis, and a following of A.D.C.'s descend the Sarai steps from Faisal's lodging and come pacing down the long path of carpets, past the guard of honour (the Dorsets, they looked magnificent) and so to the dais.... We all stood up while they came in and sat when they had taken their places on the dais. Faisal looked very dignified but much strung up – it was an agitating moment. He looked along the front row and caught my eye and I gave him a tiny salute. Then Saiyid Hussain stood up and read Sir Percy's proclamation in which he announced that Faisal had been elected King by 96 per cent of the people of Mesopotamia, long live the King! with that we stood up and saluted him. The national flag was broken on the flagstaff by his side and the band played 'God save the King' – they have no national anthem yet. There followed a salute of 21 guns.... It was an amazing thing to see all Iraq, from North to South gathered together. It is the first time it has happened in history....

There's no doubt that this is the most absorbing job that I've ever taken a hand in....

To H. B.   BAGDAD, *Sept. 11, 1921.*

Faisal's first Cabinet is formed. On the whole we are well satisfied. Out of the 9 Ministers, 6 are eminently capable men, well-fitted for their job....

Faisal has got into his new house, on the river above Bagdad. It's small but it's really very nice. On Wednesday one of the A.D.C.'s telephoned to me to ask me to dinner – I went up by launch. Have I ever told you what the river is like on a hot summer night? At dusk the mist hangs in long white bands over the water; the twilight fades and the lights of the town shine out on either bank, with the river, dark and smooth and full of mysterious reflections, like a road of triumph through the mist. Silently a boat with a winking head-light slips down the stream, then a company of quffahs, each with his tiny lamp, loaded to the brim with water melons from Samarra. 'Slowly, slowly.' the voices of the Quffahjis drift across the water. 'Don't ruffle the river lest we sink – see how we're loaded.' And we slow down the launch so that the wash may not disturb them. The waves of our passage don't even extinguish the floating votive candle each burning on its minute boat made out of the swathe of a date cluster, which anxious hands launched above the town – if they reach the last town yet burning, the sick man will recover, the baby will be born safely into this world of hot darkness and glittering lights and bewildering reflections. Now I've brought you out to where the palm trees stand marshalled along the banks. The water is so still that you can see the Scorpion in it, star by star; we'll go gently past these quffahs – and here are Faisal's steps.

And you still can't form the remotest conception of how marvellously beautiful it is.... I also rode with Nuri on Friday morning; we went down to breakfast with Haji Naji.

As we rode back through the gardens of the Karradah suburb where all the people know me and salute me as I pass, Nuri said 'One of the reasons you stand out so is because you're a woman. There's only one Khatun. It is like when Sidi Faïsal was in London and always wore Arab dress, there was no one like him. So for a hundred years they'll talk of the Khatun riding by.'

I think they very likely will.

To F. B.   BAGDAD, *September 17th, 1921.*

I'm glad you take an interest in my letters, bless you. It's not at all true that I have determined the fortunes of Iraq, but it is true that with an Arab Government I've come to my own. It's a delicate position to be so much in their confidence. I'm very careful about not obtruding myself on them. I let all the 'come hither' emanate from them. When they want to come and ask my advice I'm always there; when they're busy with other things I go about affairs of my own....

To F. B.   BAGDAD, *Oct. 17th, 1921.*

... They really are wonderful, these young Englishmen, who are thrown out into the provinces and left entirely to their own resources. They so completely identify themselves with their surroundings that nothing else has any significance for them, but if they think you're interested they open out like a flower and reveal quite unconsciously, wisdom, tact, and patience which you would have thought to be incompatible with their years....

My blue gown and cloak have arrived, they are very nice

indeed. I am so infinitely grateful for the trouble my kind family have taken about them.

To H. B.   BAGDAD, *Oct. 31st, 1921.*

What an excessive amount of trouble you take about your children and we accept it all as a matter of course — more shame to us. At any rate I do realise from time to time what it is to have someone always watching and caring for one without the care having any relation to the worth of the object it's expended on. The object is worth less than you can guess. I think I may have been of some use here but I suspect I've come very near the end of it....

To H. B.   BAGDAD, *Dec. 4th, 1921.*

Faisal privately doesn't want the Congress to be convened (its duty is to draw up the Organic law) until he has got the terms of the treaty satisfactorily settled and respective responsibilities of the British and Arab Governments defined. It's this question of responsibility which perturbs everyone; on it the position of the Advisors and indeed most other things rests. Roughly the skeleton of the problem is whether we can assume responsibility for defence if the country is attacked from without.... We must be able to satisfy the League of Nations that we can fulfil the international obligations with which the mandate entrusts us, and even if we drop the mandate and call it a treaty, that treaty must make certain reservations which the Arabs must accept....

The word Mandate produces much the same effect here as the word Protectorate did in Egypt....

But you mustn't think for a moment I have any part in settling these problems. I know about them because Sir Percy tells me about them in outline but I'm merely an on-looker and although Faisal is very friendly and agreeable he doesn't, quite rightly, consult me. I hadn't seen him for nearly 5 weeks what with his being away and my being away, and I very carefully abstain from offering advice in matters the delicate manipulation of which had much better be left to Sir Percy. All I can do and all I try to do, is to give as accurate an impression as I can of what people are saying and thinking....

I had a well spent morning at the office making out the Southern desert frontier of the Iraq with the help of a gentleman from Hayil and of Fahad Bey the paramount chief of the Anazeh. The latter's belief in my knowledge of the desert makes me blush. When he was asked by Mr Cornwallis to define his tribal boundaries all he said was 'You ask the Khatun. She knows.' In order to keep up this reputation of omiscience, I've been careful to find out from Fahad all the wells claimed by the Shammar. One way and another, I think I've succeeded in compiling a reasonable frontier. The importance of the matter lies in the fact that Ibn Saud has captured Hayil and at the earliest possible opportunity Sir Percy wants to have a conference between him and Faisal to state definitely what tribes and lands belong to the Iraq and what to Ibn Saud....

Did I tell you that Sir Percy is building an extra room on to my house? It's causing me acute discomfort at the moment but it will be a great blessing when finished.

CHAPTER 22

1922 – 23

Bagdad

To H. B.   BAGDAD, *Jan. 30th, 1922.*

During the last fortnight I've taken my health seriously in hand. I really was dreadfully run down and nearly expired of fatigue at the end of a morning in the office so I've firmly come away at 1 p.m. or thereabouts, lunched at home or with Mr Cornwallis, the Joyces or any one else I wanted to see and then gone out riding till tea time. The weather has been delicious and this programme has been just what I wanted for it has got me out every afternoon into the sun and air. Never in my experience of Iraq has there been such a spring.... To-day I rode through the Dairy Farm – and back by the gardens bordering the Tigris. Man and beast were rejoicing in the abundance of green – 'By God, I've never seen the like' I stopped to say to the shepherds. And they, 'It is the mercy of God and your presence Khatun.'

How I love their darling phrases: you know, Father, it's shocking how the East has wound itself round my heart till I don't know which is me and which is it. I never lose the sense of it. I'm acutely conscious always of its charm and grace which do not seem to wear thin with familiarity. I'm more a citizen of Bagdad than many a Bagdadi born, and I'll wager that no Bagdadi cares more, or half so much, for the beauty of the river or the palm gardens, or clings more closely to the rights of citizenship which I have acquired....

You know, Father, I shall never be content till you come out again – I want you to see the King and my new room and everything. I think your next visit should be in the spring of 1923 – I'll come to Aleppo to meet you, and take you here by motor....

To H. B.   BAGDAD, *Feb. 16th, 1922.*

I want to tell you, just you, who know and understand everything, that I'm acutely conscious of how much life has given me. I've gone back now to the wild feeling of joy in existence – I'm happy in feeling that I've got the love and confidence of a whole nation, a very wonderful and absorbing thing – almost too absorbing perhaps. You must forgive me if it seems to preoccupy me too much – it doesn't really divide me from you, for one of the greatest pleasures is to tell you all about it, in the certainty that you will sympathise. I don't for a moment suppose that I can make much difference to our ultimate relations with the Arabs and with Asia, but for the time I'm one of the factors in the game. I can't think why all these people here turn to me for comfort and encouragement; if I weren't here they would find someone else, of course, but being accustomed to come to me, they come. And in their comfort I find my own. I remember your saying to me once that the older one grows the more one lives in other people's lives. Well, I've got plenty of lives to live in, haven't I? And perhaps after all, it has been best this way. At any rate, as it had to be this way, I don't now regret it.

*

To H. B.   BAGDAD, *Feb. 16th, 1922.*

Faisal sent for me. We had a tremendous talk. He is most delightful and certainly often most amazing. I caught myself up in the middle of discussion and said to him that it was almost impossible to believe that while he had been born in Mecca and educated at Constantinople and I in England and educated in Oxford there was no difference whatever in our points of view....

Already the country is finding its feet. The stable people, the big sheikhs and nobles relying on our support of Faisal, are rallying round him and are combined. They are going to stand no nonsense from extremists and tub-thumpers....

To H. B.   BAGDAD, *March 12th, 1922.*

I spent Tuesday afternoon with the King and we had an immense talk, partly owing to the nearness of general elections, about the formation of political parties. He was

anxious – I really think that in this country it would be best –
that people of different opinions should find a platform of
agreement and start a single party with a combined policy
for the election. I've unexpectedly been thrown into the thick
of it during the last few days. On Thursday the extremists
petitioned the Interior for permission to form a party....

To H. B.   BAGDAD, *March 30th, 1922.*

During the last fortnight I have come definitely to the conclusion that I can't go on leave this summer. Things are too
much in the melting pot.... I hope you and Mother and
Maurice won't be much disappointed. I do love you so much
and I hate staying away so long.

Well now we come to the sordid but serious question of
clothes – of course, I've made no provision for the summer.
I've written to Marte (78 Grosvenor Street) by this mail telling her that if she is in time to catch you, she is to send out
by you two washing gowns, an evening gown and a hat ... if,
however, you have left before this letter arrives Mother will
open it and will tell Marte to post things I've asked her to
send me as quickly as she can so that I may find them here if
possible when I get back. But please if you possibly can bring
a hat. Elsa might choose it if the combination with Marte
fails – she is on the telephone, by the way – a ribbon hat,
black or mauvy blue and mushroom in shape. There! You'll
do your best, I feel sure, and if you can't do anything I must
just wear the topee I shall come over in....

I've received a lovely photograph of Hugo's wedding. I
think that is partly what made me feel homesick. You all
look such darlings and my two sisters so especially delightful.

Hugo's marriage to Frances Morkill took place on November
24th, 1921, at Kirby Malham in the West Riding of Yorkshire.

To F. B.   BAGDAD, *April 28th, 1922.*

I have just telegraphed to Father at Jerusalem telling him
that I'm coming over by air on the 29th and suggesting that
he should meet me at Amman on that day....

This meeting with her father took place most successfully, as arranged. He had arrived in Jerusalem, and then gone on to Amman, where he received a telephone message to say that the two official aeroplanes, in one of which Gertrude was flying, had left Bagdad at 9 a.m. and were due to arrive at Ziza between 11 and 12. He at once motored to Ziza and stood with the officials who were awaiting the aeroplanes, looking out into the eastern sky. It was an exciting moment when two small specks first appeared on the horizon and then came to a pause over the heads of the expectant group. The planes landed beautifully, Gertrude alighted and fell into her father's arms. For a little while she was dizzy, and unable to hear, then in a short time she completely recovered. Her father then told her that he and she had been invited to dine with Abdullah, King Faisal's brother, the Emir of Transjordania, who was then encamped near Amman, but that he had declined, as he did not suppose that she would feel able to do so after her long flight. But Gertrude entirely repudiated the idea of refusing, got out her evening clothes, and they went to dinner with the Emir and enjoyed themselves very much.

To F. B.   JERUSALEM, *May 10th, 1922.*

I can't tell you what a wonderful time we have had. The joy of being with Father in these surroundings and of having his amazingly acute and perceptive mind to help one in coming to conclusions! Was there ever anyone who combined as he does such wealth of experience with so fresh and vital an outlook on all and everything that he encounters? And isn't he the most delicious companion with his humanness and his charming humour and his appreciation of beauty and history and birds and flowers and all that ever was, the biggest thing to the least. I shall so dreadfully miss him when we part and I do very much regret that I'm not coming home to you, Maurice and my sisters. It's an extraordinary sense of rest, peace and understanding that one gets when one is with one's own family and it's just that which I miss so much – the intimacy and confidence in our love for one another.

Marte sent me the most excellent clothes, bless her – lovely embroidered muslin gowns to wear during the summer....

To H. B.   BAGDAD, *June 2nd, 1922*.

The Minister of the Interior telephoned to tell me that a group of extremists were planning a big demonstration against the mandate for the afternoon. The King had ordered it to be stopped and did I know where Mr Cornwallis was? With that, Mr C came in and I left him to deal with the Minister. At five Mr Cooke and I went out on another round of visits and got through some ten notables or more. There was a good deal of talk about the attempted demonstration and very plain speaking as to how this kind of thing could not be tolerated.

Oh, darling, isn't the human equation immensely interesting. I feel as if I and all of us were playing the most magical tunes on their heart strings, drawn taut by the desperate case in which they find themselves. Can they succeed in setting up a reasonable government? Can they save themselves from chaos? Their one cry is 'Help us'. And one sits there, in their eyes an epitome of human knowledge, and feeling oneself so very far from filling the bill! Poor children of Adam, they and we! I'm not sure (but perhaps that's because of my sex) that the emotional link between us isn't the better part of wisdom, but I wish I had a little more real wisdom to offer. However, Sir Percy has plenty....

To-day the vernacular press was full of Lord Apsley [who had come over as representing the *Morning Post*].

At five I took the Lord to tea with the King. I told him all that there was in the papers and he replied that he was to meet all the extremists to-morrow at Kadhimain. I gave him the lie of the land and I've no doubt he will do extremely well. For in conversation with the King he was quite admirable – I'm free to confess that I translated like an angel!... We talked over the whole mandate question with complete amity.

At the end Lord Apsley, who really is a diplomat of the highest order, said that now he wanted to come to something really serious. They all pricked their ears – 'Yes,' he said, 'a thing of real importance – when are you going to have a polo team?' They were delighted....

To H. B. BAGDAD, *June 22nd, 1922.*

Next day I went to tea with the King and had one of the most interesting talks I've ever had with him. . . .

When if ever we come up to eternal judgment, you may be very sure that we shall ultimately be graded according to the very highest point we have been able to reach. . . . Faisal on that day will come out very high. He surges up a long long way across the heavenly strand; the tide goes down again, but he has been there and left his little line of sea gold on the shore.

On Thursday I took Mrs Wilkinson to tea with some Arab ladies – I'm always taking some of our nice Englishwomen out to tea like that; it's such a help.

In the evening I had an evening party in my garden 9–11.30. Coffee and ices and talk under my lanterns. I asked about ten Arabs and five Englishmen. It was quite brought off and I shall do it again and again.

Perhaps some day you might send me a Bridge Box – I haven't one. Also possibly some patience cards?

To H. B. BAGDAD, *July 16th, 1922.*

The King and the Naqib have proclaimed to the listening Universe that they will never, so help them God, accept the mandate. H.M.G. have replied that they can conclude no treaty except by reason of the right to do so given to them by the League of Nations – i.e., the mandate.

July 17th.

Yesterday's experiences were as usual remarkable. Feeling very energetic for once, I got up at five and rode out to Karradah to breakfast with Haji Naji on scrumptious roasted fish. While I was sitting in his summer house a curious episode occurred. There strode in a youngish man in the dress of a Dervish who announced that he had come as a guest. Haji Naji replied that he was busy and bade him begone. The man blustered a little, looked sharply at me and said he had just as much right to be a guest as others and finally went out and sat down just outside a mat-walled summer house. Haji Naji called the servants and one of his sons and told them to send the man away. They failed to make him move. Presently he began to read out the Koran in a loud voice. This was more than I could bear and I went out and told him, by God, to clear out. He said 'I am reading the Holy Book.' I replied 'I know you are – get out or I shall send for the police.' He replied irrelevantly 'I rely on God.' I said 'God's a long way off and the police very near,' and with that I picked up his iron staff and gently poked him up. He made up his mind that he was beaten and saying 'Because you are here I shall go' picked up himself and his Koran and made off.... If I hadn't sent the man away Haji would have been absolutely helpless. A man who sits down on your threshold to read the Koran can only be regarded, in theory, as a blessing – you can't lift him. Curious, wasn't it? I shall tell the police to keep an eye on any dervish wandering about in Karradah....

10 p.m. I've just heard by telephone that the Ministers passed the treaty at this afternoon's meeting....

To-day the King ordered me to tea and we had two hours' most excellent talk. First of all I got his assistance for my Law of Excavations which I've compiled with the utmost care in consultation with the legal authorities. He has undertaken to push it through Council – he's perfectly sound about archaeology, having been trained by T. E. Lawrence – and has agreed to my suggestion that he should appoint me, if Sir Percy consents, provisional Director of Archaeology to his government, in addition to my other duties. I should then be able to run the whole thing in direct agreement with him, which would be excellent.

To H. B. BAGDAD, *August 15th, 1922.*

We are having a very exhausting time, physically and politically. Physically because of the incredibly horrible weather. It's not very hot, never much over 110°, but heavy and close beyond all belief. Every two or three days I get up in the morning wondering why, instead of getting up, I don't lie down and die. At the end of the day one feels absolutely dead beat. Then for a day or two one is better, for no special reason, and then again moribund. It's not only me; everyone is the same....

On Sunday 6th the King invited us to a picnic. I walked with the King through the wonderful palm gardens and out to the desert. For the sixth time I've watched the dates ripen. Six times I've seen the palms take on the likeness of huge Crown Imperials, with the yellow date clusters hanging like immense golden flowers below the feathery fronds.... The King took us back in his launch and as we slipped past the palm groves he and I laid plans to write the history of the Arab revival from first to last, from his diaries and my knowledge. It would be a remarkable tale.

Father, you do realize, don't you, how the magic and the fascination of it all holds one prisoner?...

August 16th.

This was one of the moribund days, nevertheless I've been extremely busy. Any quantity of Sheikhs came in this morning.... I really believe they are getting to work. They have parcelled out the whole country according to administrative divisions. There's a head branch in every divisional headquarter and sub-branches in every district; the sheikhs are going back to organize them. Their tails are up sky high. They declare they'll bring in the whole country.... And the sheikhs from further afield are trooping in to register themselves as members. They are the people I love, I know every Tribal chief of any importance through the whole length and breadth of Iraq and I think them the backbone of the country.

One has to take one's courage in one's hands when a wrong decision may mean universal chaos.

To H. B.   *August 27th, 1922.*

On Sunday evening August 20th we escaped from politics for a happy hour or two. The King came out bathing and picnicking with us and we had the usual party. It was my picnic and I did it beautifully. We roasted great fishes on spits over a fire of palm fronds – the most delicious food in the world – I brought carpets and cushions and hung old Bagdad lanterns in the tamarisk bushes where we kept simple state in the rosy stillness of the sunset. 'This is peace,' said the King. We lay on our cushions for a couple of hours after dinner while he and Nuri and Mr Cornwallis told stories of the Syrian campaign – I have seldom passed a more enchanting evening.

Next day we were back in the turmoil.

Wednesday was the anniversary of the accession, August 23rd. I rode with His Majesty before breakfast on Tuesday morning to see his cotton farm.... It is a tremendous cavalcade when the King goes out riding – A.D.C.'s behind us and four lancers of the body guard bringing up the rear....

... At noon on the 24th we heard that the King was down with appendicitis, in the evening his temperature was up, at 6 a.m. next day, five doctors, two English and three Arabs, were debating whether an immediate operation were necessary, at 8 they decided it was and at 11 it was successfully over....

The King has made a rapid convalescence. On Sunday he was allowed to see a selected body of notables. This was thought advisable because a rumour had been spread that he was dead. On Monday the Officers of the Iraq army offered him their congratulations on his recovery. To-day Mr Cornwallis saw him – in the presence of notables and the A.D.C.'s. There was no mention of politics....

The extreme right is just as subversive of the policy of H.M.G. as the extreme left. The one is opposed to the King and the Arab Government, the other opposed to British assistance. How are we to combine the two sharply conflicting schools of thought? If I don't specifically answer your letters it's not because I don't like having them. They are like an escape to another world. But waking and sleeping I am absorbed by what lies to my hand and the countless interviews which I conduct daily with turbaned gentlemen and tribesmen and what you please, seem to me to matter more than anything else in the world....

To H. B. BAGDAD, *September 8th, 1922.*

I spent the afternoon with the Davidsons. She is going home next week to my great sorrow. I shall miss her dreadfully. I do hope Aurelia Tod will be back this winter – it's nice to have a female friend.

September 10th.

This Sunday morning while I'm writing to you Sir Percy and Mr Cornwallis are having a momentous interview with the King, at which Sir Percy is asking him to endorse all he has done, and to give certain undertakings for the future....

Sept. 14th.

Now I must tell you that the King's momentous conversation with Sir Percy passed off very satisfactorily. He accepted and endorsed all that Sir Percy had done....

To H. B. BAGDAD, *September 24th, 1922.*

Our next excitement was the arrival of Amir Zaid, H.M.'s youngest brother to whom he is devoted. He arrived last Sunday the 17th. There was a great reception for him at the station to which we all went – notables and advisors and Arab Army and everyone you can think of....

The Mandate has been much softened for them since Mr Churchill has agreed to announce that the moment Iraq enters the League of Nations it becomes a dead letter. Now one of the clauses of the treaty is an undertaking on our part to get Iraq admitted as quickly as possible....

September 28th.

A new planet has arisen in the shape of Sir John Salmond, Air Marshal, who takes over command of all British Forces on October 1st.... He is alert, forcible, amazingly quick in the uptake, a man who means to understand the Iraq and our dealings with its people. He dined with me last night to meet Mr Cornwallis – just we three for I wanted him to get into instant touch with the Iraq government to which Mr Cornwallis belongs. We had the most enchanting evening for Sir John is delightful to talk to on any subject.

To H. B.   BAGDAD, *October 8th, 1922.*

I wrote to you on the 29th. The 30th was the first of their autumn races. We began the day, the Joyces and I, by taking the Amir Zaid to Ctesiphon.... He is so eager to find out and learn about everything – as quick and appreciative as the King. I took our breakfast which we ate under the shadow of the great walls, while I told Zaid of all the battles that had been fought there, 637 and 1914. In the afternoon we went to the races as H.M. was going. I went to Sir Percy's box and he put me next the King. After we had talked a little Sir John Salmond strolled over from his box, so I took him into H.M.'s box and we three had an hour's talk, I interpreting.

I hear the King is overjoyed at the signature of the treaty. I went up and wrote my name with respectful congratulations yesterday but I haven't yet seen him. To-day I've been translating his really beautiful proclamation which will be published in English and Arabic to-morrow together with the treaty. I wish I had more time to do it properly; it demanded better work than could be put into the twenty-five minutes allowed me....

To H. B.   BAGDAD, *October 24th, 1922.*

The Cabinet, at the request of the King, has appointed me honorary Director of Archaeology – there didn't seem to be any other way of keeping the place warm till we could afford a proper Director.

October 25th.

When I got in at six o'clock I found an urgent message from the King bidding me to dinner. Jafar, Nuri and Zaid were the party. We had a very merry dinner, during the course of which H.M. described the glories of Chatsworth, and played a game of Bridge afterwards, I teaching the Amir Zaid. I like him more and more – and I never met anyone with such exquisite manners. Incidentally, I was wearing a new gold and white gown ... so I had a modest triumph too....

To H. B.   BAGDAD, *November 1st, 1922.*

I've been figuring in my capacity as Director of Archaeology. Mr Woolley arrived on Sunday. He is a first-class
digger and an archaeologist after my own heart – i.e., he
entirely backs me up in the way I'm conducting the department. He has come out as head of a joint expedition organ-
ised by the British Museum and Pennsylvania University
and they are going to dig Ur, no less, and are prepared to
put in two years' work.... After lunch Sabih Bey and I went
to a meeting of the Cabinet which I attended for the first
time to explain and defend the Law of Excavations which I
had drafted.

To H. B.   MOSUL, *November 10th, 1922.*

It was near sunset when we reached the Levy Camp which
lies in a cup on the top of the foothills with the British flag
flying on it.... I occupied the hut of our host Captain Merry,
a simple, cheerful, self-reliant young officer.... We were
waited on by four Assyrian boys, in full native dress – striped
embroidered trousers, scarlet and yellow tassels flung over
their shoulders under the white felt zouave jacket, white
peaked caps with a white or scarlet feather at the side....

Before we left next day I inspected many of the huts – spotlessly clean, the women all dressed up in their best in antici-
pation of a visit, but their feathers are not so fine as those of
the men. I went away much impressed. Truly we are a remarkable people. We save from destruction remnants of op-
pressed nations, laboriously and expensively giving them
sanitary accommodation, teaching their children, respecting
their faiths, but all the time cursing at the trouble they are
giving us – and they're cursing us, not infrequently, for the
trouble we are giving them with our meticulous regulations.
And then behold, when left to themselves they flock to our
standards, our Captain Merrys for their chosen leaders, our
regulations their decalogue.... And on all this we gaze without amazement. It's the sort of thing that happens under the
British flag – don't ask us why, we don't know....

On the 15th I caught the train at Qaraghan and reached

Bagdad on the 16th without incident except that the train was some six hours late – you know our ways. I arrived to find a political crisis, for which I was partly prepared by letter. The Naqib has resigned. It has happened quite simply and without anyone's feelings being hurt – the Cabinet has just died of inanition. So now they are busy Cabinet making as hard as they can go and with luck I think they may have a much stronger lot than before....

To-night Sir Percy goes off to the Persian Gulf – a long postponed conference which I hope will end in the conclusion of a satisfactory treaty between Nejd and Iraq but it's rather agitating to have Sir Percy away when so many things are happening. We've had, however, very reassuring telegrams from home about the attitude they are going to take up with the Turks in defence of the Iraq frontiers....

November 23rd.

The new Cabinet is formed and is, I think very good. Yasin Pasha goes to Public Works so I shall do my Archaeological dept. with him which I shall like. H.M. and the Cabinet are determined to take a strong line. It's needed, for the Shiah mujtahids have issued fatwahs forbidding people to take part in the elections....

To H. B. BAGDAD, *December 4th, 1922.*

Do you know – àpropos of nothing at all – that I've been four times mentioned in despatches for my valuable and distinguished services in the field! It came to me as a surprise – indeed it is singularly preposterous – when I counted up the documents in order to fill up a Colonial Office Form. I hadn't realised there were so many. Apparently one of the fields I distinguished myself in was Palestine, for I was mentioned by Sir Reginald Wingate....

To H. B. BAGDAD, *December 18th, 1922.*

Major Young asked me whether I would accept appointment as Oriental Secretary, with the rest of Sir Percy's staff, till Oct. 1923 (which is to be the date of Sir Percy's own appointment). I said I would. It has turned out very much as I should have wished because it's they who have asked me to stay and not I who am clinging on. I made it very clear to Major Young that I wasn't clinging on if they did not want me. What a strange political career I've had, to be sure.... Oh for peace – peace at any price, I could almost say.

We've another problem looming on our Southern borders. You know that Ibn Saud has captured Hayil, thereby changing the balance of Arabian politics. His frontier now runs with that of the Iraq and it's as yet an undefined frontier. Sir Percy has invited him to come into conference with himself and Faisal at the earliest possible moment, and I've been laying out on the map what I think should be our desert boundaries. There's nothing I should like so much as to attend that conference of Kings but I don't suppose for a moment that Sir Percy will take me....

The conquest of Hayil will have far-reaching consequences. It will bring Ibn Saud into the theatre of trans-Jordanian politics and probably into the Franco-Syrian vista also – it's difficult as yet to see with what results. I should, however, feel much greater anxiety if I weren't so certain of Sir Percy's power to guide him. It's really amazing that anyone should exercise influence such as his.... I don't think that any European in history has made a deeper impression on the Oriental mind....

To H. B.   BAGDAD, *January 16th, 1923.*

The chief news is that Sir Percy is going home by this air mail to help the Cabinet to come to a conclusion about Iraq policy.... It is far more satisfactory that he in person should go and put the whole case to the authorities, for you see, even if they don't want to shoulder the burden they have got to learn that it's amazingly difficult to let it drop with a bump. Even the evacuation of Mosul would mean, I am convinced, that we should be faced with the problem of sixty or seventy thousand Christian refugees....

It is almost impossible to believe that a few years ago the human race was more or less governed by reason and con-

sidered consequences, before it did things. I don't feel reasonable myself – how can one when political values are as fluctuating as the currency?.... At the back of my mind I have a
feeling that we people of the war can never return to complete sanity. The shock has been too great; we're unbalanced.
I am aware that I myself have much less control over my
own emotions than I used to have. I don't really feel certain
about what I might do next and I can only hope that the
opportunity for doing impossibly reckless things won't arise,
if it did I should probably do them; at least I can't be sure
I shouldn't....

It will be dreadfully flat when I return to London, not to
be consulted about all Cabinet appointments!

To-night as I was coming back from the office very dirty
and tired, I met Sir John Salmond and Air Commodore
Borton on their doorstep and they dragged me in to a very
merry tea.... I'm much attached to the Air Force; they have
the same sort of charm that sailors have, they are so keen
and so busy with their job, and it's a job that they are always at, just as sailors are. And they are so amazingly gal-
lant. The things that they've done in this country without
anything said about them, might be a theme for epics.

To H. B.   BAGDAD, *January 30th, 1923.*

... Seven years I've been at this job of setting up an Arab
State. If we fail it's little consolation to me personally that
other generations may succeed, as I believe they must....

I've been rather busy with archaeology. First I had long
reports about Ur to write for my Minister and for the local
papers and next I've had to tackle the Oxford University expedition to Kish – I was promised a field worker and an
epigraphist and on that agreed to ask my Minister for a concession, and lo and behold, one solitary man turns up....

I feel convinced that no one, however good, can undertake single handed so big a work as the excavation of Kish,
so I've held up the concession and telegraphed for the advice
of the Joint Committee which is the highest archaeological
authority at home – for convenience, I'm a member of it....

To H. B.   BAGDAD, *March 1, 1923.*

Will you please do something for me. The King (with
whom I've just been having tea) is in perplexity as to how to
furnish a big room in the little palace that has just been built
– a reception room. It's an awkward shape for it was meant
for a dining room – 170 paces long by about 70 wide with a
monumental fireplace on one of the long sides. I've suggested
that it must be somehow broken up in furnishing it and that
he ought to make a central sitting place in the middle, opposite the fireplace, with three big handsome sofas, the middle
one the most imposing. In this dusty country it's better to
have furniture rather simple in pattern as otherwise it's difficult to clean, and we think that if we had some good drawings or pictures we could make it here. So could you perhaps
send us a selection of catalogues or drawings from some of
the best London shops by next air mail? We could get chairs
and tables out of them too and make something that would
do for the present....

I went to Ur with Major Wilson. They are closing down
for the season and we had to go in person and divide the
finds between the diggers and the Iraq....

It took us the whole day to do the division but it was extremely interesting and Mr Woolley was an angel. We had
to claim the best things for ourselves but we did our best to
make it up to him and I don't think he was very much dis-
satisfied. We, for our part, were well pleased. The best object
is a hideous Sumerian statue of a King of Lagash, about
three feet high but headless.

It has a long inscription across the shoulder in which they
have read the King's name, but it will go back to London
to be completely decyphered and then return to us....

To H. B.   BAGDAD, *April 10th, 1923.*

Thank you a thousand times for all the trouble you took
about the King's furniture. He is delighted with the pictures.
Major Wilson and I are going to have a great talk with him
to-morrow and decide what he shall order....

To F. B. BAGDAD, *April 24th, 1923.*

I went to Hillah for the night on the 14th with Major Wilson and Dr Herzfeld. We stayed with the Longriggs that night and next morning motored out about an hour to the East to see the excavations at Kish – I was inspecting, you understand. We found that Mr Mackay had done a great deal of work at one of the mounds – the one for which I had got him a permit – but it was almost certainly not the oldest part of Kish which lies under another mound about a mile away. This second mound is covered with very ancient planoconvex bricks and very ancient pottery. I'm getting permission for him to do some preliminary work there....

Haji Naji gave a luncheon party in his garden last Sunday to Sir Percy. In spite of its being Ramadhan several of the Ministers came – scarcely any of them are fasting. It was a very charming little function and Haji Naji's sorrow at parting with Sir Percy goes to my heart. But fortunately he has made great friends with Sir Henry.

All this time rather tears the heart strings, you understand, it's very moving saying good-bye to Sir Percy . . . We had the annual election of members of the Library Committee this week. I came out top. Last year I was third. They never elect any other European. That's the sort of thing that makes it difficult to leave.

To F. B. BAGDAD, *May 9th, 1923.*

This is I fear going to be a very scrappy letter for I'm rather overcome with departure....

Last week Sir Percy left – a very moving farewell....

CHAPTER 23

Bagdad

GERTRUDE is back in Bagdad after spending the summer in England.

To F. B.   BAGDAD, *Sept. 11, 1923.*

Captain Clayton came down from Mosul on Thursday, the day I posted my last letter, with the Amir Zaid. He and Mr Thomson and I dined with Haji Naji on Friday. That was a very delightful occasion, an excellent dinner spread on his roof over which nodded the tops of the mulberry trees – such broiled fish and such a lamb roasted whole and such figs from our host's garden! We dined about 7 and getting back early, the other two spent the rest of the evening with me. I had had a dinner party the night before, the Lloyds (he is Mr Cornwallis's assistant in the Interior and I like both him and his wife), Mr Jardine from Mosul, Assistant Inspector, and a nice man called Mackay in the A.P.O.C. I enjoy seeing them all again.

I've had a fearful brawl in my household – not the fault of my household fortunately. You remember Mr Thomson dismissed my gardener, Mizhir, and installed a brother in his place. When I came back Mizhir turned up at once expecting to be reinstated. I refused and finding him a day or two ago making claims to draw water at my pipe I forbade him to come into my garden. Yesterday while I was at the office and Zaya and the new gardener, Jaji Marzuq, were out being inoculated for cholera (doubly inoculated to show 'bonne volonté') did Mizhir and two other brothers come in and beat Haji Ali, my inestimable cook, over the head. Haji Ali quite rightly hauled Mizhir off to the police station next door and I who was lunching at home because of the cold in my head telephoned to a British Inspector. And then I heard shouting and screaming in the street and behold there was

Mizhir let out and one of his brothers struggling in the arms
of some privates of the Levies with the evident intention of
renewing their proceedings with me or any other victim. So
I had the police up at once and clapped all three into the
police station. So I hope that's happily concluded.

To H. B.   BAGDAD, *Sept. 17, 1923.*

It's been very touching the welcome I've had from the big
tribal people. Several of them have come in from as far as
Diwaniyah on purpose to see me and I don't think one could
mistake the fact that they're glad of my return. I feel rather
ashamed of the immense confidence they place in one when
I consider how little any of us can do really. They trust us as
they never trust their own people and they think we have
behind us the concentrated force of Great Britain entirely
at our disposal, in any matter connected with the Iraq....

To H. B.   *Sept. 25th, 1923.*

The Waring and Gillow furniture has come – it's rather
lighter in build than I expected and some of our Iraqis are
weighty people....

On Saturday there was a huge dinner party at the Palace
in honour of Sir Henry's accession to the High Commis-
sionership. I sat by Zaid who next morning sent me two
guinea pigs as a present – I felt as if I had retired into my
remotest childhood as I installed them in a cage in my
garden....

We're having great dealings with the Ministry of Pious Bequests in the matter of our library. Its finances are in a bad
way and I can't go on struggling to get money for it, so we've
conceived the idea of offering ourselves bodily to Auqaf and
are now in negotiation with the Minister who favours the
suggestion. We discussed it at length at a Committee meeting
yesterday, after which I went round to call on Mina Abdud,
a wealthy Christian lady. And there dropped in an old
Christian of high repute who is a member of the central
electoral committee. With him came the Director of Health,

and then Jafar Pasha, and we sat gossiping till it was time for me to go away.

You know I do enjoy myself here. I like being in the middle of this Arab world and on the terms I'm on with it, but I confess even now I have moments of amazement at finding how much we're in the middle of it – for instance when I looked round Sheikh Ali's luncheon table at all those turban-murbans on either side of me!

To H. B. and F. B. BAGDAD, *Oct. 1st, 1923.*

All the R'ton doings sound very pleasant, it's curious to have been so lately part of them and now to be so rapt again in to the life of Iraq. But I am immensely happy here, there's no doubt of it.... My work in the office grows more interesting – I've got all the tribal questions into my hands now....

Oct. 4th.

We had a terrific orgy last night! The dinner was excellent, Marie having supplied her best sauces and afterwards we played a preposterous game of cards invented by Capt. Clayton with pistachios for counters. Ken Cornwallis kept the score and so well that at the end everyone was proved to have won. Unfortunately no one could pocket his winnings as there was no one to pay, so we ate the pistachios and separated in peace.

The temp. is rapidly falling – it's been down a maximum of 95, very pleasant.

To H. B. BAGDAD, *October 13th, 1923.*

I've been spending most of the morning at the Ministry of Works where we are starting – what do you think? the Iraq Museum! It will be a modest beginning, but it is a beginning....

To H. B. *Oct. 30th, 1923.*

My household is in a great jig about the King's coming to dinner and Marie has quickly made a complete new set of lovely shades for the electric lights!... It has begun to rain –

it has been showery for the last two days. It's nice and early for rain; all the desert tribes will go out to pasture and keep quiet....

To H. B.   BAGDAD, *Nov. 7th, 1923.*

I seem to have been socially very busy. On Friday morning we had the formal inauguration of the American School of Archaeology. There's no concrete school as yet because there's no money and no Director and no nothing. But I made the acquaintance of a charming man, Dr Hewett, head of the American school in Mexico. He and his wife came to see me in the evening....

To H. B.   BAGDAD, *Nov. 14th, 1923.*

On Sunday I had Ken to dinner to meet Dr and Mrs Hewett. He's head of the American school in Mexico and told us most interesting things about American archaeology and anthropology. I expect you know – I didn't – that while they have all the ancient beasts they haven't ancient man. He didn't develop there and America was peopled from Asia via Behring Straits at quite a comparatively late period.

The Hewetts have now gone to Mosul. They're charming people, both of them. When they come back I'm going to take her to see an Arab family. She has never been in the East before and is deeply interested in everything.

Thank you both a thousand times for your kind shoppings and writings. In reply to Mother, I'm afraid the brocades will be too expensive but I long for the patterns to arrive.

To H. B.   BAGDAD, *Nov. 29th, 1923.*

My chief news is the arrival of Lady Dobbs. We all went to meet them at the station on Friday and found that Sabih Bey had spontaneously arranged an elegant reception, carpets on the ground and a police guard, the King's chief A.D.C. and all the officials. Poor Lady Dobbs was rather taken aback.

On Saturday afternoon we all went to the races, H.M. and Their Exs. It was Lady Dobbs' introduction to our world and she was much entertained. Lady D. is an angel to me.

We were all rather beaming on Saturday because the Cabinet had just been finally settled quite satisfactorily.... Things are going almost incredibly well....

To H. B.   BAGDAD, *Dec. 11th, 1923.*

I've made a new friend, the Director of Operations at the W.O. General Burnett Stuart, who has been out to have a look at us. I sat by him at dinner at the Air Marshal's on Thursday and told him things a General ought to know – all through dinner from beginning to end....

They go for a shooting party.

To H. B.   BAGDAD, *Dec. 31st, 1923.*

We collected beaters in the little village at bridge head and walked down the right bank of the arm of the Euphrates called Abu Shorah for 3 hours. It was glorious. The sun grew hotter and hotter as we walked through the poplar thickets and the green tamarisk scrub and thorns where the partridge lie. We got 55 brace to three guns – Rasim is nothing of a shot and that day didn't hit a bird. At the last we reluctantly decided that we must turn back, crossed the river and shot a gorgeous island, at the end of which the birds rose in great coveys. Unfortunately we had neglected to take any food with us, so having shot 3 hours down we shot 3 hours up and were rather hungry and thirsty before we got back to the cars. Not that it mattered; we had had such tremendous fun that nothing mattered. Also Mr Yapp deserves a testimonial, for he had made me such a fine pair of boots, lacing up to the knees, that though, as a rule, my skin comes off if you so much as look at it, after 6 hours of hard walking I wasn't even rubbed. My costume, I must tell you, was a most successful creation – brown boots up to the knees and a brown tweed tunic down to them. We got back to Babylon an hour after sunset, washed, dined and went to bed. The whole 6 days we were there we never saw. Babylon by daylight. We were off an hour before sunrise – aided by a full moon, and home after nightfall.

We shot for another hour after lunch and then motored home. It was a good Xmas Day spent with friends.

Altogether I think no more delightful expedition has ever been made in Iraq.

Now everyone but me has gone to a fancy dress ball and I'm ending the year by writing to you.

I must tell you a curious problem that arose – I hope you'll think I decided rightly. To-morrow Sir Henry gives an official dinner to the King, Cabinet and Advisors, a male dinner. He told me about it before I went to Babylon and I made no comment except approval. When I came back I found an invitation to myself and I went to him and asked him, as man to man, whether he wanted me to come. He said 'yes of course if you won't feel smothered.' I said I thought, as a high official in his office, I was sexless and that I ought to come and would. Sir Percy, on these occasions (levees and so on) always treated me simply as an official and I don't think there's any other way. So I'm going.

Jan. 3, 1924.

I spent New Year's Day from 10 a.m. to 5 p.m. receiving visitors. It was fatiguing but I felt rewarded when one of my guests observed with satisfaction 'the habits of the Khatun are like ours – she sits at home on the Id to receive congratulations.' The dinner party at the Residency was a very smart affair. I wore my best gown, our diamond tiara, Mother, and all my orders. Don't wish me back too much, life is being so interesting.

To H. B. BAGDAD, *Jan 9th, 1924.*

I'm not the least sorry that Labour should come in. They'll learn that it's not an easy thing to govern a large empire and they'll learn, I hope, that they don't know the nature of team work and that govt. as far as the individual is concerned is always a compromise. No one permanently has things exactly his own way of thinking except the dictator or the tyrant, who is 'ex-hypothesi' excluded. But is he?

To H. B. BAGDAD, *Jan. 22nd, 1924.*

I'll tell you the human details of my tour of inspection. I left Bagdad on Sunday 13th with J. M. Wilson and we went by train to Hillah. It was grey stormy weather and there had been rain in the night. We arrived at Hillah about 2 p.m. and found a taxi to take us the 12 miles into the desert to Kish. We began our adventures by falling into the first canal, just outside the railway station – at least our front wheel was well over the narrow bridge. However, I called up support from the station and we pushed the car over. As we went on it behaved in a fashion madder and madder. Finally when the car in the open plain began to spin round like a teetotum J.M. declared that he would not risk his precious life any longer. We walked for an hour and a half through rain and mud, to Kish where we were welcomed by Professor Langdon and Mr Mackay.

Next day Tuesday 15th, my carriage was slipped at Khidr station before dawn. After an early breakfast I went down to the river, crossed in a ferry to Khidr village and presented myself at the house of the Mudir, who provided me with a horse and escort to ride to Warka, which is Erech, the great Babylonian capital of the South. When we reached the mound we found quantities of people digging and rounded them up. They all screamed and cried when they saw me, but I gave them the salute and they were comforted. I said 'Have you any anticas?' 'No,' they answered, 'by God no.' I observed, 'What are those spades and picks for? I'll give you backsheesh for anything you have.' At that a change came over the scene and one after another fumbled in his breast and produced a cylinder or a seal which I bought for the museum at a few annas. The people came from a little village, Hasyah, about a mile away and I sent them off to bring all that was there while I examined the mounds. They returned while I was lunching on the ziggurat and I bought a quantity of terra cottas. I rode to the village and then back to Khidr and back to my carriage.

In the night I was carried down to Ur junction where I

arrived at dawn on Thursday and walked out to Ur mound in the bitter cold of the early morning, to meet Mr Woolley just coming back from the excavations to breakfast – a meal of which I partook heartily.

We spent the morning looking at their finds and at the excavations and the afternoon examining the Tell al Ubaid site which gave me the greatest sensation, I think, which in archaeology I have ever experienced.

I left Ur on Friday night, got to Bagdad on Saturday afternoon and spent the whole evening up to 1 a.m. in writing my report.

On Sunday J. M. took me to the Ministry, where I deposited all that I had brought in the Museum.

Then I went to the house of Madame Jafar Pasha to attend a meeting of a women's club which is just coming into being. I am wholly in favour of it – it's the first step in female emancipation here.

We're longing to know who is to be S. of S. But already I find myself writing to him shadow-cast-before reports and despatches quite different from those I used to write to His Grace. It is curious – one insensibly finds oneself wanting to bring out different points, better ones often. I believe I shall feel at home with a Labour Government. I have written quite a good despatch to-day about Anglo-French relations; I do hope Sir Henry will approve of it.

To H. B.   *Feb. 6th, 1924.*

This time Mother's letter has missed and I have yours of Jan. 22. Very interesting about the rly. strike; I long to hear what you think of the settlement. Also a delightful analysis of your children, only the second thing that I am I can't read, so I remain only an Imperialist. Well, if I am, I contend that it's in the best sense for I've directed all my efforts to detaching a large kingdom – for the good of the Empire! Anyhow, you're sorely tried, to be sure, but I'm glad you're fond of us.

On Sunday I spent the morning at my museum editing the labels. This sort of thing: I pick up a little marble fragment of a horse's neck and mane and find it labelled thus: 'This is a portion of a man's shoulder, marble object.'

'But,' say I, 'does a man grow a mane on his shoulder?' 'True, by God,' murmurs the Chalabi.

I forget what day it was that I was overtaken by an idea, but it came about this way. Col. Tainsh, Director of Rlys, came one morning to ask me who could possibly write a little account of all the places of interest you could get to by his railways – in view of the tourists who will come by car from Damascus, you understand. So I said I could, which was what he wanted. And thinking over it, I said to (myself) damn it all! Why shouldn't I write Murray's Guide for the Iraq. I began it that day, but I haven't so far gone on, except to write to John Murray about it. It's a good idea but I'm now rather taken aback to think of the amount of writing and writing that it will mean. What do you think?

Oh dear, I wish I weren't so cold.

To H. B.   *Feb. 13th, 1924.*

I rode home by the river through the gardens of Kadhimain, over the ground on which stood the palace of Harun al Rashid, but I wasn't thinking so much of him as of the fact that spring had come (Haji Naji sent me apricot flowers last week) the grass growing so beautifully green along the water channels and the buds showing on the pomegranates. And this naturally made me want to grow and open too, things almost impossible to do in an office.

It's rather warmer to-day. When I came in at 4 from the office I found Marie sitting in the garden looking like a female St Jerome, with a needle for a book, a slughi dog for a lion and a tame red-legged partridge standing solemnly beside her instead of a quail.

To H. B.   BAGDAD, *February 27th, 1924.*

The sensation of the week is the elections, the results of which are coming out daily. Bagdad was declared on Monday. On the whole very good and such other reports as are in are good too....

I went with my minister to see the Bagdad orphanage. It's a very touching place, 85 boys from 6 to about 14 whom they've picked up in the streets. And there they all are, dressed as boy scouts, clean and tidy and being taught. The subscription lists are really wonderful.

Not money only is given – a bag of rice, a plate of cakes, people give what they can. And it's the first time it has ever occurred to any one in Bagdad to support a public institution of this kind and not to expect that dim entity, the Govt., to do it for him. They made a tremendous fuss about our coming, of course.

To F. B.   BAGDAD, *Feb. 28th, 1924.*

My guide book is being so exciting. The part I shall not like is writing the introduction about the coinage being rupees and annas, and that kind of thing. However I haven't got to that yet.

Confidential.

This is what Sir Henry has written to the Col. Office about me in his annual report on his officers:

It is difficult to write of Miss Bell's services both to the British and Iraq Govts. without seeming to exaggerate. Her remarkable knowledge of this country and its people and her sympathy with them enable her to penetrate into their minds, while her inextinguishable faith prevents her from being discouraged by what she sometimes finds there. Her long acquaintance with the tribes and sheikhs makes her advice in the recurring crises in tribal affairs invaluable and her vitality and width of culture make her house a focus of all that is best worth having in both European and Arab society in Bagdad. She is in fact a connecting link between the British and Arab races without which there would be dislocation both of public business and of private amenities.

To H. B.   BAGDAD, *March 6th, 1924.*

Oh dear, I've been so busy that I haven't written any letters and to-morrow is the mail. On Friday after lunch J. M. Wilson and I took the so-called express and went to Ur to do the division. We arrived at 5.10 a.m. on Sat. and J.M. and I, with old Abdul Qadir, my curator walked out to Ur in the still dawn. By 8.15 when breakfast was ready I felt rather as if I had been up since the creation of the world, or at least since the time of Nabonidus. However that wasn't what we had to think about. Before 9 we started the division (it began by my winning the gold scarab on the toss of a rupee) and we carried on till 12.30, when I struck. It's a difficult and rather agonizing job, you know. We sat with our catalogues and ticked the things off. But the really agonizing part was after lunch when I had to tell them that I must take the milking scene. I can't do otherwise. It's unique and it depicts the life of the country at an immensely early date. In my capacity as Director of Antiquities I'm an Iraqi official and bound by the terms on which we gave the permit for excavation. J.M. backed me but it broke Mr Woolley's heart, though he expected the decision. I've written to Sir F. Kenyon explaining....

On Sunday I spent the whole day in the train writing the guide book to Bagdad, which I finished. I wrote 11 foolscap pages and then for the last 2 hours buried myself in a novel. We got in at 6.15, only 1½ hours late.

On Monday I had to write the fortnightly report for the Sec. of State which took from 8.15 till 5. So that was that.

I had a dinner party in the evening to meet a Mrs Harrison, an American traveller and writer and an exceptionally brilliant woman.

The following extract from a long article written by Mrs Marguerite Harrison in the *New York Times*, shows, on the other hand, the impression made on her by Gertrude.

'When I was first in Bagdad in 1923 I had the privilege of seeing Gertrude Bell on many occasions and of having several long talks with her. The first time I met her was by appointment at her office in the Administration building of the High Commission near the British Residency – across the Tigris from the present City of Bagdad....

'After waiting for a few moments I was ushered into a small room with a high ceiling and long French windows facing the river. It was the untidiest room I had ever seen, chairs, tables and sofas being littered with documents, maps, pamphlets and papers in English, French and Arabic. At a desk piled high with documents that had overflowed on to the carpet sat a slender woman in a smart sports frock of knitted silk, pale tan in colour. As she rose I noticed that her figure was still willowly and graceful. Her delicate oval face with its firm mouth and chin and steel-blue eyes and with its aureole of soft grey hair, was the face of a "grande dame". There was nothing of the weather-beaten hardened explorer in her looks or bearing. "Paris frock, Mayfair manners." And this was the woman who had made Sheikhs tremble at the thought of the Anglez!

'Her smile was completely disarming as was the gesture with which she swept all the papers from the sofa to the floor to make room for me....'

To H. B.   BAGDAD, *March 12th, 1924.*

... Saturday the 15th was the anniversary of the Nahdhah, the Arab Awakening, i.e. of their joining in the war in 1916, and the ceremonies fixed for it were (a) a review of Iraq troops, (b) the laying of the foundation stone of the central building of the University of Al al Bait, (c) the opening of the Divinity School of that University, Faisal having laid the first brick two years ago.

Mr Cooke dashed in on Thursday evening and asked me to write the leader for the papers about it. So I jumped up at 5.30 a.m. on Friday and complied. It was very important to get the right note. The functions were wonderful; for the first time I felt that we really had wakened up and become a nation. The review was at 9 on the Arab polo ground. Ken and I drove out and as we went saw the boy scouts marching along to line the roads. The whole town turned out, and the King taking the salute and looking so happy, Sir Henry, Sir John Salmond and all their staffs and all the notables, and Fahad Bey our great nomad sheikh, standing as close as possible to the King and Zaid. The troops were wonderful – as smart as could be, and all our soldiers said that they had accomplished a miracle in the last year.

What do you think, we spent a riotous evening being taught

Mah Jong by Capt. C.! We loved it and mean to go on with it when we've time. Wasn't it lucky I had it.

On Sunday Ken took us with him to the Sarai, for I was going to my museum, and there I fell into one of the worst passions I've ever been in. I found old — mending the flowers from Ur with huge blobs of plaster of Paris so that the stone petals quite disappeared in them. I told him he was never to mend anything again and sent for a friend of mine, an antiquity dealer, to repair the damage which he has done.

After that feeling rather upset, I came home and arranged flowers and played in my garden....

To H. B.   *March 27th, 1924.*

Well, my doings are not without moment. First Kish. We found an atmosphere of electric gloom and learnt afterwards that they had expected to find us such that in the first half hour Prof. Langdon would close down the excavations and Mr Mackay would find himself without a job. So I, unknowing, while eating a scrap of lunch, explained that my object was to leave, as far as possible, the tablets to them for they should be at the disposition of students. On the other hand, they would have to make up by parting with some other fine objects. 'Who decides,' said the Professor, 'if we disagree?' I replied that I did, but he needn't be afraid for he would find me eager to oblige. I said 'Come on, Professor, you'll see how it works out.' So we went to his tent where all the tablets were exposed. There was one unique object, a stone tablet inscribed with what is probably the oldest known human script. The Professor positively pressed it on me; he said he had copied it and read it and didn't mind what happened. So I took it. Then we went to a little room where all the other objects were, and began on the beads and jewels. There was a lovely pomegranate bud earring, found in the grave of a girl, time of Nebuchadnezzar, and he set against it a wonderful copper stag, early Babylonian and falling into dust. It was obvious that we here could not preserve the latter, as I explained. I took the pomegranate bud and he was pleased. So we turned to the necklaces, and we picked, turn and turn about. And thus with all the rest. The Professor grew more and more excited. It is very amusing to do I must say. And isn't it fantastic to be selecting pots and things four to six thousand years old! I got a marvellous stone inlay of a Sumerian king leading captives and not being at all nice to them, and a mother of pearl inlay of a king and his wives – inscribed with his name. The Professor got, what he longed for, a mother of pearl inlay representing a milking scene – you see I have my milking scene in the great plaque from Ur.

We worked from 1.30 to 10.30, with brief intervals for tea and dinner, choosing and packing, till I felt absolutely broken with fatigue – so tired that I couldn't sleep and when I slept dreamt restlessly. I was up at 7 and out to see the ziggurat where I met J.M. We began work again at 8 and went on till 11, by which time all was finished and packed except 3 huge Hamurabi pots which J.M. and I carried home on our knees.

I had tea with A.V.M. Higgins who had just arrived. I happened in the course of conversation to quote Herbert [Richmond] and he mentioned that in all the three services there was no one whose opinion he valued so highly. That was nice, wasn't it.

I'm writing in the middle of the night, being unable to sleep.

To H. B.   BAGDAD, *April 1, 1924.*

Well, the Assembly. The King came in looking very wonderful in full Arab dress. The Ministers followed him and sat down on either side, he sitting on the dais. He was tremendously clapped. Then he read his speech from the throne, a very fine bit of oratory and most moving. I think I have never seem him so much agitated; his voice shook. After it his procession reformed and he left.

Then they elected their President – a moment of breathless excitement. They all wrote their choice on bits of paper and dropped them into a box.

She tells that she had a dinner party where one of the guests was a somewhat enterprising storyteller.

To H. B.   BAGDAD, *April 15th, 1924.*

One of the stories I will tell you – I laughed at it too. 'How would you punctuate this sentence – Mary ran out into the garden naked?' Ken said: 'with a full stop, I hope.' 'No,' said Sir ——, 'a dash after Mary.'

On Sunday morning I went to my Museum where I had various visitors including Ken. It really is fun showing people over the museum; there are such wonderful things to be seen in it.

I've never had so many roses in my garden before – it blushes with them. And lovely carnations, stock, larkspur and things as well.

To F. B.   BAGDAD, *April 30th, 1924.*

... Summer has come and I find I want another lace gown to wear in the evenings. I would like a black one for I have a silver 'fourreau' which it will go with. So will you please send me 4½ yards of black filet lace 25 inches wide. And the great thing is to get a lace covered with pattern as much as possible, not with a big stretch of blank net at the top if you understand me.

To-day I went to the Museum in the morning where Sir Henry, Esme, and Captain Vaughan visited us. I burst with pride when I show people over the Museum. It is becoming such a wonderful place. It was a great morning because there were 6 boxes from Kish to be unpacked – the remainder of our share. Such copper instruments as have never before been handed down from antiquity; the shelves shout with them.

To H. B.   BAGDAD, *June 11th, 1924.*

We beat Cinderella by half an hour – the Treaty was ratified last night at 11.30.

To H. B. [who was in Australia]   BAGDAD, *June 25th, 1924.*

I suppose it's the reaction from the unholy excitement in which we have lived for the last few months, but whatever may be the reason, I'm feeling shockingly dull and depressed. So I'm afraid this letter won't be up to standard.

To F. B.   BAGDAD, *June 25th, 1924.*

I have been swimming so vigorously that my bathing costume is wearing out and already has to be darned. Will you please get me another. The kind I like is in two pieces, drawers and jumper, and I like it black with a coloured border of some kind round all the edges. I prefer silk tricotine to silk and I like best a square or V-shaped opening at the neck. As to colour if you see something nice in a variegated tricotine (vide enclosed – but this particular one is in silk not tricotine and I don't like that so much) it might be a pleasant change from black. But the colours should show a general tendency to dark blue or green if you understand me.

Bathing clothes are so exiguous that I think it might be sent by letter post by overland mail – they don't normally take parcels.

Ever your very affectionate (but tiresome) daughter,
GERTRUDE.

This particular order for clothes certainly was tiresome, for it was completely baffling. There were not bathing costumes to be found in two pieces, there were none to be found in tricotine, variegated or otherwise: there were very few in black or dark blue, or green, and of these none had a coloured border. Most of the costumes obtainable were in one piece, usually of bright coloured silk, with a design in gaudy embroidery on back or front, sometimes on both.

One of the least impossible of these garments was finally despatched to Gertrude. It did not give entire satisfaction, as will be seen from a subsequent letter.

Bagdad

SHE writes of her father who had gone to Ceylon to see the Richmonds. Vice-Admiral Richmond was now Naval Commander-in-Chief, East Indies.

To F. B.   BAGDAD, *July 2nd, 1924.*

Isn't it really a good thing that he should be so full of vitality and the power of enjoyment. How delightful it will be for Elsa and Herbert to have him! He is, we may admit to one another, like no one else in the world. I can't think how other daughters can bear not having him for a father.

To F. B.   BAGDAD, *July 16th, 1924.*

... I think I told you in one of my letters what I do every day. I get up at 5.30, do exercises till 5.45 and walk in the garden till 6 or a little after cutting flowers. All that grows now is a beautiful double jasmin of which I have bowls full every day, and zinnias, ugly and useful. I breakfast at 6.40 on an egg and some fruit, interview my old cook Haji Ali at 6.45 when I order any meal I want and pay the daily books. Leave for the office by car at 6.55 get there at 7. I'm there till 1.30 when I lunch with the High Commissioner – now with Nigel.

The first thing I do in the office is to look through the three vernacular papers and translate anything that ought to be brought to the notice of the authorities. These translations are typed and circulated to the H.C., the Advisers in the Arab offices, and finally as an appendix of the fortnightly reports to the Secretary of State. By the time I've done that, papers are beginning to come in, intelligence reports from all the Near East and India, local reports, petitions, etc. The petitions I generally dispose of myself; the local reports I note on, suggesting if necessary memoranda to the Ministries of Interior or Finance (mostly Interior which is the Ministry I'm most concerned with) or despatches and letters. Sometimes I write a draft at once, sometimes I propose the general outlines and wait for approval or correction. In and out of all this people come in to see me, sheikhs, and Arab Officials or just people, who want to give some bit of information or ask for advice; if there's anything important in what they have to say I inform the H.C. At intervals in the daily routine, I'm now busy writing the Annual Report for the League of Nations. I usually get a clear hour or two before lunch.

I get home about 2.30 and do nothing till 5. I don't often sleep, but I lie on a big sofa under a fan and read novels or papers. All the windows are shut and the room is comparatively cool. After 5 I go out swimming or I take a little walk or people come to see me. I very seldom ride in the summer, it's too hot in the evening and I haven't time before going to office. I dine about 7.30 on some iced soup or a bit of fish or some fruit and sometimes if I'm feeling unusually energetic I do an hour's work or I write letters. Generally I read again till about ten and then go to bed on the roof, and that's the hot weather life. And now it's time to go and have my bath before dinner. Now I come to think of it it seems rather a hermit programme. It is. I hate dining out or having people to dinner in the hot weather.

To F. B. BAGDAD, *July 23rd, 1924.*

About the bathing dress. It was my fault. I ought to have left you carte blanche about the material. Probably no one wears tricotine now – something else is the vogue. The one you sent is rather baggy but I shall be very glad of it when my present one goes into holes.

To F. B. *Aug. 5th, 1924.*

It is deadly hot and I'm as thin as a lath – I can't eat anything in the heat. But I have a glass of iced soup at 11 a.m. and find that it makes all the difference. There is another month of extreme heat and then it begins to tail off.

To H. B. BAGDAD, *Aug. 20, 1924.*

I dined with Haji Naji on his roof. It was a nice cool evening for once and we sat on the roof with the full moon so bright that we wanted no other light and the tops of the mulberry trees waving round us. Presently I glanced up and saw the moon looking a very odd shape and found that it was a total eclipse! You saw it too I expect. It's a sinister thing, an eclipse, isn't it. As we motored back the shadow spread over the moon, deepened and left the world in a threatening darkness. The people in the houses were beating pans and firing off revolvers to frighten the whale which was devouring the moon. This they ultimately succeeded in doing, but not without great trouble. It was a very long eclipse.

... Bathing in our favourite pool opposite the King's palace. To us a party of shining ones, the King, Zaid, Jafar, Nuri ... all the King's pals. They had come, some of them to bathe and all of them to picnic on the bank. Do you know it's difficult to make a curtsey with grace when you're wet in a bathing dress.

On Sunday morning I went to the Museum which I had promised to show to some teachers from Mosul. They were very much impressed and said many complimentary things about the service I was rendering to the Iraq. But what pleases me still more – since I'm blowing my own trumpet so loud – is that I have a letter from Sir F. Kenyon saying that he holds up the Iraq Department of Antiquities as the model for the manner in which the division of finds is made between excavators and the local Government and that as long as things remain in my hands he will be perfectly satisfied. I am very much relieved for I feared they would never forgive me for taking the milking plaque which was by far the best thing they found. I could do no other and I am so glad they recognized it. They have been most reasonable.

To H. B. BAGDAD, *Oct. 15th, 1924.*

I have letters from you and Mother of October 1, all about your Free Traders. You are thick in the election and I'm

longing to know your views. Upon my soul, I think I would
vote Labour if I were in England. The turning out of the
Government at a time when the peace of Europe is still on
such thin ice seems to me to be such a mean party trick. And
the programmes of the Conservatives and Liberals are poor,
hackneyed stuff, don't you think?

In October of this year Gertrude had the great pleasure of a
visit from the Richmonds, Elsa and her husband Vice-Admiral
Herbert Richmond and their daughter Mary. They were on board
the flagship *Chatham* on one of its official cruises and came up the
Persian Gulf to Basrah and then to Bagdad. This coincided with
a visit from George Trevelyan, Molly's elder son, who was on his
way to stay with the Richmonds in Ceylon and spent a week at
Bagdad on the way. His arrival was a great joy to Gertrude. It
is worth including some extracts from her letters for the interest
of seeing that she who had cared so much for her younger sisters
when they were children was ready to welcome their children as
if they had been her own.

To her sister.   BAGDAD, *October 28th, 1924.*

DARLING MOLL,

George arrived safely on Saturday at 1.30. I was delighted
to see him. We sat hand in hand talking breathlessly.

BAGDAD, *Oct. 29th, 1924.*

I have been a very poor thing this week with a touch of
bronchitis....

The excavations at Kish and Ur are opening – Kish has
already begun and Mr Woolley arrived last Saturday and
goes down to Ur to-morrow. We are all frightfully thrilled by
the discovery in India by Sir John Marshall of seals which
are exactly like Sumerian seals here. I have written to Sir
John Marshall asking him for impressions of his seals. I do
hope they will have a good season at Ur this year.

I've so little to write about because I have been seeing so
few people. But oh I'm thankful to be getting well again! I
do get so dreadfully bored when I'm ill.

To H. B. BAGDAD, *Nov. 5, 1924.*

As you may imagine, we have been having rather a rushing time, complicated by the fact that I had only just got out of bed. But I'm really beginning to feel well now.

The Richmonds all arrived on Saturday.

On Monday morning they went to Ctesiphon and I to the office. We all lunched at the Residency. Esme is back and is being kindness itself, putting her car at our disposal and so forth. After a tea party with the King, the Richmond family dined with the A.V.M., where Herbert is staying, but I didn't go as I felt still rather shaky.

On Tuesday Herbert flew to Kut and back. Elsa and Mary went shopping carpets with Elsie Sinbad and Mr Cooke, and we all lunched with the Sinbads. Then I gave a tea-party attended by 10 ladies and two of their daughters, at which Elsa and Mary shone. I hear it is likely to be the talk of the town for the next month. They dined with Jafar – I didn't go.

I feel as I did when you were here that it is almost incredible that they should actually be in Bagdad. It is also incredibly delightful. Elsa is so delicious always. She is picking up, Arabic and delights everyone with her efforts to talk it. Isn't she wonderfully quick and intelligent! And it has been so endlessly enjoyable to have her to talk to. I feel as if I had got things off my mind that had lain on it for months and months. She is amazingly well – never tired, eats enormously and is amused by everything.

Now I must go and dress for dinner.

Ever your very affectionate daughter,

GERTRUDE.

To her sister, Mary Travelyan. BAGDAD, *November 12th, 1924.*

We had the most delicious days all together when George joined us after his Northern tour....

He is wildly interested in everything. He used to sit and listen when Herbert talked of India and I of the Iraq asking us now and then of things he had not understood. He is not going to waste his time on this journey, he will come back full of new impressions and experiences and now the East looms so very large it is worth while to know something about it....

Well, I hope I have made a new friend with him. I should always like to be in close touch. Last year in England I made a new friend in Pauline and now I've got George. Isn't it nice. Kitty must be next.... [Pauline and Kitty Trevelyan.]

The *Chatham* sailed from Basrah this morning at ten. I do feel rather flat without them. All my servants adored them and one of them wept when they left.

To H. B.   BAGDAD, *Dec. 3, 1924.*

... After lunch, while I was sitting in my garden, there rolled up an American, adviser or ex-adviser to the U.S.A. on the subject of irrigation engineering and he had just been the guest of the Australian and Indian Governments! As he shook hands with me on the garden path, he observed: 'I greet the first citizen of Iraq.' Gratifying, wasn't it.

To H. B.   BAGDAD, *Dec. 10th, 1924.*

Your most beloved letter of Nov. 26th – I *was* glad to have it – it made me feel quite warm inside. I'm perfectly aware that I don't merit so much love, but the nicest thing about love is that you can have it without merit. You mustn't bother, darling, about my health. You are not reckoning with the immense elasticity which comes of being everywhere sound. I shall always be thin – an inherited characteristic; and I would rather anyhow. I don't like fat people. I really did have a very hard and lonely summer and I suppose it temporarily sapped my powers of withstanding heat. But now all my own friends are back it's very different and if we get out shooting at Xmas I shall walk eight hours a day without turning a hair.

I am told that Lionel Smith after one of the said shooting parties in which Gertrude was included said that she had outlasted them all in the matter of walking, and was as fresh at the end of the day as when she started.

To F. B.   BAGDAD, *Dec. 14, 1924.*

I've just had the little Amir Ghazi to tea, with his tutor and governess. The train and soldiers I had ordered for him from Harrod's had arrived last mail and were presented, with great success. Especially the train. He loves all kinds of machinery and in fact was much cleverer about the engine than any of us – found out where the brake was and how to make the engine go backwards or forwards. We all sat on the floor and watched it running along the rails, following it with shouts of joy. Fancy a little Mecca child introduced to the most lovely modern toys!...

To H. B.   BAGDAD, *Dec. 23rd, 1924.*

Yesterday a very interesting thing happened – I went to see the Queen. She's charming, I'm so happy to say. She has the delicate, sensitive Hashimi face (she's his first cousin, you know) and the same winning manner that he has. She had on a very nice, long tunicked brown gown made by the nuns, a long long string of pearls, and a splendid aquamarine pendant. I saw the two eldest girls who are just like her, rather shy but eager to be outgoing, one could see.

These are two of the annual testimonials about Gertrude's work sent to the Colonial Office in 1925.

1925.

To describe Miss Bell as a complete and accurate encyclopaedia on all matters concerning this country would be true – but inadequate. Her extensive and detailed knowledge of past happenings and existing personalities is sufficient in itself to make her an invaluable colleague. But beyond all this, her keen intellect and her unfailing sympathy for the struggles of the infant Iraq state enable her to play a part that could not be played by anyone else, in ensuring not only the closeness but also the cordiality of the relations between this High Commission (the officials, be they Iraqi or British) and the Iraq Government. I cannot adequately express my gratitude for the assistance I receive from her.

B. BOURDILLON.

Miss Bell's extraordinary abilities and sympathies need no further testimony from me. But I realise them even better than I did last year and am still most grateful to her for all that she has done during the critical time through which we have been passing.

H. DOBBS.

Bagdad – England

To H. B. BAGDAD, *Jan. 7th, 1925.*

I've had a week with the Queen and her court, culminating in her first reception to-day. On Saturday morning I went up to talk to her about it and on Saturday afternoon I took Esme to see her.

What with this and with preparing reports for the League of Nations delegation, I've been busy. But I did have a holiday last Friday – the only one of the season. We all went out shooting, Baqubah way – Bernard and Ken and I, Col. Joyce and Major Maclean. We started at 6.30 in freezing bitter cold and when we got out into the country it was still colder, the whole world white with hoar frost and all the waters frozen. But we enjoyed it tremendously – it looked so lovely, the green palm gardens against the white frost. We ran to the beats to keep ourselves warm and we returned 12 hours later with a bag of 150, geese, duck and snipe.

On New Year's Day, in the intervals of receiving the visits of Ministers, I made a little account of the year's expenditure. I have spent in all some £560 over and above my salary. Of this £230 (in round figures) is the cost of living here above my salary and another £79 is foods from England – also cost of living, therefore. £90 for books, papers, seeds and bulbs for my garden and various little odds and ends of that sort, and £160 for clothes – that is to say, gloves, shoes, hats, silks or stuffs for Marie to make up, for I have had no new clothes from home. On the whole I don't think it has been an extravagant year – do you?

To F. B. BAGDAD, *Jan. 15th, 1925.*

... But you know, though I love hearing of it, I don't feel that I should fit into an Xmas party. I've grown too much of a recluse. After all such years and years as I have had of being alone are bound to alter one's character. Not for the better, I admit and fear.

But there it is; if you have children and grandchildren growing up round you it is very different. I haven't had that, more's the pity....

To H. B.   BAGDAD, *January 15th, 1925.*

The Frontier Commission arrives to-morrow....

To F. B.   BAGDAD, *Jan. 28th, 1925.*

... We are still having an amazing bout of cold weather. It has frozen almost every night since Xmas and for the last three nights the temp. has been down to 18°. By day it's little above freezing point with an excruciating north wind which cuts you like a knife. I live in a fur coat except when I'm sitting before the fire in my sitting room. It's rare in this country to be longing for a little sun and warmth.

We are living through a very agitating time, feeling all of us that our destinies are in the melting pot. If good comes out of the Frontier Commission it will be mainly due to Sir Henry's extraordinarily tactful handling and the charming courtesy with which he and Esme treated them....

The Bagdadis played up splendidly. On Thursday there was a great Boy Scout function to which I went.

At the end they hoisted the Iraq flag on a tall standard. It was wonderfully moving. Some boys ran forward with the flag staff and set it up; then all the boys who carried the various scout flags ran up and formed a circle round it, while the other boys crowded in in a huge semi-circle, with the spectators crowding in behind them. When the chief Scout Master broke the flag a huge roar went up from the boys and the crowd and after it had died down the Scout Master cried out 'Three cheers for King Faisal the First!' Even out of doors they made a great sound....

To H. B.   BAGDAD, *Feb. 11th, 1925.*

This isn't going to be a very bright letter for I am suffering under the shock of a domestic tragedy with which I feel sure you will sympathize – the death of my darling little spaniel, Peter, and of his mother, Sally, who was Ken's dog. I don't know which of them I loved most, for Sally was with me all the summer while Ken was on leave. But I shall now miss Peter most – he was always with us, in the office and everywhere, and he adored me, and I him. Sally had a cold a few days ago and as Ken was going out shooting with the King I offered to take her – we neither of us, nor the vet, had any idea that it was distemper which it really was, the very worst kind that ends in pneumonia. Peter caught it and died after agonies of stifled breathing at 4 a.m. this morning – I had been up with him all night – and Sally died after the same agonies at 5 p.m. Ken and I were both with her. So you will understand that I am rather shattered. My whole household was affected to tears – they all loved them. One should not make trouble for oneself by unnecessary affections, should one, but without affections what would life be? It is difficult to know where to draw the line.

Well, that's that. They are both buried in my garden....

To H. B.   BAGDAD, *March 4th, 1925.*

I got in from Ur at 6 a.m. this morning and not having slept in the train, I slept all this afternoon till 6....

Our excavations this year, without being so sensationally exciting as they were last year, have been extremely good and there were some wonderful objects to divide. The division was rather difficult but I think J.M. and I were very fair and reasonable – I hope Mr Woolley thinks the same.

I do miss my Peter so. I longed for his little cheerful presence when I went to Ur. He would have loved that boring journey – so many dogs to look at out of the window....

To H. B.   BAGDAD, *March 11th, 1925.*

... Upon my soul I almost wish there weren't a desert route – it brings silly females, all with introductions to me....

To H. B.   BAGDAD, *March 18th, 1925.*

... Hilton Young has come.

March 25th, 1925.

On Sunday afternoon Ken and I took Hilton Young out to some marshes near the Baquba road to see birds. That was very nice. The birds played up and I brought out tea – partly in your thermos which is still one of the mainstays of existence – and Hilton Young was delighted and delightful.

Chiefly we are busy preparing for the Secretaries of State who arrive to-morrow. There are to be no end of functions for them.

To H. B.   BAGDAD, *April 1st, 1925.*

We have been remarkably busy with Secretaries of State. They arrived last Thursday and I met them at lunch on Friday and carried off Mr Amery in the afternoon to look at birds.... They are all very sympathetic and I do like Sir John Shuckburgh so much....

To F. B.   BAGDAD, *April 16th, 1925.*

The Secretaries of State left on Tuesday. I went with Mr Amery to the Museum on Monday morning and on the way back he said very satisfactory things. He said he had been much struck by the admirable relations between the British officials and the Arabs, and thought the former had done wonderful work and that the whole administration was much better than he expected. I was very glad because I felt that he was giving praise where it was due....

To H. B.   BAGDAD, *April 22, 1925.*

As for my plans, I'm thinking of coming home for a couple of months towards the end of July, so as to have two peaceful months at Rounton. If I drop into the end of a London season, I rush about so and it's not very restful. So barring accidents, that is what is in my mind....

In the evening we were mainly engaged in canvassing the merits of a little black and white puppy which Col. Prescott had offered me. She ought to have been a spaniel but she has got mixed up with an Airedale and has the oddest little ugly pathetic face and very apologetic manners. I've got her so far on appro. She is singularly intelligent and already has a passion for me. The servants all call her Peter so I've called her Petra – my poor Peter!

The King has asked me to go out to his farm near Khanaqin for a couple of days during the holidays at the end of Ramadhan. They begin on Friday or Saturday but as H.M. wants to leave on Friday afternoon I expect they will continue to see the new moon on Thursday. I shall go, I think; a couple of days out of doors would be good and it doesn't look as if it would be too hot.

To H. B.   BAGDAD, *April 29th, 1925.*

We had some emotions as to the beginning of the Id. On Thursday night no one knew whether the moon had been seen nor whether there was an Id and a levee and a departure to the King's farm (for me) next day. At 11 p.m. the guns announced the Id, for they had managed to get the moon seen at sunset, but it had taken the Qadhi all those hours to make sure that the witnesses had spoken true.

I hopped up at 6 to get Zaya and my baggage off to the station and at 8 behold me at the King's levee. I then in the course of an hour visited all the Ministers and the Naqib, went home and got into country clothes and at 10 was picked up by H.M. at the station near my house. We went up by trolley – the party was H.M., Naji Suwaidi, a Chamberlain and an A.D.C. The King's farm is a little to the N.W. of Khanaqin. We got to the nearest point to his tents at 2, having had an excellent lunch in the trolley, found horses waiting and rode up through the fields to the tents, about 20 minutes away. It was so heavenly to be riding through grass and flowers – gardens of purple salvia and blue borage and golden mullein, with scarlet ranunculus in between. After tea we went out for a walk through the crops, H.M. rejoicing over his splendid hemp and barley and wheat – they were splendid, I must say. And then we sat in the pleasant dark till dinner, after which we all went to bed. Zaya had arrived by this time and I had all my camp furniture in an enormous tent – unfortunately I shared it with innumerable sand flies.

Petra had come with me; she enjoyed herself enormously and behaved not too badly for one so young. She is going to be a nice little dog....

To F. B.   BAGDAD, *April 29th, 1925.*

Now I must go up and see the Queen about her washing silk dresses. Those sent by Moll are a great success.

To F. B.   BAGDAD, *May 20th, 1925.*

Thank heaven, I hear that Cook is opening an office here so that I shall no longer be the sole agent for tourists....

To H. B.   BAGDAD, *June 10th, 1925.*

We are in the thick of elections and so far the results are more than reasonably good, the electors choosing decent, solid men. I don't think the House will meet till the autumn; the budget is not ready and cannot be prepared until a decision on the Hilton Young report has been taken by both governments, so there's nothing for it to meet about....

Now I'm going to swim. Petra is a great swimming dog and loves it. She is a clever little thing but not as nice as Peter.

To H. B.   BAGDAD, *June 17th, 1925.*

... On Monday the Queen asked me to come and take a stroll on the bank opposite the palace. I arrived about 5.15 and we spent half an hour in desultory talk. Then I suggested that we should cross over the river, but their launch was out of order so at 6 I insisted on going over in a boat. Mme Jaudat, the Mistress of the Ceremonies had meantime arrived with her little boy, and we all went over, the two girls, Ghazi, Miss Fairley, H.M. and I. On the other bank I found that leisurely preparations for a large meal were going on, including a pile of fish waiting to be roasted ... and finally about 7 a sort of high tea was ready, sandwiches and roast fish and cakes. And as it was a very pleasantly cool evening it was agreeable to sit there and eat....

To H. B.   BAGDAD, *June 24th, 1925.*

I was cut to the heart about Anthony. [Brig.-Gen. Hon. Anthony Henley, who had died suddenly in Rumania.] I hope you will give me some news of Sylvia [his wife].

Gertrude came on leave this year and arrived in London on July 17th. She was in a condition of great nervous fatigue, and appeared exhausted mentally and physically. Sir Thomas Parkinson, M.D., our old and valued friend as well as our doctor, said that she was in a condition which required a great deal of care and that she ought not to return to the climate of Bagdad. Dr Thomas Body, M.D., of Middlesbrough, who saw her when she went north, took the same view. On Gertrude's way through London she saw Mrs W. L. Courtney, who came to dine one night at 95 Sloane Street with her and her father. She had a few minutes' private talk with Mrs Courtney and asked her to suggest something that she could do if she remained in England. Mrs Courtney wrote a few days later suggesting that Gertrude should stand for Parliament. The following letter is the reply.

To Mrs W. L. COURTNEY,
                    ROUNTON GRANGE, NORTHALLERTON, *Aug. 4.*

YOU DEAR AND BELOVED JANET,

No, I'm afraid you will never see me in the House. I have an invincible hatred of that kind of politics and if you knew how little I should be fitted for it you would not give it another thought – though it is delightful of you, all the same, to think of it. I have not, and I have never had the quickness of thought and speech which could fit the clash of parliament. I can do my own job in a way and explain why I think that the right way of doing it, but I don't cover a wide enough field and my natural desire is to slip back into the comfortable arena of archaeology and history and to take only an onlooker's interest in the contest over actual affairs. I know I could not enter the lists, apart from the fact it would make me supremely miserable.

I shall hope to see you in London before I leave – that will be about the end of September. For I think I must certainly go back for this winter, though I privately very much doubt whether it won't be the last.

Goodbye, my dear, and don't forget that I'm ever your very affectionate

GERTRUDE.

Gertrude came to Rounton, for a while, much enjoying her own gardens, and grew gradually better there. She then went to stay in Scotland with Mr and Mrs Lionel Dugdale at their shooting box, where the affectionate solicitude with which they surrounded her went far to complete her cure.

We all felt after this last visit of Gertrude to England that she had never seemed more glad to be with us all, never more affectionate and delightful to all her Yorkshire surroundings. It was a solace to her when the time came for her return to Bagdad at the beginning of October to have the company of her cousin Sylvia (Hon. Mrs Anthony Henley), for whom she cared very much.

To H. B.   *Monday, Oct. 5th, 1925.*

... Sylvia's delight in everything has been such an added zest – she has never been on a sea voyage before and her interest culminated when Captain S. took us on to the bridge last night and showed us the stars through a sextant....

To H. B.   HAIFA, *October 9th, 1925.*

We lunched happily on a balcony and on our way back walked through the old Arab town, a tiny medieval place with narrow streets, half arched over, climbing up and down a hill. It was the first really Eastern place which Sylvia had seen and she loved it. So did I. On the way back we stopped at the Monastery and at that moment a Carmelite monk came out of the door. 'That's Father Lamb,' said Mr Kennedy, 'the Father-Superior.' With that I went boldly up and said who I was – of course he had heard of me from the Carmelites at Bagdad. Our success was complete when Sylvia announced herself to be the niece of Monsignor Algernon [Stanley].

They finally land at Beyrout.

BEYROUT, *Oct. 10th, 1925.*

Then we went to the Museum where I sent in my card to the Director. He came and showed us over and opened for us the safe which contains the famous golden treasure of Byblos – about 1300 B.C. Most interesting, but what interested me more were the sarcophagi with Phoenician inscriptions said to date from the 4th millennium B.C. That's as early as our earliest inscriptions from Ur....

Oh it's fun to be me when one gets to Asia – there's no doubt of it....

To H. B.   BAGDAD, *October 14th, 1925.*

It has been so wonderful coming back here. For the first two days I could not do any work at all in the office, because of the uninterrupted streams of people who came to see me. 'Light of our eyes,' they said, 'Light of our eyes,' as they kissed my hands and made almost absurd demonstrations of delight and affection. It goes a little to the head, you know.

On Sunday afternoon Sylvia and I went to the races. It was excessively hot – it has been over 90 every day since we came back – and S. wasn't feeling very fit, though she would not hear of not going....

She was looking quite enchanting in a black and white muslin gown. She creates a sensation in Bagdad society whenever she appears. H.E. brought us back and sat talking for a bit. Sylvia then went to rest and read while I tackled some of my gradually diminishing pile of papers. At 7.30 I went in and found her very unwell and in great pain. I sent at once for a Doctor; Sinbad is still away but I got hold of Woodman whom we both like very much. Her temperature was 104!

After this, Sylvia had ups and downs of health, although able at intervals to join in seeing the people and the sights of Bagdad, all of which she enjoyed very much. It was finally decided that she ought not to remain in the East, and she returned to England in November, 1925, to Gertrude's great disappointment.

... My hat, what a social asylum bridge is!...

... Next day Sunday, I went to the Museum where I had an assignation with the two Americans. We spent a glorious hour over early pottery and all of us learnt a good deal – I know I did. On the way home I showed them a couple of medieval buildings and an 8th century marble mihrab, the oldest monument in Bagdad. They were thrilled and so was I. We went to the Diala and walked along the bank in palm groves, most lovely though why a bit of desert and a stretch of river, a few palms and a sunset should have been so lovely I don't know. It was only God's bright and intricate device I suppose....

To H. B.   BAGDAD, *Dec. 9th, 1925.*

To-day I have worked like a beaver all the morning – Bernard being away I had to do a lot of his work.... I have a terrific amount to do – the annual report and an article for the Encyclopaedia and I don't know what more.

To H. B.   BAGDAD, *December 30th, 1925.*

I've had some adventures myself. Following the example of everyone in Bagdad – nearly – I had a terrific cold in the head last week and when I wrote to you I had been indoors for two days, but I didn't tell you 'not wishing to trouble you'. Bernard was in bed with a cold too so it was all most inconvenient....

On Sunday I put on more clothes than I have ever worn before, and with a hot water bottle on my knees, went up with the King and Ken and Iltyd in a closed trolley to Khanaqin. We got to the farm about sunset, found some of the new furniture arrived and spent a happy time arranging it, the King and I. I began then to feel very tired and went to bed immediately after dinner. Next morning I felt rather bad; they all came in to see if I wanted things and were in favour of not going out shooting. However I shoo'd them off and Zaya looked after me till 5 when they came in. I felt rather better and had them in before dinner to play a game of bridge with me in bed. But the next day I was pretty bad so Ken sent for the very good local doctor only to find that he was spending Xmas away and immediately, without telling me, telegraphed to Bagdad for a doctor. By that time I wasn't taking much notice, except that I had a general feeling that I was slipping into great gulfs.... Finally at 6 arrived Dr Spencer. He brought with him a charming nurse, Miss Hannifan, who sat up with me all night. They were both of them convinced that I had got pneumonia, but not a bit of it. Next morning it was clear that it was no worse than pleurisy and a pretty general congestion. So they delayed the departure of the morning train by an hour, thus do we behave with our railway management, and took me down to Bagdad.... They sat a good deal in my compartment and amused me, I had a very comfortable journey. An ambulance met me at the station and took me straight to hospital. And lest you may think that I'm tottering about on edges of graves, I may tell you that Drs Spencer, Woodman, and Dunlop all declare that if I hadn't the most remarkable constitution I should certainly have now been dangerously ill with pneumonia.

This December and January were overshadowed for Gertrude by the deep anxiety which she shared with us about her much-loved brother Hugo. He contracted typhoid on his voyage home from South Africa with his wife and children in the autumn of 1925, and when they arrived in England on December 11th, he was desperately ill. Hope was almost abandoned. In the third week of December, however, his condition improved, and at Christmas and the New Year the cloud seemed to be lifting. Then he had a relapse. He died on February 2nd, 1926.

CHAPTER 26

1925 – 1926

Bagdad

To Hon. Mrs HENLEY.   BAGDAD, *Dec. 9th, 1925.*

... I am anxious about Hugo. My parents write me that they hear by wireless that he has pneumonia on board ship coming home and I know no more. If anything happened to him it would be such a terrible blow....

To H. B.   BAGDAD, *January 6th, 1926.*

I can't tell you how I've enjoyed reading the 'Confessions of a Capitalist'. It's a book everyone should read and I'm now going to lend it to all my friends. It contains as much good sound sense as there are sentences to the page.

That and the 3rd vol. of the Cambridge Ancient History which has just come out, have been the staples of my days, but if you want to laugh feebly I can tell you a silly ass book which will help you – 'Bill the Conqueror'; I forget the name of the talented author, but he nearly gave me a relapse and I'm sure you would feel that way too. Lionel is now seeking round Bagdad for the rest of his books. 'Bill the Conqueror' was supplied by Ken. For good simple nonsense he is not easy to beat.

To F. B.   BAGDAD, *January 6th, 1926.*

I've been having a little quiet illness of my own but it's nearly gone. I was quite bad for a day or two, but now they are all saying that they really wouldn't have bothered if they had known the kind of person they were dealing with. For three nights I had the most preposterous sort of nightmares, mostly about Iraq and the treaty and so on, but I'm pleased to remember that one was about flints, which I've been hearing about lately. You'll scarcely believe me but someone (in the nightmare) gave me a flint which had a fossil shell in it and I was so fearfully angry at anyone being such an idiot as

361

to think that a flint could have a fossil shell in it, that I had to wake myself up and say what I thought about it. I found myself saying it and afterwards thought that, 'mutatis mutandis', it was just the kind of thing that Father would do when he was ill....

To H. B. BAGDAD, *January 13th, 1926.*

The Iraq Cabinet has accepted the new treaty and I don't think there will be any difficulty about it in our Parliament.

... You need not be alarmed about our 25 years' mandate. If we go on as fast as we've gone for that last two years, Iraq will be a member of the League before five or six years have passed, and our direct responsibility will have ceased. It's almost incredible how the country is settling down. I look back to 1921 or 1922 and can scarcely believe that so great a change has taken place.... It's all being so interesting. Archaeology and my museum are taking a bigger and bigger place. I do hope this year to get the Museum properly lodged and arranged. It's such fun, isn't it, to make things new from the beginning....

To Hon. Mrs HENLEY. BAGDAD, *Jan. 25th, 1926.*

... I don't suppose you can imagine how often I have missed you and how much. Not only to talk to for myself ... we seem to have left such a lot of things untalked about, we must have wasted our time – but also when there are other people here, to throw the ball so that we may catch it and throw it back. Mr Cooke says 'she woke us all up 'and that's perfectly true, but being awake to what companionship can be like it is hard to have it snatched from me. I keep seeing in imagination all your darling ways and your charming grace and hearing echoes of your delicious voice – but there it is....

To H. B. BAGDAD, *January 27th, 1926.*

Incidentally I have read the enchanting volume of Page's 'Letters to President Wilson'. Do you remember when Lichnowsky accuses the U.S.A. of putting off the evil day in Mexico, and Page replies 'What better can you do with an evil day than put it off?'

Now do you know, that is what I feel about leaving here. I simply can't bear to think of it, and I don't....

To F. B.   BAGDAD, *3rd March, 1926.*

I feel sure you will be glad to hear that I have got the building I wanted of all others for my museum. After addressing the Prime Minister in exalted terms, His Excellency came hurrying into my office, replete with promises. He advised me to get hold of Ken whose Ministry disposes of Government buildings. What could be easier! I hauled Ken off to the place and found him the more easy to convince because it was he who first gave me a secret hint that it might be obtainable and he is now full of satisfaction that his idea has turned out so well. So we settled it all in half an hour and to-day its former occupants have almost all turned out, and I have been settling about repairs, etc. Ken observes with complacency that the Ministry of Interior, when it once gets going, sticks at nothing and indeed I am amazed at the promptness with which it has been done. Government offices don't usually move fast. I am going to lodge the Library of the American School, which will be a great advantage to us, besides being very gratifying to them and have heaps and heaps of room to show off all our things. At present you must tumble over one in order to have a glimpse of another. Oh dear, how much I should like you to see it! It will be a real Museum, rather like the British Museum only a little smaller. I am ordering long shallow drawers in chests to hold the pottery fragments, so that you will pull out a drawer and look at Sumerian bits, and then another and look at Parthian glaze, and another for early incised, then Arab incised (which I can pick up in quantities a quarter of an hour from my door) and Arab glaze and all. Won't it be nice? It is also nice to think that I shall clear the cupboards of my house of a mass of biscuit tins full of dusty fragments....

To H. B. BAGDAD, *March 3rd, 1926*.

I had Vita Nicolson [Hon. Mrs Harold Nicolson] with me for two days. She arrived on Saturday morning for breakfast and left on Sunday night after an early dinner.... She was most agreeable.

I reproduce here, by Mrs Nicolson's permission, a chapter from *A Passenger to Teheran* describing her brief visit to Gertrude.
'Gertrude Bell in Bagdad', by V. Sackville-West.

'A door in the blank wall, a jerky stop, a creaking of hinges, a broadly smiling servant, a rush of dogs, a vista of garden-path edged with carnations in pots, a little verandah and a little low house at the end of the path, an English voice – Gertrude Bell.

'I had known her first in Constantinople, where she had arrived straight out of the desert, with all the evening dresses and cutlery and napery that she insisted on taking with her on her wanderings; and then in England; but here she was in her right place, in Iraq, in her own house, with her office in the city, and her white pony in a corner of the garden, and her Arab servants, and her English books, and her Babylonian shards on the mantelpiece, and her long thin nose, and her irrepressible vitality. I felt all my loneliness and despair lifted from me in a second. Had it been very hot in the Gulf? got fever, had I? but quinine would put that right; and a sprained ankle – too bad! – and would I like to breakfast first, or a bath? and I would like to see her museum, wouldn't I? did I know she was Director of Antiquities in Iraq? wasn't that a joke? and would I like to come to tea with the king? and yes, there were lots of letters for me. I limped after her as she led me down the path, talking all the time, now in English to me, now in Arabic to the eager servants. She had the gift of making everyone feel suddenly eager; of making you feel that life was full and rich and exciting. I found myself laughing for the first time in ten days. The garden was small, but cool and friendly; her spaniel wagged not only his tail but his whole little body; the pony looked over the loose-box door and whinnied gently; a tame partridge hopped

about the verandah; some native babies who were playing
in a corner stopped playing to stare and grin. A tall, grey
sloughi came out of the house, beating his tail against the
posts of the verandah; 'I want one like that,' I said, 'to take
up into Persia.' I did want one but I had reckoned without
Gertrude's promptness. She rushed to the telephone, and as
I poured cream over my porridge I heard her explaining – a
friend of hers had arrived – must have a sloughi at once –
was leaving for Persia next day – a selection of sloughis must
be sent round that morning. Then she was back in her chair,
pouring out information: the state of Iraq, the excavations
at Ur, the need for a decent museum, what new books had
come out? what was happening in England? The doctors
had told her she ought not to go through another summer
in Bagdad, but what should she do in England, eating out
her heart for Iraq? next year, perhaps ... but I couldn't say
she looked ill, could I? I could, and did. She laughed and
brushed that aside. Then, jumping up – for all her move-
ments were quick and impatient – if I had finished my breakfast wouldn't I like my bath? and she must go to her office, but
would be back for luncheon. Oh yes, and there were people to
luncheon; and so, still talking, still laughing, she pinned on
a hat without looking in the glass, and took her departure.

'I had my bath – her house was extremely simple, and the
bath just a tin saucer on the floor – and then the sloughis began to arrive. They slouched in, led on strings by Arabs in
white woollen robes, sheepishly smiling. Left in command, I
was somewhat taken aback, so I had them all tied up to the
posts of the verandah, till Gertrude should return, an array
of desert dogs, yellow, white, grey, elegant, but black with
fleas and lumpy with ticks. I dared not go near them, but
they curled up contentedly and went to sleep in the shade,
and the partridge prinked round them on her dainty pink
legs, investigating. At one o'clock Gertrude returned, just as
my spirits were beginning to flag again; laughed heartily at
this collection of dogs which her telephone message (miracu-
lously, as it seemed to me) had called into being, shouted to
the servants, ordered a bath to be prepared for the dog I

should choose, unpinned her hat, set down some pansies on her luncheon-table, closed the shutters, and gave me a rapid biography of her guests.

'She was a wonderful hostess, and I felt that her personality held together and made a centre for all those exiled English-men whose other common bond was their service for Iraq. They all seemed to be informed by the same spirit of constructive enthusiasm; but I could not help feeling that their mission there would have been more in the nature of drudgery than of zeal but for the radiant ardour of Gertrude Bell. Whatever subject she touched, she lit up; such vitality was irresistible. We laid plans, alas! for when I should return to Bagdad in the autumn: we would go to Babylon, we would go to Ctesiphon, she would have got her new museum by then. When she went back to England, if, indeed, she was compelled to go, she would write another book.... So we sat talking, as friends talk who have not seen one another for a long time, until the shadows lengthened and she said it was time to go and see the King....'

To H. B.   BAGDAD, *March 10th, 1926.*

Last Thursday night I went up to Khanaqin to spend Friday with the King.... In the morning, a carpenter and I were busy laying down linoleum and arranging furniture....

We lunched early, went a few miles down the line on a trolley to a place in the farm where we found horses waiting, and spent the afternoon riding about....

When we got back, the drawing room and two of the bedrooms were finished. I whipped the furniture into place and the drawing room looked like a nice comfy room in an English country house. Not all the furniture is covered yet – I have now bought supplementary chintzes and silks in the bazaar to finish it off.

After dinner I left, an A.D.C. taking me to the train. The motor car, characteristically, hadn't enough petrol to reach the station, so we had to get out and walk. But there was no danger of missing the train which would have been kept waiting for me, till I turned up, unlike the North Eastern....

To F. B. BAGDAD, *March 23rd, 1926.*

... I went to tea with the Queen on Sunday to say good-bye to the little Ghazi heir apparent who is going to England to be educated. I was so sorry for her. It must be hard to send your only little boy far away into conditions of which you haven't an inkling.

I have been spending the afternoon to-day trying to learn a little about arranging a museum. Oh dear! there's such a lot to be learnt that my heart sinks. However, I know what I shall do. I shall concentrate on exhibiting the best objects properly and get the others done little by little. Meantime the new museum building has to be re-roofed, for the present mud and beams could be cut through almost by a penknife held by a determined thief. So it will be some time before I get in to the upper floor, but I shall shortly be able to begin on two downstairs rooms....

To F. B. BAGDAD, *April 6th, 1926.*

... In 30 years I don't suppose there has been such a spring – slopes and rivers of scarlet ranunculus, meadows of purple stock and wild mignonette, blue lilies, black arums and once a bank of yellow tulips. These and commoner things made the world look like a brilliant piece of enamel....

To F. B. BAGDAD, *April 14th, 1926.*

Our chief preoccupation during the past week has been water. The two days of south wind, of which I spoke with disgust in my last letter, were being more disgusting than I knew. They were melting the snows in the northern mountains and on Thursday we were in for a terrific flood. On Friday the Tigris dyke broke on the left bank – my bank – above the King's palace which it flooded. He was away at Khanaqin and his family had to be moved hastily into a house in the town. The water rushed over the eastern desert, lapping along the torn dyke and from then until now we have never been sure that it would not break through and flood the low lying parts of the town, which include my quarter! They have electric light all along and people watching and looking night and day. The big railway station on the east bank is under water and enormous quantities of merchandise waiting to go up to Persia spoilt....

The Arabs are so incurably careless; they won't shut their channels when the flood is coming down and then it finds a way in and breaks through....

This is only a flood letter I'm afraid.

I'm so sorry for the King – his nice house all spoilt....

To H. B.   BAGDAD, *April 21st, 1926.*

We are now safe from floods – as safe as we can be, for as Mr Bury observes, Bagdad cannot ever be quite safe unless it is rebuilt in another place.

The Prime Minister, I can't think why, has asked me to serve on the Government Committee for distributing relief to the peasants who were washed out above Bagdad. There's a meeting to-morrow....

Iltyd is away in Mosul where he received a telegram thus worded 'On approach of the water your house fell down' from one of his Arab officers. His house has in fact collapsed into the flood but he had moved all his clothes and things into the brick barracks nearby before he left, and these are safe. All his furniture was washed away and lost.

This is during the Strike in England.

To H. B.   BAGDAD, *May 5th, 1926.*

Everything else is swallowed up in the thought of what is happening to you. The scanty news in Reuter gives one some impression of the terrible upheaval. One peers into the future much as one did at the beginning of August, 1914 – absit omen! ...

To H. B.   BAGDAD, *May 12th, 1926.*

Your letter of April 28th, written on the eve of the strike, reached me by last mail; I wonder whether letters will have got through in the first week and fear that the next letter may be delayed. We have no news but Reuter and you may imagine how eagerly we await it. Indeed anxiety is never out of my mind; there has been word of disturbances at Middlesbrough and to-day there are railway accidents. These things don't make one feel easier.

You ask about my plans for the summer. This doesn't seem to be the moment to make any plans which involve expenditure, for I don't know whether I shall have any income or whether any of us will. My duty to the museum is of the first importance. I can't go away and leave all those valuable things half transferred and the work goes very slowly. It will take months and months, I think. I have made a little headway this week. The alterations in the building itself are finished and a few simple fittings in one of the lower rooms were ready so on Sunday morning I called on Squadron Leader Harnett to help and we placed all the big gate sockets (dull things but valuable) on the bench along the wall that had been made for them, or rather we superintended the placing of them by porters.

To H. B. BAGDAD, *May 18th, 1926.*

I had scarcely posted my letter last week, when we got news of the ending of the general strike, but that doesn't mean the ending of difficulties and you are still in the thick of them. Indeed, I don't know whether your worst difficulties are not just about to begin....

I have been very busy with my museum, but it has not got far yet. I go in at 7 a.m. and spend a couple of hours there before I go to office. On Sunday we can work until it gets too hot and fortunately it is being remarkably cool weather. In a day or two I shall have my own workroom with an electric fan which will make things easier.... As for cases, tables and things, they have not begun to materialize yet and for the moment I am occupied with the big stone objects which do not need to be behind glass.

I lunch always with Sir Henry and we discuss the affairs of the day, public and private, and then, if I have been early at the Museum, I go to sleep for a bit when I get home; and in the evening if I am alone I read Babylonian history or books about seals and things so that I may know a little better how to arrange the Museum. It sounds rather a monotonous existence, but it is inexpensive and peaceful which, I am afraid, is more than can be said for yours.

To H. B. BAGDAD, *May 26th, 1926.*

... Anyway, I take it that we shall have very little income this year.

That is not the only reason, though it's a very good one, for my wanting to stay here this summer. I hope you won't be very much disappointed. What I vaguely think of doing (but don't talk about it) is to stay with the High Commissioner till Bernard comes back in the autumn; then to resign and ask the Iraq Government to take me on as Director of Antiquities for six months or so. (I'm only Hon. Director now, you know.) I should not in any case stay much longer with the H.C.; it has really ceased to be my job. Politics are dropping out and giving place to big administrative questions in which I'm not concerned and at which I'm no good. On the other hand, the Department of Antiquities is now a full time job. The cataloguing of things from Ur and Kish for the past three years has been done and I have now nearly finished the things of this year. But the serial number of the Bagdad Museum has to be put on to everything and until each object is in the catalogue we can't number it. There are a mass of things from other places than Ur and Kish which we have not begun on. Then will come the arrangement in cases – none of which have begun to come in yet. I have moved about half the things from the old room into the new Museum and they are lying about, some on tables, some on the floor, a desolating spectacle. In the course of the next ten days it will be even worse, for by that time I hope I may have got almost everything moved over.

The afternoons, after tea, hang rather heavy on my hands. ... We can't swim yet because the river is so high and the current so strong. This last week I have sometimes gone into the Museum at 5, but it will soon be too hot to do that with any comfort and it is not really a good plan because one gets

no exercise. I did it in order to finish cataloguing the Ur and
Kish things of this year....

To H. B.   BAGDAD, *June 9th, 1926.*

... I am enclosing the catalogue of the Babylonian Stone
Room of the Museum and two picture postcards of the ex-
hibits. I forgot to mention in the catalogue that the bricks
which form the pedestal of the statue (No. 1) are blue glazed
bricks from the top of the ziggurat at Ur, remains of an
upper chamber built or restored by Nabonidus the last king
of Babylon. We brought away a lot of fragments and built
them up into a pedestal – it is most effective. The King is
going to open this room on Monday. It is the easiest of all
to arrange because it consists only of a few large objects, but
it looks extremely well and I hope it will impress the Ministers! It has indeed all the appearance of a Museum....

Thursday was a very nice day for I had the whole morning there (in the Museum) and came back to lunch and a
good rest. There was a state dinner party for the King's
birthday and a reception of about 500 people in the garden
afterwards. The party was very interesting. All the deputies
and senators and everyone one had ever known in Bagdad were there, the Ministers and most of the Arab civil
servants in ordinary European evening dress and hatless and
the religious leaders in robes and turbans. There was a
wonderful diversity....

On Sunday S/L Harnett and I had a good morning in the
Museum. After tea Ken and I went out to Karradah and
caught four exquisite swallow-tail butterflies, the first we had
seen. We were much elated.

Haji Naji is delighted with his knife and sends you a
thousand messages of thanks.

To-night the King comes to dine and play bridge....

To H. B.   BAGDAD, *June 16th, 1926.*

My principal news you have seen in the papers – the
Turkish treaty. It is almost too good to be true....

I had a nice little ceremony on Monday when the King opened the first room of the Museum.

To F. B.   BAGDAD, *June 16th, 1926.*

It is being a very grim world, isn't it. I feel often that I don't know how I should face it but for the work I'm doing and I know you must feel the same. I think of you month after month as the time passes since that awful sorrow, and realize all the time that the passage of the months can make little difference. I wish I were coming home this summer but I feel sure that when I leave I shall not want to come back here and I would like to finish this job first – indeed, I feel that I must finish it, there being no one else. But it is too lonely, my existence here; one can't go on for ever being alone. At least, I don't feel I can....

To H. B.   BAGDAD, *June 23rd, 1926.*

We are labouring under the difficulties presented by the four days' holiday of the big Id when all the Arab offices are closed and one can't get anything through. A holiday at this time of year is no good as far as holiday making goes, for it is too hot to go out on any expedition. By luck – and the vagaries of the moon – it didn't begin till Monday, so that I had Sunday morning in the Museum. I have to give my staff a holiday and I shall not be able to work there again till Saturday which is a bore. However, I brought back some cases of cylinder seals at which I have been working of an evening....

We had a terrific day on Monday. It began with a levee at the palace at 6.10. I was in an ace of going without orders, but I discovered their absence as I was waiting for the High Commissioner at the end of the Maude Bridge and dispatched a Kavass hotfoot to fetch them. The H.C. being fortunately late, they arrived in the nick of time.

I then came home, breakfasted and did an hour's work after which I set out again on visits. First the Naqib, then the Ministers, then selected notables and finally the Queen and Ali and his family....

To H. B. BAGDAD, *June 30th, 1926.*

... What an enormous waste and loss two months' coal strike must mean. It's so amazing that the world seems to go on just the same – Ascot and balls and parties are what I read of in *The Times* – or, rather, I see they are there – and extraordinarily little about things that really matter.

We are now well into the hot weather – temperature at 113° – but I am feeling it scarcely at all. Partly, I think, because we have begun bathing though the river is still very high and the current strong. It makes such a difference. We go up by launch to a place above the town where I have a little hut to undress in and get back after seven feeling both exercised and refreshed.... It is too hot now to dine indoors and play bridge and much pleasanter to lie out on the river bank and come home by launch about 10.

I often wonder how the old Babylonians with whom I now feel such a close connection passed their summer. Much as we do, I daresay, but without our ice and electric fans which add immensely to the amenities of existence. The moment of the day I don't like is going home after lunch at the hottest moment, but there is no way out of it.

Faisal has given me a bronze bust of himself by Feo Gleichen to put in the Museum. I shall set it up in the big Arab room.

There, now I must go to lunch. My letters are extremely dull, but there is really nothing to recount.

To H. B. *2nd July, 1926.*

... I don't see for the moment what I can do. You see I have undertaken this very grave responsibility of the museum – I have been writing about it ad nauseam for months. I had been protesting for more than a year that I must have a proper building; this winter one fell vacant and they gave it to me together with a very large sum of money for fittings, etc. Then first I had to re-roof it and next I was held up at least two months by the floods and the work they entailed which prevented work being done for me. Now all the very valuable objects – they run into tens of thousands of pounds and incidentally they would never have been taken out of the ground if I had not been here to guarantee that they would be properly protected, have been transferred pell-mell into the new building and there is absolutely no one but I who knows anything about them, since J. M. Wilson left. It isn't merely a responsibility to the Iraq but to archaeology in general. I could not possibly leave things in this state except for the gravest reasons. I work at it as hard as I can, but it's a gigantic task – of course I love it and am ready to give all my spare time to it. But I can't resign from my post as Oriental Secretary. And as I am a civil servant, I have only about 2 months' leave owing to me, which means a little over 9 weeks in England.

That is the whole position. In a couple of months or so I may be beginning to see daylight in the museum or at any rate a condition in which I could safely leave it for a little. Let us wait for a bit, don't you think, and see how things look.

You do realize, don't you, that I feel bound to fulfil the undertakings I gave when, at my instance the Iraq Government allowed excavations to be begun 4 years ago. The thing has grown and grown – it can't do otherwise – and whereas until last autumn I had J.M. to help me, I now have no one. All the plans that were begun before Hugo was ill even, are now bearing fruit and I'm rather overwhelmed by them. Anyhow, father, give me a little time to get things into some kind of order and then if you want me to take what leave I can I will do so. But in that case I think I should have to come back for next winter or part of it.

Except for the Museum work, life is very dull.

To H. B.   BAGDAD, *July 7th, 1926.*

... It had been very hot in the morning in the Museum but we have now changed into a north room and had a fan put into it which makes it comparatively luxurious. We can work there quite comfortably without a fan on week days when we leave at 8.30, but on Sundays when we stay until 1, it is essential to have a cool room. I have got a few standard cases and hope to have the seal case this week. But there is so much to learn; one constantly finds that the things don't exactly serve one's purpose and they have to be modified. However both we and the carpenters are learning gradually....

I have been having very busy mornings, lots of dispatches to write and long things to do. Sir Henry is delightful to work with, but he is most careful of detail and one has to pay great attention to what one is doing.

Darling I must stop now; summer does not conduce to the writing of very long letters.

To F. B.   BAGDAD, *July 7, 1926.*

... photograph of you and the little boys. They are darlings. Is not the eldest one like Hugo? In this photograph I see a great likeness....

I am so glad you like the pictures of my museum, and when in return will you give me the text of the Pageant? I want so much to read it. I wish I were at the point of having photographs of the upper rooms taken, but they are still in chaos – not so chaotic as they were, however, for most of the objects are roughly classified and ready to be put into cases. But I find arranging cases very difficult. Even the two tiny ones which I have done so far take an enormous amount of thought and rearrangement till one puts them approximately right. And then the writing of labels! Fortunately my Arab clerk writes them beautifully so I only have to give him a list of what has to go on each one and leave him to do it during the rest of the morning while I am in the office....

*

These two letters of July 2nd and July 7th were the last she wrote home. They reached England after her death.

Her strenuous self-imposed work in the museum, in the terrible heat of a Bagdad summer, added to the daily round of her duties in the office, proved too much for her slender stock of physical energy. She had never really recovered from her illness in the winter.

She died quite peacefully in her sleep, in the early morning hours of Monday, July 12th, 1926.

CHAPTER 27

Conclusion

THE tidings brought an overwhelming manifestation of sorrow and sympathy from all parts of the earth, and we realised afresh that her name was known in every continent, her story had crossed every sea. There had clustered round her in her lifetime so many fantastic tales of adventure, based on fact and embroidered by fiction, tales of the Mystery Woman of the East, the uncrowned Queen, the Diana of the Desert, that a kind of legendary personality had emerged which represented Gertrude in the imagination of the general public, to the day of her death.

At the news of her death messages were received at the High Commissioner's office from all parts of Iraq, from Bagdad, from the desert, from officials and representatives – and most of them seem to be no mere formal condolences, but to have in them a note of real sorrow.

I quote here a sentence from a moving letter from Haji Naji, for whom Gertrude felt such warm friendship, and whose garden was always her delight:

'It was my faith always to send Miss Bell the first of my fruits and vegetables and I know not now where I shall send them.'

Their Majesties sent the following message:

'The Queen and I are grieved to hear of the death of your distinguished and gifted daughter, whom we held in high regard.

'The nation will with us mourn the loss of one who by her intellectual powers, force of character and personal courage rendered important and what I trust will prove lasting benefit to the country and to those regions where she worked with such devotion and self-sacrifice. We truly sympathise with you in your sorrow.

'(Signed) GEORGE R. I.'

The Colonial Secretary, Mr Amery, paid her the rare tribute of a statement in the House of Commons.

The High Commissioner wrote the following letter to Gertrude's father about the Museum she founded in Bagdad, now called the Iraq Museum – how she would have preferred that name to any other!

HIGH COMMISSIONER'S OFFICE, BAGDAD, *6th June, 1927.*

MY DEAR SIR HUGH,

King Faisal some time ago wrote to the Prime Minister of Iraq suggesting that one of the principal rooms in the Bagdad Museum should be named the 'Gertrude Bell Room', and I understand that this has been accepted by the Iraq Cabinet.

A meeting of Gertrude's friends later decided to associate her name with the whole Museum by putting in a prominent position a brass plaque with a suitable inscription, which was to be submitted to you for approval. After you had approved it they thought of asking J. M. Wilson to design the plaque.

Yours very sincerely,

H. DOBBS.

GERTRUDE BELL

Whose memory the Arabs will ever hold in reverence and affection
Created this Museum in 1923
Being then Honorary Director of Antiquities for the Iraq
With wonderful knowledge and devotion
She assembled the most precious objects in it
And through the heat of the Summer
Worked on them until the day of her death
On 12th July, 1926
King Faisal and the Government of Iraq
In gratitude for her great deeds in this country
Have ordered that the Principal Wing shall bear her name
And with their permission
Her friends have erected this Tablet.

Gertrude was buried in the afternoon of July 12th, in the cemetery outside Bagdad, with the honours of a military funeral. 'A huge concourse of Iraqis and British,' we were told, 'were present: the High Commissioner and the whole of the British Staff, 'civil, military and Air Force, the Prime Minister of Iraq and the members of the Cabinet, and a great number of Arab sheikhs from the desert. The troops of the Iraq army lined the road, and an enormous crowd paid a last homage to one who was honoured throughout the length and breadth of the land.'

Her coffin was borne from the gate of the cemetery to the graveside by the group of young men on the High Commissioner's staff, whose names recur so often in her letters, her intimate friends and comrades, to whom her house was always a beloved centre, a meeting place and haven. Her death had come to them as an unbelievable catastrophe.

The High Commissioner, Gertrude's chief, issued an official notification of her death, in which a sense of acute grief is felt to underlie the dignified and restrained wording. I quote from it two sentences which seem to me to sum up all that can be said about her services in the East.

'She had for the last ten years of her life consecrated all the indomitable fervour of her spirit and all the astounding gifts of her mind to the service of the Arab cause, and especially to Iraq. At last her body, always frail, was broken by the energy of her soul.'

'Her bones rest where she had wished them to rest, in the soil of Iraq. Her friends are left desolate.'

*

But let us not mourn, those who are left, even those who were nearest to her, that the end came to her so swiftly and so soon. Life would inexorably have led her down the slope – Death stayed her at the summit.

*The following pages
describe other Penguin and
Pelican publications
in various series*

SELECTED PENGUINS

THE THREE HOSTAGES* – *John Buchan*

The author's most famous hero, Richard Hannay, searches for three people kidnapped by a vast criminal combine (908) 2/–

SERENADE* – *James M. Cain*

A story of love and a terrible justice, the hero an opera singer, the heroine a Mexican prostitute (902) 2/–

THE BRAVE BULLS* – *Tom Lea*

A documentary novel of the bullfight industry which the *New Yorker* described as 'one of the most dramatic and impassioned pictorial treatments of bullfighting' (922) 2/–

EDMUND CAMPION – *Evelyn Waugh*

A biography of the famous Jesuit scholar and missionary whose martyrdom disfigured the reign of Elizabeth I (955) 2/–

JANE EYRE – *Charlotte Brontë*

One of the most famous Victorian classics – a romantic tragedy that challenged the conventions of its day (960) 2/6

JASSY* – *Norah Lofts*

A realistic historical novel of the early nineteenth century (946) 2/–

THE THURBER CARNIVAL* – *James Thurber*

A selection of the best of the writings and drawings of a great American humorist (871) 2/6

* Not available for U.S.A.

PUFFIN STORY BOOKS

*

Puffin Story Books are children's Penguins. They are the same shape and size as an ordinary Penguin and about the same price (one shilling and sixpence to two shillings and sixpence), but each has its own specially designed pictorial cover. More than eighty Puffins have now been issued, many of them illustrated. They include not only established classics such as Lewis Carroll's *Alice in Wonderland*, F. Hodgson Burnett's *The Secret Garden*, and R. L. Stevenson's *Kidnapped*, but also a large number of more recent favourites and some books which have never been published before. The majority of them will probably appeal particularly to boys and girls from nine to thirteen, but there are volumes in the series for every age and every taste. Amongst recent publications, for example, are Bruce Campbell's *Bird Watching for Beginners*, a selection of *Stories and Verses** by Walter de la Mare, Eleanor Graham's anthology, *A Puffin Book of Verse*, Eleanor Doorly's *Radium Woman**, and Ann Stafford's *Five Proud Riders*.

One of Lotte Reiniger's many illustrations for King Arthur and His Knights of the Round Table, *which is newly told out of the old romances by Roger Lancelyn Green.*

* Not available for U.S.A.

*

*Two line drawings reproduced from
G. E. Pallant Sidaway's* Signs and
Symbols (PP 89)

The Puffin Picture Book series was planned twelve years ago to form a child's own library which could be bought by the child out of its own pocket money, and it now contains more than ninety books for boys and girls of all ages from four to fifteen. Its aim is to enlarge the boundaries of children's knowledge, to introduce them, by means of attractive pictures very carefully reproduced, to a variety of subjects ranging from spelling to pond life, wild flowers to woodworking, printing to the cinema, and postage stamps to sailing ships. Although none of the volumes was designed to fit any educational course, they have come to be used extensively in schools as 'background' books. Most of them (there are a few exceptions) contain thirty-two pages of plates, half in colour and half in black-and-white, and the text which accompanies them tries to strike the mean between sophistication and 'talking down'. They are oblong volumes 7⅛ by 8¾ inches, double the page size of a normal Penguin, and a few have stiff covers. The price varies between two shillings and two shillings and sixpence.

PELICANS

Pelicans, the non-fiction counterpart of Penguins, were launched in 1937 as a series of reprints of popular books with a serious, informative content. Since then their scope has widened considerably, and most of the books now appearing between the pale blue covers of a Pelican have never been published before. In all some 270 volumes have been issued, including introductions to almost every subject, a whole sub-series on the History of England, and others on Philosophy, Psychology, Religion, and Archaeology, all of which are still growing. Amongst them are:

HORSE-RACING – *Dennis Craig*

Not a punter's guide but a miniature encyclopaedia of the racing and breeding of thoroughbreds (A203)   2/-

JOHN STUART MILL – *Karl Britton*

A volume in the Pelican Philosophy series, introducing the teaching of a famous nineteenth-century political philosopher (A274)   2/-

AN OUTLINE OF EUROPEAN ARCHITECTURE – *Nikolaus Pevsner*

A well-illustrated account of the building of every period from the ninth to the twentieth century (A109)   3/6

THE GREEKS – *H. D. F. Kitto*

'The best introduction I have ever read to ancient Greece' – *Raymond Mortimer in the 'New Statesman'* (A220)   2/-

VIRUSES AND MAN – *F. M. Burnet*

An account of many common varieties of this, the smallest living organism, which is responsible for most of to-day's infectious diseases (A265)   2/-

THE ANT WORLD – *Derek Wragge Morley*

Their history, their many varieties, the organization of their society and what makes them tick (A240)   2/-